A FIELD GUIDE IN COLOR TO THE

ANIMAL
WORLD

A FIELD GUIDE IN COLOR TO THE

ANIMAL WORLD

By Dr Jiří Zahradník
and Dr Jiří Čihař

octopus

Translated by Olga Kuthanová
Graphic design by Zdeněk Weinfurter
1092 colour illustrations by A. Čepická (76), K. Drchal (47),
K. Hísek (450), J. Malý (24) and F. Severa (495)
6 line drawings by F. Severa
3/07/08/51-01

English version first published 1979 by
Octopus Books Limited
59 Grosvenor Street, London W1

ISBN 0 7064 1081 5

Printed in Czechoslovakia

Contents

Fundamentals of Zoological Nomenclature and the Classification of the Kingdom

When a layman looks through specialized and even popular scientific literature, he is often taken aback by the many technical terms – phylum, class, synonym, etc. He may have some familiarity with them, but is unable to find his bearings, to relate them to each other in the proper order or sequence. The matter is not as complex as it seems at first glance, however. All that is necessary is to learn a few basic rules about the taxonomy of animals.

What is animal taxonomy? It is a system in which all animals are arranged into groups based on overall resemblance in many features. In general it is hoped that this will reflect their evolutionary relationship. The basic taxonomic categories, or units, in descending order from the highest and most inclusive to the lowest are: kingdom, phylum, class, order, family, genus and species. Other taxa used in present-day classification are, for example, subphylum, subclass, superorder, suborder, superfamily, subfamily, subgenus, subspecies, etc.

The mutual relationship between the basic categories is clearly evident from the following examples of the classification of two well-known species: the Honey Bee *(Apis mellifera)* and the Brown Bear *(Ursus arctos)*.

Kingdom	Animal (Animalia)	
Phylum	Arthropods (Arthropoda)	Chordates (Chordata)
Class	Insects (Insecta)	Mammals (Mammalia)
Order	Hymenoptera	Carnivora
Family	Apidae	Ursidae
Genus	Bee *(Apis)*	Bear *(Ursus)*
Species	Honey Bee *(Apis mellifera)*	Brown Bear *(Ursus arctos)*

The number of examples of each category increases in descending order: there is one kingdom, but there are over 20 phyla, and many times more classes, and so on.

It took many decades before the system acquired any stability. Even today its present form is neither definite nor final. Discoveries of new species and new knowledge about the life of animals are reflected in the system, changing and adding to it. The founder of the system is rightfully considered to be the Swedish naturalist Carl Linné (Carolus Linnaeus – 1707–1778), who devoted his entire life to the study of plants and animals, and classified them according to their similarities in certain features. He published his *Systema Naturae* for the first time in 1735, at the age of 28. It was printed in Latin, which was then the only reliable language of communication in the scientific world. Linnaeus continually improved on his work and published new and further editions. Of the numerous editions it is the tenth, published in 1758, that is now considered the most important. This is because it has since been internationally agreed that the names in this tenth edition are authoritative, and all names published previously are regarded as invalid. As a result animal taxonomy dates from 1758. For the present generation Linnaeus' book is more or less only a historical document, for it includes only a small number of species, but it remains the foundation on which the entire present system has gradually been built. The importance of this basic work is borne out by the fact that it was reissued in facsimile form almost two hundred years later (in 1956) by the British Museum (Natural History), and it is to be reissued, yet again, very shortly.

One of Linnaeus' greatest contributions to systematics is the method of binominal nomenclature, the designation of every animal species by means of two names – the generic name and the specific name. For example: two similar beetles, *Carabus coriaceus* and *Carabus intricatus.* Frequently it is considered desirable to give next to the designation the name of the taxonomist who first validly published the specific name, thus: *Carabus coriaceus* L., *Carabus intricatus* L. (the letter L. stands for Linnaeus). In scientific works it is the custom to add also the date when the specific name was first validly published: *Carabus coriaceus* L., 1758.

Each new species is described from one or more specimens. Nowadays the description must include reference to the 'holotype', a single specimen specially chosen to represent the new name. Any other specimens studied by the author when describing the new species, and considered by him to belong to it, are called 'paratypes'.

It often happens that one or more taxonomists discover the same species independently of each other and each gives it a name. When this is realized, which name is the valid one? According to the law of priority, the first name that was published, complete with a description or a reference to a description of the animal, is to be taken as the valid name. Often the question of priority is indisputable, but it sometimes happens that two or more descriptions appeared in the same year, and then it is necessary to find out, if possible, the exact day of publication – not always very easy! All other names are suppressed as 'synonyms' (normally after examination of the various holotypes, to check the identities). Many species have few synonyms, but others have a great many. Some synonyms continue to be used in literature so that it is necessary to call attention to the fact (which is done in this book in many cases).

Certain complex taxonomic problems cannot be solved by the individual and for this reason an International Commission on Zoological Nomenclature has been set up, with headquarters in London, to arbitrate particularly involved cases of disputed nomenclature, issuing printed *Opinions* to this effect.

Scientific nomenclature, using properly published Latin or latinized binominal names, is the only nomenclature that is internationally valid. In addition to this the various species have other, common or vernacular names in the various languages. These are not internationally valid. Often these names are not firmly established and there is no assurance of uniformity even in the internationally used languages. As a rule, even experts are not fully acquainted with the common names used in their language, and are only capable of giving authoritative identifications by reference to the scientific nomenclature.

The Classification of the Kingdom

(listed are all the phylla and the more important classes)

Kingdom:	Animalia	
Subkingdom:	Protozoa	
Phylum:	Protozoa	
Subkingdom:	Mesozoa	
Phylum:	Mesozoa	
Subkingdom:	Parazoa	
Phylum:	Porifera	
	Classes:	Calcarea, Demospongiae, Sclerospongiae, Hexactinellida
Subkingdom:	Metazoa	
Phylum:	Cnidaria	
	Classes:	Hydrozoa, Scyphozoa, Anthozoa
Phylum:	Ctenophora	
	Classes:	Tentaculata, Nuda
Phylum:	Platyhelminthes	
	Classes:	Turbellaria, Trematoda, Cestoda
Phylum:	Nemertea	
Phylum:	Aschelminthes	
	Classes:	Gastrotricha, Rotifera, Nematoda, Nematomorpha, Kinorhyncha, Acanthocephala
Phylum:	Priapulida	

| Phylum: | Entoprocta |
| Phylum: | Mollusca |

| | Classes: | Monoplacophora, Polyplacophora, Aplacophora, Gastropoda, Scaphopoda, Bivalvia, Cephalopoda |

Phylum:	Sipuncula
Phylum:	Echiura
Phylum:	Annelida

| | Classes: | Polychaeta, Myzostomida, Clitellata |

Phylum:	Onychophora
Phylum:	Tardigrada
Phylum:	Pentastomida
Phylum:	Arthropoda

| | Classes: | Merostomata, Arachnida, Pycnogonida, Crustacea, Symphyla, Pauropoda, Diplopoda, Chilopoda, Insecta |

Phylum:	Bryozoa
Phylum:	Phoronida
Phylum:	Brachiopoda
Phylum:	Hemichordata (Branchiotremata)

| | Classes: | Enteropneusta, Pterobranchia |

| Phylum: | Echinodermata |

| | Classes: | Crinoidea, Holothuroidea, Echinoidea, Asteroidea, Ophiuroidea |

Phylum:	Pogonophora
Phylum:	Chaetognatha
Phylum:	Chordata

	Subphylum:	Tunicata
	Subphylum:	Cephalochordata
	Subphylum:	Vertebrata

| | | Classes: | Cyclostomata, Chondrichthyes, Osteichthyes, Amphibia, Reptilia, Aves, Mammalia |

The Distribution of Animals on Earth

Almost all parts of the world are inhabited by animals. Their distribution and abundance is the result of the constant changes to which the earth and its inhabitants have been subjected. Marked differences in the composition of the various faunas are the result of major, long-term processes. Particularly important, in this respect, are such processes as the joining and separation of continents and islands, the ice ages and interglacial periods, and the formation of new mountain ranges, etc. It might seem, then, that at the present time there are no significant changes taking place in the composition of the world's fauna. A new factor has appeared on the scene, however, one that previously played an insignificant role, namely Man and his developing technology. Man's influence on nature is strong: he destroys natural forests, builds over large areas, damns rivers, mines rocks, applies various poisonous agents to soil and plants (herbicides, insecticides, etc.), and so on. All this affects the structure of the living environment and will have far-reaching effects in the future.

Some animals can be seen to alter their area of distribution. About 1930 the Collared Dove (*Streptopelia decaocto*) began dispersing from its original home in the Balkans. Within the space of a few decades it has spread as far as western and northern Europe. In many places it occurs in abundance in the vicinity of Man. Man often contributes directly to the spread of animals to places where they were previously unknown. One example is the Colorado Beetle *(Leptinotarsa decemlineata)*. Originally it inhabited North America (the Nearctic region) and fed on wild plants of the nightshade family. Then it switched to potatoes, a cultivated plant of the same family. It was introduced into Europe with shipments of produce and gradually spread throughout the whole continent, becoming a new and permanent inhabitant. Many other species made their way to all parts of the world by this means, including numerous pests. Man has also been responsible for the spread of large animals from one region to another. Besides domestic animals, which he has introduced to all places he himself inhabits, and where otherwise they would mostly have only a minimum chance of existence, one example is the Muskrat *(Ondatra zibethica)*. Native to the Nearctic region, it was brought to the neighbourhood of Prague in Bohemia, whence it spread to other countries in Europe.

Man has spread many species throughout the world quite unintentionally. However, since he discovered the value of certain predaceous insects for pest control he has often introduced them purposely to that end. Introduced in this manner from Australia to North America, and later to the whole world, was the small ladybird *Novius cardinalis*. Similarly many species of beetles (e. g. ground beetles — *Calosoma*) have been imported to North America from Europe.

Man has influenced not only the distribution of many animal species, but has also been responsible for the extinction of many, either their total extermination, or just their disappearance from certain regions. A list has been compiled of those species that have become extinct. Large mammals and birds, for instance, are disappearing from Africa, and in jeopardy are the marsupials of Australia, one of the most interesting groups of vertebrate animals on our planet. Also dying out are inhabitants of smaller territories — for instance the Apollo Butterfly *(Parnassius apollo)* in Bohemia, the Gipsy Moth *(Lymantria dispar)* in Great Britain, etc.

Some species have a world-wide distribution, which has come about either naturally or with the aid of Man. Such species are termed cosmopolitan. Numerous species have a fairly large area of distribution which may include several zoogeographical regions. Many species, however, inhabit only a single region, often only a small part of that region, and to seek them elsewhere would be futile. For example, two species of apes — the Chimpanzee and Gorilla — inhabit the tropical forests of Africa, a third — the Orang-utan — inhabits the Oriental region. Kangaroos are typical inhabitants of the Australasian region, giraffes and okapis are typical of the African region, etc.

The greatest variety of animal species is to be found in the tropical and subtropical zones. From there, in both southward and northward directions through the temperate and polar zones, the number of species decreases markedly. The polar regions are inhabited only by species well adapted to survive in the extremely rugged conditions.

The science dealing with the geographical distribution of animals on the Earth is called zoogeography. It studies the relationship between animal species and the regions in which they live. To do this involves many other branches of science such as zoology, phylogenetics, palaeontology, geography, climatology, geology, etc. Zoogeographers divide the world according to the occurrence and distribution of animals into realms, which are further divided into regions, subregions, provinces, etc. Each division is characterized first by the specific fauna occurring only within its confines and secondly by the quantity of species, found also elsewhere, that it contains. The boundaries between the various regions are only approximate and where two regions meet there is always a certain intermingling of species. To date zoogeographers are not in accord as to the exact number of regions. Some believe that certain regions should be joined into one (e. g. the Palaearctic and Nearctic should be referred to jointly as the Holarctic region), whereas others (e. g. the Australasian) should be divided into several independent regions.

The division of the world into the following nine regions will be adequate for the purposes of this book:

1. The Palaearctic is located climatically in the temperate and subtropical zones. It is a very

large area which includes a great part of Europe (as far as the Arctic Circle), a large part of Asia (across Siberia and China as far as Japan, also Asia Minor, the Middle East and the Arabian peninsula as far as the Tropic of Cancer), north Africa (as far as the Tropic of Cancer) and adjacent islands (Madeira, Canary Islands, Azores, etc.).

2. The Nearctic is located in the temperate and subtropical zones of the North American continent and includes southern Canada, the USA, and the Mexican highlands. The fauna of this region is very similar to that of the Palaearctic, indicative of the fact that this continent and Eurasia once formed a single large land mass.

3. The Afrotropical region (also referred to as the Ethiopian or African region) is located primarily in the tropical zone, but does not embrace the whole of the African continent, for the northern part, as far as the Tropic of Cancer, belongs to the Palaearctic region. The Afrotropical region also includes the southern part of the Arabian peninsula, the island of Socotra and various small islands off the west coast of Africa.

Many zoogeographers include the island of Madagascar in the Afrotropical region, but the island's fauna has many unique species, and it appears to have undergone a lengthy, isolated evolution. Madagascar is therefore classified here in an independent region.

4. The Malagasy region, one of the smallest, is located in the tropical and subtropical zone. It includes Madagascar and adjacent islands. From the viewpoint of animal distribution it is a remarkable territory that at one time was part of the African mainland, but was separated from it before elements of the Eurasian fauna began to make their way into Africa. It is interesting to note that in many instances the fauna of Madagascar itself differs from that of the neighbouring islands.

5. The Oriental region (also designated as the Indian or Indo-Malayan region) is climatically located in the tropical and subtropical zones. Geographically it includes India and Pakistan, southeast Asia, and many adjacent islands: Sri Lanka, Indonesia and the Philippines. The northern boundary extends along the southern slopes of the Himalayas across northern China to the mouth of the Yangtze Kiang River. As in the other regions, the fauna is not uniform throughout the whole main territory, quite apart from the border area where there is marked intermingling with the Palaearctic fauna. Some large islands have a very similar fauna (e. g. Sumatra, Java and Borneo) which indicates that their present separation is of recent date. The same is true of Sri Lanka, which was joined to India recently (although its ancient history is separate).

6. The Neotropical region (also designated as the South American region) is located in the tropical and subtropical zone. It includes South America, Central America (the Mexican highlands mark its northern boundary) and the West Indies. It is a region rich in tropical rain forests, steppes and deserts, small and large rivers and extensive swamps, lakes and high mountain massifs.

South America was separated from the other land masses for some 60 million years, during which time an unusual fauna evolved there. Only 2–3 million years ago was it linked with North America by the Isthmus of Panama, a narrow strip of land which emerged from the sea, thereby making it possible for many animals to travel from south to north and vice versa. Central America thus became a territory containing many animal species from both continents.

7. The Australasian region is sometimes considered a single region, though it is often divided into several independent regions. Climatically it is located in the tropics, subtropics and the temperate zone. Geographically it includes Australia, Tasmania, Sulawesi (Celebes), the Moluccas, New Guinea, the Lesser Sundas, New Zealand, and the Pacific islands of Micronesia, Melanesia and Polynesia. In past geological eras the Australian continent also underwent numerous changes before acquiring its present form, which roughly dates from the Mesozoic (the Cretaceous period).

8. The Arctic region includes the northern part of Eurasia and North America (in Europe from 66 °N), the islands in the Arctic Ocean off the coast of Eurasia and North America, and Greenland and Iceland. It is roughly demarcated by the July 10 °C isotherm. Even though it is a large territory it boasts relatively little in the way of animal diversity. Only species that have adapted to the harsh climate and short period of vegetation growth are to be found there. Of the well-known carnivores, this includes the Polar Bear and Arctic Fox.

9. The Antarctic region includes the Antarctic and the subantarctic islands. This region has the lowest diversity of animal forms (of the larger animals the only ones able to survive here are the seals, penguins and albatrosses).

Survey of the Higher Units of the Classification System
Phylum: Sponges — Porifera

These are the simplest of the multicellular animals. Many are small, but some are moderately large. The largest species measures some two metres in diameter. They have widely diverse shapes. Some live singly, others form flat encrusting mats, or various shrub-like clumps or spherical masses. They are sedentary creatures, to be found in freshwaters, or (mostly) in the sea.

The body of a sponge has a very simple structure. It has no muscular, nerve, vascular or excretory systems. The body wall is composed of two layers separated by a jelly-like substance called the mesoglea. This contains a variety of cells necessary for the life processes of the organism. The mesoglea is also where the skeleton is formed. It is comprised chiefly of calcareous or siliceous spicules, together with organic spongin fibres (which in some species may form the greater part of the skeletal structure). The body of the sponge contains many small openings through which water, and with it plankton (food for the sponge), enters the body, leaving again through a single, larger opening.

Marine sponges multiply by means of eggs, from which larvae hatch. Unlike the parent sponge the larva is capable of active movement. Freshwater sponges multiply by means of reproductive bodies called gemmules.

Some 5,000 species have been described to date. These are divided into four classes and many orders.

Phylum: Coelenterates — Cnidaria

This group includes small as well as large species. Many measure only a few millimetres, whereas a large medusa may measure more than one metre across. They live singly or in colonies, and may be free-swimming or fixed. Most Coelenterates are marine, and are predators that feed on various animals. The body has a more complex organisation than that of sponges. It is enclosed by two cell layers — the outer ectoderm and inner endoderm, between which is a thin supporting layer. Sting cells containing a poisonous substance are located in the ectoderm. Inside each sting cell is a coiled, hollow, thread-like structure which whips out when the cell is touched. The tip pierces the victim and paralyses it by means of the poison. These cells occur in large numbers, chiefly on tentacles which surround the mouth. The mouth opening serves a dual function — both for the entrance of food and ejection of solid wastes.

There are two main types of coelenterates, differing in the form of the body: the polyp and the medusa. In some groups the medusa form is lacking altogether (e. g. in the Hydra), but in others the two, polyp and medusa, regularly alternate. The development of coelenterates is very complex, the general pattern being as follows: the egg, produced by a medusa, develops into a free-swimming larva. This grows into a polyp, on the top of which small, but complete medusae are formed. These detach, to grow to full size and produce eggs, so starting the cycle over again.

For a long time it was not known that medusae and polyps could belong to the same organism, and in the literature many were described as a separate species. Coelenterates also commonly reproduce by asexual means, by a process known as budding.

Some 9,000 species have been described to date. These are divided into three classes and a great number of orders and families.

Phylum: Comb jellies — Ctenophora

The members of this phylum vary in shape and size. Some species are sac-like, others flat, band-like. They range from only a few millimetres in length to more than one metre. At the anterior end of the body there are usually two tentacles with special cells called collocytes. These secrete a sticky fluid that aids in capturing prey. The body bears eight rows of comb-like plates that (together with the tentacles) propel the animal mouth forward.

Ctenophores are marine animals. They are hermaphrodites. Unlike the coelenterates there is no reproduction by asexual means, nor is there any alternation of body form. The phylum contains only two classes, the Tentaculata and the Nuda. The latter are devoid of tentacles. Only some 80 species of ctenophores have been described to date.

Phylum: Flatworms — Platyhelminthes

Most have a flattened body with internal organs located in a mesoderm. They have a nervous, excretory and reproductive system but lack any special vascular system or respiratory organs.

Some species measure only a few millimetres, others several decimetres, the longest up to 15 metres. Many are free-living species (in water, soil, etc.), others are parasites living in the organs of various animals, including Man. Parasitic species are not commonly found in the wild and therefore these are neither described nor illustrated in this book.

Platyhelminthes are usually hermaphrodites, and parasitic species produce vast quantities of eggs. Many of the parasitic species have a very complex development requiring an intermediate host (sometimes two) in addition to the main host in which they complete their life cycle.

More than 12,000 species have been described to date. They are divided into three classes and a great number of orders and families.

Phylum: Aschelminthes

Worms with long, round, unsegmented bodies. Besides small microscopic species this group also includes species that measure several tens of centimetres, the largest measuring more than eight metres. They have no respiratory or vascular systems.

Many are free-living worms found in water, damp environments, and soil; others are parasites on animals, including Man, and plants. Although inconspicuous, they are often fantastically abundant. Unlike the Platyhelminthes, the sexes are separate.

The more than 12,000 species are divided into six classes of which the Nematoda is particularly important.

Phylum: Priapulida

These are moderately large worms, the largest measuring 80 millimetres in length. They have cylindrical bodies covered with a thick cuticle which contains chitin, and strong hooks round the mouth. The mouth is situated at the tip of a retractile proboscis. There is no vascular system, but the animals do have cells containing a red respiratory pigment (haemerythrin).

These worms inhabit cold seas, buried in the mud on the sea bottom, from the littoral zone to greater depths. The sexes are separate. Small larvae emerge from the eggs, which are fertilized in the water.

Numerically this is the smallest phylum, containing only four species.

Phylum: Molluscs — Mollusca

This phylum comprises small as well as large species measuring several tens of centimetres. Largest is the giant squid *(Architeuthis dux)*, which, tentacles included, measures about 20 metres in length, and possibly more.

The body of a typical mollusc is soft and slippery, for the surface layer contains a vast number of small glands that secrete mucus. It is divided into a foot, the visceral mass, and the mantle. The foot is the most muscular part of the body and serves primarily as an organ of movement. Molluscs that move glide forward by contracting and relaxing the muscles of the foot along a path richly lubricated by secreted mucus. Some species use the foot to burrow into the ground. In those that swim it is often shaped like a fin. Located above the foot is the visceral mass, which has only a slightly developed muscular structure, but contains most of the vital organs. The edge of the mass hangs down in a fold, forming the mantle that covers the upper part of the foot. The space between it and the foot is called the mantle cavity, which contains the openings of the digestive, excretory and reproductive organs. In aquatic species the mantle cavity contains the gills.

A characteristic and important part of most molluscs is the shell, a protective cover into which the soft body can be fully retracted. Protective covers may be developed to varying degrees and need not be externally visible. The two best known types are the single

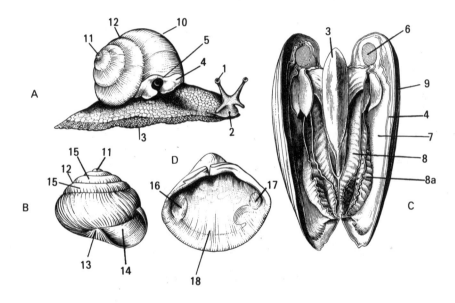

Molluscs (Mollusca): A — overall view of a gastropod (Gastropoda), B — gastropod shell, C — overall view of a bivalve (Bivalvia), D — bivalve shell; 1 — eye, 2 — mouth, 3 — foot, 4 — mantle edge, 5 — spiracle, 6 — anterior adductor muscle, 7 — mantle, 8—8a (internal and external) gills, 9 — bivalve shell, 10 — gastropod shell, 11 — apex of gastropod shell, 12 — suture, 13 — umbilicus, 14 — mouth, 15 — whorls, 16 — point of attachment of anterior adductor muscle, 17 — point of attachment of posterior adductor muscle, 18 — pallial line.

cone-shaped shell of the gastropod, which often takes the form of a spiral, and the paired bivalve shell, consisting of two halves, or valves. These may be the same size, though sometimes one is larger than the other, and need not be of the same shape. The valves may be flat or convex and can be closed by the animal by means of strong muscles. In some species the shell takes the form of loosely connected dorsal plates (e. g. in coat-of-mail shells) or else plates of varying thickness located under the skin (e. g. the well-known 'cuttle-bone' of the so called cuttle-fish). The shell of the mollusc is an inseparable part of its body for it cannot be replaced during its lifetime. As the animal grows so does the shell. It is formed primarily of an inorganic substance, calcium carbonate. On the surface, however, there is a layer of organic matter which often contains various pigments. In many species the inside layer is covered with a glossy, opalescent layer ('mother-of-pearl') of varying thickness which in some molluscs can produce pearls. The shells of some species are thin, fragile structures, in others they are thick and massive. The shape of the shell, the number of teeth in the hinge, or the presence of various teeth in the mouth of the shell serve as means for identification. Descriptions of molluscs usually include the size of the shell — in the gastropod shell its height and greatest width, in the bivalve shell its length, height and thickness, the length being measured from the hinge to the edge on the opposite side, the height from edge to edge at right angles to this line, and the thickness from apex to apex with both halves closed.

Unlike the preceding phyla, molluscs have well-developed internal organs. At the beginning of the alimentary canal there is a tongue or radula, a kind of rasp that serves to tear up food. The food then passes to the stomach, where it is digested, and undigested remnants are excreted through the anus into the mantle cavity. The nervous system consists, usually, of three pairs of ganglia joined by longitudinal and cross connectives. There are also sensory organs (eyes, organs of equilibrium — statocysts, tactile organs, etc.), as well as a developed circulatory system. As in most lower animals this is an open system, which means that the blood is mostly not confined to vessels but flows freely in the body cavity. The force that powers the circulatory system is the dorsally situated heart. The excretory organs (kidneys) also open into the mantle cavity.

Molluscs inhabit various environments: saltwater, freshwater, brackish water, and dry land. Some species are carnivorous, others herbivorous.

The sexes are usually separate, though many species are hermaphroditic. The young hatch from eggs; in some, mostly marine, species there is an intermediate larval stage.

Molluscs are of great importance to Man. In many maritime countries they are a source of food, the muscular foot being the part that is eaten. Many are collected for the pearls they contain. Shells are sold as souvenirs, those of some bivalves were long used as a medium of exchange, etc. Some species of molluscs serve as intermediate hosts in the life cycle of certain parasitic platyhelminths (e. g. the liver-fluke of the sheep — *Fasciola hepatica),* etc.

Molluscs are the second largest phylum (second only to the arthropods) in the animal kingdom. At present there are 130,000 described species recognized. In past geological periods this phylum may have been even larger, for a great many species well preserved as fossils have become extinct.

The molluscs are divided into two subphyla and seven classes. Most numerous and best known are the univalves or gastropods (Gastropoda) and the bivalves (Bivalvia). The system of orders, suborders and other groupings in not definitely established as yet.

Class: Gastropods — Gastropoda

This group has a great number of small, moderately large and large species (the shell of the largest measures as much as 60 cm). Most gastropods have a strong, muscular foot. The visceral mass is generally located inside an asymmetrical shell. The anterior part of the body forms a more or less distinct head equipped with extensible tentacles ('feelers') and a pair of eyes.

The gastropod shell, secreted by the mantle, coils in a spiral and has no inside partitions.

14

The visceral mass inside is also more or less twisted in the same way. In many species the shell is strikingly coloured. In most the spiral twists to the right, less commonly to the left. The apex is the oldest part of the shell, which grows and is added on to only at the base. In most species the shell of the adult animal can be identified by the thick recurved lip. Many species have a strong, permanent lid called the operculum. When the animal retreats inside its shell this lid fits tightly against the lip thus firmly closing the entrance.

Terrestrial species absorb oxygen from the air by means of a lung chamber. In aquatic species respiration is usually by means of gills, although many derived from terrestrial forms, have a lung chamber and must come to the surface to breathe. Also important as a means of respiration is the direct absorption of oxygen through the moist skin.

Gastropods inhabit diverse biotopes. They are to be found in the sea, in bodies of fresh as well as brackish water, and many also live permanently on dry land. Terrestrial species generally require a certain degree of moisture and therefore often conceal themselves under stones, under the bark of tree stumps, etc. The diet of gastropods shows marked diversity. Some are omnivorous, others herbivorous, and still others feed on the bodies of dead animals. Many species are predaceous and have varied techniques of capturing their prey. This group of molluscs also includes species that are parasitic.

In gastropods the sexes are separate, although their number also includes hermaphroditic forms. The eggs are laid either singly or in gelatinous masses. The egg hatches either into a larva or, where there is no larval stage, directly into a small replica of the adult.

This class of molluscs contains the greatest number of species, more than 100,000, which are divided among a large number of lower groupings.

Class: Bivalves — Bivalvia

This class includes both small and large species (the largest has a shell 1.35 metres long). Their structure differs markedly from that of the gastropods. The body is bilaterally symmetrical and greatly flattened laterally. The mantle is very well developed and enfolds the body on both sides like a cloak.

The soft body is enclosed between the two convex halves (valves) of the shell. The valves are connected on the dorsal side by a strong elastic hinge or ligament. Only rarely is the shell smaller than the body. A characteristic feature on the inside of many shells is the ingenious system of interlocking teeth called the cardo. Also apparent on the inside are the points of attachment ('scars') of the muscles which pull the valves shut. A distinctive feature on the outside is the raised area called the umbo, which is the oldest part of the shell. The outer surface may be smooth but is often patterned with concentric and radiating grooves. The growth lines formed by the addition of new shell layers at the outer edges are more darkly coloured.

In most species the two halves of the shell are practically symmetrical, but in others they are very asymmetrical (e. g. the oyster). In many marine bivalves the shells have 'ears' at the apex (e. g. genus *Pecten*).

In a live bivalve one can see the opening at the anterior end through which the animal extends its foot. At the posterior end there are two further openings: a lower one through which fresh water containing oxygen and food flows into the cavity and an upper one which serves for the discharge of waste products and water. In species that burrow in the seabed the edges of these openings are extended into muscular tubes called siphons. Many bivalves secrete an organic substance that rapidly hardens to form a tuft of filaments called the byssus, serving to attach them to an object.

Bivalves live only in water and therefore breathe by means of gills. Most species live in the sand and mud of the bottom. Some attach themselves to rocks or other objects with the byssus, others are able to burrow in stone and in wood. They feed on plankton.

Reproduction is by means of eggs, which are produced in vast numbers. This is necessary because many of the tiny planktonic larvae that hatch perish as food for other animals.

There are about 20,000 known species.

Class: Cephalopods — Cephalopoda

Cephalopods are the most highly developed and the largest of all molluscs. The body is bilaterally symmetrical, oval or sac-like. The mouth is encircled by at least eight arms or tentacles, equipped on the inner side with suckers. An external protective cover or shell is well developed only in the genus *Nautilus*. The *Nautilus* shell is divided by partitions, the animal inhabiting only the last compartment. In the other cephalopods the shell is only a vestigial structure located under the skin.

Cephalopods are predatory, marine creatures. Certain species living at considerable depths are luminescent.

Today there are a little over 700 known species, but more than 10,000 extinct species from previous geological periods are known from fossils.

Phylum: Segmented worms — Annelida

This phylum includes both small and moderately large species; the longest measures as much as 3 metres. The body is long, often vermiform, and made up of segments. The first segment is called the prostomium, the last the pygidium, and there may be as many as several hundred segments in between. Segmentation is both external and internal. The individual body segments are demarcated by partitions (septae). The effects of segmentation are apparent in the arrangement of certain body organs, primarily the renal ducts, ganglia and often the sex glands as well. The digestive system, which extends the length of the whole body, and the circulatory system are unsegmented. The latter is a closed system consisting of longitudinal and 'circular' vessels that are often visible through the skin. Most important are the dorsal and ventral vessels through which blood is conveyed towards and away from the head respectively. The blood may include a respiratory pigment usually haemoglobin (red), but sometimes a green compound, chlorocruorin.

Annelids are found in marine as well as freshwater habitats and also on dry land (often in the ground). The approximately 8,700 species are divided into three classes.

Class: Sandworms and tubeworms — Polychaeta

Members of this class range in size from several millimetres to several tens of centimetres. Species of the genus *Eunice* may measure up to 3 metres. Polychaetes have an elongated, tube-like, sometimes flattened body composed of numerous segments, most of which have a pair of fleshy, leg-like appendages called parapodia, which are sometimes shaped like fins. They may represent the precursors of the limbs of higher animals, and truly assist in movement. The parapodia are covered with tufts of bristles varying in length and thickness. The prostomium usually bears tentacle-like appendages. Many species of polychaetes are brightly coloured — red, green or blue. This is caused by pigments, including the colour of the blood or ingested food that shines through. Sessile species, which gather plankton with the aid of beautiful, fan-like tentacles, are often gregarious, forming fantastic looking 'flowering meadows'. Some species of polychaetes are luminescent.

In general polychaetes have eyes, which in many species are quite highly developed. They are located on the prostomium, the tentacles, or on the parapodia and elsewhere.

Polychaetes are chiefly marine creatures inhabiting the littoral zone, though some also descend to greater depths. In the littoral zone they live amidst seaweeds, in coral reefs, on rocks and amidst other marine animals. Many are free-swimming species, others build tubes in which they hide or else they burrow in the sand. Some remain in the tubes only for a while, others never leave them. The tubes are made of body secretions, but they may also include admixtures such as grains of sand, shell fragments, excrement, etc. The tube-dwelling animals usually cluster close together, extending only their tentacles, as already noted.

16

The diet of polychaetes depends on their way of life. Free-swimming species hunt larger animals. Those that inhabit fixed tubes feed on small organisms that come within the reach of their tentacles.

The sexes are separate. The females lay varying numbers of eggs (often several thousand) from which larvae then hatch. This class includes approximately 5,300 species.

Class: Clitellata

This class includes species ranging in length from several millimetres to several tens of centimetres (the longest species, of the genus *Megascolides*, measure 2–3 metres). The body is elongated, vermiform, segmented, and may be round or dorsoventrally flattened. There are neither anterior nor lateral appendages (parapodia). The segments may have short bristles. On certain body segments there is a saddle or clitellum which contains glands capable of secreting a cocoon. The eggs are laid inside a cocoon, which is where the further stages of development take place.

These worms are found in freshwater habitats and on dry land in damp places – in the ground, under stones, in old tree stumps and under bark, etc. They are hermaphroditic. There is no separate larval stage.

The approximately 3,400 species are divided into the following two sub-classes which are fairly easy to distinguish:

Sub-class: Earthworms and freshwater annelids – Oligochaeta

The body is long, worm-like, segmented outside and inside; each segment has at least 4 pairs of bristles. The clitellum extends across several segments. Suckers are absent. Feed on plant remnants or else are microphagous.
Example: earthworm
3,100 species

Sub-class: Leeches – Hirudinea

Body flattened, segmented on the outside. Clitellum short. Sucker at each end of body, anterior sucker round the mouth. Move with the aid of suckers, but also swim freely. Feed on blood or small animals. Most are freshwater species.
Example: leech
300 species

Phylum: Arthropods – Arthropoda

This, the largest phylum, is also very diverse. Its members range in size from several tenths of a millimetre to several centimetres; some species, however, are more than one metre long and the largest measures up to three metres (including the long legs).

Because of its great diversity it is not easy to give a brief characteristic description of the phylum. All that can be said is that the body is covered with a cuticle containing chitin. It is segmented and has varying numbers of segmented appendages. The segments of the legs and other appendages are jointed, thus allowing movement in at least one direction. The legs

17

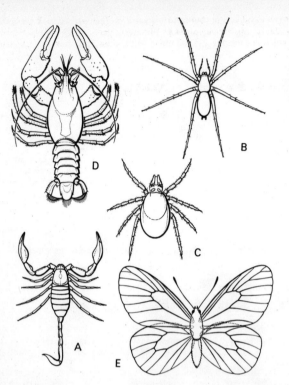

may be located both on the thorax and abdomen or only on the thorax. The head has many differently shaped appendages. Insects, which are the largest class of arthropods, often have wings as additional organs of locomotion. In some groups there are two distinct body regions — the cephalothorax and abdomen, in others there are three — head, thorax and abdomen.

The firm cuticle forms a thick external skeleton (exoskeleton). The separate pieces of the skeleton are either joined by flexible membranes or else they are fused. Each body segment is divided into a dorsal part (tergum), ventral part (sternum) and side parts (pleurae). As the animal grows it sheds its skeleton from time to time. This shedding, or ecdysis, is stimulated by the action of glands producing internal secretions (hormones).

The internal anatomy of arthropods is fairly complex. The sense organs are relatively well developed. The blood system is an open one with few vessels in which the haemolymph freely bathes the body organs. Marked diversity is exhibited by the system of respiration. Species that live in water breathe by means of gills, often located on the legs. They also obtain oxygen by diffusion through the body surface. Terrestrial species either have variously arranged lung chambers or a system of air tubes called tracheae.

Arthropods are found in widely different habitats throughout the whole world. The majority occur on dry land, with smaller numbers inhabiting waters of various types.

The sexes are generally separate, although there are some groups of arthropods that are hermaphroditic. The vast majority lay eggs, only a few species giving birth to active young. From the egg emerges either a small replica of the adult which gradually grows to reach the adult stage, or a larva which then develops into the adult form, sometimes with a discrete pupal stage in between.

Arthropods comprise many hundreds of thousands of species. They are divided according to various characteristics, chiefly the arrangement of the mouthparts or method of respiration, into four subphyla, which are further divided into several classes, numerous orders and a great many families.

Class: Spiders, ticks, mites and others — Arachnida

This class belongs to the subphylum Chelicerata and includes very small to quite large species (the largest measures 18 centimetres). The posterior end of the body, called the opisthosoma, may be without exterior segmentation or else it may be divided into segments.

There are six pairs of appendages. The third to sixth pair are fitted for walking or running. The first pair are the chelicerae, each with a basal segment and a terminal claw-like fang, often connected to a poison gland. The second pair are the pedipalps, which vary in shape. Where the chelicerae are small the pedipalps are huge, sometimes resembling the claws of a crayfish (e. g. scorpions). In other cases the pedipalps are shaped more like legs, and are used for various purposes, including feeding and sensing. Most species have several pairs of simple eyes (called ocelli), located in the centre and at the sides of the head.

Arachnids live on dry land in both damp and dry habitats. Many are predatory and hunt large prey, often larger than themselves. Some have a poisonous gland in the abdomen, instead of in the jaws, others spin webs. Many suck blood or plant sap.

The sexes are usually separate. The females lay eggs. Some species give birth to active young and are even known to tend their offspring.

There are approximately 36,000 known species. Important orders include the scorpions (Scorpionida), true spiders (Araneae), false scorpions (Pseudoscorpionida), harvestmen (Phalangida) and ticks and mites (Acari).

Class: Crustaceans — Crustacea

This class belongs to the subphylum Branchiata and includes species of varying sizes (the crab *Kampheria kampheri* with extremely long legs measures 3 metres!), with bodies that are long or short and robust. The outer cuticle sometimes contains calcium carbonate, thus forming an external skeleton that is very hard in those species.

The body of crustaceans is not composed of a uniform number of segments; on the contrary, they exhibit marked diversity in this respect. The head is rarely clearly defined, usually it is united with one or more segments of the thorax to form a cephalothorax. Some crustaceans have a dorsal shield called the carapace which covers all of the back or else shelters at least some of the segments like a roof. The last segment of the body is called the telson.

Crustaceans have three types of appendages: antennae, mouthparts, and limbs. The legs are usually located only on the thorax, but sometimes they are also present on the abdomen. The abdominal legs, however, are shaped differently from those on the thorax.

The eyes are either simple or compound. Respiration is by means of gills, the body surface, and in a few terrestrial species by means of tracheae, etc.

Many crustaceans inhabit waters of various types; some live on dry land (order Isopoda). The diet varies in accordance with the environment they inhabit. Swimming species feed on plankton, those that live on the sea bottom collect various fragments or are predaceous. Some feed on carrion. Crustaceans also include many parasitic species with a mature anatomy that is entirely different from the general pattern.

The sexes are usually separate. The egg stage is followed by a larval stage; only sometimes does a small replica of the adult emerge directly from the egg (e. g. crayfish).

The roughly 35,000 species are divided into nine subclasses, numerous superorders and orders, and a great number of families. The classification of this large class is not very stable, there being a tendency to divide it into several separate classes.

19

Class: Millipedes — Diplopoda

This class belongs to the subphylum Tracheata and includes small as well as moderately large species. The longest measures 28 centimetres. Some have an elongated, worm-like body, often flattened from above, that of others is composed of several plates (they can curl up into a ball). Some millipedes are glabrous, others have bristles. The body is made up of varying numbers of segments which are furnished with appendages. Beginning from the fifth each segment has two pairs of limbs. This indicates that these segments developed from the fusion of two original segments. Each such 'double segment' also has two pairs of spiracles (breathing vents). The number of legs varies considerably and is not constant, even within a single species. The least number is 13 pairs, though many species have several tens of pairs, as many as 300 pairs being the greatest number described to date.

Some millipedes have a number of ocelli, others are blind. They breathe by means of tracheae. The sexes are separate.

Millipedes occur in abundance under stones, amidst fallen leaves, in old tree stumps, in the ground, in caves, in gardens, greenhouses, and the like. They are nocturnal creatures that are fond of damp. They feed on rotting wood, sometimes also on young plant tissues.

The more than 7,000 species, distributed throughout the world, are divided into two orders.

Class: Centipedes — Chilopoda

This class also belongs to the subphylum Tracheata. Its members have an elongated body of moderate size (the longest species measures 27 centimetres) composed of flattened segments. The sexes are very similar in appearance.

Each segment, except for the last two, has a pair of limbs. There may be several tens of body segments. The antennae are filiform, multi-segmented. Behind the antennae are four paired appendages that function as mouthparts. Behind the large mandibles are two pairs of maxillae (the second pair is used to hold food). The fourth pair of appendages are actually the front pair of legs (of the first body segment) modified to form poison claws. The poison is fatal to many arthropods.

Reproduction is by means of eggs. Full maturity is reached after two or three years. Centipedes are nocturnal animals that hide during the daytime under stones, in the ground, in old tree stumps, under logs, etc. They are predators that capture a great number of arthropods and their larvae, earthworms and other small animals. They are warmth-loving, and so the greatest number of species is to be found in the tropics.

There are approximately 2,800 known species belonging to two separate orders.

Class: Insects — Insecta

The insect body is made up of three distinct parts: head, thorax and abdomen. The thorax usually bears three pairs of jointed legs and two pairs of wings. The body is covered with an outer protective layer called the cuticle, which is of varying thickness and composed of chitin. It forms the so-called exoskeleton (thanks to this hard skeleton many insects can easily be kept for study as dry specimens). Each of the body parts is composed of several segments, although the lines where they join are not always evident.

The head of an insect bears the antennae, eyes and mouthparts. It is thought to consist of six segments, but in the adult the segmentation is not visible. At the front is the upper lip or labrum, which covers the mandibles or upper jaws. Above it is the transverse portion called the clypeus, then comes the frons, the vertex, and last of all the occiput at the back. Laterally the head bears compound eyes of varying size, each composed of a large number of tiny individual parts called ommatidia. Some insects also have simple eyes (ocelli) on top of the head, between the compound eyes. Before the eyes are the cheeks or genae. The mandibles are·protected from below by the lower lip or labium. The antennae have a few to dozens of segments. They may vary greatly in form and are not uniform even within a single order. In the order Protura they are absent, and in some other groups of insects they may be reduced to a small stump (e. g. in some mealy-bugs).

The mouthparts take up the front part of the head. Their structure is not the same in all insects. The most common type are mouthparts adapted for chewing, consisting of upper jaws (mandibles) and lower jaws (maxillae), bounded above and below by the upper and lower lips. The mandibles may vary in size and strength and are often toothed on the inner edge. These move towards each other, from side to side. Below the mandibles are the maxillae, or second pair of jaws, to which are attached segmented appendages known as maxillary palps. The lower lip (labium) bears a second pair of appendages called the labial palps. The mouthparts, however, are often adapted to other methods of feeding, primarily for licking and sucking or piercing and sucking. In such cases the mandibles and maxillae are more or less elongated to form a proboscis (extremely long is the proboscis of certain butterflies and moths, bee-flies, some aphids and bugs, etc.).

The thorax is composed of three segments: the prothorax, mesothorax and metathorax, which may clearly be separate or more firmly joined together. Each thoracic segment bears on the underside one pair of legs; the mesothorax and metathorax also bear a pair of wings in most insects.

The legs are usually present in full number (i. e. three pairs) though sometimes one or more pairs may be reduced. The legs consist of five parts, differing in length and thickness. These are the coxa, trochanter, femur, tibia and tarsus. At the end of the tarsus, which is composed of one to five segments, are one or two claws. The legs vary in form, length and thickness according to the purpose for which they are used. They may all be identical, or a certain pair may be adapted for a specific function − for running, scraping, jumping or swimming. A special type are those adapted for seizing prey (raptorial legs).

Most insects have two pairs of wings (the anterior pair larger than the posterior). Only some have a single pair (e. g. true flies, Diptera). The commonest type is the membranous wing, consisting of two thin membranes closely applied throughout, except along certain hollow struts called veins. Wings may be glabrous, covered with hairs or with coloured scales. In many orders the first and second pair of wings differ in form and structure. For example, in beetles the front wings are altered to form special hardened covers (elytra) and only the hind wings are membranous. In the earwigs the short front wings are similarly thickened to protect the membranous hind wings folded underneath. In bugs the front wings form so-called hemelytra. The Diptera have the hind wings reduced to form minute balancing organs (halteres). In repose wings may be held in various positions. They may be folded flat above the abdomen, folded roof-like over the body or held erect above the back, etc. Some insects are primitively wingless (the Apterygota). Other groups include certain forms that are now permanently or temporarily wingless (ants, fleas, mealy-bugs, etc.) though their ancestors were winged.

The abdomen is generally the largest of the three body parts. In primitive insects there are small protuberances on the anterior segments, and in some orders there are variously formed appendages at the tail end. Some female insects are furnished with an ovipositor, which organ shows great variation in length and form.

Insects are found in widely diverse habitats throughout the world. Most species live on dry land, and only a small percentage of them inhabit water. The diet of different species includes various forms of animal life, carrion, excrements, foodstores, plant tissues, the nectar and pollen of flowers, fabrics, leather, zoological collections, etc.

The development of insects is generally one of two kinds: incomplete metamorphosis (hemimetabolic) or complete metamorphosis (holometabolic). The females of most species are oviparous and lay varying numbers of eggs. In the case of incomplete metamorphosis the larva that emerges from the egg grows and sheds its skin a number of times until it finally changes directly into an adult (imago). The larvae of insects that undergo an incomplete metamorphosis (they are often called nymphs) greatly resemble the adult. In complete metamorphosis a larva likewise emerges from the egg. It, too, sheds its skin (moults) several times, but then it turns into a pupa, which is generally immobile; this apparently quiescent stage lasts several weeks or months, after which the adult emerges. In insects that undergo a complete metamorphosis the larva does not resemble the adult at all. Several orders of very primitive insects develop without metamorphosis. The young insect is practically the same as the adult except that it is smaller and is unable to reproduce.

Insects are very important in nature's scheme of things. In the first place they are the most important agents in the pollination of flowers, a clearly vital process in the life-cycle of plants. Many species of insects feed on the larvae, pupae or adult forms of other insects that damage cultivated crops, or spread diseases. Modern science has met with success in its attempts to use these species in the control of pests — a method that in future could replace chemical agents, which have a detrimental effect on Man and his environment. Insects act as scavengers and participate in the formation of humus. Some species yield important raw materials (dyes, shellac, wax, silk) others are food for man (grasshoppers, termites). Their presence also enhances the beauty of nature and of our surroundings, despite the fact that some are harmful to Man and his economy.

Insects form the class in the animal kingdom with the greatest number of species. It is estimated that it includes more than 800,000 described forms (of this number more than 300,000 are beetles!). The number of insect species inhabiting the earth, however, is certainly much greater. Many species in the vast tropical regions await discovery and investigation. According to the modern system of classification the class is divided into three subclasses and more than thirty orders.

Phylum: Hemichordata (Branchiotremata)

Small to large marine species (the largest is 2.5 metres long) with body composed of three parts. They live singly or in colonies.

The approximately 80 species are divided into two classes.

Phylum: Echinoderms — Echinodermata

This phylum includes animals remarkable not only for their diversity of form but also for their evolution and geological age. They are classed together in one group because of several important characteristics they have in common. First is the radial body symmetry, the only instance of its kind in the animal kingdom. The basic symmetry is pentagonal (the body has five arms or furrows, or multiples thereof). Another important characteristic is the skeleton to be found in most echinoderms. Located under a thin epidermis it forms a sort of external armour of varying thickness. It is composed of calcareous plates, spines, needles, etc., the tips of which project from the skin. In many species the plates are massive and placed close together. In the sea cucumbers (Holothuroidea), however, the skeleton is composed only of tiny sclerites. The skeletons of many species are beautifully coloured. Clearly visible in live animals are the peculiar, so-called ambulacral or tube-feet, which are extensible and used for locomotion.

The internal body structure is very complex and the function of certain organs has not been satisfactorily resolved as yet.

Echinoderms adopt various positions depending on the location of the mouth, according to which they are divided into the following four groups:
1. Sea-lilies or crinoids (Crinoidea) have bodies of varying size and flowerlike form. The mouth faces upwards.
2. Starfish (Asteroidea) and brittle or serpent stars (Ophiuroidea) have the mouth facing downward.
3. Sea-urchins or sand dollars (Echinoidea) have a globular body and mouth facing downward.
4. Sea-cucumbers (Holothuroidea) have an elongated worm-like body and a lateral mouth.

Body structure of echinoderms (Echinodermata): A — sea-lily, B — starfish, C — sea-urchin, D — sea-cucumber. The ambulacral system is marked in black (according to Kaestner)

Phylum: Chordates — Chordata

The members of this phylum have an elongated, rod-shaped structure (notochord) that forms a primitive supporting axis to the body and which lies above the digestive tract and below the dorsal tubular nerve cord (central nervous system). The heart is a sac-like organ located on the ventral side of the body, posterior to the head. The respiratory organs are always closely connected with the anterior part of the digestive system — the pharynx. In the course of evolution the pharynx acquired pairs of gill slits opening to the exterior.

The phylum includes both aquatic and terrestrial species of all sizes — ranging from very small to the largest species of animals that have ever inhabited the earth. Today there are approximately 45,000 known species divided into three subphyla, several classes, and numerous orders, etc. The first two subphyla include small marine animals, the third includes marine, freshwater and terrestrial animals of all sizes.

Subphylum: Vertebrates — Vertebrata

The largest and most important chordate subphylum.

The body of vertebrates consists of three sections: the head, trunk and tail. The notochord extends only to the middle of the head and is generally present only in the embryonic stages. In some of the primitive vertebrates it persists throughout the animal's entire life. In most vertebrates it is usually replaced by a segmented backbone or spinal column that protects the spinal cord, the internal organs of the trunk being protected by ribs attached to it. The skin of vertebrates is composed of several layers. There are usually two pairs of limbs and a cartilaginous or bony skeleton.

Vertebrates are usually divided into a lower group (Anamnia) without embryonic membranes — this includes fish and amphibians, and a higher group (Amniota) with embryonic membranes — this includes reptiles, birds and mammals. The eggs of fishes and amphibians develop in water and do not need any special protection against drying out. The embryos develop freely on the yolk sac, to which they are attached by a yolk stalk and the contents of which they gradually absorb as they grow. The eggs of reptiles, birds and mammals do not develop in water and throughout the period of embryonic development are enclosed inside

23

embryonic membranes called the amnion and allantois. These are specific embryonic organs formed with the growing embryo.

The subphylum can also be divided into two superclasses – the Agnatha, or jawless, and the Gnathostomata, or jawed vertebrates. The first includes vertebrates that do not possess jaws, the second those that have an upper jaw firmly joined to or fused with the skull and a freely-moving lower jaw. The only existing class of jawless vertebrates are the cyclostomes – (Cyclostomata); all other living classes belong to the superclass Gnathostomata.

Class: Cyclostomes – Cyclostomata

These are aquatic vertebrates with a long snake or eel-like body covered with smooth skin supplied with a great number of glands. They do not have paired fins, only a single continuous fin down the length of the body. The skeleton and skull are cartilaginous. The notochord is retained throughout life; there are only the rudiments of vertebrae. On either side behind the head are 6 to 14 gill slits. The nostril is unpaired, the mouth is a jawless suctorial organ.

Cyclostomes breathe by means of their gills and feed either on small aquatic animals or are parasitic on fish. The sexes are separate. Larvae hatch from the eggs. Today there are only several dozen existing species, divided into two orders.

Class: Cartilaginous fishes (sharks and rays) – Chondrichthyes

These are aquatic vertebrates with a body that is covered with hard and sharp placoid scales similar in structure to the teeth of higher vertebrates. Behind the head are 5 to 7 pairs of gill slits through which water flows out of the gill chambers. In some cases the gill chambers are joined and open to the exterior through a single cleft. The tail fin is heterocercal (that is, the upper lobe, which contains the upturned end of the spinal column, is larger than the lower lobe). The notochord is retained in its entirety or at least in large part, in addition to the vertebrae. The skeleton is cartilaginous. The heart is two chambered. A peculiar, so-called spiral valve is to be found in the gut.

To this day more than 200 species inhabit the seas (very occasionally also fresh waters). They are divided into two subclasses and three orders.

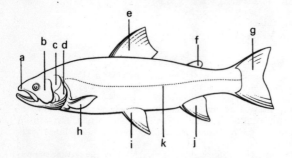

Fish external features: a – snout, b – d – opercula, composed of several bones (b – praeoperculum, c – operculum, d – suboperculum), e – dorsal fin, f – adipose fin, g – caudal fin, h – pectoral fin, i – pelvic fin, j – anal fin, k – lateral line

Class: Bony fishes – Osteichthyes

This class includes the great majority of existing fishes. The skeleton is predominantly bony; it is composed of an exoskeleton (product of the ectoderm) and a chondral (mesodermal)

skeleton, resulting from the ossification of cartilage. Fish breathe by means of gills; the gill filaments are usually attached directly to the gill arches. The gills are protected by a bony covering called the operculum. The body of fishes is usually covered with scales (but these are not placoid scales), sometimes with bony plates, while in some instances it is bare. Most fishes have a well developed air or swim-bladder. The eggs (roe) are generally fertilized outside the body; they are usually small and produced in great numbers.

There are approximately 25,000 known species of bony fish inhabiting the seas, rivers and other types of inland waters throughout the world. They are divided into two subclasses, several superorders and approximately 45 orders. Fish of two superorders are found in European waters.

Superorder: Sturgeons — Chondrostei

In these fishes only some parts of the skull are bony, the greater part is cartilaginous. The praeoperculum is absent. The tail fin is heterocercal. The notochord is retained throughout life. This group includes a single order with 25 species.

Superorder: Teleostei

These are fishes with a bony skeleton and well-developed vertebrae. The body is covered with ctenoid or cycloid scales, occasionally with bony plates, and sometimes the skin is bare. The fishes of this group have four paired gills. There is no spiral valve in the gut.

The head ends in a snout which may be blunt or elongated. The eyes are located on either side of the head and in front of the eyes are one or two pairs of nostrils. The mouth may be situated at the tip of the snout, or placed dorsally or ventrally. Behind the head, on either side, is a single gill cleft covered by a movable bony operculum. The inner sides of the gill arches bear so-called gill rakers.

The organs of locomotion are the fins, which are of two kinds: paired (pectoral and pelvic) and unpaired (dorsal, caudal and anal). The skin of the fins is supported by fin rays.

On either side of the body and head is a special sensory organ called the lateral line system. This is clearly evident as a row of dots running through the centre of the scales and branching on the head.

Today the world is inhabited by approximately 25,000 species of bony fish which are divided into more than 40 orders and approximately 430 families.

Class: Amphibians — Amphibia

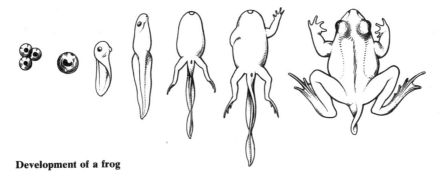

Development of a frog

25

Amphibians usually have bare skin with a great number of glands, and two pairs of limbs, which are sometimes reduced. In the adult stage they generally breathe by means of lungs and through the skin, in the larval stage by means of gills. Fertilization may take place inside or outside the body. From the egg emerges a legless larva (tadpole) which lives in water and develops legs and lungs as it grows. When metamorphosis is complete most amphibians leave the water and live on land.

Amphibians are abundant chiefly in the tropical regions, the number of species rapidly decreasing in northerly and southerly directions. There are approximately 1,900 existing species. These are divided into three orders.

Class: Reptiles — Reptilia

These are terrestrial vertebrates, some of which have reverted to life in water. Reproduction takes place on land and development of the egg likewise always takes place in an aerobic environment. There is no larval stage. The embryo is enclosed in embryonic membranes. The body temperature of reptiles varies, and the ability to regulate it is slight. The head of reptiles is joined to the body by means of a cervical section that permits marked flexibility of movement for the head. The skin is horny and forms scales or plates that protect the body. Respiration is solely by means of lungs. The limbs and their associated skeletal components have become atrophied in some groups.

The number of existing species is estimated at 4,000—5,000. These are divided into four orders.

Order: Turtles, tortoises and terrapins — Chelonia

These are reptiles with a short, broad body, encased in a hard bony shell fused with the skeleton. The surface is covered with horny plates. The upper, dorsal shell (carapace) is convex, and the undershell (plastron) is flat. The two are joined at the sides with openings for the head, legs and tail. The jaws are toothless and covered by a horny skin.

The Chelonia include both aquatic and terrestrial, carnivorous and herbivorous species. They are divided into four suborders numbering a total of approximately 250 species.

Order: Lizards and snakes — Squamata

The largest order of living reptiles, it includes species covered with horny scales that are extremely diversified in both size and form. Belonging to this group are animals with well-developed legs, excellent runners and climbers (lizards) as well as animals with variously reduced limbs, or without any limbs at all that move by crawling (snakes). Most species inhabit the tropical and subtropical regions. Snakes and lizards live on the ground, in trees and bushes as well as in water. They are mostly carnivorous and are sometimes furnished with poison fangs with which they kill their prey.

More than 4,000 species have been described to date. These are divided into two suborders and more than 30 families.

Class: Birds — Aves

Birds have a high and constant body temperature. The body surface is covered with feathers. Those that give the body its typical shape are called contour feathers. Beneath these are the down feathers that serve to insulate the animal. The forelimbs of birds are modified into wings. The jaws (bill) are usually much elongated, the bones fused and the whole covered by

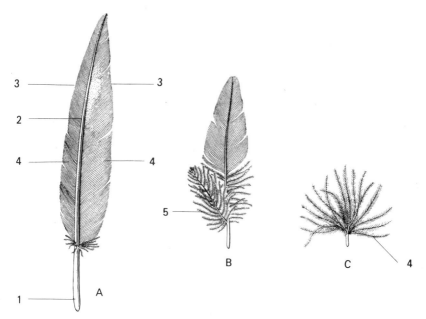

Types of bird feathers: A − flight feathers (remiges), B − tetrices (A + B = contour feathers), C − down feather; 1 − quill (calamus), 2 − shaft (rhachis), 3 − vane, web (vexellum), 4 − barbules (rami), 5 − secondary 'aftershaft' (hyporhachis)

a horny sheath. The skin of birds is dry; it has no glands apart from the uropygial or oil gland at the base of the tail. Birds are oviparous and development is direct. The embryo is encased in embryonic membranes.

Birds are distributed throughout the world and number approximately 10,000 species. They can be divided into three superorders: running birds (Ratitae), swimming birds (Impennes) and flying birds (Carinatae) − and a great many orders.

Class: Mammals − Mammalia

Mammals have a high and constant body temperature, or one that varies only slightly, and a very well developed central nervous system. The body is usually hairy, presumably to prevent heat loss. The two pairs of limbs are adapted for walking, climbing, burrowing, or for other purposes. A characteristic feature is the great number of skin glands. The sexes are separate and their reproductive organs are markedly different. The lowest group of mammals lay eggs (Monotremata) or give birth to poorly developed young (Marsupialia). The young of placental mammals (Placentalia) develop in the womb of the mother where they are nourished through a special organ − the placenta. Young mammals feed on milk produced by the mammary glands of the mother. The ear of mammals has three small bones − the hammer, anvil and stirrup − connecting the middle ear to the inner ear, and an external auditory canal terminating in the external ear. The head is joined to the spine by two occipital condyles.

Mammals are distributed throughout the world in widely diverse habitats. They number approximately 8,000 species.

27

Geological Time Chart

	Era	Period	Epoch	Number of years (in millions) since the beginning of each division
Phanerozoic 'Period of evident life'	Cenozoic	Quaternary	Holocene	0.01
			Pleistocene	2−3
		Tertiary	Pliocene	5
			Miocene	22
			Oligocene	38
			Eocene	54
			Paleocene	65
	Mesozoic	Cretaceous		130
		Jurassic		180
		Triassic		230
	Palaeozoic	Permian		280
		Carboniferous		340
		Devonian		400
		Silurian		450
		Ordovician		500
		Cambrian		570
Cryptozoic 'Period of hidden life'	Proterozoic			1800
	Archaeozoic			3500
	Astral			?

The Origin and Evolution of Animals

The number and diversity of species on the earth is the result of an extremely long period of evolution that has lasted milliards of years (one milliard is a thousand million). According to the generally recognized Oparin theory, living matter was formed from non-living matter in an oxygen-less environment at the time of the formation of the earth's crust. The first living organisms were microscopic, anaerobic, and perhaps resembled some of the bacteria and algae of the present day. It was only when there was sufficient oxygen in the earth's atmosphere that further evolution and the development of more complex organisms became possible.

28

The first living organisms that palaeontologists have succeeded in discovering to date are from the era called the Archaeozoic. They are so-called microfossils, fossilized remains of bacteria and algae preserved in extremely old geological layers. Radioactive dating has shown them to be about 3.3 milliard years old. In all probability the beginnings of life date from a far earlier time.

From the geological aspect it is not long, about 570 million years, since the beginning of the Phanerozoic, when animals already inhabited the earth. The Phanerozoic is divided into three main eras, the Palaeozoic, Mesozoic and Cenozoic.

The oldest is the Palaeozoic, which covers the period between about 570,000,000 and 230,000,000 years ago. The oldest period in this era is the Cambrian, when there was probably as yet no life on dry land, but only in the seas. These were already inhabited by many species of widely diverse invertebrates — corals, molluscs, arthropods and worms. In the Ordovician period that followed, life slowly began to make its way from the sea to dry land. In the Silurian period the first fish-like vertebrates appeared in the seas and the first small plants on land. During the ensuing period, the Devonian, animals became greatly diversified. The end of the Devonian and beginning of the Carboniferous marked the appearance of the first terrestrial vertebrates and the development of primitive vascular plants on land. The fifth period of the Palaeozoic — the Carboniferous — was the age of amphibians. The end of this period saw the appearance of the first reptiles. During the last period of the Palaeozoic — the Permian — there was great development and specialization amongst the reptiles. It also marked the appearance of the mammal-like reptiles.

The next long era, the Mesozoic, saw the full development of reptiles. Reptiles ruled dry land as well as air and water. Groups of reptiles living in the Triassic gave rise to further important groups such as the dinosaurs, plesiosaurs and ichthyosaurs, that reached their maximum development in the Jurassic and Cretaceous, becoming extinct at the end of the latter period. The Triassic also saw the beginnings of the evolution of birds and mammals from certain groups of reptiles.

At the beginning of the first period (Tertiary) of the Cenozoic era mammals and birds began to dominate the land and by the end of this period the flora and fauna of the earth closely resembled that of today. During the Tertiary birds achieved great development and to this day are a group that is on the rise in terms of evolution. Mammals achieved full development in the Tertiary and during the Quaternary. They reached an important stage with the evolution of primates, including Man. Man first appears in the fossil record in the late Miocene and early Pliocene.

The last and relatively brief period in the history of life on the earth began two to three million years ago and lasts to this day. It is the second period of the Cenozoic called the Quaternary, divided into two epochs: the earlier, Pleistocene, and the recent, Holocene, which lasts till today. The Quaternary witnessed a periodic cooling and warming of the climate, an alternation of cooler glacial periods and warmer interglacial periods. During the cold periods large parts of the earth were covered with glaciers. The early Quaternary marks the appearance of the genus *Homo* — modern Man. The evolution of Man is characteristic of this period, and that is why it is also designated as the Anthropozoic, or age of Man.

Life on our planet has had a very lengthy and complex evolution, during which the simplest microscopic organisms have changed very slowly into organisms of increasing complexity. This is not a new discovery — scholars of ancient and medieval times were already aware of the idea. The great majority of people of the ancient and medieval world, however, adhered to a literal interpretation of the Holy Bible and believed that all species of plants and animals were created when God created the world.

It was not till 1744 that Jean B. Lamarck, the well-known French zoologist, clearly set forth (one of the first to do so) the theory that animals evolved gradually, changing from simple forms to forms of increasing complexity. It was Charles Darwin, the famous English naturalist, however, who laid the foundations for the modern theory of evolution with his book 'The Origin of Species by Means of Natural Selection, or the Preservation of Favoured Races in the Struggle for Life', a theory that is called the Darwinian Theory after its author. An animal or plant species was no longer viewed as something permanent but as a unit that was continually evolving and adapting to the changing conditions of its environment.

Darwin's theory and several others greatly influenced the development of the natural sciences in the ensuing decades. Although the basis of Darwin's theory holds true to this day modern science has made many detailed aspects of it outdated.

As has already been stated, the diversity of plant and animal life today is the result of a very lengthy and gradual evolution from the simplest organisms to forms of increasing complexity. Today plants and animals form natural units called communities. A community, of course, is not only the group of animals inhabiting a certain location – it includes the whole environment in which that group lives. Usually all the organisms of a single community are biologically integrated and interdependent, forming a balanced whole. If this natural equilibrium is disrupted in any way it has far-reaching effects on the entire community.

Man has often had (and may still have!) a mistaken idea of his place in the natural scheme of things. He did not realize, or did not take cognizance of the fact that he, too, was an inseparable part of nature and not its owner and possessor. He has paid dearly many times for his reckless disregard of the environment and continues to do so time and again. What is urgently needed is for us to learn from the mistakes that appear like ugly blots throughout our history, and try to correct the harm caused by ourselves and preceding generations, as well as to prevent new mistakes that might have far-reaching and alarming effects on our environment and indeed on the whole biosphere.

PLATES

Phylum: **Sponges — Porifera**

Class: **Calcareous Sponges — Calcarea (Calcispongiae)**

Family: **Sycettidae**

1 *Sycon raphanus* — Length 5—20 mm. Ovate or globular. Body yellowish or brownish, covered with bristles. Skeleton composed of calcareous spicules. Vent (osculum) surrounded by numerous spicules. Lives in salt water where there is ample detritus. Distribution: Mediterranean coast.

Class: **Siliceous Sponges — Silicea (Demospongiae)**

Family: **Suberitidae**

2 Sea-orange *Suberites domuncula* — Diameter 40—60 mm. Globular with smooth surface. Coloured orange. Covers the shells of marine gastropods inhabited by the crab *Paguristes oculatus*. Because it grows rapidly the crab's residence increases in size thus making it unnecessary for the crab to seek a new shell. The sponge is locally abundant on the sandy bottom of seacoasts. Distribution: Mediterranean Sea, Atlantic Coasts, English Channel and North Sea.

Family: **Tedaniidae**

3 *Tedania anhelans* — Length about 70 mm. Coloured brownish, greenish or bluish. Found in abundance on muddy-sandy bottoms at depths of less than 2 metres. Distribution: Mediterranean Sea.

Family: **Freshwater sponges — Spongillidae**

4 *Spongilla lacustris* — Body soft and slippery. In sunlit waters it is green (the green coloration is caused by green algae, usually of the genus *Pleurococcus*), otherwise it is yellowish-grey or brownish. In spring and summer it is very plentiful. It coats stones, submerged branches, etc. Later it grows larger and produces shrub-like formations with branches of diverse length. The size of the sponge depends on the size of the object on which it lives. Clumps of this species smell of iodine or mud. Propagation is by means of gemmules, which are globular cells that overwinter after the sponge has died and form a new sponge in spring. The skeleton of this freshwater sponge is often sought out by various insect larvae, chiefly of the genus *Sisyra*, the larvae of caddis flies (Trichoptera) and many other animals. Distribution: Palaearctic, Nearctic and African regions (in freshwater lakes).

5 *Spongilla fluviatilis* — Forms veneers of varying thickness and size on stones and various submerged plants. Inhabits calm fresh waters as well as brackish waters. It overwinters. Distribution: the Palaearctic and Nearctic.

Family: **Spongiidae**

6 Bath Sponge *Spongia officinalis* — One of the best-known forms. Diameter 15—20 cm (sometimes even more). Soft, composed of spongin fibres, coloured red, brown, green, greyish-violet to black. Found near the coast at shallow depths of approximately 10—50 metres. It is firmly anchored to one spot. Because of its soft skeleton it is collected, dried and sold on the market. The related Honeycomb Sponge *(Hippospongia communis)* is also collected for commerce but its coarser skeleton makes it better suited for cleaning school blackboards, etc. Distribution: Mediterranean Sea.

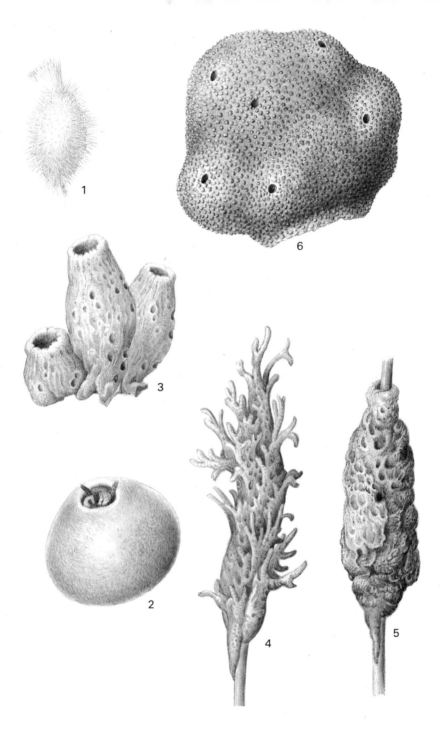

Phylum: **Coelenterates — Cnidaria**

Class: **Polyps — Hydrozoa**

Family: **Hydridae**

1 *Pelmatohydra oligactis* — Length 30 mm. Colour brownish. The single body opening, which serves both as a mouth and vent, is surrounded by several tentacles. These may be stretched out to great lengths and are furnished with special sting cells containing a coiled thread-like structure which whips out and numbs the victims the hydra feeds on. These consist mainly of unicellular and various other small animals. Lives in fresh waters. Adults appear in autumn and winter. Reproduction is by means of eggs and by budding. In the latter case a bud forms on the body which later detaches to form an independent individual. Distribution: much of Europe (north to Finland and Great Britain).

2 *Hydra viridissima* — Length 10—15 mm. Body opening surrounded by 6—12 tentacles. The hydra is coloured green by the algae which live within it, in a close symbiotic relationship. Widespread in fresh waters, in light places, amidst vegetation. Distribution: from the Balkans across central Europe to the north.

Family: **Campanulariidae**

3 *Obelia geniculata* — Makes a clump of variously-formed individuals. The clump is up to 40 mm high and comprises both true polyps and medusae that successively detach themselves and float amidst the plankton. The whole clump is protected by a firm cover (theca). Reproduction is rather complex (as in other species). The medusae produce eggs; these develop into polyps on which new medusae are formed (this type of reproduction, in which there is an alternation of an asexual with a sexual generation, is called metagenesis). This species is very plentiful on algae (mainly of the genus *Laminaria*) and on the sea bottom near the coast. Distribution: Atlantic coast of Europe, Mediterranean, North and Baltic Seas.

Family: **Aglaopheniidae**

4 *Aglaophenia tubulifera* — Individuals arranged in clumps up to about 50 mm high and resembling a bird feather. The species is locally abundant on rock walls at depths of 1 to 2 metres. Distribution: shores of western Europe.

Class: **Jellyfish — Scyphozoa**

Order: **Semaeostomae**

Family: **Pelagiidae**

5 Compass Jellyfish *Chrysaora hyoscella* — Body about 300 mm in diameter. The margin of the fairly flat disc bears 32 lobes and 24 marginal arms. The yellow-white disc is patterned with 16 brownish radiating lines. Feeds on fish, other medusae, arrow-worms, etc. Locally abundant. Distribution: Mediterranean Sea, Atlantic coast of Europe, also the North Sea.

Family: **Ulmariidae**

6 Common Jellyfish *Aurelia aurita* — Body 400 mm in diameter, furnished with numerous short arms. Round the mouth are four long, flat arms. A plentiful species that often floats in groups near the shore. Feeds only on small animal life (plankton). Distribution: Mediterranean Sea, Atlantic coast of Europe, North and Baltic Seas.

Order: **Rhizostomae**

7 *Rhizostoma pulmo* — Disc markedly convex, 200—800 mm in diameter, whitish, with bluish-violet margin. On the frilled part of the eight mouth arms there are numerous sting cells. This species, the largest of European jellyfish, occurs near the coast in abundance, often in large congregations, in winter and spring. Distribution: Mediterranean, Atlantic, North and west Baltic Seas.

34

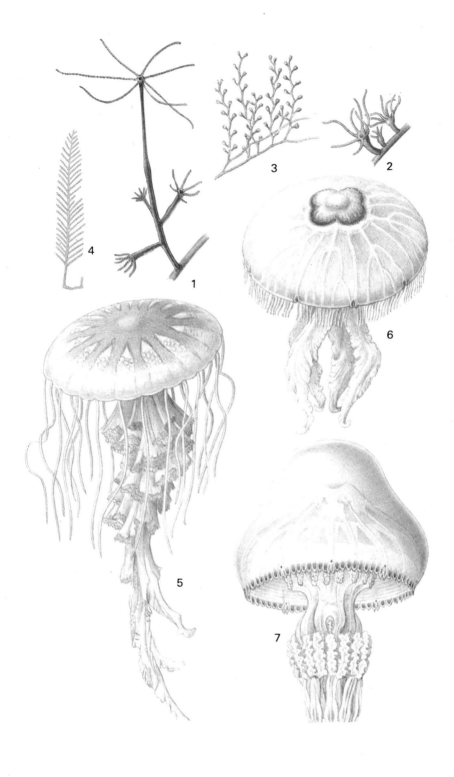

1

2

3

4

5

6

7

Phylum: **Coelenterates — Cnidaria**

Class: **Anthozoa**

Subclass: **Hexacorallia**

Order: **Sea anemones — Actiniaria**

1 Snake-locks Anemone *Anemonia sulcata* — Height 10−20 cm. Has a great number of stinging tentacles (150−200) up to 100 mm in length. Coloured yellowish-brown to bright green. Occurs in abundance by the coast to depths of about 6 metres. Lives on rocks in places where there is ample light. Feeds on molluscs, crustaceans and small fish. Distribution: Mediterranean Sea, Atlantic coast of Europe as far as the English Channel and west Scotland.

2 'Parasitic' Anemone *Calliactis parasitica* — Height 100 mm. Previously known also under the generic name *Adamsia*. White, yellow as well as brown. Lives attached to the shells of marine molluscs (often *Buccinum* or *Murex*), very often these inhabited by the hermit crab *Eupagurus bernhardus*. If the crab abandons the shell and moves to another, the anemone moves with it. Both appear to profit from this relationship: the crab moves the anemone around and provides scraps of food, and the anemone probably protects the crab with its stinging tentacles. Locally abundant in shallow as well as deep water. Distribution: Mediterranean Sea, rarer around northern coasts.

3 Daisy Anemone *Cereus pedunculatus* — Height 60−90 mm. Yellow-brown to white, upper third of the body furnished with numerous whitish suction pads. Approximately 700 tentacles arranged in 8 rows, inside tentacles longer than those on the outside. Lives attached to stones, rocks, shells, etc. at shallow depths by the shore. Locally very abundant. Viviparous. Distribution: Mediterranean Sea, Atlantic coast north to Scotland and English Channel.

Order: **Ceriantharia**

4 *Cerianthus membranaceus* — Length 200 mm. Tube-like, elongate, variously coloured (from white to brown to violet) body furnished at upper (mouth) end with about 130 tentacles arranged in 4 rows. Noted for its power of self-regeneration. Occurs along the sea coast at depths of 1−35 metres. Distribution: Mediterranean Sea.

Subclass: **Octocorallia**

Order: **Alcyonaria**

5 Dead Men's Fingers *Alcyonium digitatum* — Forms colonies, measuring up to 200 mm, composed of polyps, each furnished with 8 branching arms. The polyps are white and retractile, capable of completely concealing themselves inside the calcareous skeleton. Colonies may be whitish, orange, yellow or pink, depending on the colour of the skeleton. Occurs on the sea bottom, often attached to the shells of oysters. Distribution: Atlantic coast from Biscay northwards and North Sea.

Order: **Pennatularia**

6 Phosphorescent Sea-pen *Pennatula phosphorea* — Length 200 mm. Forms colonies comprising a great number of individuals. The whole greatly resembles a branching bird feather. The skeleton is red, the polyps white. Occurs on sandy sea bottoms. Luminescent: when brought to the surface the slightest touch will cause that region to 'light up', the light spreading until the whole is aglow. Distribution: cosmopolitan.

Phylum: **Comb jellies — Ctenophora**

Class: **Nuda**

Order: **Beroidea**

7 *Beroe cucumis* — Length 160 mm. Coloured pink, front end rounded with wide mouth; has no tentacles or sting cells. Floats freely in the sea and feeds on other comb jellies. Distribution: Mediterranean, Atlantic and northern Seas.

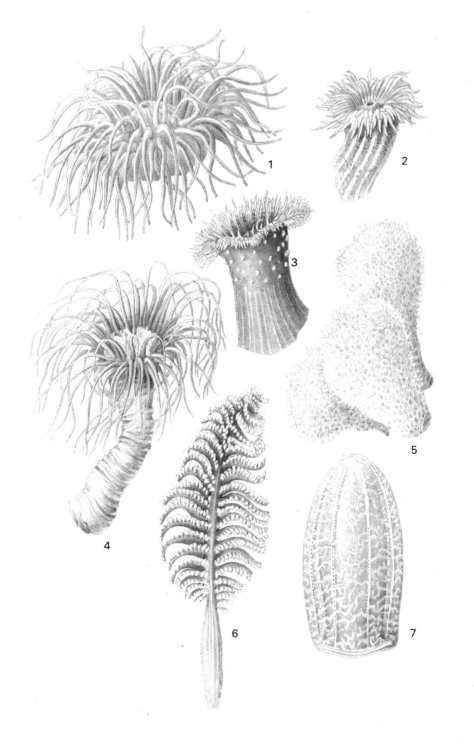

Phylum: **Platyhelminthes**

Class: **Turbellarian flatworms — Turbellaria**

Order: **Planarians — Tricladida**

1 *Planaria gonocephala* — Length up to 25 mm. Nowadays generally classed in the genus *Dugesia*. Body elongate, brownish, blackish-brown or greyish-brown with ear-like growths at the front end. The distance between the eyes is about the same as that between the eyes and edge of the body. A freshwater species found in clean, flowing water. When it moves, the body continually changes shape. Feeds on minute organisms. Because the alimentary canal does not have an anal opening undigested food remnants are expelled through the mouth. This flatworm, like all other species, is noted for its powers of self-regeneration. Distribution: Palaearctic region.

2 *Dendrocoelum lacteum* — Length 26 mm. Coloured milky white. The distance between the eyes is greater than that between the eyes and edge of the body. A freshwater species, found under stones in clean, slow-flowing or still waters, also in brackish waters. Distribution: Europe, as far north as Scandinavia.

3 *Polycelis cornuta* — Length 18 mm. Striking because of its greatly elongated 'ears'. Furnished with many eyes arranged parallel to the front edge of the body. Distribution: much of Europe, but absent in the north.

Phylum: **Aschelminthes**

Class: **Nematodes — Nematoda**

Order: **Rhabditida**

4 Vinegar Eel or Worm *Turbatrix aceti* — Length 0.8−2.4 mm. Found in old fermenting vinegar and in tree sap. Female bears about 50 young worms. Distribution: worldwide.

Order: **Oxyurida**

5 Pinworm *Enterobius vermicularis* — Length ♂ 0.5−1 cm, ♀ 1.5−2 cm. Male is distinguished from the female by having spicules on the hind end, which is coiled. Parasite in the large intestine of man. At night it emerges, remaining around the anus, where the female lays as many as 12,000 microscopic eggs. Man may become infected either by means of unclean fruit to which the eggs easily adhere, or by contact with dirt (true chiefly of children). Inadequate personal hygiene may result in continued reinfection. Itching caused by the parasite when laying eggs leads to scratching. Eggs which adhere to the fingers then find their way to the mouth and digestive tract, where they change into larvae that moult several times. The disease caused by pinworms is called oxyurasis. This parasite is still relatively common in countries with poor hygiene. However, it often affects small children in more civilized countries. Distribution: cosmopolitan.

Phylum: **Priapulida**

6 *Priapulus caudatus* — Length 30−80 mm, sometimes more. Flesh-red in colour. Elongated, cylindrical body with front part, which comprises about one quarter of the body length, furnished with numerous cuticular hooks. Lives in the littoral zone where it burrows in the mud. A predaceous species, it feeds on various animals. Distribution: Atlantic, North and west Baltic Seas, coasts of the Nearctic and Neotropical regions.

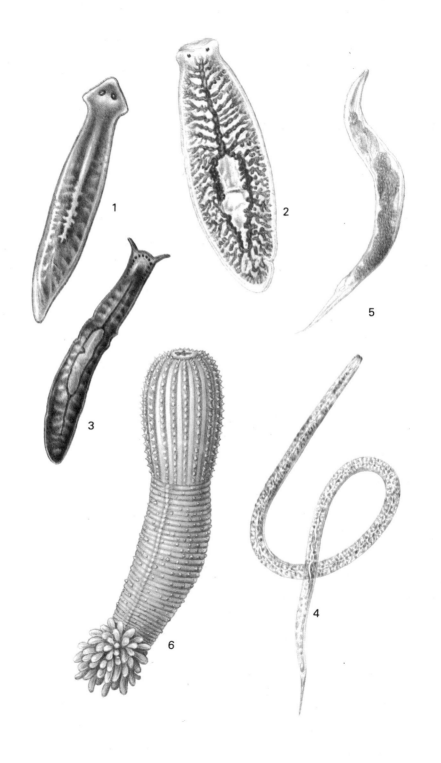

Phylum: **Molluscs — Mollusca**

Class: **Coat-of-mail shells — Polyplacophora**

Family: **Chitons — Chitonidae**

1 Grey Mail-shell *Lepidochitona cinereus* — Length 10—22 mm. Oval body with broad foot. Dorsal part of the body covered by eight overlapping calcareous plates, the first and eighth marked with radial and concentric patterns. Plates usually greyish-brown, greenish or reddish. They have a certain freedom of movement and enable the animal to curl up into a ball when danger threatens. The animal, however, usually attaches itself firmly to a rock or other solid object. It feeds on algae. Distribution: Mediterranean, Atlantic and North Sea shores, abundant along the coast of Great Britain.

Class: **Gastropods — Gastropoda**

Order: **Archaeogastropoda**

Family: **Ear shells — Haliotidae**

2 Green Ormer or Sea Ear — *Haliotis tuberculata* — Shell 80—90 mm long, 60 mm high, flat, marked with radial and concentric grooves. At the outer edge is a row of about five to seven holes through which the animal extends tactile filaments. The inside of the shell is lined with a thick layer of mother-of-pearl. The broad foot is furnished with a large number of lateral filamentous outgrowths. Found in shallow water with a stony bottom where it adheres firmly to the underside of stones. Breeds in August and September. Diet consists of vegetable matter, chiefly algae. It is edible but is gathered mainly for the valuable mother-of-pearl. This is the only species of the genus *Haliotis* on the European coast. Distribution: Atlantic coast north to Channel Islands, Mediterranean Sea, Canary Islands, Azores, Senegal. Does not occur in the North Sea.

Family: **Fissurellidae**

3 Slit-limpet *Emarginula huzardi* — Shell 13—20 mm long, whitish, shaped like a pointed cap, with a network pattern of radiating ribs crossed by finer concentric grooves. Found on the hard sea bottom at shallow depths, generally under stones. Feeds on algae. Distribution: Mediterranean Sea.

Family: **Patellidae**

4 Common Limpet — *Patella vulgata* — Shell 50—60 mm long, outer surface tinged green or brown, with rough ridges, interior glossy (nacreous), with alternate white and brown rays. Clings firmly to stones, leaving them only at night to feed on plant material. Edible. Distribution: Atlantic (including Great Britain), North Sea and Mediterranean coasts.

Family: **Trochidae**

5 Variegated Topshell *Gibbula divaricata* — Shell 23 mm high, about 19 mm across, has 6 inflated whorls. The top whorls are smooth; bottom whorls have spiral ridges. Colour greenish-yellow with lines of carmine red spots. Found in the sea at shallow depths under stones or amongst seaweed on which it feeds. Distribution: Coasts of Mediterranean Sea and Atlantic north to English Channel.

6 *Monodonta articulata* — Shell moderately large, 30—50 mm high, 24—42 mm wide, strong, composed of 6 (sometimes 7) whorls, very varied in coloration. Closed by a calcareous operculum. Found in abundance on rocky coasts, often on stone harbour constructions. Distribution: Mediterranean Sea, Portugal.

40

Phylum: **Molluscs — Mollusca**

Class: **Gastropods — Gastropoda**

Order: **Mesogastropoda**

Family: **Viviparidae**

1 Common River Snail *Viviparus viviparus* — Shell thin-walled, 32—40 mm high, 24—30 mm wide, with sharp-pointed apex and ovate mouth closed by an operculum. Running around the asymmetrically placed nucleus of the operculum are concentric growth lines. There is a notch at the top left of the operculum. A freshwater species, found in calm water with dense vegetation. Distribution: Europe (from northern Italy, Spain and Portugal to southern Scandinavia, Great Britain) east to the Urals and the Caucasus.

2 *Viviparus contectus* — Shell 30—32 mm high, 23—24 mm wide, resembles the foregoing but is less massive and the apex is not as pointed. A freshwater species, generally found in slow-flowing waters. Distribution: much of Europe and Great Britain. In Germany it occurs in large rivers (Rhine, Main, etc.).

Family: **Littorinidae**

3 Common or Edible Periwinkle *Littorina littorea* — Shell 15—40 mm high, greyish with brown lines, composed of 6—7 whorls, with pointed apex, and an operculum with which the animal closes the aperture at low tide. Lives in the tidal zone along the coast on stones, vegetation and harbour constructions. An edible species and widely gathered. Distribution: Coasts of the Atlantic, Mediterranean, North and Baltic Seas, eastern coast of the U.S.A (introduced).

4 Small Periwinkle *Littorina neritoides* — Shell 4—10 mm high, about 3 mm wide, composed of 5 whorls and furnished with operculum as protection against desiccation. Lives largely above upper shore (in splash zone), especially in crevices; commonest in areas exposed to strong wave action. Distribution: Atlantic Sea along the coast of Europe and Great Britain, North Sea, Mediterranean Sea, Madeira.

Family: **Epitoniidae**

5 Common Wentletrap *Clathrus clathrus* (often known under the generic names *Epitonium* or *Scalaria*) — Shell about 30 mm high, 12 mm wide, composed of 12—15 whorls, decorated with very striking ridges crossing each whorl at right angles. The oval mouth is closed by an operculum. Found on muddy and sandy sea bottoms at depths of as much as 100 metres. Distribution: coasts of Atlantic, Mediterranean, North and Baltic Seas.

Family: **Calyptraeidae**

6 Chinaman's Hat *Calyptraea chinensis* — Shell 7 mm high, 29 mm wide, thin-walled, milky white, apex in the centre. Found at shallow depths attached to small stones, shells and similar solid objects. Distribution: European coast of the Atlantic, Mediterranean Sea.

7 Slipper Limpet *Crepidula fornicata* — Shell 20 mm long, up to 47 mm wide. Shape depends on the object to which the animal is attached. When young it is mobile; later, however, it becomes firmly attached. The animals live in piles or chains — the lowest individuals are females, the top individuals males and those in the middle are hermaphrodites. Found at shallow depths, where it is often a pest of oyster beds, smothering the oysters and competing with them for food. Distribution: in Europe along the coast of Great Britain since 1880 (when it was introduced there from the U.S.A., together with oysters); in Holland since 1929; later it spread to further parts of the Atlantic coast of Europe. Native to the Nearctic region.

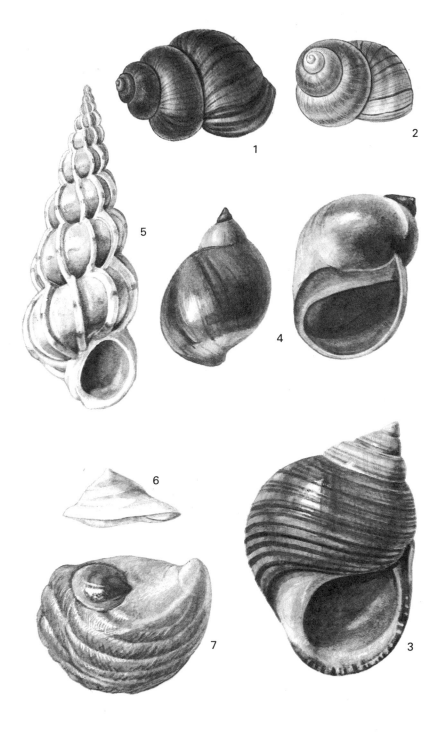

Phylum: **Molluscs — Mollusca**

Class: **Gastropods — Gastropoda**

Order: **Neogastropoda**

Family: **Muricidae**

1 *Murex trunculus* — Shell about 100 mm high, with broad siphonal canal. Lives on muddy sea bottoms. One of the species which once served as a source of the dye known as Tyrian purple. Distribution: Mediterranean Sea.

2 Sting Winkle or Oyster Drill *Ocenebra erinacea* — Shell about 60 mm high, thick-walled, yellowish white to dark brown, oval mouth terminating in a siphonal canal. Surface covered with large spines (hence its Latin name: *erinaceus* means hedgehog). Found on hard sea bottoms at shallow depths. Breeds in May and June. A predaceous species that feeds on various molluscs (e. g. oysters) and barnacles. It is collected for its edible fleshy foot, and the ornamental shells are often sold in seaside towns as souvenirs. Distribution: Mediterranean Sea, Atlantic coast from western Scotland to the Azores and Madeira.

Family: **Thaididae**

3 Common Dog Whelk *Nucella lapillus* — Shell 35—45 mm high, thick-walled, aperture oval with thickened lips and toothed outer margin. A predaceous species that feeds on crustaceans and sometimes molluscs, especially mussels. Lives on rocks in the littoral zone. Distribution: Atlantic, English Channel and North Sea, and the north African coast.

Family: **Buccinidae**

4 Common Whelk *Buccinum undatum* — Shell up to 110 mm high, 65 mm wide, heavy, with large mouth, 6—8 whorls and rich surface sculpture. Ground colour greyish-yellow overlaid with a thin, dark brown organic layer. Found in the lower tidal zone as well as at depths of as much as 200 metres on sandy and muddy bottoms. Individuals that dwell at greater depths have a thinner shell. In comparison with other molluscs the diet of this species is somewhat unusual, as it will feed on both dead and living animals. Carrion can be used to bait it. The eggs are laid in large capsules, about a thousand in each, but only a few develop into mature individuals, for the larvae that hatch earlier feed on the remaining eggs in the capsule. A plentiful species, gathered for its fleshy foot which serves as food. Distribution: coast of the Atlantic and North Sea, rarely in the Mediterranean.

Family: **Nassariidae**

5 Netted Dog Whelk *Nassarius reticulatus* — Shell about 30 mm high, conical, pointed, with spiral pattern of broad flat ribs. The white inner and outer lips are polished, the outer lip having 12—14 'teeth'. A common species found in abundance on soft or sandy sea bottoms. Distribution: Mediterranean Sea, European coast of the Atlantic, North Sea and west Baltic.

Family: **Conidae**

6 Mediterranean Cone Shell *Conus ventricosus* (often named C. *mediterraneus*) — Shell up to 57 mm high, colour variable, sometimes brownish-yellow, at other times olive-brown. Usually has a whitish band and brownish spots. Common on rocky coasts amidst vegetation. Distribution: Mediterranean Sea, west African coast.

44

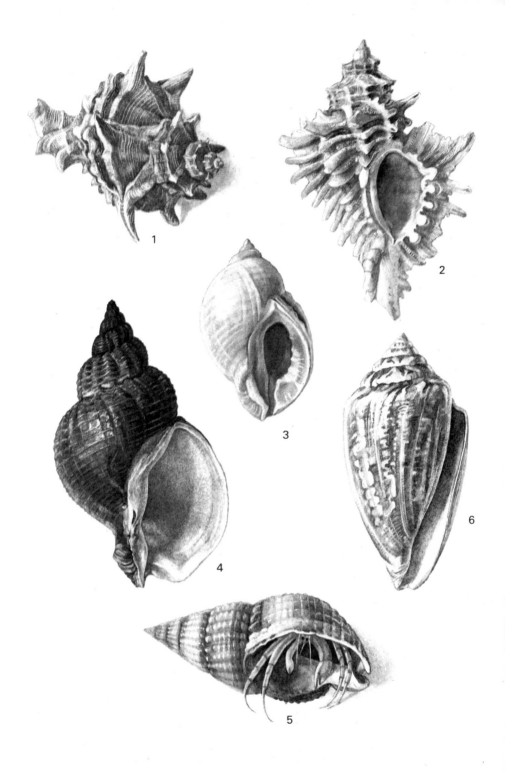

Phylum: **Molluscs — Mollusca**

Class: **Gastropods — Gastropoda**

Order: **Basommatophora**

Family: **Lymnaeidae**

1 Dwarfed Lymnaea *Lymnaea truncatula* — Shell 7—14 mm high, 3.5—6.3 mm wide, small, conical, elongate, composed of 5—5 1/2 whorls separated by a deep suture. A common species in ponds, pools, ditches, and irrigation ditches. Lives on vegetation (algae). Sometimes climbs up above the water surface or lives in mud. This snail serves as an intermediate host for the liver fluke *(Fasciola hepatica)*, which cannot complete its life cycle without first parasitising the snail. Distribution: Palaearctic and Nearctic regions.

2 Great Pond-snail *Lymnaea stagnalis* — Shell up to 60 mm high, 22—30 mm wide, large, composed of 7—7 1/2 whorls. The shape and colouring show considerable variation, although it is usually yellowish-brown or grey. This snail lives in calm, fresh, sometimes also brackish waters at low elevations, where it is a general feeder, often predaceous. Distribution: Palaearctic and Nearctic regions.

3 Ear Pond-snail *Lymnaea auricularia* — Shell 25—30 mm high, 20—30 mm wide, broad, composed of 4 whorls. The top three are small, the bottom one is broad. The mouth is wide. Lives in stagnant waters with rich vegetation, sometimes also in very slow-flowing rivers. Distribution: large part of Europe, north and east Asia, North America (introduced).

Family: **Planorbidae**

4 Ram's-horn *Planorbarius corneus* — Shell 11—13 mm high, 25—33 mm wide, composed of 4 1/2—5 whorls, top part more concave than bottom part, dark brown, often sculptured with a network pattern. This species inhabits calm or gently flowing waters with rich vegetation. It is not found at higher elevations. Distribution: much of Europe, the Caucasus, Asia Minor, eastern Siberia.

5 Margined Trumpet-snail *Planorbis planorbis* — Shell 3.5—4 mm high, 12—17 mm wide, composed of 5 1/2—6 whorls, and furnished with a keel on the underside. Found at lower elevations in calm waters with vegetation. Distribution: Palaearctic and Nearctic regions.

6 *Segmentina nitida* — Shell 1.5—1.8 mm high, 5—7 mm wide, tiny, flat, composed of 4 1/2—5 whorls. The mouth is shaped like a heart laid on its side. A common species, found in pools, ditches, ponds and bogs. Distribution: much of the Palaearctic region.

Family: **Ancylidae**

7 Fresh-water Limpet *Ancylus fluviatilis* — Shell 4.7—7.3 mm long, oval, the apex extended backward and to the right. It is thin-walled and marked with radial grooves. This species lives on stones in clean flowing streams, feeding on algae and aquatic moss, chiefly in foothills and mountains. Because of the increasing pollution of water courses it has disappeared from many localities. Distribution: Europe, the Caucasus, Transcaucasia, north Africa.

46

Phylum: **Molluscs — Mollusca**

Class: **Gastropods — Gastropoda**

Order: **Stylommatophora**

Family: **Pupillidae**

1 *Pupilla muscorum* — Shell 3—4 mm high, 1.8—2 mm wide, small, thick, reddish-brown. Mouth furnished with one or two small teeth. A common species that lives on dry grassy slopes, particularly on chalky-loamy substrates. Often found under stones. Distribution: Eurasia, north-west Africa, North America.

Family: **Vertiginidae**

2 *Truncatellina cylindrica* — Shell 1.8—2 mm high, circa 1 mm wide, cylindrical, composed of 5—6 finely grooved whorls, yellow-brown in colour. Lives in dry grassy steppes, dry meadows and on rocks, but is not to be found in forests. Distribution: Europe as far as 60° N, the Caucasus, Transcaucasia, Asia Minor, north Africa.

3 *Vertigo pygmaea* — Shell 1.5—2.2 mm high, 1.2—1.5 mm wide, glossy brown, mouth furnished with 5 teeth (sometimes only 4 or as many as 6). Favours meadows and hedgerows, also found on rocks. Distribution: Europe (excepting the north and south), the Caucasus, Transcaucasia, western Asia, North America.

Family: **Valloniidae**

4 *Acanthinula aculeata* — Shell 1.8—2.1 mm high, 2—2.3 mm wide, horn-brown, composed of 4 whorls, the last two covered with ridges bearing small spines. Found in forests amidst damp leaves, in decaying wood, etc. Distribution: Europe (absent in northern Scandinavia), the Caucasus, Transcaucasia, north Africa.

5 *Vallonia costata* — Shell 1.3 mm high, 2.1—2.7 mm wide, yellow-grey, with radial ribs (there may be as many as 36 on the last whorl). A common species in meadows and on rocks. Distribution: Palaearctic and Nearctic regions.

6 *Vallonia pulchella* — Shell 1.3 mm high, 2—2.5 mm wide, almost circular in outline, whitish yellow-grey. Found in moist locations, in meadows, hedgerows, under stones, etc. Distribution: Palaearctic and Nearctic regions.

Family: **Enidae**

7 *Zebrina detrita* — Shell 20—22 mm high, 9—10 mm wide, glossy white, sometimes marked with brown stripes. A warmth-loving species found chiefly on calcareous soils. Distribution: from southern to central Europe (which marks the northern limit of its distribution), Iran.

Family: **Succineidae**

8 Large Amber Snail *Succinea putris* — Shell 16—22 mm high, 8—11 mm wide, composed of 3—4 whorls, yellowish, thin, semi-transparent, mouth about 2/3 the height of the entire shell. Lives in riverine forests, on reeds and water plants, chiefly at lower elevations. Distribution: Europe, western and northern Asia.

Phylum: **Molluscs − Mollusca**

Class: **Gastropods − Gastropoda**

Order: **Stylommatophora**

Family: **Clausiliidae**

1 Door-shell *Clausilia dubia* − Shell 12−13 mm high, 2.8−3 mm wide, elongate, spindle-shaped, resembling the shell of many other species. Exact identification is possible only with the aid of a magnifying lens which allows detailed examination of the mouth characteristics. Shell is thickly covered with transverse grooves crossed by fine spiral grooves. Found in moist locations, on rocks (common in ancient ruins) and old tree stumps. Distribution: western Europe, from the northern Balkans to southern Scandinavia, Great Britain.

2 *Ruthenica filograna* − Shell 7.5−9 mm high, 2−2.2 mm wide, composed of 9−10 convex whorls separated by a suture and covered with comparatively few ribs. Inhabits damp woods with abundance of decaying leaves. Not found on tree trunks. Distribution: southern Alps, mountains of Saxony, Thuringia, eastern Harz, Carpathians, northwestern part of Balkans, as far east as Moscow.

3 *Cochlodina orthostoma* − Shell 12−13 mm high, 3 mm wide, brown, marked with fine ribs. A common species found on moss-covered rocks and on the trunks of sycamores *(Acer pseudo-platanus)* and beeches in broadleaved forests. Distribution: in Europe from the Carpathians, across the Baltic countries, Finland, east to the Ukraine.

4 *Macrogastra plicatula* − Shell 10−15 mm high, 2.8−3 mm wide, slender, ribbed and covered with fine spiral ridges. Found in forests from lowlands to mountainous elevations amidst fallen leaves, on tree trunks, in stumps, on rocks and on walls. Distribution: from northern Italy to southern Scandinavia, eastern France; absent in some parts of the German lowlands.

Family: **Endodontidae**

5 Rounded Snail *Discus rotundatus* − Shell 2.4−2.8 mm high, 5.8−7 mm wide, yellow-brown marked with reddish-brown stripes. A common species found in forests amidst fallen leaves, under old wood, under stones, etc., also plentiful in ancient ruins. Distribution: much of Europe (in the north, southern Scandinavia and Lithuania), north Africa.

Family: **Zonitidae**

6 Crystal Snail *Vitrea crystallina* − Shell about 2 mm high, 3−4 mm wide, composed of 4 1/2−5 whorls, the last about 1 1/2 times broader than the preceding one. Lives in moist locations under old fallen leaves, in decayed stumps and moss. Found from lowlands to mountainous elevations. Distribution: much of Europe and northwest Africa.

Family: **Vitrinidae**

7 Pellucid Glass-snail *Vitrina pellucida* − Shell about 3.5 mm high, 4.9−6 mm, wide, glassy, smooth, composed of 3−3 1/2 whorls. Shell very delicate, barely large enough to contain the animal. A very common and widespread species. Lives in both damp as well as dry localities − in forests, steppes, on rocks, meadows and cultivated land. Hides under old fallen leaves, stones and in moss. Distribution: Eurasia (also Iceland), North America.

Phylum: **Molluscs — Mollusca**

Class: **Gastropods — Gastropoda**

Order: **Stylommatophora**

Family: **Arionidae**

1 Large Black Slug *Arion ater* — Length 120—150 mm. Colour variable — orange, brick red, brown or black. Foot is red or yellowish on the edge, and crossed with dark lines. Found in moist localities, chiefly in broadleaved forests. An omnivore, it feeds on vegetable matter as well as living and dead animals. Distribution: in Europe from the northern part of the Iberian peninsula to southern Scandinavia, Great Britain and Iceland.

2 Dusky Slug *Arion subfuscus* — Length 60—70 mm. Ochre yellow to orange with striking but indistinct dark band on either side of the body. On the shield are dark markings resembling a lyre. Foot grey, crossed by dark lines. Inhabits broadleaved as well as coniferous forests. Burrows under the bark of old trunks where it seeks the moulds on which it feeds. Fond of mushrooms and various fruits. Distribution: much of Europe (except the southern part of the Balkans, the Iberian peninsula and Italy).

Family: **Limacidae**

3 Field Slug *Deroceras reticulatum* — Length 50—60 mm. Ground colour greyish, yellowish-white or brownish-red, marked with a dark network pattern. Found in moist locations, in forests, meadows, fields and gardens; it hides amongst leaves, under stones, logs, etc. An omnivore that causes damage in gardens and greenhouses. This and related species and genera are often mistaken for members of the family Arionidae by the layman. However, there are marked differences between the two, for instance in the location of the spiracle: in the Arionidae it is located in front of the point marking half the length of the shield whereas in the Limacidae it is located behind the midway point. *D. reticulatum* was formerly classed with *D. agrestis* as a single species. Distribution: worldwide.

4 *Lehmannia macroflagellata* — Length about 50 mm. Resembles the related species *L. marginata* in whose company it is sometimes found. Inhabits mountain, mostly broadleaved (beech) forests, occurring also above the forest limit to altitudes of 2,000 metres. Distribution: central Europe (Carpathian and Sudeten mountains).

5 Great Grey Slug *Limax maximus* — Length 120—150 mm. One of the largest of slugs. Coloured pale grey to whitish with 1—3 rows of dark spots on either side of the body. The shield is also covered with dark spots; the dorsal keel is a light hue. Secretes a colourless mucus. Partial to parks and gardens, less fond of forests. Often found in cellars. Feeds on detritus, particularly fat and other animal remains (including molluscs). Distribution: Mediterranean region, France, the Alps, Carpathians, Balkans, northern Great Britain, Lithuania, Scandinavia (introduced), north Africa.

6 *Bielzia coerulans* — Length 100—120 mm. Noted for its colour — blue, violet to almost black without any dark markings. The dorsal keel is quite pronounced. A well-known mountain species, commonly found under the bark of old trees, stones and fallen leaves. Distribution: Carpathian and Sudeten mountains.

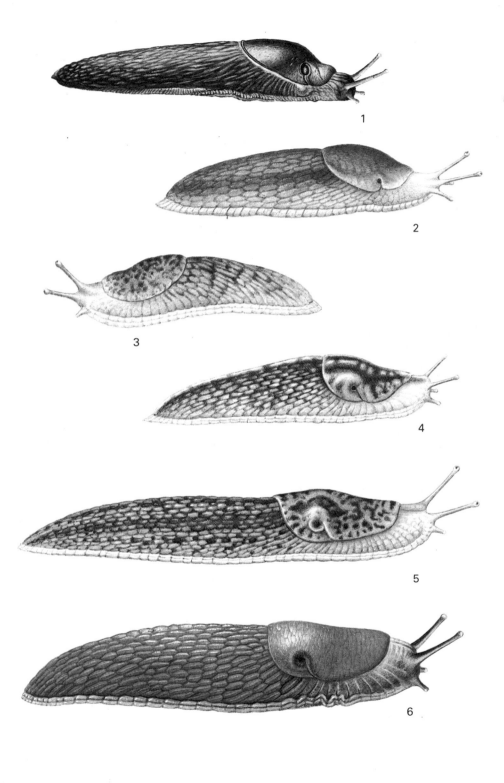

1

2

3

4

5

6

Phylum: **Molluscs — Mollusca**

Class: **Gastropods — Gastropoda**

Order: **Stylommatophora**

Family: **Helicidae**

1 Heath Snail *Helicella itala* (also known as *H. ericetorum*) — Shell 7—8 mm high, 15—16 mm wide, whitish-yellow, composed of 5 1/4—5 3/4 whorls. May be unicolorous but is usually marked with pale brown translucent bands. A warmth-loving species, it is found on dry hillsides, chiefly with a calcareous substrate. Distribution: western and central Europe.

2 *Helicella obvia* (also known as *H. candicans*) — Shell about 8 mm high, 16 mm wide, composed of 5 1/2—5 3/4 whorls, white, with dark opaque bands sometimes broken up into narrow stripes or spots. Likes warm and dry situations and is therefore found on unforested hillsides and railway embankments. It will also tolerate cooler localities and thus easily becomes established in new regions to which it is introduced. Distribution: southeastern and central Europe, in Germany in the upper Rhine region, Thuringia and Harz, less frequent in the north German lowlands.

3 *Perforatella bidentata* — Shell 7 mm high, 10 mm wide, glossy brown, composed of 7 whorls. The mouth has two teeth on the lower edge (hence the scientific designation *bidens*). Found in lowlands, in moist locations, including riverine forests, and alder stands. Distribution: central and eastern Europe, Germany (eastern Holstein, along the Main River, etc.) and the Baltic countries.

4 *Perforatella incarnata* — Shell 9—10 mm high, 13—16 mm wide. The broad, low cone is coloured greyish-yellow to reddish brown, with a finely grained surface. A damp-loving species, it is found amongst fallen leaves in forests and on herbaceous plants. Occurs also on cultivated land. Distribution: western and central Europe, southern Scandinavia, northern Balkans. Absent in Great Britain.

5 *Trichia unidentata* — Shell 5—6 mm high, 7—8 mm wide (fairly high compared to that of several related species), horn-brown, covered with short hairs. Mouth furnished with a single large tooth. Lives in mountain and submontane forests in damp situations, amongst fallen leaves and under stones. Distribution: northern limestone Alps, mountains of southern Germany, the Bohemian Forest (Šumava Mts.), Giant Mountains (Krkonoše), etc.

6 Bristly Snail *Trichia hispida* — Shell 4.5—5 mm high, 7—8.5 mm wide, composed of 5—6 whorls, greyish-brown to reddish brown, covered with hairs up to about 0.3 mm in length. Fond of moist localities; found chiefly at lower elevations in meadows, lowland alder groves and gardens, concealed in moss, amongst leaves, under stones, in old walls. Distribution: the whole of Europe (north as far as the Arctic Circle), including the Caucasus.

7 Cheese Snail *Helicodonta obvoluta* — Shell 5 mm high, 11 mm wide, flat, covered with hairs. Mouth three-lobed in shape. A warmth-loving species found in forests on calcareous substrates. Conceals itself amidst old fallen leaves, under stones and old wood. Distribution: western and central Europe, including northern Balkans, Great Britain, and Italy.

54

Phylum: **Molluscs — Mollusca**

Class: **Gastropods — Gastropoda**

Order: **Stylommatophora**

Family: **Helicidae**

1 Lapidary Snail *Helicigona lapicida* — Shell 7.5−8.5 mm high, 16−17 mm wide, lentil-shaped, greyish-brown, usually covered with reddish-brown spots. Found chiefly in foothills on beech trunks, palings, old walls and rocks. Distribution: in Europe from the northern part of the Iberian Peninsula to southern Scandinavia, Great Britain, Baltic countries.

2 Copse Snail *Arianta arbustorum* — Shell 18−21 mm high, 18−25 mm wide, fairly large, pale or dark brown, yellow spotted, with a dark band. Mouth circular with broad white edge. Found in damp forests from lowland to mountain elevations. Lives to the age of five years. Feeds on the leaves of various herbaceous plants and on fruits. Distribution: the Pyrenees, France, Great Britain, central Europe north of the Alps, Scandinavia, Baltic countries, the Ukraine.

3 *Isognomostoma isognomostoma* — Shell about 6 mm high, 10.5 mm wide, brownish, fairly flat, covered with comparatively long hairs. Mouth is three-lobed, a shape caused by the teeth and lamellae. Found in mountain and submontane forests in stony locations. Plentiful also amongst fallen leaves and under logs. Distribution: mountains of central Europe and Pyrenees.

4 Brown-lipped Snail *Cepaea nemoralis* — Shell 17−18 mm high, 22−23 mm wide. Mouth about as high as it is wide, reddish-brown to black. Coloration very variable, yellow, white, pink or brown, with or without up to five bands. Found in gardens and parks, also in open woodlands, particularly abundant in hedgerows. Distribution: western and central Europe, British Isles, southern Scandinavia, Lithuania, northern Balkans.

5 White-lipped Snail *Cepaea hortensis* — Shell 15−16 mm high, 19−21 mm wide, patterned with dark stripes, mouth greater in width than in height, with pale edge. Shows very similar variation to *C. nemoralis*. Found in moist locations in forests and groves, cultivated land, hedgerows, etc. Distribution: central and western Europe, British Isles, southern Scandinavia, southern Finland, North America.

6 Roman, Apple, or Edible Snail *Helix pomatia* — Shell about 40 mm high and 40 mm wide, yellow-brown, patterned with 5 darker stripes that are not always distinct, and composed of 4 1/2−5 whorls. This is one of the best known snails. Does not reach maturity until the third or fourth year. As with many snails, it is a hermaphrodite (having both male and female sexual organs). Eggs measure about 5.5 mm in diameter and are enclosed in a calcareous cover. Occurs chiefly in warmer locations in woodlands and on cultivated land. Feeds on various herbaceous plants. In some places it is raised on farms for food. Distribution: western, central and south-eastern Europe, southern Scandinavia, Great Britain, Baltic countries.

7 Common Garden Snail *Helix aspersa* — Shell about 35 mm high, 38 mm wide, yellow with 5 dark stripes. Very common in gardens, where it is a pest of vegetables. Distribution: western Europe, Mediterranean region.

Phylum: **Molluscs — Mollusca**

Class: **Tusk shells — Scaphopoda**

Family: **Dentaliidae**

1 Common Tusk Shell *Antalis entalis* — Shell 30—50 mm long, resembles a small elephant tusk. Related species have similar shells. Principal identifying characteristics are the size of the shell (in some species it measures less than 5 mm), and above all the surface markings. The white, slightly curved shell of this species is marked by 18—20 longitudinal grooves. These are sometimes reddish. The shell is open at both ends. The Tusk Shell lives buried in muddy or sandy sea bottoms with only the posterior, pointed end projecting. It is found down to depths of several hundred metres. Diet consists chiefly of various species of one-celled foraminiferans which it captures in the sand with its mobile tentacles. Eggs hatch into freely-floating larvae. It is found in abundance. Distribution: Atlantic, English Channel and North Sea.

2 *Antalis vulgare* — Shell about 60 mm long, matt milky-white, marked with a great many fine longitudinal grooves. It is bluntly truncated at the end and does not have a notch. Found on the sea bottom in sediment at depths down to 70 metres. Reproduces in April and May. Distribution: Mediterranean Sea, central part of the Atlantic coast.

Class: **Bivalves — Bivalvia**

Dimensions in this section give the length of the shell, (i. e. from the anterior to the posterior margin), the height (i. e. from edge to edge at right angles to the foregoing), and thickness (i. e. from apex to apex with both halves closed).

Order: **Nuculoida**

Family: **Nut Shells — Nuculidae**

3 Common Nut-shell *Nucula nucleus* — Length 12 mm, height 9 mm, thickness 5.6 mm. Surface of shell yellowish-white, inside walls have a nacreous gloss. Lower margin is finely toothed. Found in abundance in coarse sediments on sea bottoms down to depths of 150 metres. Distribution: European coast of the Atlantic from Portugal to Norway, Mediterranean Sea, Black Sea, westerly and southeasterly coasts of Africa.

Family: **Nuculanidae**

4 Beaked Nuculana *Nuculana minuta* — Length about 14 mm, broadly rounded at the front, narrow, elongate at the rear. Surface covered with bold, concentric grooves. Found on sea bottoms of muddy sand and gravel at depths of 10—180 metres. Distribution: Widely distributed in northern hemisphere, in Europe south to English Channel. Reaches California, Japan and Nova Scotia.

Order: **Arcoida**

Family: **Ark shells — Arcidae**

5 Noah's Ark Shell *Arca noae* — Length about 70 mm, height 30 mm, thickness 36 mm. Shell is longish, boat-shaped, outer surface pale grey to brown, interior usually dark brown. Surface marked with raised concentric growth lines and radiating ridges. Margin of the hinge is long and straight and covered with numerous large teeth. A common species found at various depths (from lower shore to 100 metres) on stony and sandy bottoms, often in the shells of other molluscs or on rocks. An edible mollusc, it is widely gathered and offered for sale at fish markets. Distribution: Mediterranean and Atlantic.

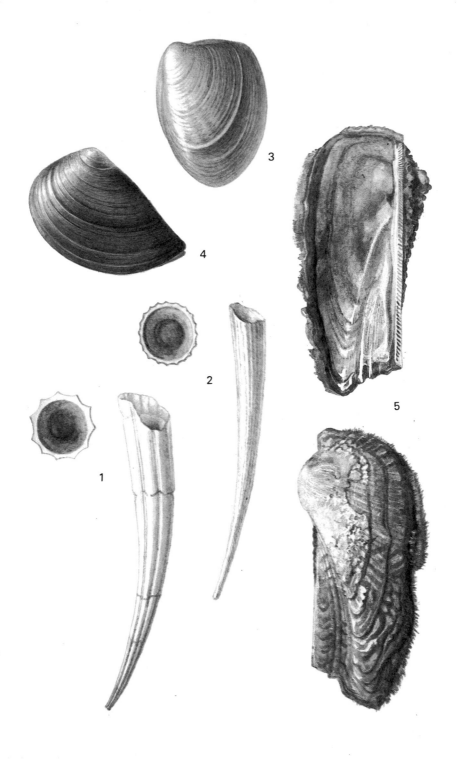

Phylum: **Molluscs — Mollusca**

Class: **Bivalves — Bivalvia**

Order: **Mytiloida**

Family: **Mussel shells — Mytilidae**

1 Common Mussel *Mytilus edulis* (sometimes a more southerly species, *M. galloprovincialis,* is separated from *M. edulis*) — Length 60—80 mm, height 40 mm, thickness 35 mm. The shell is wedge-shaped, the surface smooth, blue-black or yellow-brown with darker growth lines. The inside of the shell is bluish-white or bluish-grey. Very plentiful on coastal rocks and harbour constructions. It attaches itself firmly to objects by the aid of its byssal threads, thus anchoring the shell to withstand the impact of waves. The diet consists mostly of minute planktonic organisms. It reproduces in May and June. The larvae also live on plankton. One of the molluscs that has been gathered and consumed as food for ages past. It is frequently cultivated, together with oysters *(Ostrea).* In maritime countries it is often sold at fish markets. Distribution: coasts of the Black and Mediterranean Seas, the British Isles, California and Japan. Absent from the high Arctic.

Order: **Pterioida**

Family: **Pinnidae**

2 Fan-mussel *Pinna nobilis* — Length 700—900 mm. The shell is shaped like a cudgel. The surface, particularly in young individuals, is covered with a great many scales arranged in rows. The inside walls have a pearly gloss. Individuals are found at depths of more than 3 metres on sandy coasts with the pointed end embedded in the sand. They are also anchored to the bottom by the aid of long byssal threads. An edible species of excellent quality commonly sold at fish markets. Distribution: Mediterranean and Atlantic Seas.

Family: **Scallops — Pectinidae**

3 Fan Shell *Pecten jacobaeus* — Length 130—150 mm, height 120 mm, thickness 30 mm (but usually smaller). The shape of the shell resembles that of other species of the family. It is extremely beautiful. The surface of each valve is ornamented with 14—16 radiating ribs. As in other species, the right and left valves differ in colour as well as shape; one is convex, the other flat. The 'ears' on both are almost symmetrical. This edible species is found on sandy sea bottoms at depths of more than 25 metres. Distribution: Mediterranean Sea and off the Canary and Cape Verde islands.

4 Queen Scallop *Aequipecten opercularis* — Length 80 mm, height 75 mm, thickness 24 mm. Surface of each valve marked with 19—22 raised radiating ribs. Coloration very variable. Found on firm sandy, muddy or shelly sea bottoms, down to about 180 metres. Like some other species of scallop, it swims well. A popular delicacy and thus widely gathered. Distribution: Atlantic coast of Europe, Mediterranean Sea, Azores and Canary Islands.

5 Variegated Scallop *Chlamys varia* — Length 50—60 mm, height 60—65 mm, thickness 18 mm. Coloration is variable, generally yellowish-white, red, brown or completely dark. Surface of each valve is marked with 25—35 radiating ribs bearing raised thorn-like plates. The ears are strongly asymmetrical. Generally found on sandy bottoms to depths of about 80 metres; also occurs on coral formations. An abundant species that is regularly harvested. Distribution: European Atlantic coast from Spain to Denmark, Mediterranean Sea, to the Cape Verde Islands and Senegal.

Phylum: **Molluscs — Mollusca**

Class: **Bivalves — Bivalvia**

Order: **Pterioida**

Family: **File shells — Limidae**

1 File Shell *Lima lima* — Length 35 mm, height 50 mm, thickness 18—22 mm. A beautiful shell with quite prominent ears, it is thick-walled and porcelain white both outside and inside. Surface ornamented with 19—24 ribs radiating from the apex, bearing projecting scales arranged in concentric rows coincidental with the growth lines. Between the ribs are smooth, deep furrows. A plentiful and common species found on stony bottoms, frequent also amongst marine sponges and in layers of coral (Anthozoa). Distribution: Mediterranean Sea, coast of southwestern Europe, Canary and Cape Verde Islands, North America, etc.

Family: **Saddle oysters — Anomiidae**

2 Saddle-oyster *Anomia ephippium* — Length 50—65 mm, height 50—60 mm, thickness 18—20 mm. Shell thin, brownish-red to brownish-yellow. Surface marked with concentric, irregular furrows and ribs. Lower valve has a byssal opening. On the inside wall of the valve are three muscle scars (an important means of separating it from related species). Found at shallow depths, from low water to about 150 metres, attached to wood and other hard objects on the sea bottom. Distribution: Black and Mediterranean Seas, in the Atlantic from Norway and Iceland to the Cape Verde Islands and south to Ghana. Also in the South Atlantic.

Family: **Oysters — Ostreidae**

3 Common Oyster *Ostrea edulis* — Diameter of shell 70—150 mm. Valves thick, irregularly rounded, not identical. Lower valve is firmly cemented to the substrate. Lives on firm, hard bottoms, from low water down to depths of 80 metres in the sea. A gregarious species, it often forms oyster 'banks'. Lives to an age of about 10 years, sometimes more. Feeds on minute planktonic organisms which it strains from the water. A hermaphrodite, it is protandric, producing first spermatozoa, then eggs, then spermatozoa, and so on, throughout its lifetime. The larvae swim freely in the water before finding a suitable place (rock, shell, etc.) to settle and continue growth. Oyster colonies are the home of many other species of animals, many of which predate the oysters (e. g. starfish). Throughout their area of distribution oysters occur in many different forms, previously described as separate species. *O. edulis tarentia* (3a) has a transversely oval shell and fine lamellae on the surface of the upper valve. *O. edulis adriatica* (3b) has a transversely ovate shell. The upper valve is covered with large lamellae arranged in dense rows. The oyster was and still is of great commercial value in maritime regions, where it is harvested and sold on the market. It is also cultivated in special 'oyster beds'. At one time the western coast of Europe was fringed with an almost continuous belt of oyster banks. The intensive harvesting of oysters, however, has greatly damaged this community, so that nowadays oysters are entirely absent in many places. In recent years, thanks to the limiting of certain methods of harvesting, the colonies are gradually being restored. Distribution: Atlantic coast of Europe, Arctic Circle, coast of north Africa, the Black and Mediterranean Seas.

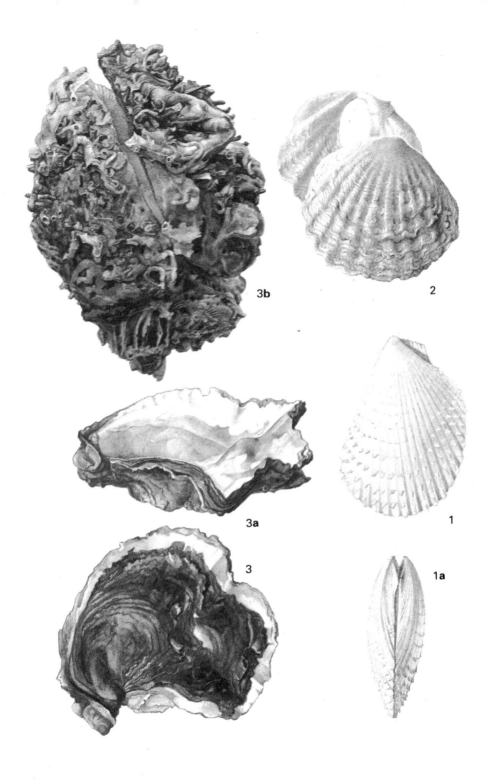

3b

2

3a

1

3

1a

Phylum: **Molluscs — Mollusca**

Class: **Bivalves — Bivalvia**

Order: **Unionioida**

Family: **Swan mussels — Unionidae**

1 Swollen River Mussel *Unio tumidus* — Length 70—80 mm, height 36—40 mm, thickness 23—26 mm. Shell glossy greenish-brown, broadly rounded at the front, pointed at the rear. Lower edge is rounded (in which it differs from *U. pictorum,* the Painter's Mussel, which has a straight lower edge). Found in abundance in quiet and slow-flowing waters (in ponds, backwaters of rivers). There are several geographical races within its area of distribution, e. g. *U. tumidus depressus (= rhenanus)* in the Rhine River and its left-bank tributaries. Distribution: Europe (absent in the south and mountain belt of central Europe), Transcaucasia, western Siberia.

2 Swan Mussel *Anodonta cygnea* — Length 170—220 mm, height 84—120 mm, thickness 52—60 mm. Shell thin, broadly oval or elongated, greenish-yellow. Found on the muddy bottom of ponds, rivers and reservoirs. Has many forms. As in other species, the eggs hatch into small parasitic larvae called glochidia which infest fish. After a while they leave their hosts to live freely in water. Distribution: Eurasia (absent in the Mediterranean region), North America.

Family: **Pearl mussels — Margaritiferidae**

3 Pearl Mussel *Margaritifera margaritifera* — Length 120—150 mm, height 50—72 mm, thickness 30—45 mm. Dull, blackish-brown. Found only in clean streams in lowland country and foothills. Lives to an age of 60—80 years. Because of water pollution this species is rapidly decreasing in numbers in many places. It forms genuine pearls, once collected for the jewellery trade. Distribution: Europe, Siberia, Kamchatka, North America.

Order: **Veneroida**

Family: **Astartes — Astartidae**

4 Furrowed Astarte-shell *Astarte sulcata* — Length 19 mm, height 15 mm, thickness 8 mm. Shell marked with concentric ribs. Plentiful on the seacoast, where it burrows in mud and gravel down to considerable depths. Distribution: from the Cape Verde Islands to Norway, Mediterranean Sea, Iceland and S. E. Greenland, North America.

Family: **Freshwater cockles — Sphaeriidae**

5 Horny Orb-shell *Sphaerium corneum* — Length 12—15 mm, height 10—11 mm, thickness 7.5—9 mm. Common in quiet or slow-flowing waters (also in mill races, bogs, etc.). Shell thin, marked with concentric grooves. Distribution: Palaearctic region.

6 Lake Orb-shell *Sphaerium lacustre* — Length 8—9.3 mm, height 6—7.6 mm, thickness 4—4.3 mm. A plentiful species. Found in muddy, calm and slow-flowing waters. Distribution: Palaearctic region.

7 River Pea-shell *Pisidium amnicum* — Length 8—10 mm, height 6—7 mm, thickness 4—5 mm. One of the largest members of this genus, which includes many other, extremely small species that are difficult to identify. The valves of this species are quite convex, thick, coloured yellow or brown. Found in fine mud on the bottoms of rivers and larger streams. Distribution: most of Europe, northern Asia, north Africa.

1

7

6

2

5

3

4

Phylum: **Molluscs — Mollusca**

Class: **Bivalves — Bivalvia**

Order: **Veneroida**

Family: **Dreissenidae**

1 Zebra Mussel *Dreissena polymorpha* — Length 20—30 mm, height 13—15 mm, thickness 17—20 mm. Shell is pointed and has a keel extending from the front to the hind edge. It is attached by the aid of byssal threads to various objects (stones, wooden posts, etc.) in rivers, lakes and canals. A plentiful species, it often occurs in large colonies. Originally it made its home in the rivers of the Black and Caspian Sea regions but was later spread or introduced to other areas (rivers in West Germany, Austria, Czechoslovakia, Sweden, Denmark, Great Britain, etc.).

Family: **Cockles — Cardiidae**

2 Common Edible Cockle *Cerastoderma edule* — Length 30—50 mm, height and thickness about 30 mm. Striking shell with broad ribs crossed by darker concentric stripes. Lives shallowly embedded in sandy bottoms, from midtide level to just below low-water mark. Capable of jumping with the aid of its foot. In winter it is commonly found in fish markets and is popular as food. Distribution: European seas, Canary Islands, North America.

3 Spiny Cockle *Acanthocardia aculeata* — Length up to 80 mm, height 75 mm, thickness 50 mm. Shell has 20—22 broad ribs set with stout spines. Found in both shallow and deeper waters of the coast. A plentiful species, harvested and sold in markets. Distribution: Mediterranean Sea, Atlantic coast from Morocco to south-west coast of Great Britain.

4 Rough Cockle *Acanthocardia tuberculata* — Length 65 mm, height 65 mm, thickness 50 mm. Shell coloured a dirty yellow with brownish-black concentric rings. Surface marked with 21 or 22 rounded ribs. Burrows in muddy sand and gravel bottoms. An edible species. Distribution: Atlantic coast of Europe and Mediterranean Sea, Madeira, Canary Islands.

5 Prickly Cockle *Acanthocardia echinata* — Length 55 mm, height 50 mm, thickness 38 mm. Surface patterned with 18—22 ribs bearing knobs and spines. Found on soft sea bottoms down to depths of as much as 360 metres. Sold in markets. Distribution: Atlantic coast from Canary Islands to Iceland, Norway and Greenland, occasionally in the Mediterranean Sea.

Family: **Venus and carpet shells — Veneridae**

6 Smooth Venus *Callista chione* — Length 80—110 mm, height 65—85 mm, thickness 41—48 mm. Surface dirty grey to brown, almost smooth with darker radiating bands. Lives embedded in clean sand, offshore down to about 130 metres, extending only its siphons above the surface. The water sucked by the siphon provides the animal with oxygen and food — minute organisms of the plankton. A tasty, edible species harvested and sold in markets. Distribution: Mediterranean Sea, Atlantic coast from the Canary Islands to Ireland.

7 Warty Venus *Venus verrucosa* — Length 40—70 mm, height 39—68 mm, thickness 27—48 mm. Shell very thick, surface marked with rugged concentric ridges crossed toward the anterior and posterior margins by radiating ribs. Burrows in sand or gravel bottoms. An edible species, harvested and often sold in fish markets. Distribution: Mediterranean Sea, European and African coast of the Atlantic, southeast Africa.

8 Smooth Artemis *Dosinia lupinus* — Length 25—30 mm, height 25—30 mm, thickness 12—14 mm. Shell whitish to yellowish, smooth with only the growth lines discernible. Burrows quite deeply in sand, muddy sand or shell-gravel, from intertidal zone down to 125 metres. Very plentiful. Distribution: Canary Islands, Mediterranean Sea, Atlantic coast of Europe as far as northern Norway, the Faroes and Iceland. South to Ivory Coast.

Phylum: **Molluscs — Mollusca**

Class: **Bivalves — Bivalvia**

Order: **Veneroida**

Family: **False Angel Wings — Petricolidae**

1 American Piddock *Petricola pholadiformis* — Length 60—80 mm, height 25—32 mm, thickness 20—25 mm. Shell whitish, thin, surface marked with irregular concentric lines and at the anterior margin by radial ribs. Lives at shallow depths where it bores into hard clay, chalk, stiff mud, peat-moss, limestone or soft sandstone. Distributed along the eastern coast of North America; in 1890 introduced into Europe (Great Britain), nowadays occurs on the western coast of Europe (in Holland since 1905), and western coast of Africa.

Family: **Wedge shells — Donacidae**

2   Banded Wedge Shell *Donax vittatus* — Length 35 mm, height 14—18 mm, thickness 10—12 mm. Shell white to yellowish-brown, surface marked with concentric lines and radiating ribs. Lives from low-water mark down to depths of about 20 metres. The empty shells are often found on the seashore. Distribution: Mediterranean Sea, European coast of the Atlantic as far as Norway, off the Canary Islands, Morocco.

Family: **Scrobiculariidae**

3 Peppery Furrow Shell *Scrobicularia plana* — Length 50—55 mm, height 40 mm, thickness 15 mm. Shell thin and flattened, generally whitish or yellowish-white. Burrows about 10—16 cm deep in soft bottoms extending only the siphons through which it also receives food. Shells are often found on the seashore. Harvested and sold in markets. Distribution: Mediterranean Sea, Atlantic coast of Europe from Norway to the Canary Islands and Senegal.

Family: **Tellins — Tellinidae**

4 Thin Tellin *Tellina tenuis* — Length up to 25 mm, height 15—17 mm, thickness 5—6 mm. Shell thin, yellowish-white or rose coloured, sculptured with concentric bands. Inside walls are pink. A plentiful inhabitant of sandy coasts, often food for larger fish. Distribution: Mediterranean Sea, Black Sea, Sea of Azov, Atlantic coast of Europe as far as northern Norway, Morocco.

Family: **Trough shells — Mactridae**

5   Rayed Trough Shell *Mactra corallina* — Length 40—60 mm, height 34—45 mm, thickness 16—28 mm. Shell whitish with concentric lines, sometimes also radiating bands. Interior is white. Found in sandy (rarely soft) bottoms at depths of 5—30 metres; often cast up on the shore by waves. Regularly sold in markets. Distribution: Black Sea, coast of Mediterranean, west coast of Europe north from Norway to Iberian Peninsula, south to Senegal.

Family: **Razor shells — Solenidae**

6 Sword Razor *Ensis ensis* — Length 115—160 mm, height 18—21 mm, thickness 12—16 mm. Shell strikingly long and narrow, slightly curved with blunt ends, glossy yellow-white or greenish-brown, with reddish-brown bands marking the growth lines. Lives in fine or silty sand bottoms, usually buried just below the surface with only the siphons extending, although it may burrow to a depth of one metre. Edible, often harvested. Distribution: from the Mediterranean to the North and Baltic Seas.

7 Pod Razor Shell *Ensis siliqua* — Length 180—200 mm, height 28—33 mm, thickness 10—11 mm. Shell resembles that of the preceding species, but is longer and almost straight, whitish with violet bands, and a conspicuous diagonal pattern. Plentiful in sandy bottoms. Sold in fish markets, as is *E. ensis*. Distribution: Atlantic coast from Morocco to the Baltic and southern Norway.

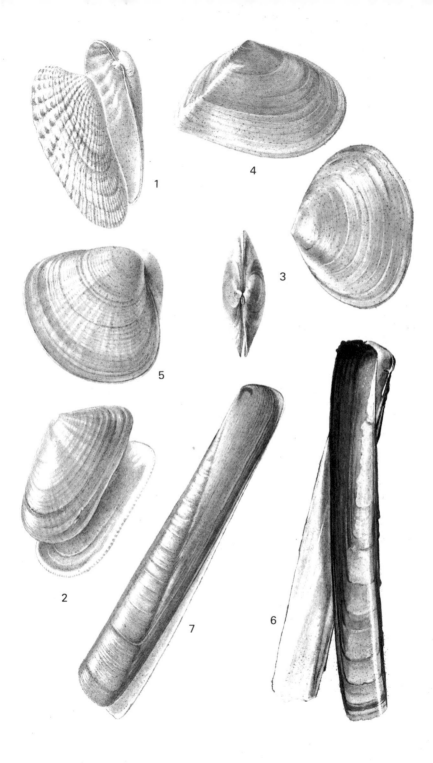

Phylum: **Molluscs — Mollusca**

Class: **Bivalves — Bivalvia**

Order: **Myoida**

Family: **Gapers — Myidae**

1 Sand Gaper *Mya arenaria* — Length 100—130 mm, height 60—73 mm, thickness 40—45 mm. Shell oval, rounded at the front end, tinted brown. Lives buried about 20 cm deep in sand or mud on the sea bottom, extending only its long, massive siphon sometimes as much as four times the length of the shell. An edible species, harvested for food. Very adaptable to the varying salinities of the European seas. Distribution: coasts of northern Europe, North America, Japan, the Black Sea.

Family: **Gastrochaenidae**

2 Flask Shell *Gastrochaena dubia* — Length 20 mm, height 10 mm, thickness 8 mm. Shell white to brown, with short anterior end, and enlarged, elliptical hind end. Bores holes into various kinds of hard matter, including rocks and dead shells of other molluscs (e. g. oysters). It cements limestone fragments into a flask-shaped jacket around its shell and siphonal tubes. Distribution: European Atlantic coast, Black Sea, Mediterranean Sea.

Family: **Piddocks — Pholadidae**

3 Common Piddock *Pholas dactylus* — Length 90—150 mm, height 33 mm, thickness 20—35 mm. Shell white with yellowish epidermis, elongated, narrowing to a point at the front end, rounded at the hind end, surface sculptured with numerous concentric and radiating ribs. Drills corridors in soft rock and wood. A luminescent mucus is secreted by the mantle and siphonal tubes. Edible species. Distribution: Mediterranean Sea, Black Sea, Atlantic coast of Europe (to Norway), Morocco.

Family: **Ship worms — Teredinidae**

4 Common Ship Worm *Teredo navalis* — Body measures 100—200 mm in length. This species differs markedly in appearance from all the ones described and illustrated on the preceding pages. The shell is reduced and looks like a helmet on the broadened front end of the body which is very long and snake-like. The animal bores in wood with the aid of the helmet. It feeds on the sawdust produced during the process and also on plankton which it obtains through tubes. The mantle secretes a thin calcareous tube round the body. Where they occur in large numbers their drilling can cause great damage, particularly to harbour constructions and ships. Disastrous damage was caused by Ship Worms to the merchant and war fleets of ancient times. Distribution: cosmopolitan.

Class: **Cephalopods — Cephalopoda**
Order: **Decabrachia**
Family: **Cuttles — Sepiidae**

5 Common Cuttle *Sepia officinalis* — Length 30—40 cm. In spring it occurs in large numbers near the shore, later in deeper waters. The eight arms around the mouth are furnished with suction pads arranged in 4 rows and the two longer tentacles with 5—6 larger suckers (in which it differs from related species). The shell is a greatly reduced, spoon-shaped structure located under the skin — the well-known 'cuttle-bone'. The Cuttle is a predator. When threatened by danger it ejects a dark pigment. An excellent swimmer, it propels itself through the water by the undulating motion of the narrow fins and by the powerful ejection of water from the mantle cavity. It forms several races (*S. officinalis filliouxi* lives in the North Sea and during the spawning season swims to the coast of Holland). Distribution: from the Mediterranean to the North Sea.

Family: **Squids — Loliginidae**

6 Long-finned Squid *Loligo vulgaris* — Length 50 cm. Has an internal shell the same as the cuttlefish. The elongate body is furnished with fairly large fins. Distribution: Atlantic Ocean, Mediterranean Sea, occasionally in the North and Baltic Seas.

70

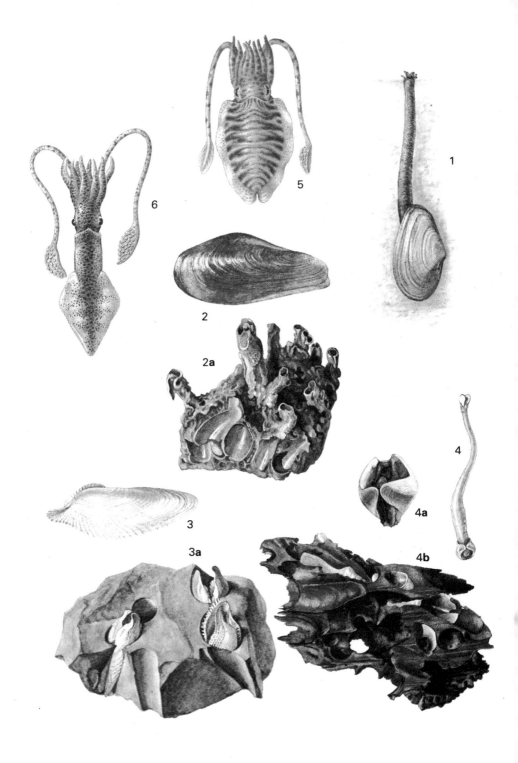

Phylum: **Segmented Worms — Annelida**

Class: **Polychaeta**
Order: **Errantia**
Family: **Aphroditidae**

1 Sea Mouse *Aphrodite aculeata* — Length 100—200 mm, width 50 mm. Body elongate, oval, covered with numerous bristly hairs. Side bristles glow with the colours of the rainbow, dorsal bristles form a dense cover entirely concealing the dorsal plates that serve to protect the soft body. Lives on soft sea bottoms. Feeds on minute animals. Distribution: Atlantic coast of Europe, North, Baltic and Mediterranean Seas.

Family: **Nereidae**

2 Ragworm *Neanthes diversicolor* — Length 60—120 mm, width 2—6 mm. Long, elongated body composed of 70—120 segments. Colour variable, ranging from yellow, orange and green to reddish. Lives in muddy sand sea bottoms of shallow coastlines where it digs a tube about 30 cm long. Tolerates brackish water. Feeds on dead marine animals. Distribution: European Atlantic coast, North, Baltic, and Mediterranean Seas.

Order: **Sedentaria**
Family: **Arenicolidae**

3 Lugworm *Arenicola marina* — Length 150—200 mm. Body narrowed toward the hind end, coloured yellowish-brown, olive green or brown. The striking red gills usually number 13 pairs. Found in soft sea bottoms. Digs tubes to a depth of 30 cm in which it lives, feeding on sand containing minute organisms. Very plentiful. Its place of occurrence is easily identified by the small holes and coiled casts. Distribution: European Atlantic coast, North and Baltic Seas; rarely also in Mediterranean.

Family: **Serpulidae**

4 *Protula tubularia* — Length up to 50 mm. Body composed of 100—125 segments. Lives concealed in a tube with only the numerous brightly coloured tentacles extending. The tubes are often attached to rocks, shells or stones. Distribution: Atlantic coast, English Channel, Mediterranean Sea.

Class: **Clitellata**
Subclass: **Oligochaeta**
Family: **Naididae**

5 *Stylaria lacustris* — Length 5.5—18 mm. Body transparent. Found in abundance in fresh water amidst vegetation. Also tolerates brackish water. Distribution: Eurasia, North America.

Family: **Tubificidae**

6 *Tubifex tubifex* — Length 25—30 mm. Coloured red. Lives in tubes of cemented mud, particularly in polluted waters. Used as food for aquarium fish. Distribution: Palaearctic, Nearctic, Oriental and Australasian regions.

Family: **Enchytraeidae**

7 *Enchytraeus albidus* — Length 20—40 mm. Yellowish-white. Lives in compost, by the banks of ponds and brooks, amidst vegetation, under stones and on the seacoast. Feeds on the roots of houseplants in flowerpots. Reproduces very rapidly. Cultivated as food for aquarium fish and cage birds. Distribution: worldwide.

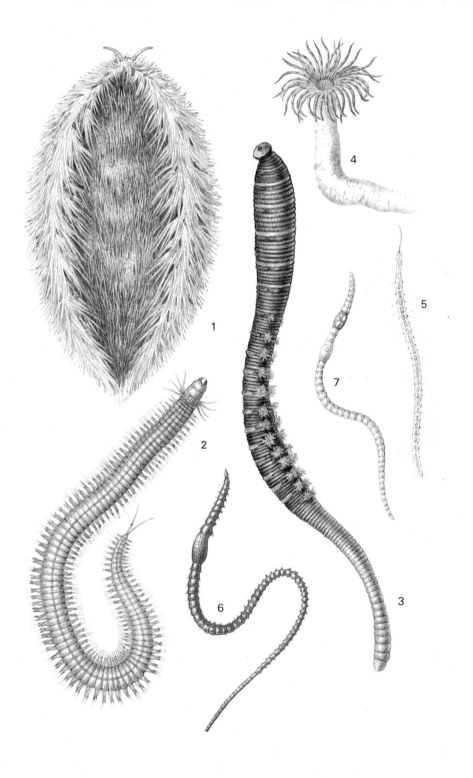

1

4

5

2

7

6

3

Phylum: **Segmented Worms — Annelida**

Class: **Clitellata**

Subclass: **Oligochaeta**

Family: **Earthworms — Lumbricidae**

1 Common Earthworm *Lumbricus terrestris* — Length 90—300 mm, width 6—9 mm. Body composed of 110—180 segments, hind end flattened. Found chiefly in loamy soils. Like all other species of earthworms it burrows in the soil and is important in aerating and fertilizing it. Like other earthworms this species is hermaphroditic. Reproduction is by means of eggs laid in a cocoon which is produced by the raised band (clitellum) on segments 32—37. Distribution: Europe, introduced to other continents.

2 *Lumbricus rubellus* — Length 60—150 mm, width 4—6 mm. Reddish-brown, red or reddish-violet. Clitellum located on the segments 27—32. Plentiful in moderately moist, humus-rich soils, and amidst fallen leaves. Distribution: Europe, introduced throughout the world.

3 *Aporrectodea caliginosa* — Length 60—170 mm, width 4—5 mm. A very common and plentiful species. Colour quite variable (greyish-blue, grey, pink, brown). Number of body segments also very variable, ranging from 100 to more than 200. Distribution: Europe.

4 *Aporrectodea rosea* — Length 25—150 mm, width 3—4 mm. Coloured flesh pink. Found in dry and moist soils. Distribution: Europe.

5 *Eisenia lucens (= E. submontana)* — Length 90—135 mm, width 5—6.5 mm. Segments marked with brown stripes. Found under the bark of old broadleaved trees and tree stumps (chiefly beech), in rotting wood and in moss in submontane and mountainous regions. Plentiful. Capable of luminescence. Distribution: central Europe, northern Balkans, U.S.S.R.

6 *Octolasium lacteum* — Length 30—180 mm, width 2—8 mm. Generally coloured milky-grey, less often reddish-brown. Plentiful in all types of soil, but not found in sand. Distribution: native to Europe, introduced to other continents.

Subclass: **Hirudinea**

Family: **Leeches — Hirudinidae**

7 *Haemopis sanguisuga* — Length 60—100 mm. Coloured greenish-brown, may have a yellowish band on either side of the body, but does not have reddish-brown longitudinal stripes. Hermaphroditic, like all leeches. Common in quiet and slow-flowing waters. Predaceous, hunts smaller animals which it swallows whole. Does not suck blood. Distribution: all Europe.

Family: **Herpobdellidae**

8 *Herpobdella octoculata* — Length 60 mm, width 8 mm. Colour variable — from brown to dirty green. Body segments marked with yellow or yellow-white spots. Found in calm and slow-flowing waters, tolerates also polluted waters. Feeds on various aquatic animals. Distribution: Europe.

Phylum: **Arthropods — Arthropoda**

Class: **Arachnida**

Order: **Scorpions — Scorpiones**

Family: **Chactidae**

1 *Euscorpius carpathicus* — Length 40 mm. Coloured brown. Requires warm conditions, like other scorpions. Elongated tail with poison claw at the end. Head furnished with chelicerae and pedipalps, resembling the claws of a crab. With the aid of the pedipalps it captures various arthropods which it then transfers to the chelicerae. Distribution: southern, southwestern and central Europe, the Balkans, Caucasus, Asia Minor, north Africa.

Order: **True spiders — Araneae**

Family: **Eresidae**

2 *Eresus niger* — Length ♂ 8—11 mm, ♀ 9—16 mm. The sexes differ in coloration; female is blackish-brown, male is black, the upper surface of the abdomen red with four large black spots. A warmth-loving species. Female makes vertical burrow, from which extends a tough sheet of silk threads to snare beetles and grasshoppers, on which the spider feeds. Distribution: Europe (north to Denmark and Great Britain), Transcaucasia, Turkestan, Altai.

Family: **Daddy longlegs spiders — Pholcidae**

3 *Pholcus opilionoides* — Length 4.5—5 mm. Commonly found in buildings, stables, under stones, etc. Female carries cocoon containing eggs in the chelicerae. Distribution: central and southern Europe (absent in Great Britain), Turkestan, China.

Family: **Sparassidae**

4 *Micrommata roseum* — Length ♂ 8.5—9.5 mm, ♀ 11—13 mm. Abdomen green, in males it has a red stripe. Does not spin a web; captures prey with its front legs. In spring it may be plentiful amidst fallen leaves, later on shrubs. Distribution: Palaearctic region.

Family: **Crab spiders — Thomisidae**

5 *Diaea dorsata* — Length 5—7 mm. Striking because of its green colouring, only the top of the abdomen is brown. From May on plentiful in shrubby oak stands and coniferous forests. Distribution: Europe, the Caucasus, Turkestan.

6 Flower-Haunting Spider *Misumena vatia* — Length ♂ 4 mm, ♀ 10 mm. Very common on flowering daisies and other Compositae, where it sits in wait for insects. Female able to change the colour of the body (over 2—3 days) according to the colour of the object on which she is resting. Favours either white or yellow flowers. Distribution: the Palaearctic and Nearctic regions.

Family: **Jumping spiders — Salticidae**

7 Zebra Spider *Salticus scenicus* — Length 4.5—7.5 mm. Abdomen marked with dark stripes. A warmth-loving, jumping species common on sunny walls and rocks. Distribution: Europe, Siberia, north Africa, North America.

1

3

5

6

4 ♀

2 ♂

7

Phylum: **Arthropods — Arthropoda**

Class: **Arachnida**

Order: **True spiders — Araneae**

Family: **Wolf spiders — Lycosidae**

1 *Alopecosa aculeata* — Length about 5 mm. Has many related species in Europe. Very common in forests. Captures prey without the aid of a web. Female makes a greenish-yellow cocoon about 6 mm long for the eggs. Distribution: the Palaearctic and Nearctic regions.

2 *Xerolycosa nemoralis* — Length 5—7 mm. Cephalothorax marked with a pale parallel-sided band covered with fine white hairs. Female lays about 60 eggs in a whitish cocoon. A very plentiful species in dry locations — in coniferous woods, clearings, heaths, etc. Distribution: the Palaearctic region.

Family: **Pisauridae**

3 *Pisaura mirabilis* — Length 11—13 mm. Abdomen elongate, light brown with double zig-zag band composed of dark and pale spots. Found chiefly in sunny places at lowland elevations — on herbaceous plants and shrubs, in forests and forest-steppes. Before copulation the male captures a victim (a fly), spins silken threads around it and presents it to the female. The eggs are laid in a globular, pale blue-green cocoon. At first the female carries it in the mandibles, later she spins a web between two leaves, places the cocoon under this shelter and stands guard alongside. Distribution: the Palaearctic region.

Family: **Agelenidae**

4 Water Spider *Argyroneta aquatica* — Length 8—15 mm. Lives gregariously in calm or slow-flowing, clean waters with abundant vegetation. An air-breather, it renews its supply of oxygen at the water surface. Bubbles of air are held fast in the hairs on the abdomen and the ventral side of the cephalothorax. It spins bell-like structures amidst the aquatic vegetation into which it puts bubbles with oxygen brought from the surface; it also spends most of its time inside the bell. During the egg-laying period the female reinforces the bell, spins a kind of ceiling inside on which she places the cocoons containing the eggs, herself then keeping watch in the bottom half of the bell. Distribution: Europe (from northern Italy to Scandinavia), Siberia, central Asia, New Zealand.

5 House Spider *Tegenaria ferruginea* — Length 9—14 mm. One of the largest of 'domestic' spiders. Found in the neighbourhood of man in cellars, sheds, on walls, as well as in dim, undisturbed corners. Spins a horizontal web up to 1/2 metre across in which it captures its prey. Resembles *T. domestica* from which it is distinguished chiefly by the reddish coloration on the upper surface of the abdomen, and longer legs. Distribution: Europe, Siberia.

Family: **Tetragnathidae**

6 *Tetragnatha extensa* — Length 8.5—12 mm. Found usually in characteristic outstretched position, on the leaves of aquatic plants by the banks of ponds. Spins a web. Distribution: almost worldwide.

Family: **Orb web spiders — Araneidae**

7 *Araneus cucurbitinus* — Length 6.5—7.5 mm. Occurs in May and June on shrubs and conifers. Identification features are the 4—5 pairs of dark dots on the vivid green or yellowish abdomen. Distribution: the Palaearctic region.

8 Garden or Diadem Spider *Araneus diadematus* — Length ♀ up to 17 mm. Variable in colour. There are many similar large species. Found in abundance on shrubs and trees where it spins its beautiful orb web. Distribution: the Palaearctic and Nearctic regions.

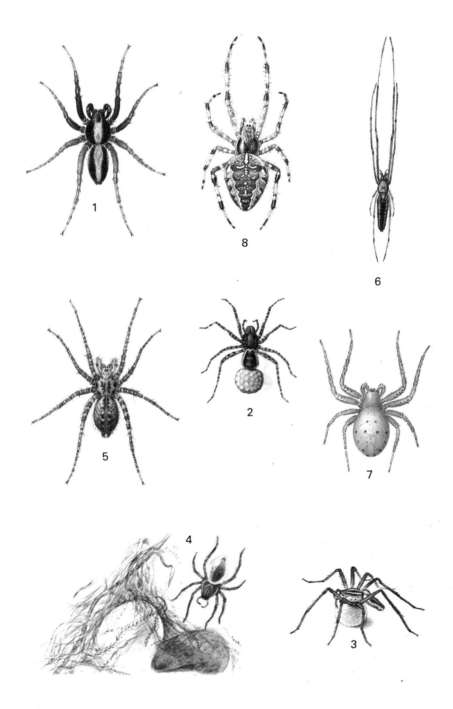

Phylum: **Arthropods — Arthropoda**

Class: **Arachnida**

Order: **False scorpions — Pseudoscorpiones**

Family: **Chthoniidae**

1 *Chthonius ischnocheles* — Length 1.6—2.5 mm. Distinguished by its claw-like pedipalps and large chelicerae which it uses to cut up its food. Found under stones and in litter. Distribution: Europe, north to Denmark and Sweden.

Family: **Cheliferidae**

2 Common False Scorpion *Chelifer cancroides* — Length 2.6—4.5 mm. Has greatly developed pedipalps. Feeds on various small species of insects. Although it also occurs under bark and in the nests of birds it is most often found in human dwellings. Distribution: cosmopolitan.

Order: **Harvestmen — Opiliones**

Family: **Phalangiidae**

3 *Phalangium opilio* — Length 6—9 mm. Back greyish to rufous-brown with darker longitudinal stripe constricted at two points. Individuals living in open locations (e. g. in fields) are a lighter colour. A common species found on the ground, on trees, rocks, telegraph poles, etc. Feeds on living as well as dead animals and plant tissues. Female often devours the male. The eggs overwinter. Adults may be seen from the end of May to November. Distribution: Europe, Siberia, central Asia, north Africa, North America.

4 *Opilio parietinus* — Length 5—8 mm. Body ovate. Female greyish, with faint pattern down the middle of the body. Male yellowish. A synanthropic species, found in sheds, cellars, on fences, walls, etc. It rests with legs outspread. Adults may be seen from the end of August until November. Distribution: Eurasia and the Nearctic region.

Order: **Mites — Acari**

Family: **Parasitidae**

5 *Parasitus coleoptratorum* — Length about 1—1.2 mm. Coloured orange. Larvae live chiefly on the underside of the bodies of dung beetles *(Geotrupes)* which carry them to piles of horse dung where they find food: the larvae of flies and small aschelminths. Distribution: Europe.

Family: **Ticks — Ixodidae**

6 Sheep or Castor-Bean Tick *Ixodes ricinus* — Length ♀ 4 mm, after sucking blood as much as 10 mm. Generally plentiful. Young larvae climb up on shrubs whence they drop on the first host, generally a bird nesting on the ground or a lizard, sucking its blood for 3—5 days. The larva then changes into a nymph (the next stage) on the ground. The nymph likewise sucks blood, but from a mammal, leaving it after a certain time to change into the adult form or imago. The female must suck blood before laying eggs. The male does not suck blood. Distribution: worldwide.

Family: **Trombidiidae**

7 *Trombidium holosericeum* — Length 4 mm. Coloured a striking bright red, body covered with fine velvety hairs. Found in upper soil layers. Larvae are parasitic on insects. Distribution: Europe.

80

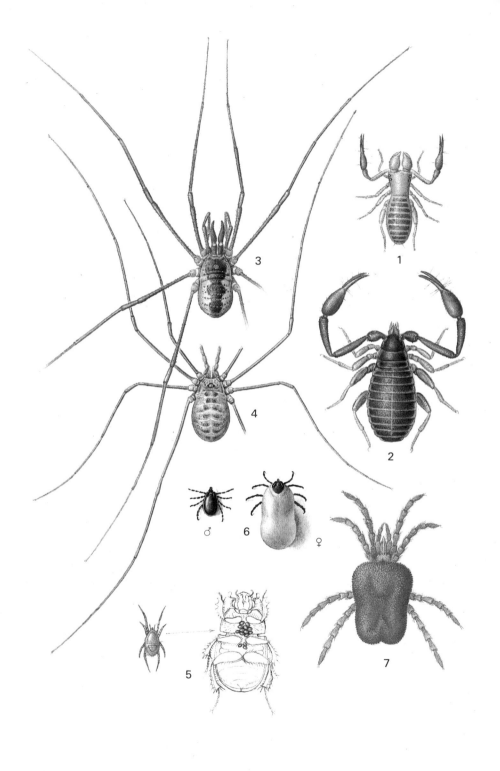

Phylum: **Arthropods — Arthropoda**

Class: **Crustaceans — Crustacea**

Order: **Anostraca**

Family: **Chirocephalidae**

1 *Siphonophanes grubii* — Length 12−28 mm, including appendages which measure 3 mm. Found locally in early spring in snow melt water where it flows through leaf litter. Adults live from February until May. Distribution: central Europe, eastern France, Denmark.

Order: **Notostraca**

Family: **Triopsidae**

2 *Triops cancriformis* — Length up to 10 cm (including caudal spines which are the same length as the body). Body composed of 32−35 segments, the last 4−7 without legs. It is largely covered by the broadly rounded shield-like carapace. Found in puddles, sometimes together with the similar species, *Apus apus,* from April until September. Distribution: much of the Palaearctic and Nearctic regions (does not occur above 60° N).

Order: **Water fleas — Cladocera**

Family: **Daphnidae**

3 Water Flea *Daphnia pulex* — Length ♀ 1.5−4.5 mm, ♂ 1.2−1.8 mm. A very common species. Body covered by an upper shell with coarse sculpturing. Found in forest pools, tolerates even the polluted water of village ponds. Feeds on detritus and various algae. This planktonic species is important as food for fish. Distribution: the Palaearctic and Nearctic regions.

Order: **Copepoda**

Family: **Cyclopidae**

4 *Macrocyclops fuscus* — Length 1.8−4 mm. Another species of the fresh water plankton. Found in water with dense vegetation. Distribution: Europe.

Order: **Amphipoda**

Family: **Gammaridae**

5 Common Freshwater Shrimp *Gammarus pulex,* now often named *Rivulogammarus pulex* — Length 12−15 mm. Body laterally compressed (flattened), arched, coloured greyish-yellow. Found in flowing, clean water, in springs under stones, etc. Can swim in various positions. Distribution: much of Europe and Asia Minor.

Order: **Isopoda**

Family: **Sow bugs or woodlice — Oniscidae**

6 *Oniscus asellus* — Length up to 18 mm. Body dark grey, marked with light spots down the middle. A variable species, found in large numbers in damp places in forests, buildings, under stones, amidst damp leaves, etc. Distribution: much of Europe and North America.

7 *Porcellio scaber* — Length up to 16 mm. Extremely variable. Ground colour yellowish with grey markings. Common in damp places both in the open and in buildings. Distribution: cosmopolitan.

Family: **Armadilliidae**

8 Pill Bug *Armadillidium vulgare* — Length up to 15 mm. Coloured grey, sometimes spotted. Found in drier places, under stones, old logs, in old walls. Distribution: almost worldwide.

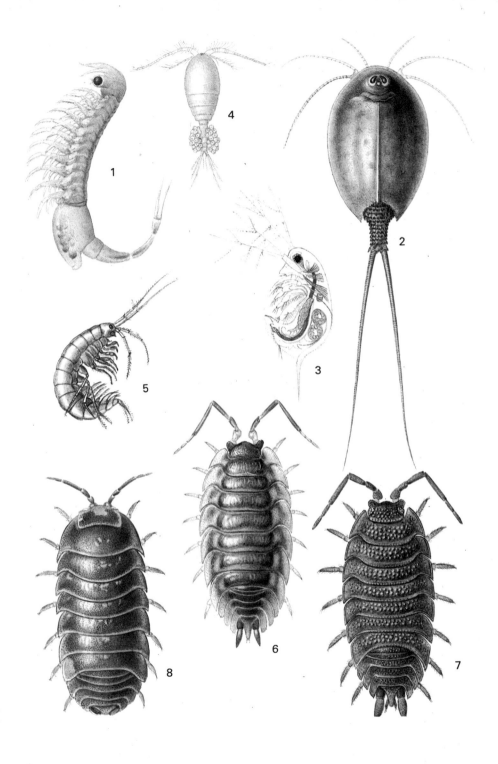

Phylum: **Arthropods — Arthropoda**

Class: **Crustaceans — Crustacea**

Order: **Decapoda**

Family: **Shrimps — Crangonidae**

1 Common Shrimp *Crangon crangon* — Length 40—50 mm. Greyish-yellow, yellow or greenish, sometimes dark brown on the upper side. A nocturnal creature that lives buried in the sea bottom during the daytime. Found along seacoasts from lower shore to depths of 10—50 metres; often very plentiful. In summer it often swims up rivers against the current to brackish waters. Feeds on small animals, algae and detritus. Female lays eggs in April — June and October—November. Caught and consumed as food, also used as bait and for making fishmeal. Distribution: Mediterranean, coast of western Europe (abundant in the North and Baltic Seas), eastern coast of North America.

Family: **Lobsters — Astacidae**

2 Common Lobster *Homarus gammarus,* also known as *H. vulgaris* — Length 300—500 mm. Inhabitant of rocky and stony seacoasts to depths of about 40 metres. Has large, unequal pincers (one is less massive). Forages for food at night; feeds on various marine animals (molluscs, other crustaceans). Eggs are laid in July — August. Widely captured as a great delicacy. In some places its numbers have shown such a marked decline that certain countries have taken protective measures to halt this trend. Distribution: Mediterranean Sea, Atlantic coast of Europe, and the North and Baltic Seas.

3 River Crayfish *Astacus astacus* — Length 120—160 mm. In recent years its numbers have undergone a marked decline both due to the pollution of water courses (it needs clean water) and diseases. It lives in flowing as well as still waters, burrowing in the banks (under roots of trees) or hiding under stones. It feeds on smaller animals (small fish, tadpoles) and on carcasses. The female lays several dozen eggs which she carries with her on the underside of the abdomen. Distribution: from central Europe to southern Scandinavia.

Family: **Hermit crabs — Paguridae**

4 Common Hermit Crab *Pagurus bernhardus* — Length about 35 mm. It has a soft abdomen and seeks out the abandoned shells of marine gastropods for protection, inserting its rear end into the shell and carrying it about with it. It is found on the seashore and on sandy or stony sea bottoms, sometimes at fairly great depths. Feeds on small animal organisms and detritus. Distribution: Atlantic coast of Europe as far as the North and Baltic Seas, and the Mediterranean.

Family: **Swimming crabs — Portunidae**

5 *Portunus holsatus* — Length about 40 mm. A moderate-sized crab with smooth, grey-green carapace. Found by the seacoast as well as at greater depths; locally abundant. Distribution: Atlantic coast of Europe as far as the North Sea.

Family: **Grapsidae**

6 Chinese Mitten Crab *Eriocheir sinensis* — Length about 75 mm. Has large pincers; those of males are thickly covered with hairs. A marine crab, it travels against the current up rivers, but reproduces only in salt water. Distribution: Yellow Sea. At the beginning of this century introduced into Europe where it is spreading up the Elbe, Ems and Weser rivers. Through the Elbe it has now extended its range as far as the lower reaches of the Vltava River. Atlantic north from English Channel, North and Baltic Seas.

Phylum: **Arthropods — Arthropoda**

Class: **Millipedes — Diplopoda**

Family: **Polydesmidae**

1 *Polydesmus complanatus* — Length 15—23 mm, width 2.3—3.2 mm. A common species found in damp places, e. g. alder groves and broadleaved forests under the bark of old stumps. Distribution: central Europe, north to central Sweden.

Family: **Blaniulidae**

2 *Blaniulus guttulatus* — Length 7.5—16 mm, width 0.4—0.7 mm. Body composed of numerous segments and having as many as 103 pairs of legs. Whitish to yellow-grey, glossy, with a row of carmine-red spots running along the sides of the body, one pair of spots to each segment. Does not have ocelli. Lives in the ground, in gardens and greenhouses, and is herbivorous. In gardens it feeds on damaged fruit (strawberries, fallen apples), in which it often occurs in greater numbers. Not harmful. Distribution: much of Europe (north as far as Scandinavia and the British Isles), Canada.

Family: **Iulidae**

3 *Iulus terrestris* — Length 17—23 mm, width 1.5—2.1 mm. Has up to 89 pairs of legs. Body elongate, black or black-brown, lighter on the sides. Legs yellowish-white. Head bears 42 ocelli. Common in damp places — amidst fallen leaves in woodlands and gardens, under stones, etc. Distribution: Europe, from the Balkan Peninsula north to Scandinavia, Lithuania, Estonia.

4 *Schizophyllum sabulosum* — Length 15—47 mm, width 1.6—4 mm. Common species, easily identified by the two longitudinal bands composed of yellow-red spots. On the last body segment there is an apparent 'tail'. Found from spring until autumn in various locations (in forests, in chalky and sandy places, under stones and on the branches of trees). Distribution: all Europe.

Class: **Centipedes — Chilopoda**

Family: **Lithobiidae**

5 *Lithobius forficatus* — Length 20—32 mm. Likes dark and damp places. Common under stones, under bark and under old logs. Rapidly disappears in the dark when disturbed. A predaceous species that feeds on various arthropods (including members of its own species), earthworms, etc. Female deposits the yellow-white eggs singly. Young larva has only 7 pairs of legs; their number increases with successive moults. Adult centipedes also moult but they do not develop further legs. Distribution: north temperate region, widely introduced elsewhere.

Family: **Geophilidae**

6 Necrophloephagus *Geophilus longicornis* — Length 20—40 mm. Common species. Has up to 57 pairs of legs. Female noted for her care of the offspring. She coats eggs with a special secretion which encases them, and then curls around them in a spiral, protecting them against infection as well as enemies. During this period she does not feed. She also tends the young larvae until their second moult when they are capable of fending for themselves. They reach maturity after two years. Distribution: all Europe, north Africa, Siberia, introduced to North America.

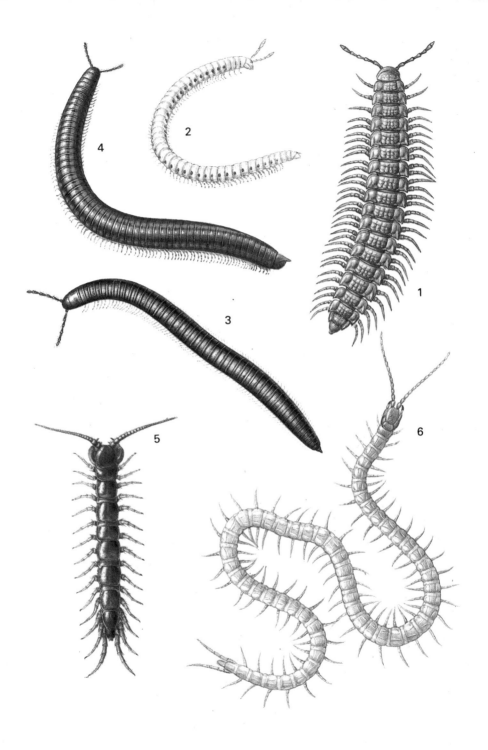

Phylum: **Arthropods — Arthropoda**

Class: **Insects — Insecta**

Order: **Japygids — Diplura**

Family: **Campodeidae**

1 *Campodea fragilis* — Length 3.5 mm. Blind. Has two caudal setae shorter than the body. Lives in damp places in the ground, under wood, under stones, sometimes also in anthills. Distribution: cosmopolitan.

Order: **Springtails — Collembola**

Family: **Poduridae**

2 *Podura aquatica* — Length 1.1—1.5 mm. Very common. In spring, when the snow melts, it occurs in large numbers on the surface of puddles. Distribution: Eurasia, North America.

Order: **Bristle-tails — Thysanura**

Family: **Lepismatidae**

3 Silver-fish *Lepisma saccharina* — Length 7—10 mm. Synanthropic. In central Europe it is found in households, pantries, warehouses and libraries, in southern Europe it lives in the open. A nocturnal species that runs rapidly. Body covered with fine greyish scales. Distribution: worldwide.

Order: **Mayflies — Ephemeroptera**

Family: **Ephemeridae**

4 *Ephemera danica* — Length of body 15—24 mm, caudal cerci 14—40 mm. Wings brownish with darker spots. Adults on the wing from May until August (most abundant in June). Larvae frequent flowing water in hilly country. Distribution: most of Europe.

Order: **Dragonflies and damselflies — Odonata**

Family: **Agriidae**

5 *Agrion virgo* — Length of body 50 mm, wingspan 70 mm. Wings of male are a glossy blue-green, wings of the female are brownish. When at rest they are held together, above the body. The sexes can also be distinguished by the pterostigma near the apex of the wings, present only in the female. Adults are on the wing from May until September, around streams and rivers. Not noted for sustained flight; often rests on shoreline vegetation. Female deposits about 300 eggs in the tissues of various aquatic plants such as *Sagittaria, Butomus, Sparganium,* etc. Nymphs live in water. When full-grown they climb out of the water, and after a while the adult emerges. Development takes two years; the nymphs overwinter twice. Distribution: Eurasia.

6 *Agrion splendens* — Length 50 mm, wingspan 70 mm. Resembles preceding species both in shape and size of body. Males have a broad blue or greenish-blue band on the fore and hind wings. The wings of the female are pale green, transparent, with pterostigma. Found near flowing water from April until mid-September, up to mountainous elevations. Nymphs grow to a length of about 20 mm, and overwinter twice, development taking two years. Distribution: Europe, Middle East, north Africa.

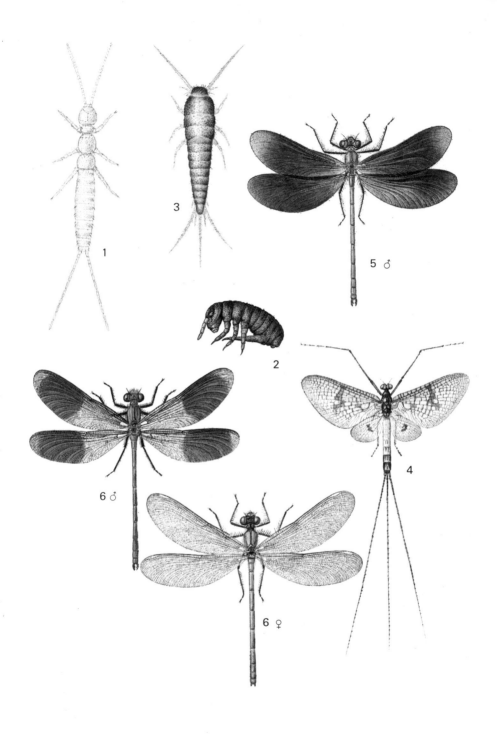

1

3

5 ♂

2

6 ♂

4

6 ♀

Phylum: **Arthropods — Arthropoda**

Class: **Insects — Insecta**

Order: **Dragonflies and damselflies — Odonata**

Family: **Coenagriidae**

1 *Pyrrhosoma nymphula* — Length 35 mm, wingspan 45 mm. Body reddish-black; black thorax marked with 2 red longitudinal stripes, reddish abdomen marked with black pattern. Adults on the wing from April until August, near calm or very slow-flowing waterways. Female deposits eggs in various plants by the waterside, usually accompanied by the male. Development of the nymph takes one year. Distribution: Europe and Asia Minor.

Family: **Aeshnidae**

2 *Aeshna cyanea* — Length 65—80 mm, wingspan 95—110 mm. One of the commonest members of the family. Excellent flier. Male has distinctly notched hind wings, blue dorsal patches on the last abdominal segments, green patches on the others. The wings of the female are not notched and all the abdominal patches are green. Adults on the wing from spring until early November. Often leaves the vicinity of water, even visiting cities. Eggs overwinter. Development of nymph takes two years. Distribution: much of Europe as far as northern Sweden, Asia Minor, north Africa.

Family: **Gomphidae**

3 *Gomphus vulgatissimus* — Length 45—50 mm, wingspan 60—70 mm. On the wing from May till July, near water, on meadows, clearings and forest rides. Female flies close above water, occasionally submerging the abdomen to release eggs, which fall to the bottom. Distribution: Europe and Asia Minor.

Family: **Libellulidae**

4 *Libellula quadrimaculata* — Length 40—50 mm, wingspan 70—85 mm. There is a dark patch on the node of each wing (4 patches in all, hence its scientific name). Very common round calm bodies of water from May to August. Larva hibernates twice. Distribution: Eurasia, North America.

5 *Sympetrum sanguineum* — Length 35—40 mm, wingspan 50—60 mm. Occurs round calm bodies of water until October. Fond of warm situations on banks by the waterside, on shrubs, etc. Development takes one year. Distribution: Eurasia, north Africa.

Order: **Stoneflies — Plecoptera**

Family: **Perlidae**

6 *Perla burmeisteriana* — Length 17—28 mm, wingspan 55—58 mm. Distinguished by dark thorax and light abdomen. Adults fly near water. Distribution: central and southern Europe, the Balkans, western Europe.

Order: **Earwigs — Dermaptera**

Family: **Labiidae**

7 Small Earwig *Labia minor* — Length 5—9 mm. Common in fields, meadows, forest margins and greenhouses from spring till autumn. On the wing during the day, it flies readily unlike other European earwigs. Distribution: almost worldwide.

Family: **Forficulidae**

8 Common Earwig *Forficula auricularia* — Length 14—23 mm. During the daytime conceals itself under stones, logs, amidst fallen leaves, old rags, etc. Common in buildings. Feeds on plant as well as animal matter, often on aphids. In autumn the female deposits several dozen eggs in an underground chamber, watching over them and cleaning them constantly; she also broods over the young nymphs. Distribution: worldwide.

90

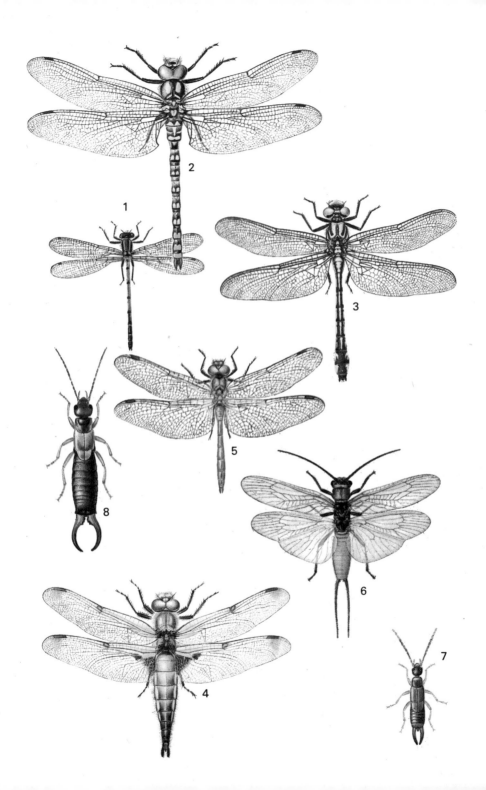

Phylum: **Arthropods — Arthropoda**

Class: **Insects — Insecta**

Order: **Cockroaches — Blattodea**

Family: **Blattidae**

1 Dusky Cockroach *Ectobius lapponicus* — Length 7—10 mm. Common in woodlands. Eggs are laid in oothecae about 3 mm long. Distribution: Europe, western Siberia.

2 Common Cockroach *Blatta orientalis* — Length 18—30 mm. Nocturnal, warmth-loving. Occurs in human habitations where it feeds on various remnants, etc. Male has 2 pairs of wings (shorter than the abdomen), female has only wing stumps. Eggs are deposited in oothecae 7—12 mm long. There are as many as 10 nymphal stages. Adult lives only one year. This cockroach is generally not considered to be harmful, but it is unpleasant, soils foodstuffs and may transmit diseases. Distribution: worldwide.

Order: **Crickets and bush crickets — Ensifera**

Family: **Bush crickets — Tettigoniidae**

3 Great Green Bush Cricket *Tettigonia viridissima* — Length 28—42 mm. Occurs from July to October on shrubs, meadow and field plants. Climbs up trees for the night. Feeds on various insects. Female has large ovipositor with which she lays about 100 eggs in the ground; eggs overwinter. Males stridulate both during daytime and at night. Distribution: Europe, the Caucasus, Asia Minor, Siberia, north Africa.

4 Wart-biter *Decticus verrucivorus* — Length 24—44 mm. Found in meadows, fields, heaths, etc. Feeds on various insects, sometimes also plant tissues. Adults occur from June till September. Eggs overwinter. Distribution: Eurasia.

Family: **True crickets — Gryllidae**

5 Field Cricket *Gryllus campestris* — Length 20—26 mm. Adult found from May to July in underground chambers which it excavates in warm places, e. g. meadows and hedgerows. Feeds on small insects and plant tissues. Female lays eggs over a period of several days. Nymphs live gregariously at first but later each excavates a separate chamber in which to hibernate. Males stridulate most intensely during the mating period. Distribution: central and southern Europe, southern Great Britain, western Asia, north Africa.

6 Ground Cricket *Nemobius sylvestris* — Length 7—10 mm. Found from June to September amidst fallen leaves in woodlands. It is usually the nymph that hibernates. Distribution: Europe including Great Britain (central Europe marks its northern boundary), north Africa.

Family: **Mole crickets — Gryllotalpidae**

7 Mole Cricket *Gryllotalpa gryllotalpa* — Length 35—50 mm. Adapted to life underground (front pair of legs modified as burrowing limbs) but surfaces during the mating period. In both sexes the folded hind wings extend beyond the end of the abdomen. Adults found from April to October, in meadows and gardens. Good flier and swimmer. Generally feeds on various insects (including cockchafers), if need be also on plant tissues. Eggs are laid in an underground chamber, where the female broods over them as well as the newly emerged nymphs. Hibernates either in the nymphal or adult stage. Distribution: Europe, western Asia, north Africa, North America (introduced).

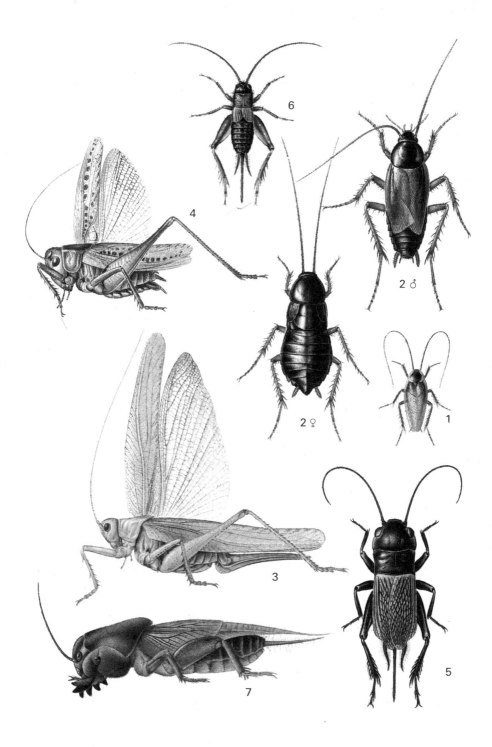

Phylum: **Arthropods — Arthropoda**

Class: **Insects — Insecta**

Order: **Locusts and short-horned grasshoppers — Caelifera**

Family: **Grouse-locusts — Tetrigidae**

1 *Tetrix subulata* — Length 7—10 mm. Found in abundance in damp and rather dry locations from lowlands to mountainous elevations. Herbivorous like other members of this order. Distribution: Europe, Siberia, north Africa, North America.

Family: **Catantopidae**

2 *Calliptamus italicus* — Length 14—34 mm. Occurs in dry meadows and fallow land, feeding on broadleaved plants. Adults found from July to September. Distribution: Mainly southern and central Europe, Asia Minor, Middle East (Syria), north Africa.

Family: **Acrididae**

3 *Psophus stridulus* — Length 23—32 mm. Adults found from June to October chiefly in mountain country in meadows and clearings. The scientific name given to it by the Swedish naturalist C. Linné is derived from the grating sounds so characteristic of the species. Both sexes stridulate; stridulation that is most pronounced, however, is the song of the male in flight. In recent years it is disappearing in the wild. Distribution: Europe (absent in Scandinavia and British Isles), Siberia.

4 Migratory Locust *Locusta migratoria* — Length 33—65 mm. Throughout its range occurs in several geographic races, differing in colour. Each race has two phases; sedentary and migratory. At high population density the sedentary phase gives rise to the migratory and vice versa. This phenomenon is also known in several other locusts that are feared pests mainly in tropical and subtropical regions. The migratory locust was formerly a severe pest in Europe and still is in Africa, for locust 'bands' consume great quantities of green food. Swarms of these locusts can descend on the land and destroy entire crops. History in Europe records countless such invasions against which man was almost powerless. Locusts spread to central Europe from the Danube River region where conditions were conducive for production of the migratory forms. Nowadays it occurs in Europe locally, and only sporadically. Distribution: Europe (except the north), much of Asia, Africa, Madagascar.

5 *Oedipoda caerulescens* — Length 15—28 mm. Hind wings usually blue with dark broad band before the apex (may be yellow or even pinkish in some individuals); in this it resembles several other species such as *Sphingonotus caerulans*. Found from July to September in dry places, heaths, steppes, on dry hillsides, etc. Distribution: Europe (except British Isles), Asia Minor, Middle East, north Africa.

6 Stripe-winged Grasshopper *Stenobothrus lineatus* — Length 16—25 mm. Found in meadows, heaths, forest rides, etc. Noted for its marked variability of colour. Stridulation of male is not very loud. Distribution: Europe as far as southern Sweden and southern Great Britain, western Asia, Siberia.

Phylum: **Arthropods — Arthropoda**

Class: **Insects — Insecta**

Order: **True bugs — Heteroptera**

Family: **Pentatomidae**

1 *Graphosoma lineatum* — Length 9—11 mm. Characteristic black stripes on a red ground colour. Warmth-loving, found on flowering Umbelliferae and other plants. Distribution: southern and central Europe, Asia Minor, Middle East.

2 Bishop's Mitre *Aelia acuminata* — Length 7—9.5 mm. A common and plentiful species that emerges from its winter shelter in April. Found on grass blades, including cereals, on which the eggs are laid in spring. Nymphs change into adults in August. Distribution: Eurasia and north Africa.

3 *Palomena viridissima* — Length 12—14 mm. Similar to the Green Shield Bug *(P. prasina)* but differs by having the third antennal segment about one-fourth shorter than the second, whereas in *P. prasina* they are of the same length. Found on shrubs and trees. Adults hibernate. Distribution: much of Europe (rare in the north and absent in British Isles), Asia, including northern India.

4 Brassica Bug *Eurydema oleracea* — Length 5—7 mm. Marked colour variability. Ground colour metallic green or blue with red, yellow, white or orange spots. Found mostly on Cruciferae. Adults hibernate. Distribution: Eurasia.

5 *Picromerus bidens* — Length 11—14 mm. Found in broadleaved forests in July and August. Feeds on the larvae of various insects, e. g. the caterpillars of Lepidoptera. Eggs overwinter. Distribution: the Palaearctic region.

Family: **Squash bugs — Coreidae**

6 *Mesocerus marginatus* — Length 12—14 mm. Found in damp places chiefly on sorrel, dock, blackberry, groundsel, etc. Distribution: Europe, Asia Minor, central Asia.

Family: **Cotton stainers — Pyrrhocoridae**

7 Firebug *Pyrrhocoris apterus* — Length 7—12 mm. One of the first insects to appear in spring. In congenial weather even in late winter at the base of trees in parks, tree avenues, etc., usually in great numbers. Feeds on plant juices and on dead or living insects. Distribution: Eurasia, north Africa, Central America and elsewhere.

Family: **Damsel bugs — Nabidae**

8 *Nabis rugosus* — Length 6—7 mm. A very plentiful species on expanses of grass. Predaceous on smaller plant-eating insects. Adults hibernate under grass. Distribution: the Palaearctic region.

Family: **Blood-sucking and bed-bugs — Cimicidae**

9 Bed-bug *Cimex lectularius* — Length 3.5—8 mm. Well-known, annoying species that sucks the blood of man. Can go without food for several months. An itching red spot appears round the point of puncture. Active at night, concealing itself under pictures, peeling wallpaper, etc. during the day. Found primarily in unclean, poorly kept dwellings, hotels and army barracks. Female successively deposits some 100—200 eggs but must suck her fill of blood before doing so. Distribution: cosmopolitan.

96

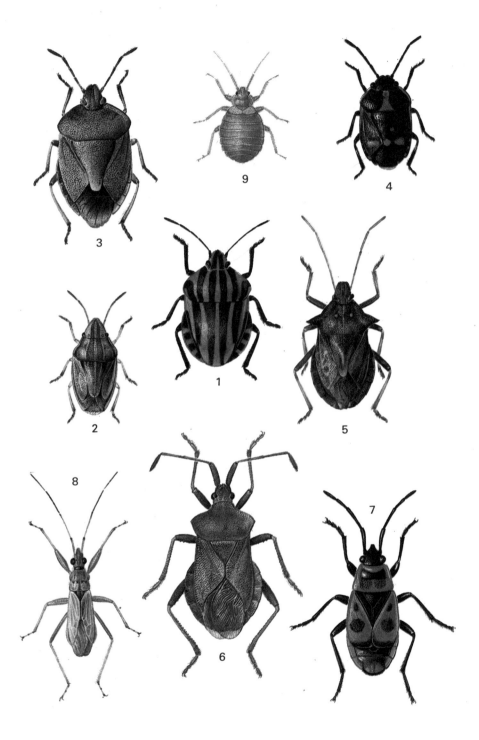

Phylum: **Arthropods — Arthropoda**

Class: **Insects — Insecta**

Order: **True bugs — Heteroptera**

Family: **Flower bugs — Anthocoridae**

1 Common Flower Bug *Anthocoris nemorum* — Length 3—4.5 mm. Very common in deciduous woodlands and gardens. Feeds on various insects (aphids, scale insects) as well as other arthropods (e. g. mites), sometimes also sucks the sap of plants. Adults hibernate; may be found in early spring on catkins. There are 1—3 generations a year. Distribution: most of Europe, Asia Minor, northern Asia, north Africa.

Family: **Capsids — Miridae**

2 *Phytocoris tiliae* — Length 6.1—6.9 mm. Lives on various trees, e. g. oak, lime, ash, apple. Feeds on the small larvae of insects, mites, etc. Adults found in July and August. Distribution: Europe, (except the far north), north Africa.

3 *Lygus pratensis* — Length 5.8—6.7 mm. Very common species which emerges from its winter shelter in early spring. Destructive pest of fruit tree crops. There are 1—2 generations a year. Distribution: entire Palaearctic region.

4 *Deraeocoris ruber* — Length 6.5—7.5 mm. Very variable in colour. Found on deciduous trees and herbaceous plants. Adults and larvae feed on aphids and other small insects. Eggs overwinter. Distribution: Europe, north Africa, North America.

Family: **Water-striders or pond-skaters — Gerridae**

5 *Gerris gibbifer* — Length 10—13 mm. Common on the surface of pools and puddles. There are 2 generations a year. Resembles several other species that live in the same environment. Adults hibernate. Distribution: Europe (absent or rare in the north), Middle East, north Africa.

Family: **Backswimmers — Notonectidae**

6 *Notonecta glauca* — Length 14—16 mm. Has a short, strong beak with which it can bite painfully. Found in calm water, e. g. ponds, pools, puddles, amidst vegetation. Eggs are deposited in the stems of aquatic plants from winter to spring. Adults found from summer onward; predaceous. Forms several geographic forms within its range. Distribution: Europe, the Caucasus, north Africa.

Family: **Water scorpions — Nepidae**

7 *Nepa cinerea* — Length 18—22 mm. Predaceous species, also named *N. rubra*. Fore legs modified to serve as grasping organs. There is a long breathing tube at the hind end of the body. Found in quiet and slow-flowing waters in the mud by the shore. Adults hibernate. After hibernating the female lays eggs in the stems and leaves of aquatic plants. Distribution: much of Europe.

Family: **Creeping water-bugs — Naucoridae**

8 Saucer Bug *Ilyocoris cimicoides* — Length 15 mm. Inhabits calm and slow-flowing waters. Adults hibernate. Eggs are deposited in the tissues of aquatic plants in April and May. Distribution: much of Europe, the Caucasus.

98

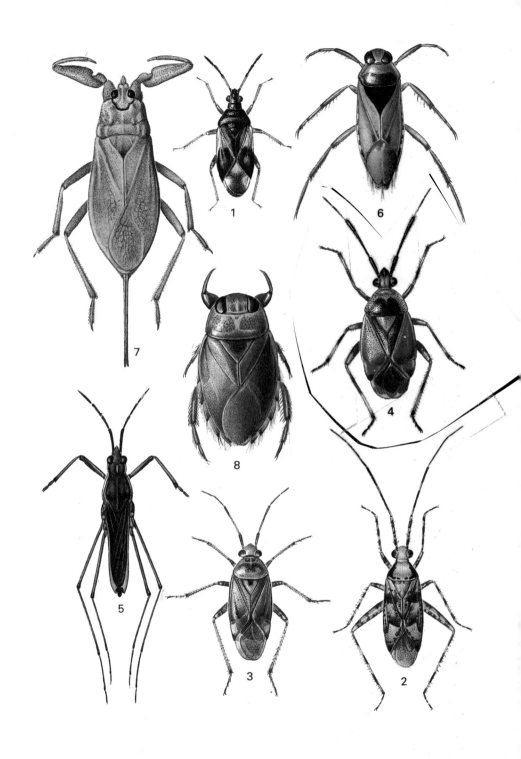

Phylum: **Arthropods — Arthropoda**

Class: **Insects — Insecta**

Order: **Homoptera**

Suborder: **Cicadinea**

Family: **Cicadas — Cicadidae**

1 *Tibicen haematodes* — Length 26—38 mm, span of fore wings 75—85 mm. One of the largest of European cicadas. Likes warm situations, partial to vineyards. Male makes very loud sounds. Distribution: southern and central Europe, the Caucasus.

Family: **Spittle-bugs or frog-hoppers — Cercopidae**

2 *Cercopis vulnerata* — Length 9.5—11 mm. Occurs in abundance on various plants in June and July. The larvae, encased in foamy matter, live on plant roots. Distribution: all Europe.

Family: **Leaf-hoppers — Cicadellidae (Jassidae)**

3 *Cicadella viridis* — Length 5—9 mm. Common in July and August in damp locations, meadows, forest rides, etc. Distribution: the Palaearctic and Nearctic regions.

Suborder: **Aphidinea**

Family: **Aphids — Aphididae**

4 *Myzus cerasi* — Length 2 mm. Found on cherry leaves. In some years it occurs in huge numbers, coating leaves or young annual shoots and sucking the sap, causing the leaves to curl. Important enemies of aphids are lady-birds and hover-fly larvae. Distribution: cosmopolitan.

Family: **Adelgidae**

5 *Adelges viridis* — Length 1.7—2 mm. Produces pineapple-shaped galls on young spruce shoots. The gall is composed of a great many small chambers in which the development of the nymph takes place. Life-cycle of the species is very complex. Distribution: Europe.

Suborder: **Scale insects — Coccinea**

Family: **Ensign coccids — Ortheziidae**

6 *Orthezia urticae* — Length of female 2.5—3.5 mm; with egg sac 8—10 mm. Generally found on nettles *(Urtica)*. Male has one pair of wings, female is wingless and her body is covered with symmetrically arranged white waxy plates. The female forms a long egg-sac at the end of the abdomen, containing the eggs which she carries with her. Distribution: Eurasia.

Family: **Eriococcidae**

7 *Cryptococcus fagi* — Length 0.8—1 mm. Forms large colonies on the trunks of beech trees. Locally very abundant. Distribution: Europe, Asia Minor, Armenia, North America.

Family: **Armoured scales — Diaspididae**

8 *Chionaspis salicis* — Length 1.9—2.5 mm. Polyphagous, very common on alder, willow, mountain ash, blueberry, etc. Red, flat females are covered by a white scale. Distribution: the Palaearctic.

Suborder: **Psyllinea**

Family: **Jumping plant lice — Psyllidae**

9 Apple Sucker *Psylla mali* — Length 3.5 mm. Found on apple trees. The flat nymphs, which are very injurious to the leaves, also excrete large amounts of sweet honeydew which causes the leaves and flower-buds to become sticky. Distribution: almost worldwide.

100

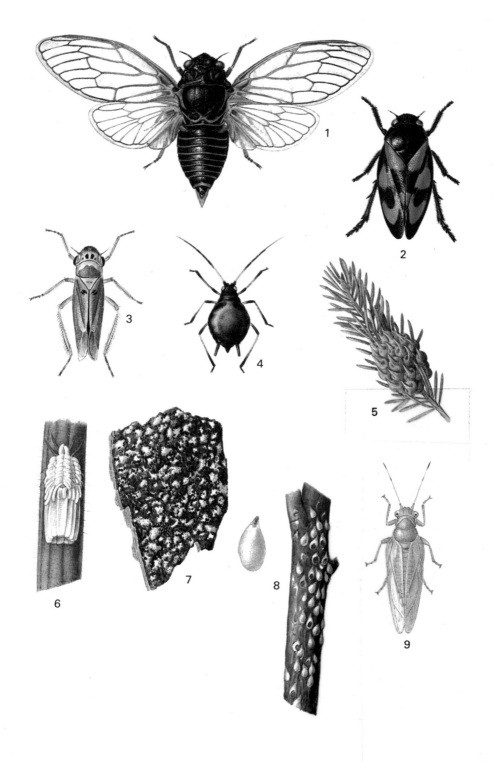

Phylum: **Arthropods** — **Arthropoda**

Class: **Insects** — **Insecta**

Order: **Alder flies and snake flies** — **Megaloptera**

Family: **Sialidae**

1 Alder Fly *Sialis lutaria* — Length 10—15 mm, wingspan 25 mm. Wings folded roof-like over abdomen when at rest. Flight cumbersome. Found on vegetation near water. Eggs are laid on aquatic vegetation or stones. Larvae live in water and feed on small aquatic animals. When full-grown the larva climbs out of the water, begins breathing by means of tracheae and pupates in the soil. Development takes about one year. Distribution: Europe (except the southeastern part), Siberia.

Family: **Raphidiidae**

2 Snake Fly *Raphidia notata* — Length about 15 mm, span of fore wings 25—29 mm. Resembles several other specie. in whose company it occurs. Both sexes have an extremely long prothorax, the female has a long, narrow ovipositor. Found in forests on shrubs and ground vegetation. Larvae have a greatly flattened body and live under the bark of trees as well as on leaves. The adults and larvae are predaceous. They are beneficial in forestry. Distribution: northern and central Europe (absent in the Balkans and Iberian Peninsula).

Order: **Lacewings and ant lions** — **Planipennia**

Family: **Chrysopidae**

3 Green Lacewing *Chrysopa perla* — Length 10 mm, wingspan 25—30 mm. Very common in forests from May to September. Coloured blue-green, longitudinal veins in the wings are green. Adults and larvae are predaceous, feeding on aphids. Distribution: Europe.

4 *Chrysopa flava* — Length 15 mm, wingspan 35—45 mm. Found in forests and gardens from June to September. Distribution: Europe, north Africa, North America.

Family: **Osmylidae**

5 *Osmylus chrysops* — Length 25 mm, wingspan 37—52 mm. Adults on the wing at night near flowing water. The larva, which overwinters, is amphibious, and is a predator of fly larvae. Distribution: Europe as far north as Scandinavia.

Family: **Ant lions** — **Myrmeleontidae**

6 *Myrmeleon formicarius* — Length 35 mm, wingspan 65—75 mm. Slightly resembles a dragonfly. Adults on the wing from June to August, always in the evening, in coniferous forests in sandy localities. Larva excavates a fairly large pit in the sand, buried in the bottom of which it waits for prey (often ants) to fall in. Larva hibernates once or twice and pupates in a cocoon. Distribution: most of Europe, north to southern Norway and Sweden (absent in British Isles).

Family: **Ascalaphidae**

7 *Ascalaphus libelluloides* — Length 20—25 mm, wingspan 45—53 mm. The Ascalaphidae differ from other neuropteroid insects by having long, clubbed antennae. A very warmth-loving species and an excellent flier. Adults on the wing from June to August. Distribution: southwestern Europe (Bohemia marks its northeastern boundary), northwest Africa.

Phylum: **Arthropods — Arthropoda**

Class: **Insects — Insecta**

Order: **Beetles — Coleoptera**

Family: **Tiger beetles — Cicindelidae**

1 Green Tiger Beetle *Cicindela campestris* — Length 12—15 mm. Often occurs in abundance on field paths, forest rides, in hedgerows and sandy localities. On the wing from early spring, but flies only short distances. Like other related species it is carnivorous, feeding on various insect larvae as well as adult insects. The larva is also predaceous. It excavates a burrow, perhaps 30 cm long or even longer, in a soil bank, remaining at the mouth of the burrow and closing the entrance with its head. Captured victims are pulled inside where they are eaten. When fully grown the larva pupates at the bottom of the burrow. Distribution: all Europe, Siberia, north Africa.

Family: **Ground beetles — Carabidae**

2 *Cychrus caraboides* — Length 15—23 mm. Found in damp forests from lowlands to mountainous elevations (up to about 2000 metres). Hides under logs, stones and beneath the bark of tree stumps. Predaceous. It does not chew or swallow its prey, but decomposes it first by regurgitating a small amount of digestive juice after which it can suck up its meal in liquid form. This is a common way of feeding in ground beetles. Distribution: much of Europe.

3 Violet Ground Beetle *Carabus violaceus* — Length 18—34 mm. Has a striking narrow, violet or greenish to blue-green, flattened rim round the edges of the elytra and scutum. Locally common, chiefly in damp forests, occasionally also found in fields and gardens up to mountainous elevations. Distribution: practically all Europe, the Caucasus, western Siberia.

4 *Carabus hortensis* — Length 23—30 mm. A good character for identifying this species are the conspicuous gold spots on the elytra. A damp-loving species, it hunts in woodlands and gardens at night, concealing itself during the day. Distribution: much of Europe, south as far as Greece, east to the Urals (absent in some parts of western Europe).

5 *Carabus auratus* — Length 20—27 mm. Easily mistaken for *C. auronitens,* from which it differs by the ridges on the elytra. Found in fields and gardens where it hunts various, sometimes fairly large animals, e. g. cockchafers, the larvae of the Colorado beetle, etc. Appears early in spring, as it hibernates in the adult stage. Distribution: western and part of central Europe. In eastern Europe it is replaced by *C. auronitens.*

6 *Carabus cancellatus* — Length 18—27 mm. Occurs in fields and forests where both adults and larvae are important in controlling various harmful insects. Has become rare in some regions due to application of insecticides. Easily mistaken for certain related species. Distribution: much of Europe (absent in British Isles, which lack many other large ground beetles), Siberia.

7 *Carabus glabratus* — Length 22—32 mm. Found in damp forests up to mountainous elevations. Unlike many other ground beetles it is active even during the day. Distribution: all Europe as far as the Urals.

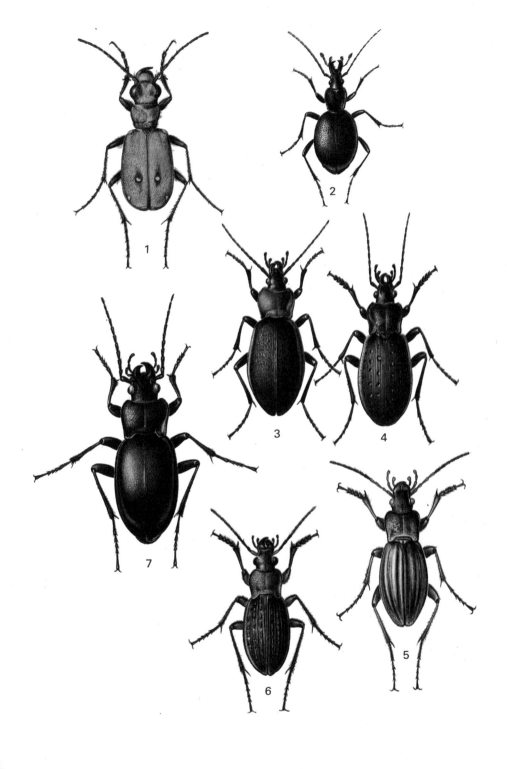

Phylum: **Arthropods — Arthropoda**

Class: **Insects — Insecta**

Order: **Beetles — Coleoptera**

Family: **Ground beetles — Carabidae**

1 *Notiophilus biguttatus* — Length 5 mm. A very common small ground beetle of European forests (which contain many different species). Like many relatives it has strikingly large eyes. Distribution: the Palaearctic region.

2 *Agonum sexpunctatum* — Length 7—9 mm. Notable for its metallic colour, which is often variable. Scutum is usually green and the elytra golden-red, but in some individuals the scutum is blue and the elytra bronze, blue-violet or entirely black. Found chiefly in foothills and mountains under stones, in hedgerows, forests and field paths. Distribution: much of Europe, Siberia.

3 *Pterostichus niger* — Length 16—21 mm. Common in fields, forests and gardens. In Europe there are many similar, black species. Distribution: Europe, the Caucasus, Siberia.

4 *Harpalus rufipes* — Length 14—16 mm. Elytra thickly covered with yellowish hairs. Common in fields, on field paths and under stones. Referred to as *H. pubescens* in older literature. Distribution: the Palaearctic region.

Family: **True water beetles — Dytiscidae**

5 *Graptodytes pictus* — Length 2.3 mm. Found in pools with rich vegetation. Distribution: much of Europe.

6 *Ilybius fenestratus* — Length 11—12 mm. Common in river back-waters, pools and small forest springs. Distribution: northern part of southern Europe, central and northern Europe as far as Lapland, Siberia, North America.

7 *Acilius sulcatus* — Length 16—18 mm. Marked differences between the sexes as in other diving beetles. The male has suction discs on the front legs, the female has furrowed elytra. Common chiefly in pools, ponds and calm waters of rivers. Also in large puddles. Tolerates polluted water. Adults and larvae are predaceous. Respiration is by means of tracheae and, like other diving beetles, it must come up for air. Distribution: from central Italy and northern Spain to northern Europe, Transcaucasia, Siberia, north Africa.

8 Great Diving Beetle *Dytiscus marginalis* — Length 35 mm. Found mostly in ponds but also in garden pools. Hunts small animals and even feeds on carrion. It is not a pest in ponds for it feeds only on diseased and weakened fish. Larva has a large flat head, large mandibles, and is predaceous. When full-grown it climbs out of the water and burrows in the soil of the shore, where it pupates in a cocoon. Adults live to an age of about 18 months. Distribution: much of Europe (usually absent in the Balkans), the Caucasus, Siberia, Japan, North America.

Family: **Whirligig beetles — Gyrinidae**

9 *Gyrinus natator* — Length 5—7 mm. The eye is divided by a partition into two parts — an upper part for seeing over the surface and lower for seeing down into the water. Occurs abundantly on the surface of ponds, where individuals swim around one another in a swirling motion. Distribution: Europe, Siberia, Mongolia, north Africa.

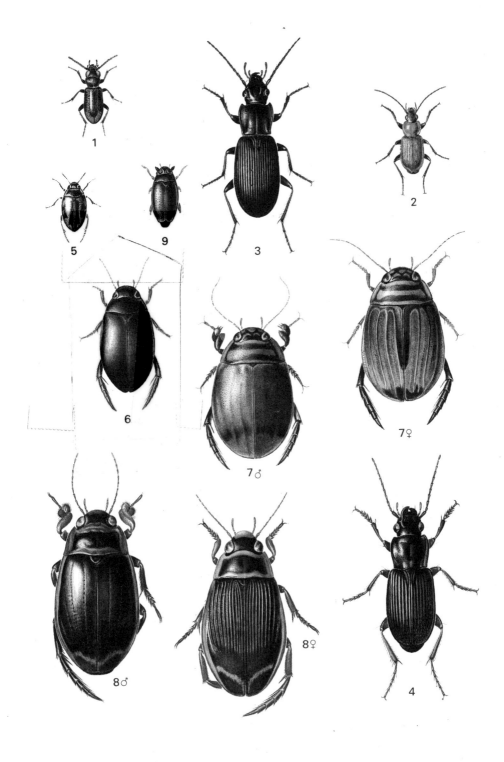

Phylum: **Arthropods — Arthropoda**

Class: **Insects — Insecta**

Order: **Beetles — Coleoptera**

Family: **Hydraenidae**

1 *Hydraena riparia* — Length 2.2—2.4 mm. Small, elongate water beetle with greatly developed maxillary palpi, which are larger than the antennae located behind them. There are many similar species in European waters. Distribution: from central Italy to central and northern Europe.

Family: **Water-scavenger beetles — Hydrophilidae**

2 Great Silver Beetle *Hydrous piceus* — Length 34—47 mm. Found chiefly in quiet waters — ponds, river backwaters, forest pools, etc. with abundant aquatic vegetation, the only food on which the adult beetle feeds. The larva, however, is predaceous and feeds on small animals. It must come up for air, as with the true diving beetles; unlike the latter, however, it obtains air on the surface by way of a special cleft at the side of the body. Its short, club-shaped antennae are used to help break the surface film in this complex operation. For egg-laying the female spins a remarkable case in which the eggs are deposited. The case, furnished with an upright chimney and containing some 50 eggs, is attached to a leaf floating on the water surface. The larvae live in water. When fully grown they climb out and bury themselves in the ground to pupate. Until recently it was considered a pest of fish-fry. It was believed that it killed the young fish by means of a needle-sharp spine on the underside of the body, and was relentlessly persecuted and killed so that now it is rare or even extinct in many places where it was recently abundant. In some countries (e. g. West Germany) it is protected by law. European waters are also inhabited by a similar species — *H. aterrimus,* which is somewhat smaller. Distribution: the Palaearctic region.

3 *Hydrophilus caraboides* — Length 14—18 mm. Locally abundant in river backwaters, in ponds, and in pools with abundant vegetation, on which the beetle feeds. Unlike many (particularly small) species that only move about on the bottom or amidst the vegetation, it is a good swimmer. Distribution: the Palaearctic region.

4 *Sphaeridium scarabaeoides* — Length 5.7 mm. Although its morphological characteristics place it in this family, unlike many 'water-scavenger beetles' it is not aquatic but lives on dry land, where it seeks out fresh cow dung. The larvae are grub-like. Distribution: the Palaearctic and Nearctic regions.

Family: **Histeridae**

5 *Hister impressus* — Length 4—7 mm. Formerly referred to as *H. cadaverinus.* One of the commonest members of the family. Feeds on carrion, but also attracted to decaying plant remnants (old mushrooms, etc.) and fermenting sap that oozes from fresh tree stumps or injured and felled trees. Distribution: much of the Palaearctic region.

6 *Hister quadrinotatus* — Length 6—8 mm. There are two red patches on each elytron, the foremost located at the outer corner. Sometimes the two patches fuse together. The beetle lives in cattle dung, where it sometimes occurs in large numbers, feeding on fly larvae. Distribution: Europe to the Caucasus and the Middle East.

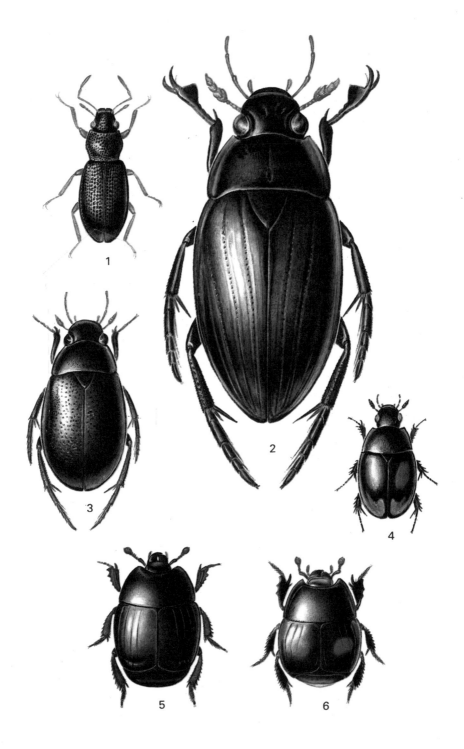

Phylum: **Arthropods — Arthropoda**

Class: **Insects — Insecta**

Order: **Beetles — Coleoptera**

Family: **Carrion beetles — Silphidae**

1 Burying Beetle *Nicrophorus vespillo* — Length 10—24 mm. One of several very similar species of burying beetles with orange patches on the elytra. Like its relatives, it seeks out small dead animals (vertebrates) and buries them, thus providing a food store for the offspring. The carcass disappears below ground within several hours. Nearby the female makes a tunnel in which she lays about 10 eggs. The larvae emerge within a few days and, sensing food nearby, they make their way to the carrion. Unable to feed themselves at first, they have to wait until the female puts a drop of liquid in their mouths. Later they are able to manage without her aid. The larvae are fed by the mother after every moult. After about a week they pupate and the adult emerges two weeks later. Distribution: much of the Palaearctic and Nearctic regions.

2 *Nicrophorus humator* — Length 18—28 mm. Distinguished from the larger *N. germanicus* by the red-clubbed antennae (*N. germanicus* has black-clubbed antennae). Distribution: Europe, the Caucasus, Syria and north Africa.

3 *Oiceoptoma thoracicum* — Length 12—16 mm. Easily identified by the red scutum. Very common on dead animals, decaying plant matter (old mushrooms) and in excrement. Distribution: Europe, Siberia, Japan.

4 *Aclypea opaca* — Length 9—12 mm. Sometimes regarded as a pest, for it feeds on sugar beet. Usually not harmful, however, for it feeds chiefly on various grasses, even weeds. Now locally rare. Adult appears in early spring. Distribution: all Europe, northern and central Asia, North America.

Family: **Rove beetles — Staphylinidae**

5 *Oxyporus rufus* — Length 7—12 mm. Appears in forests as early as May, but most abundant in July and August when mushrooms, in which the larva lives, are plentiful. The beetle is carnivorous and hunts various insects in mushrooms, in which it excavates tunnels. Often found perching on the underside of the cap. Distribution: much of Europe, the Caucasus, Siberia.

6 *Staphylinus caesareus* — Length 17—25 mm. Resembles other rove beetles with brown elytra. Feeds on various larvae and dead animals, as well as decaying plant matter. Appears in spring. Most abundant at higher elevations, absent or rare in lowland country. Distribution: Europe, North America.

7 *Creophilus maxillosus* — Length 15—25 mm. Predaceous, like many other rove beetles. Found in dung, piles of rubbish and on carrion, where it hunts insect larvae. Distribution: the Palaearctic, Nearctic and Oriental regions.

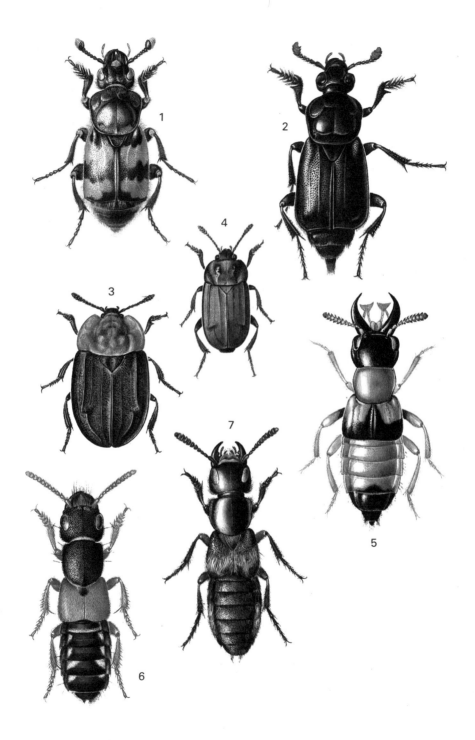

Phylum: **Arthropods — Arthropoda**

Class: **Insects — Insecta**

Order: **Beetles — Coleoptera**

Family: **Stag beetles — Lucanidae**

1 Stag Beetle *Lucanus cervus* — Length of male (with mandibles) 30—75 mm, female 25—40 mm. One of the largest of European beetles. Female has strong functional mandibles, those of the male are huge and branched, furnished with teeth and used not for biting, for the beetle feeds on sap oozing from injured trees, but as weapons in jousts for the female. In some males the mandibles are less developed (f. *capreolus*). The female burrows in stumps of old oaks, sometimes also other broadleaved trees (beech, elm, etc.), where she lays her eggs. The larva is round, plump and feeds on the wood of the stump. The larval stage often lasts as long as five years. A full-grown larva reaches 100 mm in length. It makes a hard cell about itself, in which it pupates in the earth. The beetle emerges in autumn but hibernates in the cell, not appearing until the following June and living until July. During the past two decades its numbers have markedly declined, for many of its localities in old oak forests have been destroyed. In some central European countries it is protected by law (GFR, GDR, Czechoslovakia). Distribution: most of Europe.

2 *Sinodendron cylindricum* — Length 12—16 mm. Likewise notable for its marked sexual dimorphism. Male has a distinct recurved 'horn' on the head, female only a small bump. Inhabits broadleaved forests in foothills and mountainous regions. Adults found in June and July. Distribution: Europe, Siberia.

3 *Systenocerus caraboides* — Length 10—14 mm. Coloured metallic green, blue-green, blue-violet to blue-black. Beetles are on the wing on sunny days in spring; locally abundant, chiefly in oak and beech woods. Distribution: western and central Europe.

Family: **Chafers and dung beetles — Scarabaeidae**

4 *Aphodius fimetarius* — Length 5—8 mm. Found from early spring in horse and cattle dung, where the eggs are laid. Full-grown larva burrows into the ground to pupate. Distribution: Eurasia, north Africa, North America.

5 Lousy Watchman *Geotrupes stercorarius* — Length 16—25 mm. Like many related species it is noted for its care of the offspring. Adults excavate a vertical shaft about 50 cm long to which the female adds several side shafts. Each of these is about 20 cm long and broadened at the end to form a chamber in which a single egg is laid. The entire side-shaft is filled with excrement on which the larva feeds, there being more than it can consume. Development takes two years. Distribution: the Palaearctic region.

6 *Geotrupes vernalis* — Length 12—20 mm. Likewise prepares a nest for its offspring but of a different kind from that of the previous species. First it excavates a funnel-shaped pit and at the bottom several horizontal tunnels about 20 cm long which are filled with excrement. Only then do the beetles excavate a vertical tunnel from the bottom of the pit to a depth of about 50 cm, ending in a chamber in which the single egg is laid. The entrance is then plugged with excrement. The white larva slowly feeds on the food store. Like other species this beetle removes excrement and contributes to the formation of humus. Distribution: Europe, Asia Minor.

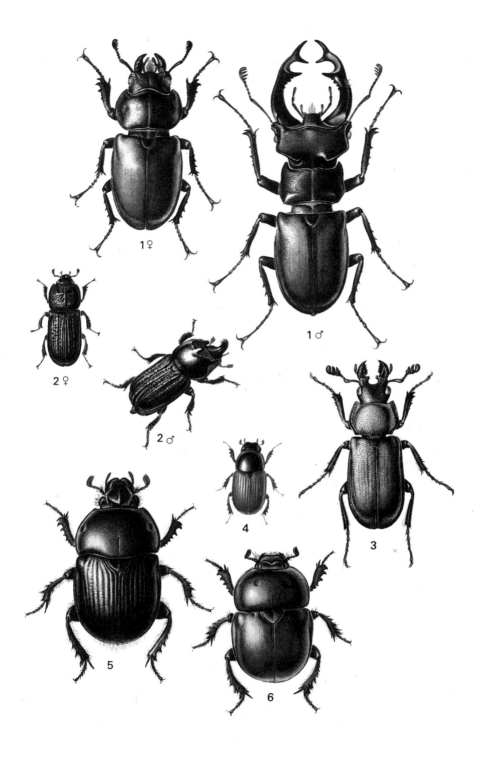

1 ♀   1 ♂

2 ♀   2 ♂

4

3

5   6

Phylum: **Arthropods — Arthropoda**

Class: **Insects — Insecta**

Order: **Beetles — Coleoptera**

Family: **Chafers and dung beetles — Scarabaeidae**

1 *Serica brunnea* — Length 8—10 mm. On the wing from June (in the south from May) to August. During the day it conceals itself under bark, in moss, under stones, etc., emerging at dusk. It occurs in large groups. Attracted to light, it often flies to illuminated windows. Eggs are laid in the ground at a depth of several centimetres, usually in sandy soil but also in garden beds, etc. Larvae similar to grubs of the cockchafer but smaller. They grow to a length of about 20 mm and then pupate in the ground. Development takes one year. Distribution: much of Europe, north as far as the Arctic Circle, southern Siberia, north Africa.

2 *Amphimallon solstitialis* — Length 14—18 mm. Active in the evening and at night. In July often occurs in large swarms in meadows, forest margins, round trees in parks and avenues. Development takes three years. Distribution: the Palaearctic region.

3 Cockchafer or Maybug *Melolontha melolontha* — Length 20—30 mm. Formerly commonest of the large beetles, but because of the intensive campaign waged against it in the recent past it has become an unknown species in places, or else occurs only sporadically. In some European countries, however, it still causes damage even today. The male has antennae with large 'fans' composed of 7 lamellae; those of the female are small with only 6 lamellae. The eggs are laid in the ground. The larvae (grubs) feed on plant roots. Development takes 2—3 years. Adult emerges in autumn but hibernates and does not appear until spring. Distribution: much of Europe, except Spain and southern Italy.

4 *Euchlora dubia* — Length 12—15 mm. On the wing in localities with sandy and sandy-loamy soil. Most abundant in July. Very active on warm days. Distribution: from southern Italy to southern Sweden and Finland.

5 Garden Chafer *Phyllopertha horticola* — Length 8—11 mm. Very common in gardens, forest margins, hedgerows, etc. where it is on the wing in June. Fond of flowering roses, nibbling the edges of the blossoms. Distribution: Europe, Siberia, Mongolia.

6 *Tropinota hirta* — Length 8—11 mm. Found on Compositae from April onwards — first on hawkweed, later on daisies. Larvae live in the ground and feed on old grass roots, and so they are not harmful. Distribution: Europe, Asia Minor, the Middle East, North America (introduced).

7 Rose Chafer *Cetonia aurata* — Length 14—20 mm. Found in spring on flowering roses, elder, etc. Flies with elytra folded but with outspread hind wings. Larvae generally found in rotting wood of beech and oak stumps, and in garden compost heaps, very occasionally also in ant nests. Larvae inhabiting nests of the wood ant are usually those of the closely related *Potosia cuprea*. Development takes one year. Distribution: Europe (except the extreme north), Asia Minor, Syria, Siberia.

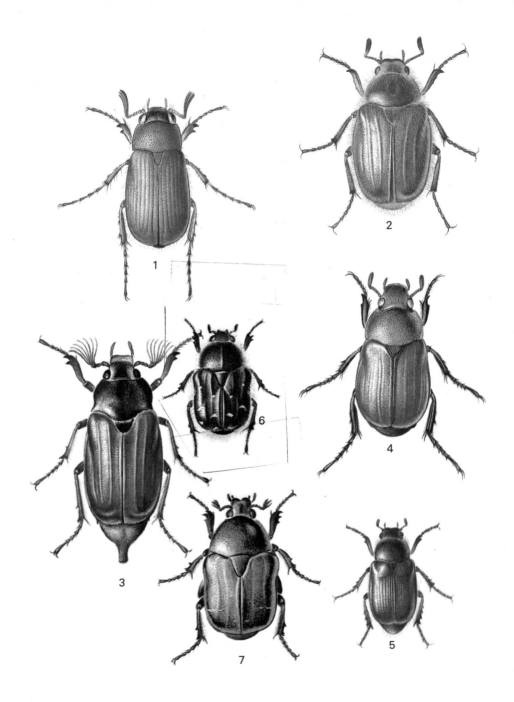

Phylum: **Arthropods — Arthropoda**

Class: **Insects — Insecta**

Order: **Beetles — Coleoptera**

Family: **Pill beetles — Byrrhidae**

1 *Byrrhus pilula* — Length 7.5—11 mm. If danger threatens it feigns death, withdrawing its legs and antennae into crevices on the underside of its body, and thus changing into a motionless ball. Common in fields and forests. Distribution: the Palaearctic region.

Family: **Metallic wood-borers — Buprestidae**

2 *Anthaxia nitidula* — Length 5—7 mm. Quite common in warm regions. Visits flowering hawk-weed, wild rose, etc. Larval development takes place in dying fruit trees. Distribution: central and southern Europe (absent in the north), Asia Minor, north Africa.

3 *Buprestis rustica* — Length 12—18 mm. Sometimes fairly plentiful in open coniferous forests. Distribution: northern part of southern Europe, central and northern Europe, the Caucasus, southern Siberia.

4 *Agrilus pannonicus* — Length 10 mm. Found from May to July in young oak thickets, clearings, forest margins and on stumps or felled oak trunks. Larvae live under the bark of dying branches or under stones. Distribution: Europe (rarer in the north), the Caucasus, Asia Minor, Iran, north Africa.

5 *Trachys minutus* — Length 3—3.5 mm. Locally abundant on flowers and willow leaves. Larvae are leaf-miners. Distribution: Europe (except the north), the Caucasus, Asia Minor, Siberia.

Family: **Click beetles — Elateridae**

6 *Agrypnus murinus* — Length 11—17 mm. Elytra and scutum covered with tiny whitish and yellowish scales; their quantity determines the colour of the beetle. Some specimens so densely covered with scales that they are almost white. Adults are found from spring until autumn in forests, gardens, meadows and fields up to mountain elevations. The larvae, commonly known as 'wireworms' (this applies to many click beetle larvae), feed on various plant roots. Distribution: Europe, the Caucasus, Siberia, North America.

7 *Athous vittatus* — Length 8—10 mm. Usually has bands on the elytra, but in some specimens these are absent and the elytra are unicolorous — yellowish-brown to dark brown. A common beetle found in broadleaved forests in lowlands and foothills, sometimes also in mountains. Distribution: Europe, the Caucasus, Asia Minor.

8 *Selatosomus aeneus* — Length 10—17 mm. Always has a metallic sheen but variable in colour — usually greenish or coppery, sometimes blue, blue-violet or black. Adult beetles found from early spring to late autumn on plants in meadows, hedgerows, field paths, etc. Larvae live in the ground. May sometimes cause damage to cultivated plants. Distribution: Europe and Siberia.

9 *Corymbites purpureus* — Length 8—14 mm. Has characteristic raised, longitudinal ribs on the elytra. Cannot be mistaken for any similar species. Found on various deciduous shrubs in foothills, from early spring on. Locally common. Distribution: central and southern Europe, Asia (Iran, the Himalayas, etc.).

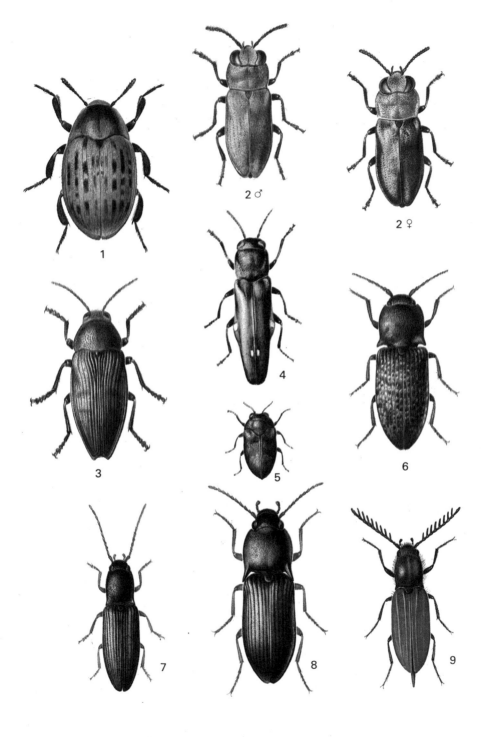

1

2 ♂

2 ♀

3

4

5

6

7

8

9

Phylum: **Arthropods — Arthropoda**

Class: **Insects — Insecta**

Order: **Beetles — Coleoptera**

Family: **Fireflies and glow-worms — Lampyridae**

1 Common Glow-worm *Lampyris noctiluca* — Length: Male 11−12 mm, female 16−18 mm. There are very marked differences between the sexes. Male has membranous wings and elytra, and can fly; female is wingless and crawls only on the ground. Both sexes have a complex light organ on the underside of the body which emits a bright light in wave lengths of 518−656 nm. Light is produced by a complex chemical process in which oxygen, conveyed by the tracheae, plays an important role. The larvae, which also emit light, grow to a length of 23 mm. They live in grass and are carnivorous on snails and slugs. Distribution: from the Mediterranean to central Scandinavia, the Caucasus, Siberia, China.

Family: **Soldier beetles — Cantharidae**

2 *Cantharis fusca* — Length 11−15 mm. Found on leaves and flowers, where it hunts aphids. The black larvae, which are also predaceous, are the stage in which winter is passed. May sometimes be found on snow where they have been washed up or blown by the wind from their winter shelters. Distribution: Europe, from northern Spain and Italy to southern Scandinavia.

3 *Rhagonycha fulva* — Length 7−10 mm. Differs from similar light-coloured species chiefly by having dark antennae and dark-tipped elytra. Beetles found in large numbers in late summer, on flowering Umbelliferae in meadows. They hunt aphids and small insect larvae. Distribution: Europe (except the far north), the Caucasus, Syria.

Family: **Lycidae**

4 *Dictyoptera aurora* — Length 7−13 mm. Found on forest undergrowth and on stumps, chiefly in foothill and mountain localities. Distribution: Europe, across Siberia to Korea and Japan.

Family: **Museum beetles — Dermestidae**

5 Larder Beetle *Dermestes lardarius* — Length 7−9.5 mm. Originally it lived in the wild and even today may be found occasionally in the nests of certain birds. Gradually, however, it became Man's associate and nowadays is generally found in his vicinity — in dwellings, warehouses, museums, dove-cotes and bee-hives. The beetle itself is not harmful but the 'woolly' larvae feed on various man-made products (fabrics, leather, specimens in zoological and entomological collections, etc.). Distribution: cosmopolitan. Introduced by Man to regions where it was previously non-existent.

6 *Attagenus pellio*. Length 4−5.5 mm. A synanthropic species found in households and warehouses. Appears as early as February and March, later common on flowers. The larvae, which have a long tail at the tip of the abdomen, are feared pests of furs, fabrics and zoological collections. Distribution: worldwide.

7 Carpet Beetle *Anthrenus scrophulariae* — Length 3−4.5 mm. Covered with fine, coloured scales that give it its characteristic coloration. Adult is harmless, lives on flowers. Outside the growing season it is quite common in households, where the larval stage is spent. Larvae feed on furs, carpets, fabrics, feathers and natural history collections. The most feared pest of collections, however, is not this species but *A. verbasci*. Distribution: much of Europe, the Middle East, North America, etc.

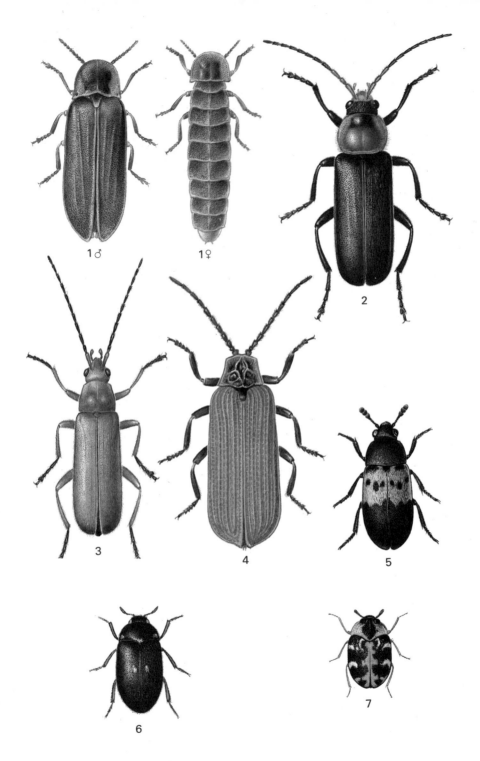

1♂   1♀

2

3   4   5

6   7

Phylum: **Arthropods — Arthropoda**

Class: **Insects — Insecta**

Order: **Beetles — Coleoptera**

Family: **Anobiidae**

1 Woodworm or Furniture Beetle *Anobium punctatum* — Length 3—5 mm. Development takes place in old wood — in floors, furniture, rafters, etc. The related Death Watch Beetle *(Xestobium rufovillosum)* makes a peculiar ticking sound that is very penetrating, particularly in the quiet of the night. Woodworm beetles, after emerging from the pupae, climb out of the wood through a hole around which the female later lays eggs, and through which the young larvae will enter the environment in which they pass their entire lives. They bore tunnels in the wood, which is their sole food. Cellulose, which is hard to digest, is processed with the aid of symbiotic organisms that live in special gut diverticula of the beetles. Distribution: the Palaearctic, Nearctic and Australasian regions.

Family: **Spider beetles — Ptinidae**

2 *Ptinus fur* — Length 2—4.3 mm. Noted for the marked differences in shape and colour between the sexes. Usually found in households, stables, attics and outhouses. Common also in bird nests. Distribution: the Palaearctic region, North America.

Family: **Checkered beetles — Cleridae**

3 *Thanasimus formicarius* — Length 7—10 mm. Found from spring till autumn on stacked wood and felled logs, where it hunts bark beetles. Beneficial, for it kills great numbers of potentially harmful insects. Distribution: Eurasia, north Africa, North America (introduced).

Family: **Melyridae**

4 *Malachius bipustulatus* — Length 5—6 mm. Common on grasses and other flowering plants the whole summer long. When danger threatens it protrudes peculiar reddish pouches (vesicles) from the sides of the body. Distribution: Europe, Asia Minor, Siberia.

Family: **Lymexylidae**

5 *Hylecoetus dermestoides* — Length 6—18 mm. Adult beetles live only 2—4 days. Larvae develop in the wood of oak and beech, chiefly in stumps, where they bore long, narrow tunnels. They do not feed on wood but on ambrosia fungi. Distribution: central and northern Europe, Siberia.

Family: **Flower beetles — Nitidulidae**

6 *Meligethes aeneus* — Length 1.5—2.7 mm. Found very early in spring on various flowers, later visits rape, feeding on its tender leaves and buds. Eggs are laid in the rape flowers. Full-grown larvae pupate in the ground. Distribution: the Palaearctic and Nearctic regions.

7 *Pocadius ferrugineus* — Length 2.8—4.5 mm. Found in puffballs, in which fungi the entire development takes place. Distribution: Europe, the Caucasus.

8 *Glischrochilus quadripunctatus* — Length 3—6.5 mm. Occurs under bark and on injured tree trunks oozing sweet sap. Feeds chiefly on bark beetles. Distribution: Europe, Siberia.

9 *Pityophagus ferrugineus* — Length 4—6.5 mm. Lives under the bark of trees where it hunts bark beetles. Distribution: the coniferous forests of central Europe to the northern Balkans and the Caucasus.

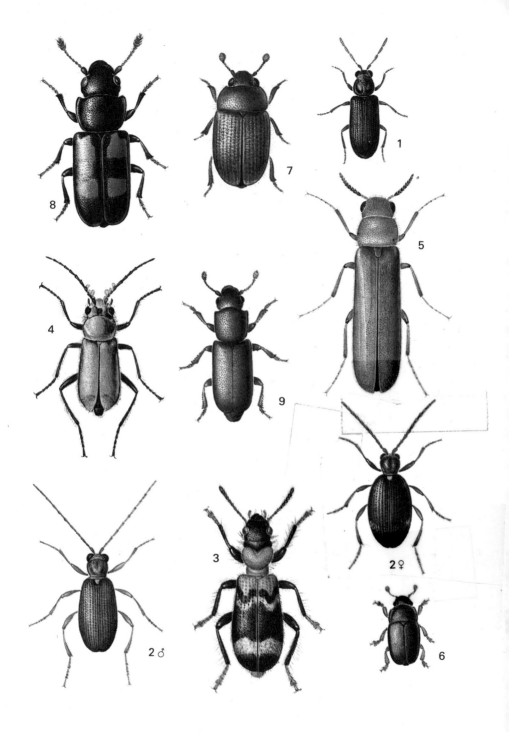

Phylum: **Arthropods — Arthropoda**

Class: **Insects — Insecta**

Order: **Beetles — Coleoptera**

Family: **Cucujidae**

1 *Uleiota planata* — Length 4.5—5.5 mm. Has extremely long antennae. When danger threatens it points the antennae forward and feigns death. Lives under the bark of various trees, mostly broadleaved species. Distribution: southern part of the Palaearctic region.

Family: **Byturidae**

2 Raspberry Beetle *Byturus tomentosus* — Length 3.2—4 mm. More often encountered then the beetle is the elongate larva, commonly known as the raspberry fruit-worm. Found chiefly in the fruit of the raspberry (less often in blackberries). Adult beetles rest on raspberry and blackberry blossoms. Distribution: the Palaearctic region, except the northern part.

Family: **Shining flower beetles — Phalacridae**

3 *Olibrus aeneus* — Length 2.5—2.8 mm. Common in late summer on flowering camomile *(Matricaria chamomilla)*, foodplant of the larvae. Distribution: Europe, from northern Italy to Lapland, Siberia.

Family: **Ladybirds — Coccinellidae**

4 Two-spot Ladybird *Adalia bipunctata* — Length 3.5—5.5 mm. Very variable in colour. Typical individuals have red elytra with a black spot on each. In some, however, the black colour prevails. Often hibernates in dwellings. The new generation occurs from July on. Both beetles and larvae are predaceous and destroy large numbers of aphids. Distribution: much of the Palaearctic region, introduced into North America.

5 Seven-spot Ladybird *Coccinella septempunctata* — Length 5.5—8 mm. One of the commonest and most beneficial of beetles. Adults and larvae found on plants attacked by aphids, on which they feed. Larva is elongate, grey-blue with black and yellow or orange spots. It pupates on a leaf. Adult beetles hibernate, often in greater numbers, under bark, stones, in clumps of grass, etc. They appear very early in spring on the first sunny days. Distribution: Europe, Asia, north Africa.

6 Eyed Ladybird *Anatis ocellata* — Length 8—9 mm. Very variable in number and shape of spots. Found from lowlands to mountainous elevations, chiefly in coniferous forests, where it hunts aphids. Larvae are spotted red. Distribution: Europe, the Caucasus, Siberia, Japan, introduced to North America.

7 *Thea vigintiduopunctata* — Length 3—4.5 mm. Easily distinguished from the other species by the bright yellow elytra with 22 black spots. Often found in mountain regions. Distribution: southern part of the Palaearctic region.

8 *Chilocorus renipustulatus* — Length 3—4.5 mm. Distinguished by the large red spot on each elytron. The related species *C. bipustulatus* also has two red spots on the elytra, but the spots are elongate. Often found on tree trunks covered with scale insects (Diaspididae), on which it feeds. Distribution: the Palaearctic region.

Family: **Endomychidae**

9 *Endomychus coccineus* — Length 4—6 mm. Found in beech woods, often in large numbers, under the mouldy bark of felled trees or in tree fungi. Distribution: Europe; in the south only at higher altitudes.

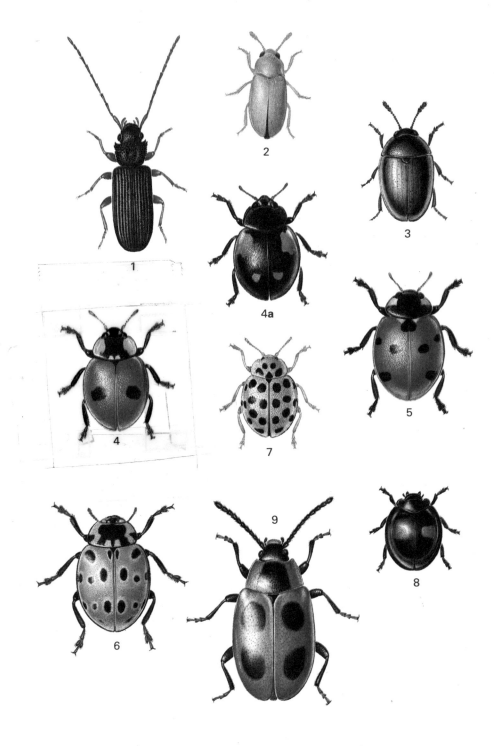

1

2

3

4a

4

7

5

9

6

8

Phylum: **Arthropods — Arthropoda**

Class: **Insects — Insecta**

Order: **Beetles — Coleoptera**

Family: **Colydiidae**

1 *Bitoma crenata* — Length 2.6—3.5 mm. Common under the bark of old stumps, where it usually occurs in great numbers. Feeds on insect larvae, e. g. of bark beetles. Distribution: the Palaearctic region.

Family: **Darkling beetles — Tenebrionidae**

2 Mealworm *Tenebrio molitor* — Length 15 mm. Entire development takes place in flour. Female lays several hundred eggs, which she covers with a protective sticky secretion. The larvae, which emerge 1—2 weeks later, grow rapidly. They are the well-known 'mealworms' used as food for birds and pet animals. Distribution: cosmopolitan.

Family: **Lagriidae**

3 *Lagria hirta* — Length 7—10 mm. Found in damp vegetation in meadows, alongside paths and streams. Distribution: Europe, Siberia.

Family: **Cardinal beetles — Pyrochroidae**

4 *Pyrochroa coccinea* — Length 14—15 mm. Head and scutellum are black (unlike the related *P. serraticornis*, in which they are red). Beetles are found in May and June on flowers, stumps and felled trees. Larvae are very flat and live under the bark of dead wood, stumps, etc. Distribution: northern part of southern Europe, to southern Scandinavia.

Family: **Mordellidae**

5 *Variimorda fasciata* — Length 6—9 mm. Distinguished from related species by the grey-brown pattern on the elytra. Found on flowers. Distribution: Europe, the Caucasus, Asia Minor, Iran, etc.

Family: **Oil and blister beetles — Meloidae**

6 *Meloe violaceus* — Length 10—32 mm. Has a complex life cycle. Female lays a great number of eggs, for many young larvae die at the very start. The tiny larvae are called triungulins — because they have three strong claws on the feet. These were once believed to be a separate animal species. The triungulins crawl up on flowers and await the arrival of their host insects, species of solitary bees. They are carried to a nest where the next stage of development takes place, the so-called caraboid larva, which feeds on honey. This stage is followed by a quiescent stage called the pseudo-pupa, which moults again to form a legless grub, which then changes into a pupa, from which the adult beetle finally emerges! The pseudo-pupa is an additional stage to the normal insect sequence, and this type of metamorphosis has been called hypermetamorphosis. The body of these beetles contains the pharmacologically active substance cantharidin. Far more cantharidin, however, is contained in the body of the Spanish Fly *(Lytta vesicatoria)*, another member of this family. Distribution: Europe, Siberia.

Family: **Oedemeridae**

7 *Oedemera podagrariae* — Length 8—13 mm. Elytra diverge at the back to reveal the folded membranous wings underneath. Males have very stout hind femora. Adult beetles are found in summer on flowers. They greatly resemble small long-horned beetles. Distribution: much of Europe, Asia Minor, Siberia.

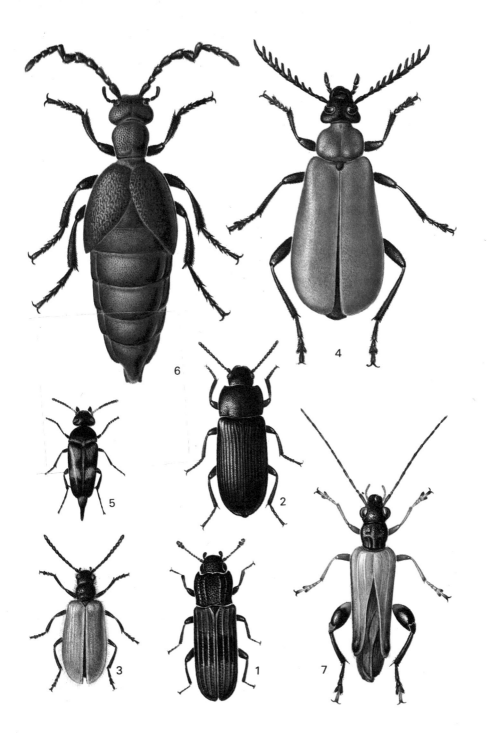

Phylum: **Arthropods — Arthropoda**

Class: **Insects — Insecta**

Order: **Beetles — Coleoptera**

Family: **Long-horned beetles — Cerambycidae**

1 *Prionus coriarius* — Length 18—45 mm. As in other long-horned beetles, there is marked sexual dimorphism. The antennae are relatively small, but those of the male have 12 segments and are strongly serrate, whereas those of the female have 11 segments and are comparatively slender and slightly serrate. The beetles emit rasping sounds by rubbing the margins of the elytra against the hind legs. They are found in old broadleaved and coniferous forests, and are on the wing at dusk from spring until autumn, being most abundant in August. The eggs are laid on tree trunks and in old stumps. The larvae grow to about 50 mm in length before pupating in the stump. The beetles are hunted by various nocturnal animals; the elytra of these beetles are often found on the floor of forest rides during periods when the beetles are abundant. Distribution: much of Europe, the Caucasus, Middle East, western Siberia, north Africa.

2 *Rhagium inquisitor* — Length 10—21 mm. Found from lowlands to mountainous elevations, in coniferous forests. Adult beetles are locally abundant from spring until July on logs and flowers. Larvae live under the bark of spruce trees, where they pupate in cells lined with wood shavings. The beetles emerge in autumn, but remain in the pupal cells for the winter, appearing in the spring. Distribution: Europe, western Siberia, North America.

3 *Leptura rubra* — Length 10—19 mm. The sexes differ in shape, size and colour. The male is more slender, smaller, with dingy-yellow elytra and black scutum. The female is larger, stouter and coloured orange-red. The antennae also differ in form. A very common species. On the wing in summer, settling on flowers, stumps, felled logs and stacked wood. The larvae generally develop in old stumps, in which they bore tunnels, and in which they later pupate. Adult beetles bite their way out through a circular opening. Distribution: Europe, Siberia, north Africa.

4 *Strangalia maculata* — Length 14—20 mm. The elytra are yellow with various large, dark blotches. Adult beetles are plentiful from May to August on flowers in forest meadows. Development usually takes place in broadleaved trees. Distribution: Europe, the Caucasus, Transcaucasia, Syria, Iran.

5 *Strangalia melanura* — Length 6—9.5 mm. Common from May to September on various flowers. Larval stage is passed in trees. Distribution: Europe, the Caucasus, Transcaucasia, Siberia, Mongolia.

6 *Spondylis buprestoides* — Length 12—24 mm. Body strikingly robust, mandibles large, antennae short. During the day it hides under the bark of stumps, under logs, etc., flying out in the evening. The larvae develop in old pine stumps. Distribution: Europe, Asia Minor, Siberia, China, Japan.

7 *Tetropium castaneum* — Length 9—18.5 mm. Found in spruce woods. Adult beetles fly from May to July. The female lays 80—120 eggs under the scales of spruce bark. Larva lives beneath the bark at first, later boring into the wood. When fully grown it excavates a chamber at a depth of 2—4 cm in which it pupates. The beetle usually infests diseased trees. Distribution: Eurasia.

126

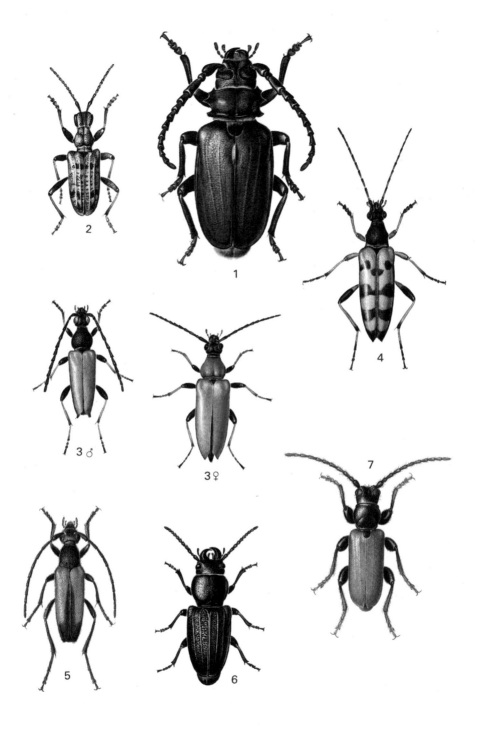

Phylum: **Arthropods — Arthropoda**

Class: **Insects — Insecta**

Order: **Beetles — Coleoptera**

Family: **Long-horned beetles — Cerambycidae**

1 *Cerambyx cerdo* — Length 24—53 mm. One of the largest of European beetles. Occurs in old, broadleaved, chiefly oak forests in June and July. Adults fly at dusk and at night, concealing themselves by day under bark and in tunnels in old trees. In flight the beetles make a considerable noise. The female lays about 80 eggs in oak bark. The young larva must bite its way through the tough bark to the phloem, and later to the heart wood, where it pupates in a hook-shaped tunnel. It grows to a length of 70—90 mm. Development takes 3—5 years. The beetle emerges in summer, but remains within the wood until the following year. At present its numbers are declining because of the rapid disappearance of its original habitats. It is protected by law in some countries (GDR, Czechoslovakia). Distribution: Europe.

2 *Molorchus minor* — Length 6—16 mm. This, and certain other species are unusual amongst cerambycids in that the elytra cover only part of the abdomen. Adults are plentiful from April to July, on flowering plants (usually Umbelliferae). Larvae develop in dead trunks and branches of spruce and pine trees, in which they bore zig-zag tunnels. Distribution: Europe, the Caucasus, Transcaucasia, Asia Minor, the Middle East, Siberia, Japan.

3 Musk Beetle *Aromia moschata* — Length 13—34 mm. Usually coloured green to blue-green, although sometimes the blue colour prevails. Beetles have a strong musky smell; they rest on flowers and felled trees. Development usually takes place in the wood of willows. Distribution: Europe, Siberia, Japan.

4 House Longhorn *Hylotrupes bajulus* — Length 7—21 mm. A summer, sun-loving species. Found in coniferous forests. Sometimes occurs also in attics and households, having emerged from the house timbers or furniture. Larva lives in wood for several years. Distribution: cosmopolitan.

5 *Callidium violaceum* — Length 8—16 mm. Usually the elytra are blue, but they may be green or reddish-violet. Adults are found from May to August, in spruce forests. Larvae develop under bark and pupate in wood. Beetles often emerge from house timbers and rafters in attics, which may then harbour several ensuing generations, for the larvae can thrive even in dead wood. Distribution: the Palaearctic region.

6 *Pyrrhidium sanguineum* — Length 8—12 mm. Found on felled oak logs, in which eggs are laid from April onwards. Beetle easily identified by the velvety red hairs covering the whole body. Distribution: central and southern Europe, the Caucasus, Asia Minor, Middle East, north Africa.

7 *Plagionotus arcuatus* — Length 6—20 mm. Coloration resembles that of a wasp. The yellow patches and bands on the elytra vary in shape. Adult beetles are found during May and June in oak woods, where they fly busily and rest on felled logs. The female lays some 30 eggs which she inserts with her ovipositor into cracks in bark. The larva makes its way into the phloem where it bores tunnels up to 2 metres long that become filled with dust. When full-grown it measures up to 40 mm in length. In spring, after hibernating, it bores into the wood and pupates at a depth of several centimetres. Distribution: Europe, Transcaucasia, Asia Minor, north Africa.

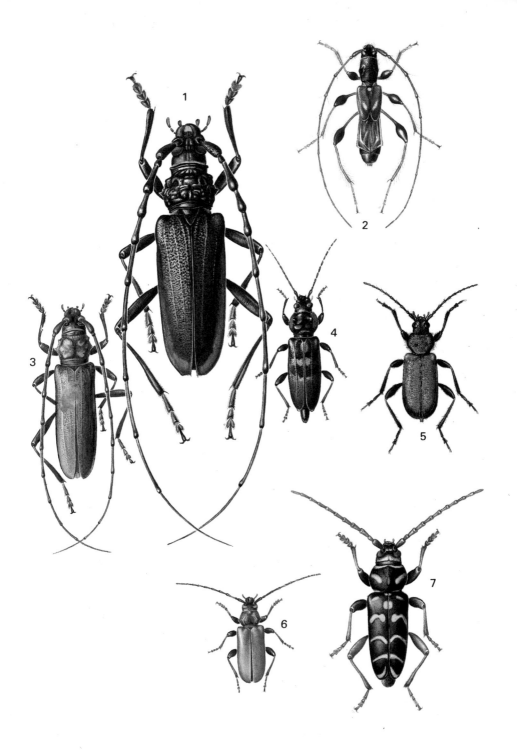

Phylum: **Arthropods — Arthropoda**

Class: **Insects — Insecta**

Order: **Beetles — Coleoptera**

Family: **Long-horned beetles — Cerambycidae**

1 *Dorcadion pedestre* — Length 11—17 mm. Differs from most cerambycids by having a robust body and short antennae as well as different habits, for the larva does not live in wood but feeds on the roots of various grasses. Adult beetles are very common in sandy localities, from April to June. Distribution: eastern part of central Europe and the Balkans.

2 *Acanthocinus aedilis* — Length 12—20 mm. Sexes markedly different. The body of the female is terminated by a blunt, truncate ovipositor; the antennae are about 1 1/2 times the length of the body. The antennae of the male are up to 5 times longer than its body. It is one of the first spring cerambycids, appearing on pine logs as early as March and April. Its colouring blends with that of the log. In spring the female lays about 40 eggs in the bark of pines, first of all biting a hole with her mandibles and then inserting her ovipositor. The larva bores irregular tunnels, and pupates either in the bark or in a pupal-cell made within the wood. The pupa is easily identified by the antennae, which are coiled into a loop. The beetle emerges in autumn and hibernates in the pupal cell. Distribution: Europe, Siberia, eastern Asia (Korea, Mongolia, etc.).

3 *Leiopus nebulosus* — Length 6—10 mm. An inconspicuous and common cerambycid of broad-leaved forests. Beetles appear as early as April when they emerge from the pupae. Larva develops in dry, slender trunks and stronger branches of broadleaved trees, chiefly hornbeam, oak, beech, etc. It bores zig-zag tunnels under the bark, which become filled with dust. Distribution: central and northern Europe.

4 *Saperda populnea* — Length 9—15 mm. Found in May and June on aspen and other poplars, sometimes also on willows. The branches of such trees and shrubs are covered with swellings caused by the larvae. When laying eggs the female bites several transverse furrows in the surface, and then a hole in the bark, trimming the edge and shaping it like an upturned horseshoe, inserting her ovipositor and depositing a single egg in each hole. The larva feeds on the plant tissues which grow rapidly as a result of the irritation. At some time in the second year the larva penetrates inside the branch. The swellings formed on the branch eventually become woody. The larva pupates inside the branch and the adult emerges through a circular hole. Distribution: much of Europe, Transcaucasia, Asia Minor, Siberia, Korea, north Africa, North America.

5 *Oberea oculata* — Length 15—21 mm. Readily identified by the long narrow body and two dark spots on the scutum. Beetles found on willow and sallow from June to September. Larva develops in young twigs, boring a tunnel about 3 cm long. Distribution: Europe, Siberia.

6 *Tetrops praeusta* — Length 3—5 mm. Found on various flowering plants from April to July. Larva develops in the twigs of roses, hawthorn and fruit trees. Infested twigs die back from the tips and the bark falls off. Distribution: Europe, Transcaucasia, Asia Minor, north Africa.

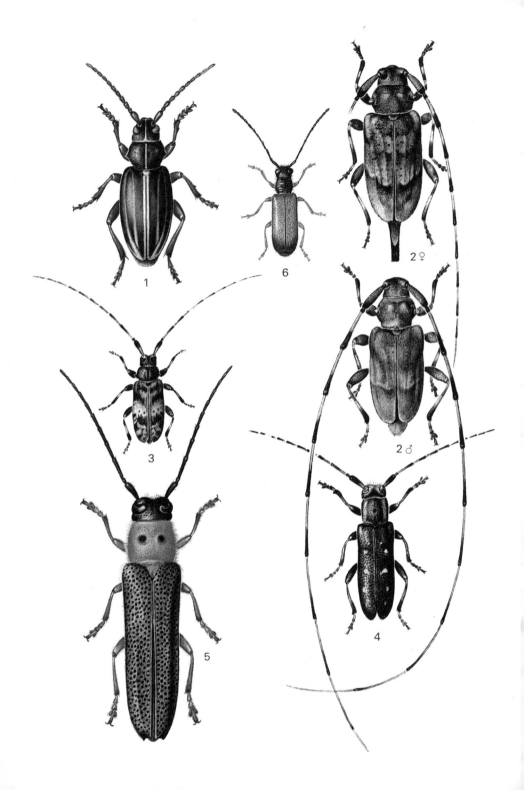

1

6

2 ♀

3

2 ♂

5

4

Phylum: **Arthropods — Arthropoda**

Class: **Insects — Insecta**

Order: **Beetles — Coleoptera**

Family: **Bruchidae**

1 *Bruchus pisorum* — Length 4—5 mm. Common pest of peas. Beetles appear in spring in gardens and fields, after hibernating either in stored seeds or outside. They feed on the stamens and young petals of blossoms. Eggs are laid on young pea pods and covered with a sticky substance by the female to prevent their being washed off by rain. Only a single larva can develop inside each seed, boring its way there from the outside of the pod. It is pink at first, and provided with legs. Once inside the seed it moults, changing both in colour and form, becoming white and legless. Distribution: originally probably the Mediterranean, but introduced to all parts of the world together with the host plant.

Family: **Leaf beetles — Chrysomelidae**

2 *Oulema melanopa* — Length 4—4.8 mm. In some regions regarded as a pest of grain fields; elsewhere it occurs only in small numbers. Found chiefly on oats and barley, from early spring. Both beetles and larvae feed on the leaves of the host plants. Eggs are laid on the leaves along the length of the primary vein. Distribution: Europe, Siberia, north Africa, and North America (where it was introduced and has since become a pest).

3 *Lilioceris lilii* — Length 6—8 mm. Very similar to the related *L. merdigera*, from which it differs in having a black head (the head of *L. merdigera* is red). Found in gardens, on cultivated plants of the family Liliaceae, usually on white lilies on the leaves of which both beetles and larvae feed. Female begins laying eggs in April, continuing to do so until autumn. Some females hibernate and lay further eggs again the following spring. When full-grown the larva abandons the host plant and burrows into the ground to pupate. There are generally 2—3 generations a year. Distribution: Europe, Asia, north Africa.

4 *Smaragdina cyanea* — Length 4.5—6.5 mm. Common from May to July, chiefly on sorrel. Distribution: Europe.

5 *Cryptocephalus sericeus* — Length 7—8 mm. The head of this and related species is concealed by the scutum, so that it is better seen from the side (this character is reflected by the scientific name, which is derived from two Greek words: *kryptos,* meaning hidden, and *kéfalé,* meaning head). The beetle is usually metallic green, but it is sometimes golden, purple or blue. Common in summer on flowering hawkweed, field scabious, yarrow and other plants in hedgerows, meadows, etc. Distribution: from northern Italy to the north of Europe, Asia Minor, Siberia.

6 *Cryptocephalus moraei* — Length 3—5 mm. Glossy black with yellow patches which sometimes merge across the junction of the elytra to form a transverse band; in some cases only the front or the hind patches so merge. Beetles common on blossoms in sunny localities. Distribution: Europe.

132

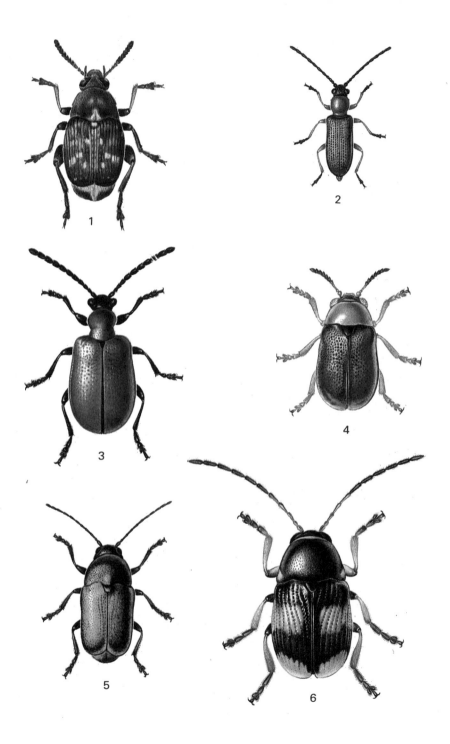

Phylum: **Arthropods — Arthropoda**

Class: **Insects — Insecta**

Order: **Beetles — Coleoptera**

Family: **Leaf beetles — Chrysomelidae**

1 *Chrysolina coerulans* — Length 6.5—9 mm. Coloured a beautiful metallic blue to blue-green. Beetles and larvae found on mint in damp meadows and alongside streams in piedmont and mountainous regions. Distribution: southern and central Europe, Asia Minor, central Asia, southern China.

2 *Chrysolina staphylaea* — Length 6.5—9 mm. Common throughout the summer on plants of the family Labiatae. Often found crawling on field paths. Distribution: the Palaearctic and Nearctic regions.

3 *Chrysolina fastuosa* — Length 5—6.5 mm. An outstandingly beautiful beetle. Like other chrysomelids it is herbivorous. Distribution: Eurasia.

4 *Plagiodera versicolora* — Length 2.5—4.5 mm. Usually coloured blue, sometimes blue-green or coppery. Beetles and larvae found on leaves of willow and poplar (larvae strip the leaves). Distribution: much of the Palaearctic region, North America, part of the Oriental region.

5 *Chrysomela aenea* — Length 6.5—8.5 mm. Colouring is variable — usually green, sometimes blue or golden-red. Beetles and larvae found on the leaves of alder. Distribution: Europe (absent in the Mediterranean), Siberia, Mongolia, northern China, Japan.

6 *Phyllodecta vulgatissima* — Length 4—5 mm. Emerges very early in spring, and is abundant until autumn on the leaves of willow, where the larval stage is also passed. Distribution: northern and central Europe, Siberia, Korea, North America.

7 Colorado Beetle — *Leptinotarsa decemlineata* — Length 8—9 mm. A member of the European fauna for only about a century. Formerly a greatly feared pest in potato-growing regions. Native to North America where the beetles and larvae fed on the leaves of wild plants of the family Solanaceae. In the 19th century, when potatoes began to be cultivated in North America on a large scale, the beetle switched to this plant and also sought it out in regions to which it was introduced. It also occurs on other solanaceous plants such as deadly nightshade *(Atropa belladonna),* jimson weed *(Datura stramonium)*, tobacco *(Nicotiana tabacum)*, etc. In Europe it is being increasingly found in places quite distant from farmland (e. g. in the Krkonoše — Giant Mountain National Park, the High Tatras, etc.). The beetles hibernate. Female lays eggs early in spring and throughout the summer. She cements them in batches to the leaves of the host plant. Larvae are conspicuously coloured bright red with two rows of black spots on the sides. After three moults they change to orange. When full-grown the larva leaves the host plant and burrows into the ground to pupate. The beetle emerges after two weeks, remaining in the ground one week more before flying out. In central Europe it has 1—2 broods a year, depending on the climatic conditions. It has been spread throughout the world by Man.

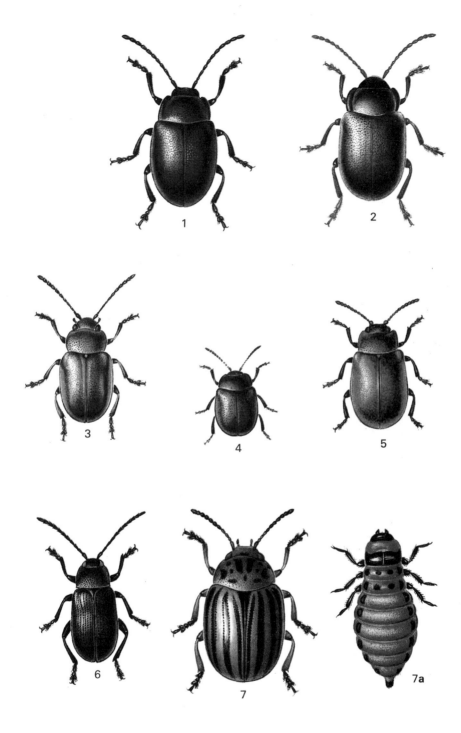

Phylum: **Arthropods — Arthropoda**

Class: **Insects — Insecta**

Order: **Beetles — Coleoptera**

Family: **Leaf beetles — Chrysomelidae**

1 *Galeruca tanaceti* — Length 6.5−11 mm. Very abundant from spring to autumn. Crawls rather cumbersomely, and is often to be found on forest and field paths. Distribution: western part of the Palaearctic region.

2 *Agelastica alni* — Length 6−7 mm. Very abundant from springtime, on alder, where the larvae are also later found. Both beetles and larvae feed on the leaves, the larvae stripping them bare. Adults hibernate. Distribution: the Palaearctic region (original range), introduced to North America.

3 *Phyllobrotica quadrimaculata* — Length 5−7 mm. Found in damp places, on the edges of bogs, etc. There are usually 4 black spots on the elytra; in some individuals the spots at the base may be absent. The four spots serve to distinguish it from the related *P. adusta*, which has only two dark spots at the tips of the elytra. Distribution: Europe.

4 *Cassida viridis* — Length 7−10 mm. Live beetles are bright green, but in mounted specimens the green colour gradually fades to yellow. At rest the antennae and legs are concealed beneath the scutum and elytra. A herbivorous species, it is found on plants of the Labiatae (dead-nettle) family. Female lays eggs in batches of 8−15 on leaves, cementing them together with a protective secretion and then enclosing the batch in a protective layer. Larva is coloured the same as the adult. The margin of the body is fringed with spines and the caudal end bears a forked appendage. It pupates on leaves. Adult emerges after about a week; it hibernates. Distribution: much of the Palaearctic region.

Family: **Weevils — Curculionidae**

5 *Otiorhynchus niger* — Length 6.5−10 mm. Found in spruce woods in piedmont and mountainous country. Eggs are laid in the ground. Larvae feed on various small roots. Distribution: central and southern Europe.

6 *Polydrusus sericeus* — Length 6−8 mm. Beautifully coloured. Evident in its full glory only when viewed through a magnifying lens or microscope that reveals the gleaming, greenish-gold scales. Abundant in May and June on various broadleaved trees; very common on birch, also inhabited by other species of weevils. Distribution: from southern Europe to southern Scandinavia, Siberia.

7 *Polydrusus mollis* — Length 6−8.5 mm. Resembles the preceding species but the scales are coppery reddish-brown, sometimes greenish-grey. Beetles abundant in spring on the young twigs of broadleaved trees and shrubs. With its strong beak, furnished at the end with mandibles, it bores into leaf buds to get at the contents on which it feeds. Found also on young spruce and pine shoots. Males have not been found in central Europe and it is therefore assumed that reproduction is parthenogenetic. Distribution: Siberia and from the Balkans to the north of Europe.

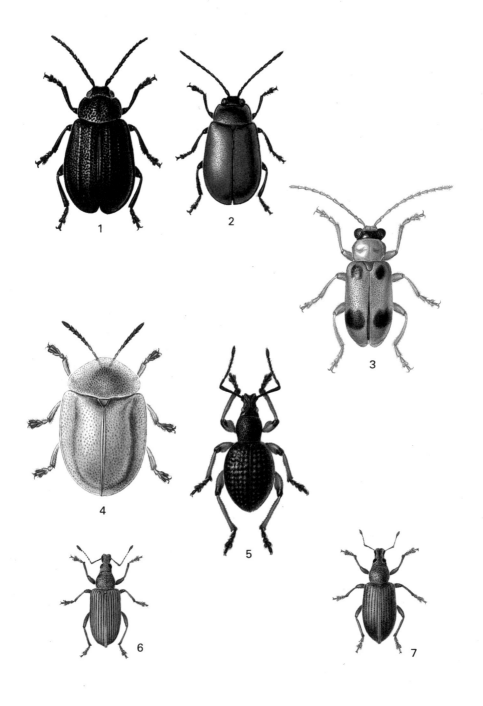

Phylum: **Arthropods — Arthropoda**

Class: **Insects — Insecta**

Order: **Beetles — Coleoptera**

Family: **Weevils — Curculionidae**

1 Pine Weevil *Hylobius abietis* — Length 7.3—13.5 mm. Common and abundant in pine forests. Adult lives to an age of 2—3 years. Hibernates under felled logs, amidst fallen leaves, in stumps, etc. and emerges in spring. Feeds on the bark of young pine trees, which it bites off in spirals. In summer it moves to old pines where it feeds on the bark of branches. Larva develops in pine stumps, in which it also pupates after hibernating. Distribution: Europe, Siberia, Japan.

2 *Liparus glabrirostris* — Length 14—21 mm. One of the largest of European weevils. Found in piedmont and mountainous regions, generally on the leaves of butterburs round streams and in forest margins. Very similar to *L. germanus*. Distribution: central and southwestern Europe, northern Italy.

3 Apple Blossom Weevil *Anthonomus pomorum* — Length 3.4—4.3 mm. Found in fruit orchards. Larva, which lives in apple blossom buds, seen more often than beetle. The adult beetle bites its way out and settles on the foliage on which it feeds. Distribution: much of Europe, north Africa (Algeria), North America (introduced).

4 *Curculio venosus* — Length 5—7.5 mm. Found on oak. Larva develops in acorns which, as a result, fall prematurely. Pupates in the ground. Distribution: Europe, the Caucasus, Asia Minor.

5 *Cionus scrophulariae* — Length 4—5 mm. Locally abundant on figwort in summer. Distinguished from related species by the pale-coloured scutum and dark spots in the centre of the elytra. Distribution: Europe, the Caucasus, Asia Minor, the Middle East, Turkestan.

Family: **Attelabidae**

6 *Byctiscus populi* — Length 3.8—6 mm. Metallic green, sometimes blue or black. Male differs from female by having two forward-facing spines on the scutum. Found on aspen and poplar, less often on other broadleaved trees. Larva develops in leaves which the female 'sews' into a tube. Pupates in the ground. Distribution: Eurasia.

7 *Deporaus betulae* — Length 2.5—4 mm. Common on birch. Male differs from female by having remarkably stout femora. Female makes striking leaf cases in which the eggs are laid and larval development takes place. Distribution: much of Europe, Siberia, Mongolia, north Africa.

Family: **Bark beetles — Scolytidae**

8 Large Pine Shoot Beetle *Tomicus piniperda* — Length 3.5—4.8 mm. Found under the bark of pine trees where the female bores a 10—12 cm long main gallery. Adults hibernate, emerging very early in spring and settling on felled pine trunks. Distribution: the Palaearctic region.

9 Spruce Bark Beetle *Ips typographus* — Length 4.2—5.5 mm. Best known of the Scolytidae, even though other species are often more plentiful. Often found in large numbers after strong winds or snow storms leave trees uprooted in their wake. Usually infests spruce about 60 years old, occurring on younger trees only in times of high population density. Males are polygamous, usually having two females, and they construct burrows composed of two branches to accommodate them. Distribution: Europe, Asia Minor, Siberia, Korea, northern China.

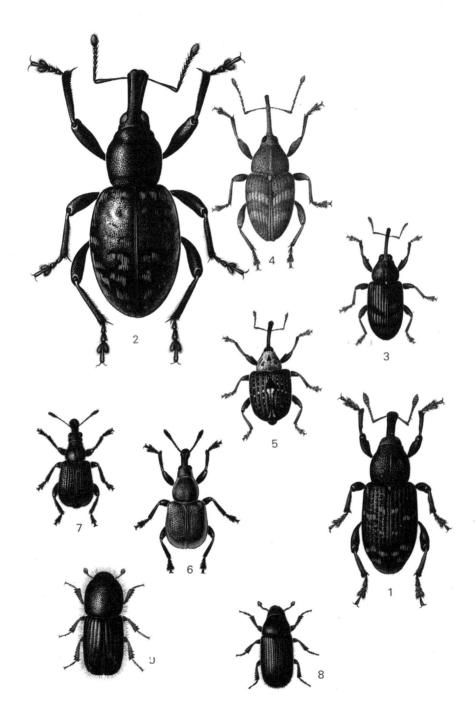

Phylum: **Arthropods — Arthropoda**

Class: **Insects — Insecta**

Order: **Hymenoptera**

Family: **Diprionidae**

1 Pine Sawfly *Diprion pini* — Length 7—10 mm. Found in pine forests where there are weak and diseased trees. Females usually remain on branches, but the males fly actively. Female deposits about 150 eggs in all, making an incision in the pine needle with her ovipositor and laying as many as 20 eggs in a row in the slit. Larvae live and feed on pine needles. There are 1—2 generations a year. Larvae of the second generation pupate either in crevices in the bark or in the soil. They hibernate once or twice before pupating. Distribution: central and northern Europe, Spain, north Africa.

Family: **Typical sawflies — Tenthredinidae**

2 *Tenthredo zonula* — Length 9—10 mm. Important identification feature is the yellow first segment of the antenna. Very common on flowering Umbelliferae in early summer. Distribution: Europe, Asia Minor, north Africa.

3 *Rhogogaster viridis* — Length 10—13 mm. Bright green, often with dark stripe on the abdomen. Similar to *R. picta* but lacks the black patches on the sides of the body. Larva is herbivorous, adult beetle predaceous. Usually common, in forests, fields and in gardens. Distribution: all Europe and temperate regions of Asia as far as Japan.

4 *Caliroa cerasi* — Length 5 mm. Development takes place on cherry trees. Eggs are laid under the leaf epidermis. The larva, which strips the leaves, is black and smells of ink. It pupates in the ground. Distribution: Eurasia, northern and southern Africa, North America and Australia (introduced).

Family: **Horntails or wood wasps — Siricidae**

5 *Sirex juvencus* — Length 14—30 mm. Very similar to *S. noctilio* except that its antennae are orange. Larva generally develops in the trunks of pine or spruce. Distribution: all Europe, Japan, north Africa, the Nearctic and Australasian regions.

Family: **Ichneumon flies — Ichneumonidae**

6 *Rhyssa persuasoria* — Length 18—35 mm. One of the largest members of this family. Female has an ovipositor 30—35 mm long. Found in forests. Female flies about felled logs inhabited by the larvae of wood wasps of the genus *Urocerus, Xeris, Sirex,* etc. drilling her way to them with her ovipositor and laying an egg in each. The larva that hatches then feeds on the host larva. Distribution: Europe, North America.

7 *Pimpla instigator* — Length 10—24 mm. Larvae of this and many other related species are parasites of the caterpillars of various Lepidoptera. Distribution: Europe, north Africa.

8 Yellow Ophion *Ophion luteus* — Length 15—20 mm. Abdomen laterally compressed. Common even in gardens, often flying into illuminated rooms through open windows. Eggs are laid in the caterpillars of various Lepidoptera (e. g. of the Black Arches Moth). Distribution: entire Palaearctic region.

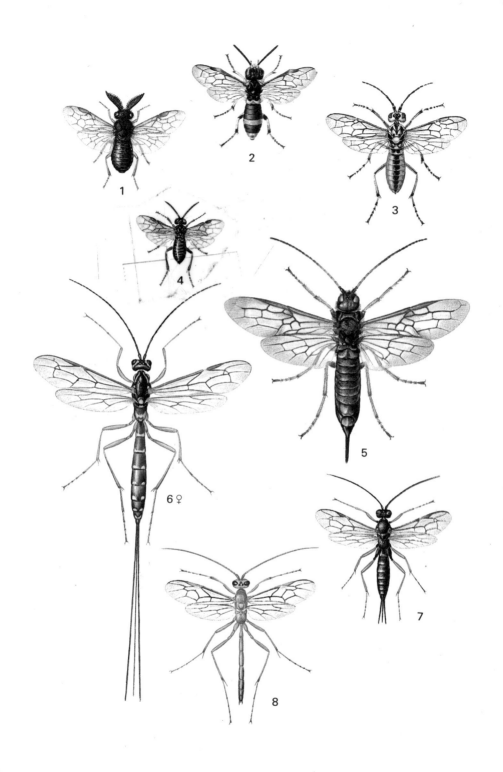

1

2

3

4

5

6 ♀

7

8

Phylum: **Arthropods — Arthropoda**

Class: **Insects — Insecta**

Order: **Hymenoptera**

Family: **Gall wasps — Cynipidae**

1 Oak-apple Gall-fly *Biorhiza pallida* — Sexual generation measures 1.7−2.8 mm, asexual genera-tion 3.5−6 mm. Like all gall wasps it has a complex life cycle, and marked differences in body form between the sexual and asexual generations. Produces two types of galls: on the roots, and on the branches of oak. Those on the branches, called oak apples, are very striking, up to 40 mm across and shaped like a potato. Inside this gall the sexual generation develops, the males and females emerging in June. After pairing, the female, which is usually wingless, burrows into the ground where she lays eggs on slender oak roots. These eggs give rise to entirely different, roundish galls, inside which only females develop. These emerge in the winter of the following year, climbing to the tips of the branches and laying eggs in the buds, which give rise to the oak apple galls. Distribution: Europe, Asia Minor, north Africa.

2 *Cynips quercusfolii* — Sexual generation measures 2.3−2.5 mm, asexual generation 3.4−4 mm. Makes cherry-like galls on oak leaves. These are green, yellow or reddish and placed singly or in batches on the underside of the leaf. In autumn the galls fall to the ground together with the leaves and the females that have developed inside emerge from November to February. These lay eggs in buds, which give rise to small galls in which males and females of the sexual generation develop. In May and June the females of this generation lay eggs on the underside of leaves, which give rise to the cherry-like galls. These were formerly used to make ink. Distribution: Europe, Asia Minor.

3 *Andricus lignicolus* — Asexual generation measures 4−4.5 mm. Found on young oak twigs where it induces formation of hard galls inside which the asexual female develops. Distribution: Europe, Asia Minor.

4 Artichoke Gall-fly *Andricus fecundator* — Sexual generation measures 1.5−1.9 mm, asexual generation 4.3−4.8 mm. Another species to be found on oak. Produces two types of galls. Asexual females develop inside the artichoke galls on the twigs. They emerge in late autumn or spring, and lay eggs on male catkin buds. Their offspring — the sexual generation — develop inside tiny galls in the flowers. They mature in May and the gall wasps emerge in June. Distribution: Europe, Asia Minor.

5 Spangle Gall-fly *Neuroterus quercusbaccarum* — Sexual generation measures 2.5−2.9 mm, asexual generation 2.4−2.8 mm. Found on oaks. Females of the sexual generation lay eggs on the underside of leaves inducing the formation of spangle galls. In autumn they fall to the ground and the adults, all asexual females, emerge from them the following March. These lay eggs in the male catkin flower buds of the oak, inducing the formation of little spherical 'currant' galls in which the sexual generation develops. The adults emerge in June. Development takes one year. Distribution: Europe, Asia Minor, north Africa.

6 Robin's Pincushion Gall-fly *Diplolepis rosae* — Length 3.7−4.3 mm. Produces a single type of gall, called robin's pincushion or bedeguar gall, on roses. It varies in size, is green at first turning to yellow and red later. The gall is composed of several chambers. As a rule only females emerge; males are rare. The galls are also inhabited by large numbers of other hymenopterous insects that have varying relationships to the rightful inhabitants. Distribution: Europe.

142

1♀

1

2♀

2

3

5

4

6♀

Phylum: **Arthropods — Arthropoda**

Class: **Insects — Insecta**

Order: **Hymenoptera**

Family: **Scoliidae**

1 *Scolia quadripunctata* — Length 10—18 mm. Has a variable number of yellow patches on the abdomen, usually four, but sometimes fewer or more. Adult wasps visit flowers and feed on the nectar. The larvae feed on the body tissues of various scarabaeid larvae, e. g. of the genus *Tropinota, Cetonia, Anisoplia,* etc. Distribution: Europe (except the far north), Channel Islands, the Caucasus, Transcaucasia, Iran, Egypt, Algeria.

Family: **Velvet ants — Mutillidae**

2 Large Velvet Ant *Mutilla europaea* — Length 10—15 mm. Distinguished from related species by the front abdominal segments which are bluish and unspotted. Male is winged, female wingless. Larvae are parasites in the nests of bumblebees. Distribution: the Palaearctic region.

Family: **Cuckoo wasps — Chrysididae**

3 Ruby-tailed Wasp *Chrysis ignita* — Length 7—10 mm. Beautiful metallic colour. Coloration rather variable. Front part of the body is blue-green to blue, abdomen gold, reddish-gold or purple. Adults rest on flowering Umbelliferae and sun-warmed walls. Larvae are parasitic on the larvae of various wasps and bees (families Eumenidae, Vespidae, Sphecidae, Apidae). Distribution: much of the Palaearctic region.

Family: **Ants — Myrmicidae**

4 *Manica rubida* — Length 5—9 mm (worker). Found in foothills and mountains. Nests under stones and in the ground. Sting is quite painful. Distribution: southern and central Europe.

Family: **Ants — Formicidae**

5 *Lasius fuliginosus* — Length 3—5 mm. Builds sponge-like nests in hollow trees. Well-tended paths usually lead from these nests. Distribution: Eurasia, North America.

6 Wood Ant *Formica rufa* — Length 6—11 mm. Occurs in spruce forests. The nest proper is located underground, but above it the ants make a large mound of pine needles and various fragments. The nest contains three castes: workers, males and females. The female does not build her own nest. She either joins a nest of her own species, or else seeks out a nest of the related *Formica fusca*. For a temporary period the nest then contains two types of inhabitants but gradually the offspring of the Wood Ant prevail. The Wood Ant destroys large numbers of various harmful larvae and is important in maintaining the balance of nature. It is sensitive to chemical agents and in recent years its numbers have been rapidly declining in many places. In some countries it is therefore protected by law (GFR and GDR, Czechoslovakia). Distribution: Europe (absent in the south), the Caucasus, Siberia, North America.

7 *Camponotus ligniperda* — Length 7—14 mm. One of the largest European ants. Similar to *C. herculeanus*. The nest is made by the female without the aid of another species of ant. It is located in stumps and in the living wood of conifers, chiefly spruce. The chambers are excavated along the annual rings. Distribution: central and northern Europe.

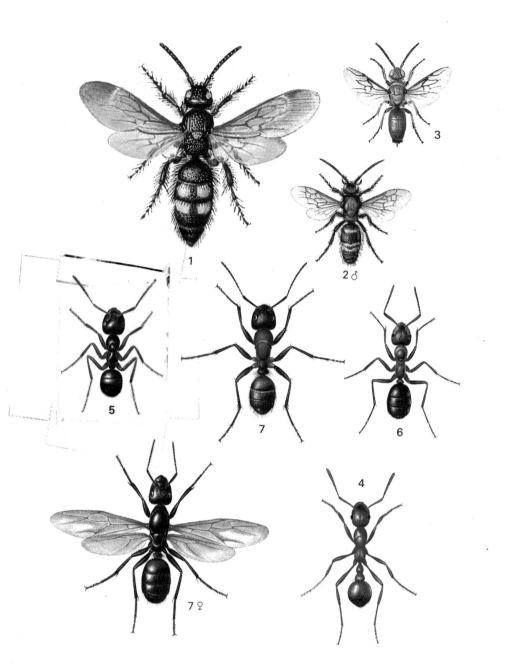

1

3

2 ♂

5

7

6

4

7 ♀

Phylum: **Arthropods — Arthropoda**

Class: **Insects — Insecta**

Order: **Hymenoptera**

Family: **Spider-hunting wasps — Pompilidae**

1 *Anoplius viaticus* — Length 7—20 mm. Locally abundant on flowering Umbelliferae. Larvae feed on spiders which the female hunts, paralyzes and carries to the underground nest. Distribution: all Europe.

Family: **Eumenidae**

2 Potter Wasp *Eumenes pomiformis* — Length 10—16 mm. Very similar to *E. subpomiformis*. The yellow pattern on the dark body shows considerable variation. Female is noted as an excellent builder. She makes a flask-like nest with a narrow neck, attaching it to a plant, to a twig or under bark, and stocking it with several small caterpillars which later serve as food for the larvae. The flasks are favourites of cuckoo-wasps (Chrysididae) which try to insert their eggs unobserved, and thus it sometimes happens that another insect eventually emerges instead of the rightful offspring. Because there are several generations a year the adult wasps are found from spring until autumn. Distribution: the Palaearctic and Nearctic regions.

3 *Odynerus spinipes* — Length 9—12 mm. Occurs in late spring. Female hunts *Phytonomus* larvae with which she stocks the nest. The nest is a small chamber, which she excavates in a soil bank with a small tube cemented of bits of earth round the entrance. The egg is suspended by a slender thread from the ceiling of the chamber. Distribution: all Europe, Asia Minor, Siberia, north Africa.

Family: **Vespidae**

4 Hornet *Vespa crabro* — Length 19—35 mm. Builds a large nest which in time contains a whole colony of hornets. The community, like that of other wasps, lives only one year. It is started in spring by the fertilized queen after hibernation. She makes the first cells herself, and feeds the larvae, later these tasks are performed by the workers. They build further tiers, feed the larvae and clean the nest. Various insect larvae are the mainstay of their diet. At the end of the summer the nest also contains males. This heralds the end of the hornet community for most of the population dies in the autumn. Only the young, fertilized females survive the winter. Distribution: the Palaearctic and Nearctic regions.

5 German Wasp *Paravespula germanica* — Length 10—19 mm. Very common. Nests underground, often in the abandoned nest of a mouse, mole, etc. The complete nest contains as many as 3,000 individuals. Like the hornet, the German Wasp hunts flies, caterpillars, etc. as food for its larvae. It also sucks nectar and in autumn visits ripe fruits. Distribution: the Palaearctic and Nearctic regions.

6 Common Wasp *Paravespula vulgaris* — Length 11—20 mm. Resembles the German Wasp but has a dark triangle on the face (clypeus) instead of the three separate spots. Likewise nests in the ground. Distribution: the Palaearctic region (chiefly in the more northerly part) and North America.

7 *Polistes nimpha* — Length 12 mm. Makes a small nest attached to a plant by a stalk. Distinguished from the similar *P. gallicus* by having the underside of the terminal abdominal segment coloured black instead of yellow. Distribution: the Palaearctic region.

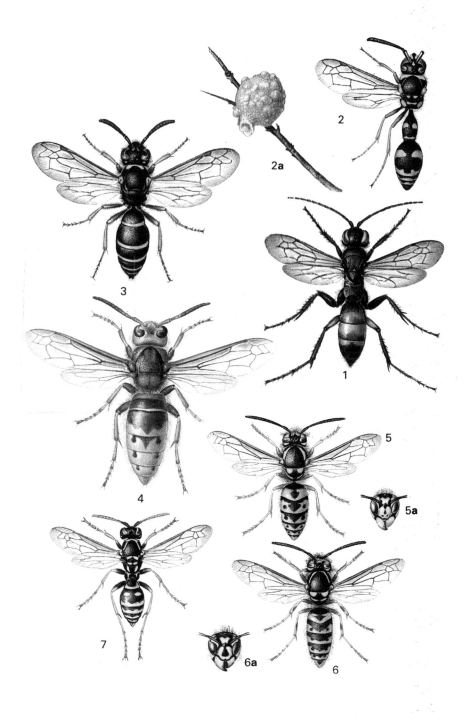

Phylum: **Arthropods — Arthropoda**

Class: **Insects — Insecta**

Order: **Hymenoptera**

Family: **Digger wasps — Sphecidae**

1 Slender-bodied Digger *Crabro cribrarius* — Length 11—17 mm. Found in summer on flowering Umbelliferae. Like other sphecids, it has a complex life cycle. Female hunts various species of flies which she paralyzes and carries to the nest, storing them there for the future larvae to feed on. The nest is made in rotten wood, or in the soil. Distribution: much of the Palaearctic region.

2 Bee-killer Wasp *Philanthus triangulum* — Length 12—18 mm. Found chiefly in warm places where the female makes the nest. She excavates a main tunnel 20—100 cm long, with several lateral tunnels, each ending in a cell. Each nest contains 5—7 such cells, in which the larvae develop. The larva does not lie on the bottom of the cell, but clings to the cell in a horizontal position, to protect itself from damp and mould. The larvae feed solely on honey bees. The female wasp captures the bees on flowers, first paralyzing them and then carrying them off to the nest. Two bees suffice as food for a male larva, but a female requires three. The brood of a single mother will consume about 20 bees. The female wasp also uses the bees as food for itself, sucking the honey from their bodies before taking them to the nest. Distribution: the Palaearctic region (except the northern parts).

3 Sand Tailed-digger *Cerceris arenaria* — Length 9—17 mm. Found in sandy localities. Hunts larvae of various weevils (Curculionidae) as food for its offspring. Distribution: much of Europe.

4 *Ammophila sabulosa* — Length 16—28 mm. Found until late autumn on flowering plants in sandy localities. Nest is excavated by the female in sand. Inside she places a paralyzed caterpillar, on which she lays an egg and then carefully closes and conceals the entrance. Distribution: much of the Palaearctic region.

Family: **Bees — Apidae**

5 Tawny Mining Bee *Andrena fulva* (also known as *A. armata*) — Length 12 mm. This bee has a strikingly thick coat of brownish-red hairs. On the wing in early spring, when fruit trees are in blossom. Nests on field paths, often found also in city parks and gardens, where, in some measure, it supplements or serves as a substitute for the honey-bee, which is less often found in large cities. Distribution: scattered across northwestern Europe from Great Britain to central Europe and Bulgaria; in southern Europe only at higher elevations.

6 Spurred Panurgus *Panurgus calcaratus* — Length 8—9 mm. A generally common and striking little black bee usually found on flowering dandelion and other yellow composites. It crawls on its side between the individual florets and so becomes covered all over with pollen. Distribution: almost all Europe.

7 *Halictus quadricinctus* — Length 15—16 mm. Adults emerge from the pupae in autumn and occur on flowers. The males die the same year, after mating; the fertilized females hibernate, returning to the flowers again in spring. Nest is located in soil banks. Distribution: Europe.

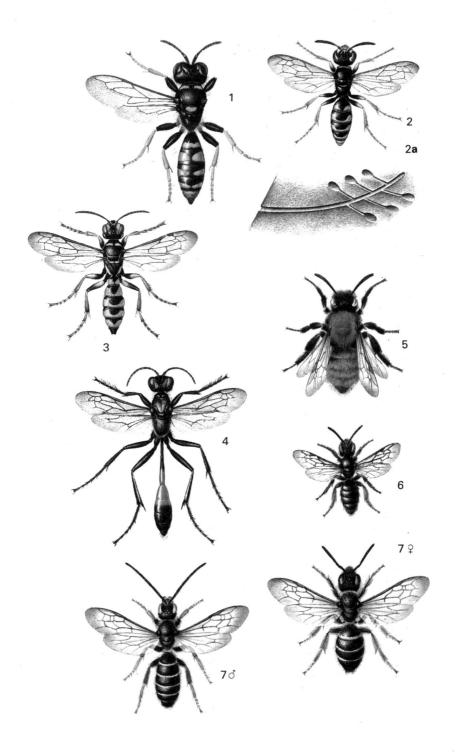

1

2

2a

3

5

4

6

7 ♀

7 ♂

Phylum: **Arthropods — Arthropoda**

Class: **Insects — Insecta**

Order: **Hymenoptera**

Family: **Bees — Apidae**

1 *Melitta leporina* — Length 11—13 mm. Common on flowering clover and lucerne in July and August. Nest consists of a small number of underground cells filled with pollen on which the larvae feed. The larva pupates in a cocoon. Distribution: northern and central Europe.

2 Hairy-legged Mining Bee *Dasypoda altercator* (also known as *D. hirtipes*) — Length 13—15 mm. Found on flowering hawkweed, field scabious, etc., in July and August. Nest consists of a number of underground cells. Each contains a ball of pollen supported on three 'legs' so that it does not touch the ground and so become mouldy. Egg is laid on the ball of pollen, on which the larva feeds. Distribution: much of the Palaearctic region.

3 Carpenter Bee *Xylocopa violacea* — Length 21—24 mm. Very similar to the related *X. valga*. One of Europe's largest bees. Adults hibernate. In spring the female makes the nest in an old trunk or branch. First she excavates a short tunnel to enter the wood, then a vertical tunnel some 15—30 cm long, which she divides into about 15 cells. She stocks each with pollen for the larva to feed on. The full-grown larva pupates in the cell and when the adult emerges it cuts its way out through the side wall. If the wall is too thick it waits until the bees in the upper part of the tunnel hatch and then climbs out after them. Distribution: southern Europe and southern part of central Europe (Rhine region, Slovakia).

4 *Bombus pomorum* — Length of female 20—24 mm. Like other bumblebees, it lives in colonies. The nest is made by the female after hibernating. She cements the first cells for stores of food and for the eggs. Later the workers that hatch (they are smaller) take over the task of building the nest and feeding the larvae. Males appear in the autumn. After that all the inhabitants die except for the fertilized females. In spring the queens visit flowering primroses, deadnettle, etc.; the males are abundant in autumn in fields of clover. Protected by law in Czechoslovakia. Distribution: central Europe, Siberia.

5 Large Red-tailed Bumblebee *Bombus lapidarius* — Length of female 20—25 mm. Differs in coloration from most other common species. Female emerges from her winter shelter in April. The nest is often built under stones, or in crevices between bricks of country dwellings, etc. The nest is often infested by the parasitic cuckoo-bee *Psithyrus rupestris* that does not build its own nest. Distribution: Eurasia.

6 Buff-tailed Bumblebee *Bombus terrestris* — Length of female 24—28 mm. Nest is built deep in the ground. Females fly early in spring and are common on catkins. Distribution: Europe, Asia Minor, northern Asia, north Africa.

7 Honey Bee *Apis mellifera* — Length 14—18 mm. Lives in colonies numbering 40,000—80,000 individuals, each 'ruled' by a queen which lays the eggs. The nest is built and cleaned and the larvae fed by the workers. Their lifespan is short and during that time they perform various tasks — collecting pollen and nectar, feeding grubs, cleaning the hive, etc. The males (drones) appear in summer. The life of bees and their remarkable habits have been the subject of intensive study, recently most notably by the Nobel Prize winner Prof. Karl von Frisch. Distribution: worldwide.

Phylum: **Arthropods — Arthropoda**

Class: **Insects — Insecta**

Order: **Caddis flies — Trichoptera**

Family: **Rhyacophilidae**

1 *Rhyacophila vulgaris* — Length 7—9 mm, wingspan 24—32 mm. Larval stage passed in fast-flowing streams. Adults on the wing in late summer and autumn until October. Distribution: all Europe except the north.

Family: **Leptoceridae**

2 *Athripsodes cinereus* — Length 7—7.5 mm, wingspan 20—24 mm. Flies from June to autumn round slow-flowing waters and ponds. Larvae make slender portable cases. Distribution: the Palaearctic and Nearctic regions.

Family: **Phryganeidae**

3 *Phryganea grandis* — Length 15—21 mm, wingspan 40—60 mm. Found in summer from lowland to mountain elevations round calm bodies of water. Larvae live in calm water and build cases of plant fragments up to 40 mm in length. At first they live on the bottom, later on aquatic vegetation. They feed on insect larvae. Distribution: the Palaearctic and Nearctic regions.

Order: **Butterflies and moths — Lepidoptera ***

Family: **Swift Moths — Hepialidae**

4 Ghost Swift *Hepialus humuli* — 20—35 mm. Found from June to August in damp places in meadows and forests. Male and female differ in size and colouring of the wings. Female deposits eggs in flight. The caterpillar burrows in the ground where it feeds on the roots of dandelion, coltsfoot, sorrel and other plants. It pupates in the ground. Distribution: much of the Palaearctic region (north to the Arctic Circle), the Middle East.

Family: **Incurvariidae**

5 *Nemophora degeerella* — 7—8 mm. Flight is jerky, slow. Flies in forest undergrowth. Male has remarkably long antennae. Distribution: Europe.

Family: **Goat Moths — Cossidae**

6 Leopard Moth *Zeuzera pyrina* — 18—35 mm. Male is smaller than female. Antennae of female are filiform; the basal section of the male antenna is plumose. Caterpillars live in the branches and trunks of various broadleaved trees. They hibernate once or twice. Distribution: southern and central Europe, temperate regions of Asia, north Africa.

Family: **Burnets and Foresters — Zygaenidae**

7 *Agrumaenia carniolica* — 12—15 mm. Coloration and number of spots on the wings show marked variability. On the wing in sunny places from June to August. Caterpillar found from August onward on bird's-foot trefoil *(Lotus corniculatus)* and *Onobrychis viciaefolia*. After hibernating it pupates in a parchment-like cocoon. Distribution: Europe, north to Lithuania (absent in Great Britain). Also found in Transcaucasia, Asia Minor, Iran.

8 Six-spot Burnet *Zygaena filipendulae* — 14—18 mm. Many colour forms exist. On the wing in July and August from lowland to mountain elevations. Caterpillars feed on Papilionaceae. Distribution: Europe and Transcaucasia.

* (In this section measurements give the length of the forewing.)

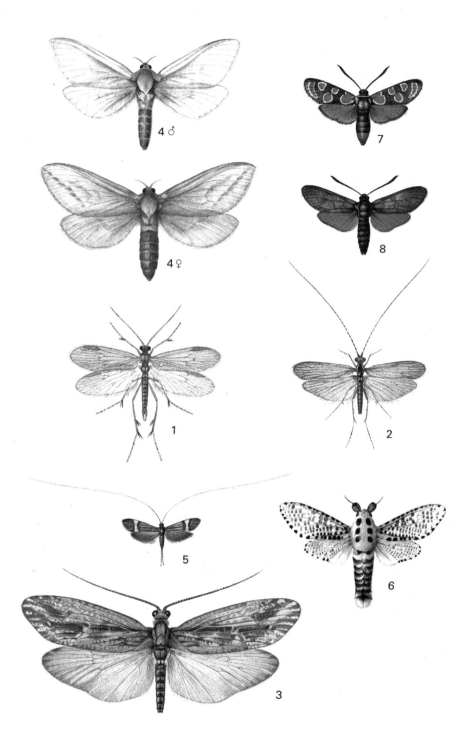

Phylum: **Arthropods — Arthropoda**

Class: **Insects — Insecta**

Order: **Butterflies and moths — Lepidoptera**

Family: **Bagworms — Psychidae**

1 *Apterona crenulella* — 6—7 mm. Occurs chiefly in the so-called *helix* form which is parthenogenetic. In southern Europe the bisexual form also exists. Caterpillars make coiled cases resembling small snail-shells. Often found on twigs in great numbers. Distribution: much of Europe and western Asia.

Family: **Tineidae**

2 Tapestry Moth *Trichophaga tapetzella* — 6—8 mm. Found in association with Man. Caterpillars are troublesome pests of woollen fabrics, felt, etc. Distribution: cosmopolitan.

3 Common Clothes Moth *Tineola bisselliella* — 4—8 mm. Occurs in houses chiefly in spring, often in great numbers. The moth itself is not harmful, but its presence indicates that somewhere the larvae have made holes in fabrics, furs, etc. Distribution: worldwide.

Family: **Lyonetiidae**

4 *Lyonetia clerkella* — 4—6 mm. A very common little moth. Caterpillars live in the leaves of various broadleaved trees where they make serpentine mines in which they deposit their dark excrement. When full-grown the larva leaves the mine and pupates on the leaf. There are 3 generations a year. Moths of the third generation hibernate. Distribution: much of the Palaearctic region.

Family: **Clearwings — Sesiidae**

5 Hornet Clearwing *Sesia apiformis* — 15—20 mm. Often found on poplars fringing streams, as the caterpillars feed on poplar wood. The larval stage takes 2 years. The first year the caterpillar lives under the bark, the second year it tunnels into the wood at the base of the trunk, and also into roots. Distribution: the Palaearctic region (original range), North America (introduced).

Family: **Yponomeutidae**

6 *Yponomeuta padella* — 9—10 mm. A summer species. It lays eggs in batches on the twigs of hawthorn, plum, etc. and covers them with a protective layer which later also serves to shelter the small caterpillars. Larvae hatch in the autumn, hibernate and in spring feed on buds, later moving to the leaves. They live in a communal web where they also pupate. Distribution: the Palaearctic region.

Family: **Tortricidae**

7 Codling Moth *Cydia pomonella* — 7—9 mm. A pest in some regions. The moth is not harmful; troublesome are the pink caterpillars that live in apples and pears. They grow to a length of about 20 mm, then they leave the fruit and find shelter for the winter. There are usually 2 generations a year, sometimes more. Distribution: cosmopolitan.

8 Green Oak Tortrix Moth *Tortrix viridana* — 9—11 mm. Flies from June to August in the tops of oaks. Female lays eggs on young oak twigs. These overwinter and in spring the small larvae emerge, first of all entering the buds and later feeding on the leaves, often stripping them bare and leaving only the skeletal veins. Oak, however, is not their only host plant. Distribution: much of Europe, Asia Minor.

154

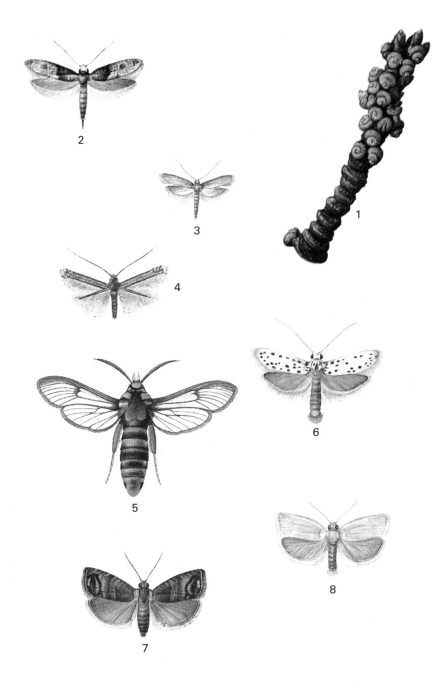

Phylum: **Arthropods — Arthropoda**

Class: **Insects — Insecta**

Order: **Butterflies and moths — Lepidoptera**

Family: **Alucitidae**

1 *Alucita desmodactyla* — 5—6 mm. Each wing is divided into six plumes (24 plumes in all). Flies from June to August. Larvae feed on the flowers of *Stachys*. Distribution: southern Europe, including the southern parts of central Europe.

Family: **Pyralidae**

2 Mediterranean Flour Moth *Ephestia kuehniella* — 10—12 mm. Found chiefly in mills, storehouses and houses. Larva generally lives in flour. It is a pest not so much because it feeds on the grains but because the cocoons soil the flour. It also feeds on other foodstuffs, fabrics, etc. Distribution: cosmopolitan, introduced into Europe in the 19th century.

3 Meal Moth *Pyralis farinalis* — 8—12 mm. There are two transverse zig-zag bands on each of the whitish-grey hind wings. Larvae found in mills, stores of grain, bakeries, etc. where they feed on flour, grain and straw. Locally still abundant, but no longer considered as important a pest as before. Distribution: Eurasia, North America, Australia.

Family: **Skippers — Hesperiidae**

4 Large Skipper *Ochlodes venata* — 14—17 mm. A single generation (in the south there are 2 or 3 generations) on the wing from July to August. Unlike the Silver-spotted Skipper the male does not have a black patch with silvery streak on the fore wing. Caterpillar feeds on grasses. It hibernates. Distribution: Eurasia.

5 Grizzled Skipper *Pyrgus malvae* — 10—11 mm. There are 2 generations between April and August. Usually found in forest clearings, forest margins and on paths from lowland to mountainous elevations. Larvae feed on raspberry, strawberry, *Potentilla reptans* and other plants. They are concealed in rolled leaves. Distribution: from the Balkans to southern Scandinavia, Asia.

6 Chequered Skipper *Carterocephalus palaemon* — 13—14 mm. There is only one generation; on the wing from May onward in forest margins, along pathways and in damp meadows. Found even in mountains (in the Alps up to 1,500 metres). Larvae feed on grasses, favouring couch grass and brome grass, as well as on ribwort plantain. They hibernate. Distribution: common in certain parts of Europe, elsewhere absent or rare (e. g. in northern Germany, northwestern and southern Europe), Asia (to the Amur), North America.

7 Dingy Skipper *Erynnis tages* — 13—14 mm. 1—2 generations, flies on sunny paths, in glades and sometimes also in gardens. Larvae feed on bird's-foot trefoil *(Lotus corniculatus)*, crown vetch *(Coronilla varia)*, *Eryngium campestre*, etc. They hibernate. Distribution: chiefly southern and central Europe, Great Britain, rarely in the northern parts of the continent — northern Germany, Lithuania, etc. Also found in northern Asia.

1

2

3

4

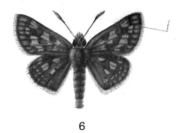

5

6

7

Phylum: **Arthropods — Arthropoda**

Class: **Insects — Insecta**

Order: **Butterflies and moths — Lepidoptera**

Family: **Swallow-tails and apollos — Papilionidae**

1 Swallow-tail *Papilio machaon* — 34—45 mm. In most of Europe there are 2 generations, in the north and in mountain regions only one, in the south also a partial third so that adults are on the wing from April to August, those of the third generation even in September and October. Its numbers in the wild are rapidly declining. Occurs even in mountains and is often found flying around the highest points in a landscape — on hilltops, round tall spires, etc. Larva is brightly coloured. Feeds on fennel, caraway, wild carrot, and in regions where they are cultivated on citrus plants. Forms several geographic races within its range (e. g. in Europe ssp. *gorganus,* in Great Britain ssp. *britannicus,* etc.) In some countries it is protected by law (Czechoslovakia, GDR). Distribution: much of Europe (rare in Great Britain), temperate regions of Asia, north Africa, North America.

2 Scarce Swallow-tail *Iphiclides podalirius* — 35—45 mm. Flies from spring to September in forest margins, fields and gardens, most often on warm, sunny limestone hillsides. Caterpillars feed on blackthorn, hawthorn and fruit trees. In many countries it is protected by law (GFR and GDR, Czechoslovakia), but its numbers continue to decline hand in hand with the eradication of its most favoured habitat (hedgerows with blackthorn and hawthorn). There are 1—2 generations a year. Distribution: much of Europe (absent in the north and Great Britain, even though it occasionally strays there), Transcaucasia, Asia Minor, Iran, western China.

3 Southern Festoon *Parnassius polyxena* — 20—30 mm. Flies in April and May, close to the ground, in warm situations. Larvae feed on various species of birthwort (*Aristolochia*) from May. After about 4 weeks they pupate. The pupa hibernates. In Czechoslovakia and other countries it is protected by law. In the literature it is also known by the generic name *Zerynthia* and the specific names *hypsipyle* or *hypermnestra.* Distribution: southern and southeastern Europe, the Balkans, Greece and Albania. In central Europe, Austria and southern Czechoslovakia mark the northern limit of its range.

4 Apollo *Parnassius apollo* — 34—50 mm. Flight slow and lethargic. Found in mountainous regions, usually resting on thistles of the mountain slopes and meadows. Flies in July and August. Caterpillar feeds on stonecrop (*Sedum*) and house-leek (*Sempervivum*). It hibernates and then pupates in spring. This species exhibits marked variability; some 600 different forms have been described. Its numbers are markedly declining and in some places (e. g. Bohemia) it has become extinct. In many countries it is protected by law (GFR and GDR, Czechoslovakia). Distribution: most of Europe (excluding British Isles), east across the Alps and Carpathians to Turkey, Syria, the Ukraine, Altai, parts of China and Mongolia.

5 Clouded Apollo *Parnassius mnemosyne* — 27—32 mm. Flies from May till July in meadows, alongside streams and pathways, from lowland to mountain elevations. Caterpillars feed on *Corydalis;* they emerge only on sunny days. This butterfly is likewise rapidly declining in numbers and is therefore protected by law in some countries (GFR and GDR, Czechoslovakia). Distribution: Europe, (excluding British Isles), the Caucasus to Iran and east through central Asia, reaching as far as the Urals in the USSR.

Phylum: **Arthropods — Arthropoda**

Class: **Insects — Insecta**

Order: **Butterflies and moths — Lepidoptera**

Family: **Whites and yellows — Pieridae**

1 Large White *Pieris brassicae* — 29—34 mm. Most often found in gardens, fields and meadows. Female differs from male in having black dots on the fore wing. In the male only the apex of the fore wings is coloured black. There are 2—5 generations, sometimes even more, depending on the conditions; in central Europe generally only 2 (April-May, July-August). The female lays 200—300 eggs on the underside of the host plants, mainly cabbages (in which it can be a pest) and other crucifers. When full-grown the caterpillars leave the plant and hide in a sheltered place to pupate. Pupa is pale-green with dark spots. Distribution: much of the Palaearctic region, including the Canary Islands and northwestern China, Chile (introduced).

2 Small White *Pieris rapae* — 20—26 mm. May be seen from spring to autumn, for there are 2—3 generations. Members of the first generation are smaller than those of the summer generation and also the dark pattern on the wings is less pronounced. Host plants of the caterpilars are various species of Cruciferae, including cabbages, of which it can be a serious pest. The pupa hibernates. Distribution: Eurasia, north Africa, North America (introduced), Australia and New Zealand (introduced).

3 Green-veined White *Pieris napi* — 20—25 mm. A very common and extremely variable species. There are 2 (in the south 3) generations that fly in fields, gardens, clearings, forest margins etc. Caterpillar feeds on the leaves of Cruciferae (although rarely on crop plants), at first only in the centre, later also from the edges. Distribution: the Palaearctic and Nearctic regions.

4 Black-veined White *Aporia crataegi* — 32—35 mm. There is only 1 generation, on the wing from May to July. Formerly the caterpillars were feared pests of fruit trees, but nowadays it is much rarer and in some places even extinct (e. g. British Isles). Distribution: most of Europe, the temperate regions of Asia, Korea, Japan, north Africa.

5 Orange Tip *Anthocharis cardamines* — 21—25 mm. Male has a large orange patch at tip of each forewing, female has a smaller black patch. In central Europe there is a single generation on the wing from April to June, where it occurs up to mountain elevations. Caterpillar feeds on the leaves of various wild Cruciferae, on the underside of which the females lay their eggs. It generally pupates on the plants. Distribution: the Palaearctic region.

6 Clouded Yellow *Colias croceus* — 22—28 mm. A migrant species. In Europe the Alps mark the northern limit of its permanent range, beyond that it occurs only as a vagrant. It arrives in central Europe in April and May producing 2 to 3 generations there. Caterpillar feeds on the leaves of Papilionaceae, including clovers and trefoils. In autumn some of the butterflies return south. The remainder die, as do the caterpillars. Distribution: most of Europe, in the north occasionally as far as Sweden and Finland, Asia Minor, the Middle East, north Africa, Canary Islands, Madeira.

7 Brimstone *Gonepteryx rhamni* — 27—30 mm. Appears very early in spring. Male is bright yellow, female greenish white. Caterpillar feeds on buckthorn (*Rhamnus*). Butterflies of the new generation emerge in mid or late summer, but fly only a while, after which they hibernate, to appear again in the early spring and lay their eggs. Distribution: Europe, Asia Minor, the Middle East, eastern Siberia, north Africa.

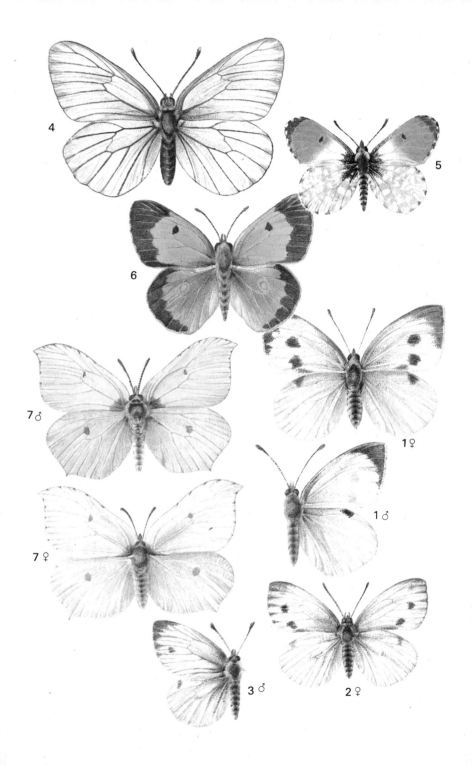

4

5

6

7♂

1♀

7♀

1♂

3♂

2♀

Phylum: **Arthropods — Arthropoda**

Class: **Insects — Insecta**

Order: **Butterflies and moths — Lepidoptera**

Family: **Blues, coppers and hairstreaks — Lycaenidae**

1 Green Hairstreak *Callophrys rubi* — 15—17 mm. Wings coloured a striking green on the underside. Flies in spring from March to June; in Africa there is a second, partial generation. Butterflies found up to mountainous elevations. Caterpillar is polyphagous. The pupa hibernates. Distribution: Europe — far to the north of Scandinavia, Siberia, Asia Minor, north Africa.

2 Small Copper *Lycaena phlaeas* — 14—16 mm. Flies in meadows, fields, gardens, parks and other fairly open places. There are 1 or 2 (in the south more) generations a year. Caterpillars feed on sorrels (*Rumex acetosella, R. acetosa*) and marjoram (*Origanum vulgare*). Distribution: Europe, temperate regions of Asia, Japan, north Africa, Ethiopia, North America.

3 Scarce Copper *Heodes virgaureae* — 18—20 mm. The wings of the male (both fore and hind) are orange with only the edges bordered black, but the females have a much darker patterning. There is only one generation that flies from June to August, from lowland to mountainous elevations, most often in open woodlands, glades, clearings and meadows, where they settle on flowering ragwort (*Senecio), Eupatorium cannabium,* etc. The eggs overwinter. Caterpillars emerge in April and are found on sorrels, their host plant, until June. Distribution: Europe (absent in British Isles, southern Italy, southern Greece, etc.), Asia Minor, central Asia, and the Far East.

4 Sooty Copper *Heodes tityrus* — 15—17 mm. As in many related species, the male and female differ in colour. There are 2 generations (April-May, July-August), in the south also a partial third generation. Common in meadows and fields, found also in the Alps up to elevations of 2,000 metres. Caterpillar feeds on various sorrels, etc. Distribution: Europe (absent in British Isles, many Mediterranean islands and Scandinavia), Transcaucasia, the Altai, Asia Minor.

5 Mazarine Blue *Cyaniris semiargus* — 16—18 mm. The male wings are coloured blue-violet on the upperside; the female wings are brown. Flies from late June to July in forest rides. Occurs also in mountains (in the Alps at about 2,500 metres). Caterpillars feed on clover, *Anthyllis,* melilot, and other plants of the family Papilionaceae. They pupate after hibernation. Distribution: Europe (very rare in Spain and Portugal, extinct in British Isles), temperate parts of Asia, Mongolia, Morocco.

6 Common Blue *Polyommatus icarus* — 14—18 mm. Very abundant. Male and female differ in the coloration of the wings (although the female can be almost as blue as the male). There are 1 (in the north) to 3 (in the south) generations a year, depending on the geographical location. Found from lowlands to mountainous elevations. Caterpillars feed on clover (*Trifolium*), rest-harrow (*Ononis*) and greenwood (*Genista*). Distribution: the Palaearctic region.

6 ♀

5 ♀

5 ♂

6 ♂

1

3a

3 ♀

1a

3 ♂

4

2a

2

Phylum: **Arthropods — Arthropoda**

Class: **Insects — Insecta**

Order: **Butterflies and moths — Lepidoptera**

Family: **Nymphalidae**

1 Purple Emperor *Apatura iris* — 35—40 mm. Very similar to the related *A. ilia*. Found in July and August in damp forests. Both sexes fly round the tree tops, but the males will descend into forest rides to drink from puddles, also visiting dung and carrion. Caterpillars feed on various species of willow, generally sallow. They hibernate. Distribution: Europe, local in Great Britain and Scandinavia, occasional visitor to Finland (absent in the southern Balkans and southern Italy), temperate parts of Asia, Japan.

2 Southern White Admiral *Limenitis reducta* — 26—31 mm. This warmth-loving species is fond of sunny hillsides. There are 1, 2 or 3 generations a year, depending on the location. In central Europe there is only one generation. Caterpillars feed on the leaves of honeysuckle (*Lonicera*). They hibernate and then pupate the following spring. Distribution: chiefly southern and central Europe (absent in the north); 50° N marks its northern limit. Also occurs in the Caucasus, Transcaucasia, and the Middle East.

3 Pearl-bordered Fritillary *Clossiana euphrosyne* — 21—25 mm. Distinguished from the similar *C. selene* by the number and arrangement of the pearly patches on the underside of the wings. In northern Europe and at higher elevations there is 1 generation, in warmer localities 2 (April—June, July—September). Found on flowers in forest clearings, glades and margins. Caterpillars found on violets; they hibernate. Distribution: Europe (absent only on certain Mediterranean islands), temperate parts of Asia, Kamchatka.

4 High Brown Fritillary *Fabriciana adippe* — 29—34 mm. Common from June to August on flowers in glades, clearings, and forest rides. Only 1 generation occurs. Found even in mountains. Caterpillars feed on the leaves of violets. Distribution: Europe (absent in the far north and on certain Mediterranean islands), temperate parts of Asia, Japan, north Africa.

5 Silver-washed Fritillary *Argynnis paphia* — 33—38 mm. Most plentiful in July and August on flowering thistles and blackberry blossoms in clearings, forest rides, forest margins, etc. Wings of male are rufous-brown with black pattern on the upper side. The females are similar, though slightly lighter in tint, and lack the 3—4 dark 'scent-brand' stripes of the male fore wing. There are silvery bands on the underside. In the Mediterranean islands (Sardinia, Corsica, Elba, etc.) there exists a form with reduced silver bands. This butterfly also has an alternative colour form in the female, the dark greenish-grey f. *valesina*. Eggs are laid chiefly on the trunks of pine and spruce trees, sometimes also on violets, on which the caterpillars feed. Caterpillars hibernate and then pupate in May or June. Distribution: Europe (absent in the northern part of Great Britain, in northern Scandinavia and southern Spain), Algeria, temperate parts of Asia, east to Korea and Japan.

164

Phylum: **Arthropods — Arthropoda**

Class: **Insects — Insecta**

Order: **Butterflies and moths — Lepidoptera**

Family: **Nymphalidae**

1 Painted Lady *Cynthia cardui* — 27—31 mm. Flies in dry meadows, steppes and fields, avoids forests, often known as *Vanessa cardui*. A migrant that arrives in central Europe from the south in early April. Progeny of this generation return south again in autumn. Migration of this butterfly has been widely studied, particularly in Great Britain. Caterpillar feeds chiefly on nettle and thistles. Distribution: almost worldwide, absent only in South America.

2 Red Admiral *Vanessa atalanta* — 27—30 mm. Found on flowers in forest margins, clearings, meadows, parks and gardens from spring to autumn. In late summer found also on over-ripe fruit where it sucks the sweet juice. Flies to central Europe from the south. North of the Alps it sometimes hibernates but most individuals die. Caterpillars generally feed on nettles. Distribution: Europe (absent in northern Scandinavia), Asia Minor, north Africa, North and Central America.

3 Camberwell Beauty *Nymphalis antiopa* — 35—45 mm. Butterflies emerge after hibernation very early in spring. Progeny of this generation on the wing from June to autumn. This large and beautiful nymphalid flies in sunny forest margins, clearings, forest rides, round water; it also visits gardens and is found even in mountains. Caterpillars feed on the leaves of willow, birch, elm, poplar, etc. Distribution: Europe (except southern Spain, the Mediterranean islands and Ireland — vagrant only in Great Britain), temperate parts of Asia, North America.

4 Large Tortoiseshell *Nymphalis polychloros* — 29—33 mm. Butterflies emerge from their winter shelters very early in spring. Their progeny fly from June into broadleaved forests, parks and gardens, settling on flowers and trees oozing sap. Caterpillars feed on the leaves of various broadleaved trees. Distribution: Europe (absent in Ireland, much of Great Britain and northern Scandinavia), Asia Minor, the Himalayas, north Africa.

5 Small Tortoiseshell *Aglais urticae* — 23—28 mm. Emerges from its winter shelters (caves, cellars, attics and outbuildings) in March. Progeny of this generation are on the wing from June and sometimes even on fine October days. Found from lowland to mountain elevations in clearings, meadows, forest margins, parks and fields. Caterpillar feeds on nettles. Distribution: Europe, temperate regions of Asia, to Japan.

6 Peacock Butterfly *Inachis io* — 27—35 mm. Emerges from its winter shelter in spring and basks in the sun. Offspring from this hibernating generation fly from July to September. Caterpillar feeds on nettles. Distribution: Europe (absent in northern Scandinavia), temperate parts of Asia, to Japan.

7 Comma Butterfly *Polygonia c-album* — 22—25 mm. White pattern on the underside of the hind wings resembles the letter 'C'. Butterflies hibernate and fly from March. Caterpillar feeds on nettles, black and red currant, hops, elm, and other plants. Distribution: Europe (absent in northern Scandinavia and northern part of Great Britain), temperate parts of Asia, China, Japan, north Africa.

Phylum: **Arthropods — Arthropoda**

Class: **Insects — Insecta**

Order: **Butterflies and moths — Lepidoptera**

Family: **Browns — Satyridae**

1 Marbled White *Melanargia galathea* — 23—28 mm. Wings whitish or yellowish with variable dark bands and patches. There are many colour forms and geographic races. The butterflies fly in June and July, sometimes also in August, settling on field scabious in forest margins and forest rides, on shrub-covered hillsides and railway embankments. Eggs are laid in flight or freely on plants. The caterpillars feed on grasses. They hibernate and then pupate in May or June. Distribution: Europe (except Scandinavia, northern Germany, Ireland and northern parts of Great Britain), the Caucasus, northern Iran, north Africa.

2 Woodland Ringlet *Erebia medusa* — 23—24 mm. Flies in May and June (in mountains even later), in glades and clearings up to elevations of 2,500 metres. Caterpillars feed on grasses. They hibernate and then pupate the following spring. Distribution: Europe (absent in the north, British Isles, southwest and much of Italy), Asia Minor.

3 Meadow Brown *Maniola jurtina* — 22—28 mm. Flies from June to August in lowlands and mountains, in meadows, fields, forest margins and clearings. Caterpillars feed on grasses; they hibernate. Distribution: Europe (except the far north), Asia Minor, the Middle East, north Africa.

4 Speckled Wood *Pararge aegeria* — 22—25 mm. Flies along forest margins, forest rides, and in clearings from lowlands to mountainous elevations. There are several geographical races (in Great Britain, for instance, ssp. *tircis*). Caterpillars feed on grasses. Distribution: Europe (except northern Scandinavia), Asia Minor, central Asia, north Africa.

Family: **Lasiocampidae**

5 Lackey Moth *Malacosoma neustria* — 13—20 mm. Flies from June to August in broadleaved woods and fruit orchards. Eggs are laid in dense rings round slender twigs. Caterpillars feed on the leaves of various trees. Distribution: the Palaearctic region (except the northern part).

6 Oak Eggar *Lasiocampa quercus* — 26—37 mm. There are several colour forms. Flies in oak and mixed woodlands or over heaths and moors, mostly during July and August. Caterpillar or pupa hibernates, some individuals even doing both, in successive years, so taking two years to complete development. Distribution: southern and central Europe (including British Isles), Asia Minor, Transcaucasia, Siberia.

7 Pine Lappet Moth *Dendrolimus pini* — 25—36 mm. Colouring ranges from light to dark. Flies from late June to August in pine forests. Female always lays eggs in batches of about 50 on the bark of pine branches, only occasionally on the trunk or needles. Development takes 1 or 2 years. Distribution: much of Europe, China, Japan.

Phylum: **Arthropods — Arthropoda**

Class: **Insects — Insecta**

Order: **Butterflies and moths — Lepidoptera**

Family: **Lemoniidae**

1 *Lemonia dumi* — 25—29 mm. Flies from August till November at the edges of forests or in meadows. Eggs are whitish and speckled black. Caterpillars feed on various Compositae. They are brown, hairy and have black, elongate patches on the sides of the body. They grow to a length of 60—70 mm and they pupate either under fallen leaves or in the ground. Distribution: from the Balkans to southern Scandinavia, the Urals.

Family: **Saturniidae**

2 Great Peacock Moth *Saturnia pyri* — 60—72 mm. Largest European moth. Coloration rather variable. Male distinguished from the female by the pectinate antennae. On the wing at night in April and May in vineyards, fruit orchards and sometimes in parks. Caterpillar differs in colour at the various stages of its development. It is found on fruit trees and on ash. It grows to a length of 120 mm and then pupates either in the forks of branches or on the ground. The pupa hibernates. Distribution: southern Europe (central Europe marks its northern limit — absent in British Isles), Asia Minor, the Middle East.

3 Emperor Moth *Saturnia pavonia* — 28—40 mm. The wings of the female are all similar in colour; the male has yellow-orange hind wings and pectinate antennae. May hybridise with related species. On the wing from April to June, males even on sunny days. Caterpillars found from May to August chiefly on blackthorn, rose, blueberry, raspberry, willow and heather. They grow to a length of about 60 mm and then pupate inside a brownish or whitish cocoon. Distribution: all Europe, the palaearctic part of Asia.

Family: **Drepanidae**

4 Pebble Hooktip *Drepana falcataria* — 16—18 mm. Flies from spring until August in deciduous groves, clearings, heaths and alongside streams. In the north there is 1 generation (in May and June), in the south also a second (in July and August). Caterpillars feed on the leaves of alder and birch. They grow to a length of 25—30 mm. The pupa hibernates. Distribution: Europe, north as far as Scandinavia.

Family: **Thyatiridae**

5 Peach Blossom *Thyatira batis* — 18—19 mm. Readily identified by the pink patches on the wings. Flies from May to July in clearings, forest margins, gardens and parks. There are 1 or 2 generations. Caterpillars feed on raspberry and blackberry. Distribution: Europe to Scandinavia, Finland, Estonia, Transcaucasia, Siberia, Korea, western China, Japan, northern India.

170

1

2

3 ♀

3 ♂

4

5

Phylum: **Arthropods — Arthropoda**

Class: **Insects — Insecta**

Order: **Butterflies and moths — Lepidoptera**

Family: **Geometridae**

1 Large Emerald *Geometra papilionaria* — 21—29 mm. Flies from June to August at the edges of broadleaved or mixed woodlands. Caterpillars feed on birch, hazel, alder, beech, mountain ash. Distribution: central and northern Europe, Asia Minor, Siberia, Japan.

2 Lace Border *Scopula ornata* — 11—12 mm. Found from April to August, in 2 or 3 generations, in dry localities. Caterpillars feed on thyme (*Thymus*), marjoram (*Origanum*), speedwell (*Veronica*), yarrow (*Achillea*), etc. Distribution: Europe from the south to Scandinavia, Asia, the Amur region, north Africa.

3 Riband Wave *Idaea aversata* — 14—15 mm. The typical form has a broad dark band on the wings, but this is absent in f. *spoliata* shown in the illustration. As in many other geometrids there are 2 generations, and the moth is on the wing from May to September in open woodlands and clearings. Caterpillar is polyphagous and able to go without food for a long time. Distribution: Europe (except the far north and certain regions on the Iberian Peninsula), Transcaucasia, Asia Minor, the Middle East.

4 Treble Bar *Aplocera plagiata* — 18—23 mm. Found on dry and warm hillsides, in steppes and forest margins in 2 generations, from May to October. Locally abundant. Caterpillar feeds on St. John's Wort (*Hypericum perforatum*). Distribution: much of the Palaearctic region.

5 Clouded Border *Lomaspilis marginata* — 12—14 mm. Variable patterning on the wings. One, sometimes also a partial second, generation occurs from April to August. Found in forest margins, valley meadows, along rivers, etc. Caterpillars feed on leaves of various willows, sallow, hazel, aspen, birch, etc. Distribution: Europe, central Asia, southeastern Siberia.

6 Mottled Umber Moth *Erannis defoliaria* — 22—26 mm. There are several colour forms. On the wing from late September to early December in forests and gardens. Caterpillars feed on the leaves of various trees. Distribution: from northern Italy to southern Scandinavia, Transcaucasia.

7 Peppered Moth *Biston betularia* — 21—32 mm. Best known and often most abundant is the almost black form *carbonaria* found in the vicinity of industrial cities. Another form — *ochrearia* — has ochre wings. Flies at night in May and June. Caterpillars feed on the leaves of oak, poplar, elm, pear, rose, blackthorn, etc. Distribution: Eurasia.

8 Bordered White Moth *Bupalus piniaria* — 19—22 mm. Found in pine and mixed coniferous forests. On the wing from April to July. From time to time the caterpillars are destructive to pine stands. The pupa hibernates. Distribution: northern and central Europe, Transcaucasia, Siberia.

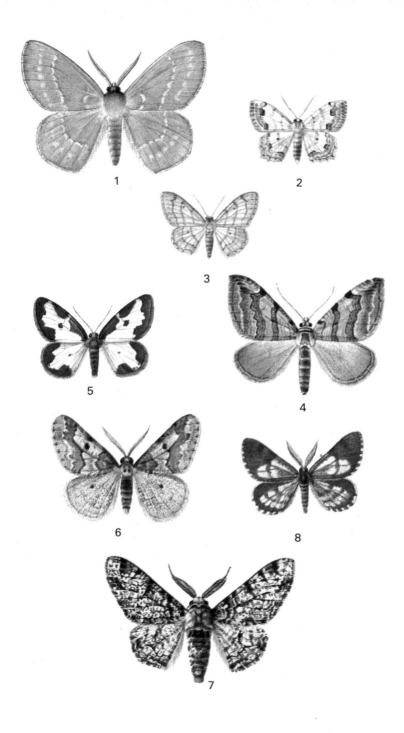

Phylum: **Arthropods — Arthropoda**

Class: **Insects — Insecta**

Order: **Butterflies and moths — Lepidoptera**

Family: **Hawk moths — Sphingidae**

1 Eyed Hawk *Smerinthus ocellatus* — 33—44 mm. Has a striking dark-pupilled and dark-bordered eye-spot on each hind wing. Found in woods and groves, where it flies from late at night until dawn. One generation, on the wing from May to July (in the south a second generation on the wing until October). Caterpillars feed on the leaves of willow, poplar, lime, blackthorn and various fruit trees. They reach a length of 90 mm by autumn and then pupate in the ground. Pupa is a glossy, dark brownish-red. Distribution: most of Europe, Transcaucasia, Asia Minor.

2 Lime Hawk *Mimas tiliae* — 30—40 mm. Colour varies from greenish to reddish-brown to dark olive. The broad band on the fore wings may also be divided into two separate patches. Locally still common. In central Europe there is 1 generation from April to July, in the south a second generation from August to October. Found in lime-tree avenues, forest margins and parks up to mountainous elevations. Eggs are greenish. Caterpillars feed chiefly on the leaves of lime and also other trees (ash, birch, oak). When full-grown they burrow in the ground where they pupate in a sturdy cell. The pupa hibernates. Distribution: much of the Palaearctic region.

3 Death's Head Hawk *Acherontia atropos* — 45—60 mm. Named after Atropos, eldest of the three fates in Greek mythology. The common name in various languages refers to the startling pattern on the thorax which resembles a human skull. Native to the tropics. Commonly migrates to southern Europe but is a less frequent visitor to central Europe. Will fly into a lighted room. Also visits beehives to taste honey. Females found in potato fields where they lay their eggs on the leaves of potato plants (also on other Solanaceae) on which the caterpillar feeds. In autumn, when fully grown, the caterpillar burrows into the ground where it pupates in a large earthen cell. Many pupae do not survive the winter. Distribution: Africa, Madagascar. Flies far to the north of Europe, to Transcaucasia, Iran, etc.

4 Pine Hawk *Hyloicus pinastri* — 33—45 mm. Fore wings greyish with brownish patches and three dark streaks. Pattern is variable and the streaks may be absent. In the frequent melanistic individuals the wings are completely dark. Found in pine forests, where the caterpillars feed on pine needles. They pupate at the base of the trunk, either in the ground or on the surface. Distribution: temperate parts of Eurasia.

5 Bedstraw Hawk *Hyles gallii* — 32—35 mm. There are usually 2 generations (May—June, August—October). Coloration slightly resembles that of the Spurge Hawk, with which it sometimes hybridises. Caterpillars are polyphagous but are partial to bedstraw (*Gallium*). Distribution: temperate regions of Eurasia (very occasionally visits the British Isles), and the Nearctic region.

1

2

4

5

3

Phylum: **Arthropods — Arthropoda**

Class: **Insects — Insecta**

Order: **Butterflies and moths — Lepidoptera**

Family: **Hawk moths — Sphingidae**

1 Privet Hawk *Sphinx ligustri* — 44—50 mm. Flies at dusk from May, around flowering lilac, where it sucks the nectar. At night is attracted to light; during the day rests on stones or fences. Eggs are pale green. Caterpillar hatches after about 10 days and usually feeds on the leaves of privet (*Ligustrum*), lilac (*Syringa*) or snowberry (*Symphoricarpus*). It rests on the plant with front part of body raised, thus resembling a sphinx. After 4—6 weeks it reaches a length of 10—12 cm and burrows in the ground, where it pupates. The pupa hibernates. Distribution: Europe (except the arctic regions and Ireland), temperate parts of Asia.

2 Elephant Hawk *Deilephila elpenor* — 25—32 mm. On the wing from May to June, a partial second generation in August, in the late evening and at night round flowering petunia, phlox, soapwort, viper's bugloss, etc. It sucks the nectar in flight. May also be attracted to lepidopterist's 'sugar'. Female lays about 100 glossy green eggs, singly on the underside of the foodplants, chiefly great hairy willow-herb, bedstraw, grapevine, etc. The full-grown larva measures 7—8 cm. It changes into a yellow-brown, dark-spotted pupa. Distribution: the Palaearctic region.

3 Narrow-bordered Bee Hawk *Hemaris tityus* — 19—21 mm. Wings are transparent. Flies by day, chiefly around mid-day, in meadows and on hillsides where there are plenty of flowers. 1 or 2 generations a year (May—June, July—August). Caterpillars generally found on field scabious (*Knautia*) or scabious (*Scabiosa*). Distribution: Europe (except the far north), the Altai.

Family: **Prominents — Notodontidae**

4 Puss Moth *Cerura vinula* — 28—36 mm. Found from late April to July in meadows, along streams, and in parks. In the north (Scandinavia) there are dark-coloured forms. The striking, large caterpillar (which has whip-lash tails and a mask-like 'face') grows to a length of 7—8 cm. It feeds on the leaves of willow, poplar and aspen and pupates in a sturdy cocoon which is reinforced with particles of wood and bark. The pupa hibernates. Distribution: the Palaearctic region.

5 Buff-tip Moth *Phalera bucephala* — 24—32 mm. Resembles *P. bucephaloides,* which, however, has a larger yellow spot at the apex of the fore wings and another striking yellow spot on the costa. One generation (in the south two), on the wing in woods and parks. Caterpillar feeds on broadleaved trees (lime, willow, poplar, birch, alder, oak etc.).Grows to a length of about 60 mm and then pupates in the ground. The pupa hibernates. Distribution: Europe (except the far north), Asia Minor, Siberia, northeast Africa.

Family: **Thaumetopoeidae**

6 European Processionary Moth *Thaumetopoea processionea* — 13—18 mm. Found in oak woods. On the wing mostly in July and August. Eggs overwinter. Caterpillars emerge in spring and live communally in nests on branches. At night they leave the nest and crawl in rows over trunks and branches to feed on the leaves. Distribution: most of central and southern Europe (absent in British Isles), Asia Minor.

Phylum: **Arthropods** — **Arthropoda**

Class: **Insects** — **Insecta**

Order: **Butterflies and moths** — **Lepidoptera**

Family: **Tussock moths** — **Lymantriidae**

1 Pale Tussock Moth *Dasychira pudibunda* — 20—29 mm. Fore wings greyish with darker, variable pattern. Flies from April to June (or July) on the edges of broadleaved forests, in parks and gardens. Caterpillars found from July to October on various broadleaved trees and shrubs. In autumn they pupate in a cocoon reinforced with caterpillar hairs. The pupa hibernates. Distribution: chiefly central and western Europe, Transcaucasia, Siberia and as far east as Japan.

2 Vapourer Moth *Orgyia antiqua* — 11—15 mm. Male winged, female stout with only wing stumps. In the north 1 generation (on the wing in July and August), southward 2 or 3 generations (July—October). Caterpillars feed on various broadleaved trees and shrubs (oak, beech, sallow, fruit trees). They grow to a length of 30 mm. Distribution: much of Europe, Transcaucasia, Siberia, northern China, Japan, North America.

3 Brown-tail Moth *Euproctis chrysorrhoea* — 17—22 mm. Both male and female usually white-winged, but sometimes the fore wings are marked with small black dots. On the wing from June to September, in gardens and other places. Eggs are laid on the top and underside of leaves and on branches of broadleaved trees. The young caterpillars live communally on branches in fairly large nests woven of silk fibres. There they hibernate and continue their development in spring. They pupate in a loose cocoon. Distribution: Europe north to Sweden and Lithuania, the Caucasus, Transcaucasia, Asia Minor, north Africa.

4 White Satin Moth *Leucoma salicis* — 22—26 mm. Found in June and July in poplar avenues, parks and along streams bordered by poplars and willows on which the caterpillars feed. Distribution: Europe, Asia Minor, central Asia, Siberia, north Africa.

5 Black Arches Moth *Lymantria monacha* — 19—27 mm. Hind wings almost a uniform brown, fore wings richly patterned with dark variable markings. Melanistic forms are quite common. Adults occur from June to September, chiefly in conifer stands, sometimes also in broadleaved woods. Caterpillars may occur in vast numbers and cause catastrophic damage. Nowadays, however, such calamities are rare and in many places this moth has become extinct. Distribution: from the west across central Europe to the east, Transcaucasia, Siberia, and Japan.

6 Gipsy Moth *Lymantria dispar* — 18—36 mm. Found in summer in broadleaved forests, sometimes also in gardens. Female covers the eggs with a layer of hairs, the whole slightly resembling a tree fungus. Caterpillars feed on the leaves of various trees. Distribution: much of Europe (now extinct in British Isles), Transcaucasia, Siberia, north Africa, North America (introduced in 1868 and now a pest in certain places).

Phylum: **Arthropods — Arthropoda**

Class: **Insects — Insecta**

Order: **Butterflies and moths — Lepidoptera**

Family: **Tiger moths — Arctiidae**

1 Speckled Footman *Coscinia cribraria* — 15—21 mm. On the wing from June to August over heaths and in pinewood clearings. Caterpillar feeds on small plants, e. g. dandelion, plantain, etc. Distribution: Europe, temperate parts of Asia.

2 *Rhyparia purpurata* — 20—26 mm. There are several forms differing in the colour of the hind wings (red, yellow or orange, always with dark spots) and patterning of the fore wings. On the wing in June and July in damp localities. Eggs are small and yellowish. Caterpillar feeds on various herbs (bedstraw) and woody plants (heather), etc. It grows to a length of about 45 mm, hibernates and then pupates. Distribution: Europe (less common in the west, absent in British Isles), Asia Minor, northern Asia, Transcaucasia, Japan.

3 Garden Tiger *Arctia caja* — 26—37 mm. Several colour forms occur. Fore wings are yellowish-white to ochre with a dark pattern (may be yellow-brown), hind wings are vermilion or ochre with dark patches. On the wing in July and August, in the south there is a partial second generation. The stout caterpillar, which has long russet hairs, feeds on raspberry, blueberry, heather, blackthorn, and many other plants. Distribution: almost all Europe, Asia Minor, the Middle East, Siberia, Japan, Pamir, North America.

4 Cream-spot Tiger *Arctia villica* — 28—32 mm. Flies in June and July in sunny places. Found in several colour forms. Caterpillars feed on various herbs, deadnettle, yarrow, strawberry, etc. Distribution: Europe (now disappearing in some places), the Middle East.

5 Scarlet Tiger *Callimorpha dominula* — 21—27 mm. Orange spot on each fore wing may vary in size; sometimes it is absent. Flies by day in woodland meadows and near water. Caterpillars feed on deadnettle, nettle, buttercup, forget-me-not, and other plants. Distribution: Europe (absent in some parts of western and northern Europe), the Urals, Caucasus, Transcaucasia.

6 Jersey Tiger *Euplagia quadripunctaria* — 26—30 mm. Found on rocky and stony hillsides and valleys (chiefly with limestone substrate) where it is on the wing in August. Caterpillar is polyphagous, and is the stage which hibernates. Distribution: Europe (except the far north), Asia Minor, the Middle East, western Asia.

7 Cinnabar Moth *Tyria jacobaeae* — 18—21 mm. Named after ragwort (*Senecio jacobaea*), foodplant of the bright yellow and black caterpillars. The larvae can also sometimes be found feeding on the leaves of butterbur and coltsfoot. They pupate in autumn. The pupa hibernates. Adult moths found from July to September, in damp situations. Distribution: Europe, Asia as far as the Altai.

Phylum: **Arthropods — Arthropoda**

Class: **Insects — Insecta**

Order: **Butterflies and moths — Lepidoptera**

Family: **Noctuidae**

1 Turnip Moth *Agrotis segetum* — 16−21 mm. Very variable in size and colouring. Hind wings whitish to greyish, fore wings light grey, light brown, or black-brown with darker pattern. 1 or 2 generations, depending on climatic conditions. On the wing until October and November, in fields and gardens. Female lays several hundred eggs. Caterpillar is polyphagous, found on grasses, vegetables (a pest of turnips and swedes), etc; full-grown it measures up to 50 mm. Distribution: Eurasia, South Africa, North America.

2 Heart and Dart Moth *Agrotis exclamationis* — 17−19 mm. Besides the dark kidney-shaped patch on the fore wing there is another that resembles an exclamation mark (hence its scientific name). Colour varies from pale grey to greyish-black. One or 2 generations. Female lays about 800 eggs. Caterpillar is polyphagous, often found on grasses. Distribution: Eurasia.

3 Large Yellow Underwing *Noctua pronuba* — 26−29 mm. Striking orange-yellow hind wings edged with a broad dark band. One generation in the north, 2−3 farther south. Adult moths sometimes found as late as early November. Female lays several hundred eggs in batches on small plants. Caterpillar is polyphagous, grows to a length of 50−60 mm. Distribution: the Palaearctic region.

4 Cabbage Moth *Mamestra brassicae* — 19−23 mm. Very common in fields and gardens. Flies at night. Caterpillars feed on vegetables, including peas, lettuce and cabbage, and may cause damage; they are also recorded from oak and birch. Distribution: Eurasia.

5 Grey Dagger Moth *Acronicta psi* — 16−21 mm. Pattern on the fore wings resembles the Greek letter 'psi', hence the scientific name. Very common. Occurs in 1 or 2 generations, until September. Caterpillars feed on the leaves of various trees and shrubs. Distribution: All Eurasia except the north.

6 Dark Arches *Apamea monoglypha* — 22−26 mm. Below the margin of the fore wings is a light pattern with a clearly evident letter 'W'. On the wing from June to September. Caterpillars found on various grasses, sometimes also on cereals. Distribution: Europe (absent in the north), Asia Minor, Siberia.

7 Silver Y Moth *Autographa gamma* — 17−21 mm. Markings on the fore wings resemble the Greek letter 'gamma'. Common from spring to November in fields, meadows and gardens. Flies by day and at night. Adult moths from the south and southeast arrive in central Europe by spring. There they produce 1 or 2 generations and these moths return south in summer and early autumn. Caterpillar is polyphagous; when very numerous it may cause damage to certain cultivated plants. Distribution: the Palaearctic and Nearctic region, Ethiopia.

8 Dark Crimson Underwing *Catocala sponsa* — 30−33 mm. Found chiefly in oak woods, but also visits parks and gardens. On the wing from late July to September. Caterpillar feeds on the leaves of oak. It grows to a length of 70 mm. Distribution: Europe.

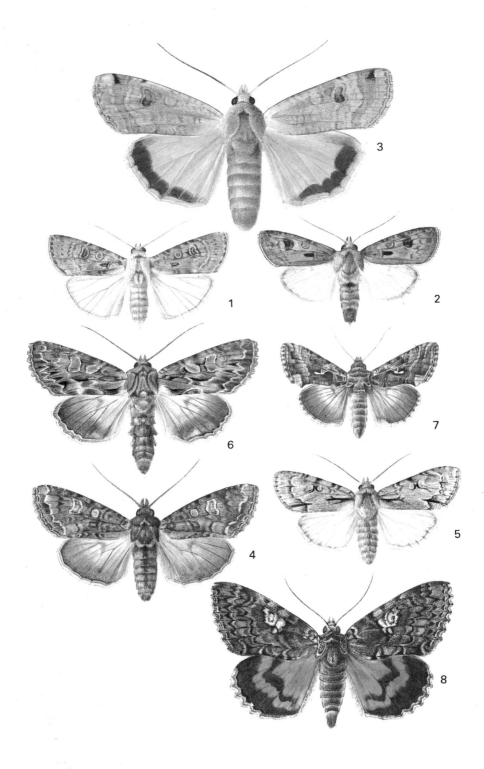

Phylum: **Arthropods — Arthropoda**

Class: **Insects — Insecta**

Order: **Scorpion flies — Mecoptera**

Family: **Panorpidae**

1 Scorpion Fly *Panorpa communis* – Length 20 mm, wingspan 25 – 30 mm. Resembles several other species. As in other species male has pincers-like clasping organ at the tip of the abdomen. Found in large numbers from spring to autumn, in waterside vegetation and forest undergrowth. Adults and larvae are predaceous. Distribution: Europe.

Order: **Two-winged flies — Diptera**

Family: **Crane flies — Tipulidae**

2 Daddy Longlegs *Tipula oleracea* — Length 15–23 mm. There are 2 generations a year. Eggs are laid in the ground where the larval stage is passed. Larvae feed on plant roots, especially of grasses, and pupate in the ground. Distribution: Europe, north to central Scandinavia, more plentiful in western Europe, north Africa, North America (introduced).

Family: **Mosquitoes — Culicidae**

3 *Aedes vexans* — Length 4 mm. One of the commonest of mosquitoes. Found from May to autumn. Visits houses and cattle-sheds. Females are persistent blood-suckers. There are several generations a year. Larvae found in ponds, pools, puddles, etc. Distribution: Eurasia and North America, where it transmits the St Louis encephalitis virus.

Family: **Gall-midges — Cecidomyidae**

4 *Mikiola fagi* — Length 4–5 mm. An inconspicuous, small fly, on the wing in March and April. Best known for the galls produced by the larvae and located on the upper side of beech leaves. They are coloured green, yellowish and reddish, about 4–12 mm long and shaped like small skittles. Distribution: Europe.

Family: **Soldier flies — Stratiomyidae**

5 *Stratiomys chamaeleon* — Length 14–15.5 mm. Found in marshes, damp meadows and hedgerows, where it visits various flowering plants. Eggs are laid on the underside of the leaves of aquatic plants. Larvae live in water, and are predaceous. Distribution: central and southern Europe, Transcaucasia, Siberia.

Family: **Horse flies — Tabanidae**

6 *Tabanus bromius* — Length 11.5–16 mm. Similar to many other species. Female distinguished by the characteristic pattern on the frons between the eyes. In the male the eyes are close together and there is no pattern. Adults very abundant from June to August in meadows near water. Female sucks the blood of animals and Man, male feeds on plant juices. Distribution: Europe.

7 Cleg *Haematopota pluvialis* — Length 8–12 mm. Flies from spring to autumn on pathways and in forests. Female attacks warm-blooded animals (including Man) and sucks their blood. It is particularly aggressive before a storm. Found in many areas, including the Alps and Tatras. Distribution: the Palaearctic region.

8 *Chrysops caecutiens* — Length 7.5–11 mm. Distinguished from other species by the markings on the abdomen. Common in summer in damp localities. Female sucks the blood of Man, cattle and horses. Distribution: Europe, Siberia.

184

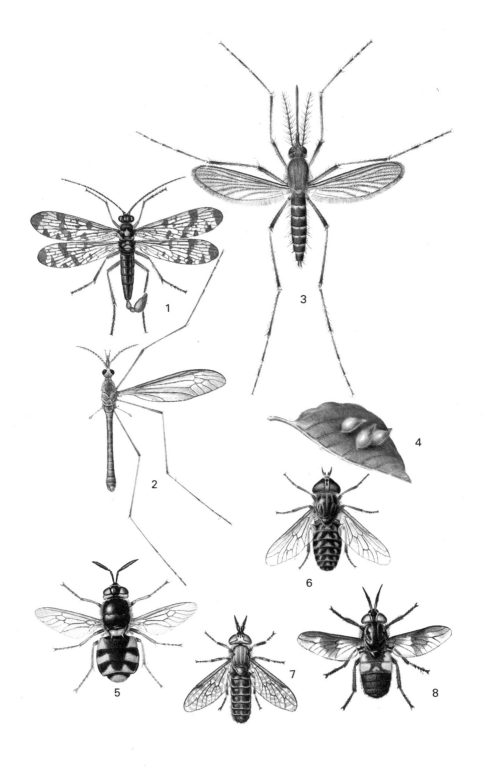

Phylum: **Arthropods — Arthropoda**

Class: **Insects — Insecta**

Order: **Two-winged flies — Diptera**

Family: **Snipe flies — Rhagionidae**

1 *Rhagio scolopacea.* Length 13—18 mm. It and related species somewhat resemble scorpion flies in general appearance. Often rests on logs and tree trunks with head turned towards the ground and front part of the body raised. Adults found from May to August. Larvae live in the ground. They feed on various insects and decaying matter. Distribution: most of Europe.

Family: **Robber flies — Asilidae**

2 *Asilus crabroniformis* — Length 16—30 mm. Found from June to September in forests, where it hunts various insects. It pierces its victims and sucks their juices. Distribution: the Palaearctic region.

3 *Laphria flava* — Length 16—25 mm. Waits for arrival of prey on logs or plants. Adults most plentiful in June and July. Distribution: all Europe.

Family: **Bee flies — Bombyliidae**

4 *Bombylius major* — Length 8—13 mm. Somewhat resembles a small bumblebee. On the wing in early spring, April and May, on flowering plants, where it sucks the nectar. An excellent flier, with strikingly long proboscis. Larvae are parasites in the nests of certain solitary bees, e. g. of the genera *Andrena, Colletes,* etc. Distribution: the Palaearctic and Nearctic regions.

Family: **Hover flies — Syrphidae**

5 Drone Fly *Eristalis tenax* — Length 15—19 mm. With its robust body and dark colouring it resembles a bee, for which it is often mistaken. Flies from spring until late autumn; settles on flowers. Larvae live in dung heaps, foul water, cess pools, decaying carcasses, etc. The 'rat-tailed maggot' larva is grey, plump, with a 20—30 mm long breathing tube at the hind end. Distribution: cosmopolitan.

6 *Myiatropa florea* — Length 12—16 mm. Many individuals have distinctive markings on the thorax that somewhat resemble the 'skull' on the thorax of the Death's Head Hawk Moth. In others these markings are not particularly distinct. Common on flowers throughout almost the entire growing season. Distribution: much of the Palaearctic region.

7 *Volucella pellucens* — Length 15—16 mm. Visits various flowers from April to October. Larval development takes place in the nests of the Common Wasp and German Wasp. In autumn, when the wasp colony dies, the larva burrows in the ground, where it hibernates and then pupates in spring. Distribution: Eurasia.

8 *Scaeva pyrastri* — Length 14—19 mm. Resembles several other species, chiefly *S. selenitica,* for which it might easily be mistaken in the wild. Partial to flowering plants of the carrot family. Found from lowlands to mountainous elevations. Distribution: much of Eurasia, north Africa and North America.

9 Hover Fly *Episyrphus balteatus* — Length 11—12 mm. Flies in various habitats in gardens, parks and forests. Very abundant. Settles on flowers and pollinates them. Distribution: the Palaearctic and Austro-oriental regions.

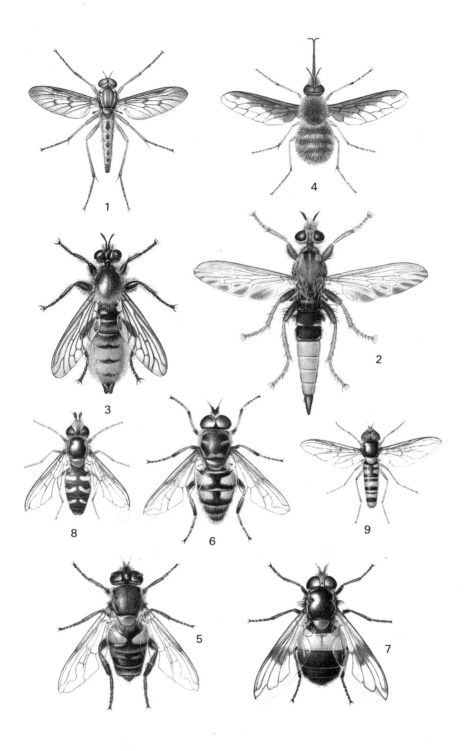

Phylum: **Arthropods — Arthropoda**

Class: **Insects — Insecta**

Order: **Two-winged flies — Diptera**

Family: **Tephritidae**

1 *Rhagoletis cerasi* — Length 3.5—5 mm. A well-known fly of cherry orchards and groves. Found from May, often until July. Larva develops in the cherry fruit and gradually tunnels its way to the pip. It grows to a length of about 6 mm, leaves the fruit and burrows in the ground where it pupates. The pupa hibernates. One of the methods of avoiding damage by the larva is timely harvesting of the fruit. Distribution: Europe (absent in British Isles), the Caucasus.

Family: **Fruit-flies — Drosophilidae**

2 Vinegar-fly *Drosophila melanogaster* — Length 2 mm. Very similar to related species. Found in their company in fields, gardens and households, round rotting refuse, fruit juices, beer, bottles of wine, etc. This species has been much used in genetic experiments. Distribution: worldwide.

Family: **Anthomyidae**

3 Cabbage-root Maggot *Delia brassicae* — Length 5.5—7.5 mm. There are 2—3 generations a year. The pupa hibernates. Adults emerge in spring. Eggs are laid in batches on the ground as well as on wild and cultivated cruciferous plants. Larvae live in the ground, feed on the roots and finally tunnel into the host plant, where they pupate. Destructive of crops. Distribution: Europe, North America.

Family: **Dung-flies — Scatophagidae**

4 Yellow Dung-fly *Scatophaga stercorarium* — Length 9—11 mm. Sexes differ in colour. Male is covered with honey-coloured hairs, females with greyish-green hairs. Found on dung heaps and round excrement, from lowlands to mountainous elevations. Feeds on various insects. Larvae found in dung, on which they feed. Distribution: the Palaearctic regions.

Family: **Muscidae**

5 Common House-fly *Musca domestica* — Length 7—9 mm. Adult hibernates and emerges in spring. A synanthropic species (found in the vicinity of Man), which unlike many other such flies does not bite. Feeds on liquid food of various kinds. Female lays about 150 eggs, usually on foul-smelling animal and vegetable matter, in which the larval stage is passed. Larva pupates in the ground. Because there are several generations a year it is a plentiful and often troublesome species, spreading bacteria and other disease organisms. Distribution: worldwide.

6 Stable-fly *Stomoxys calcitrans* — Length 5.5—7 mm. Found chiefly in the country. Unlike the Common House-fly, it bites severely; the piercing mouthparts are clearly visible. Feeds on the blood of various mammals, including Man. Eggs are laid in excrement. There are many generations a year, increasing in number the farther south the locality. Distribution: cosmopolitan.

7 Lesser House-fly *Fannia canicularis* — Length 5—7 mm. Characteristically flies around hanging lamps inside houses. Very plentiful from spring until winter. Distribution: worldwide.

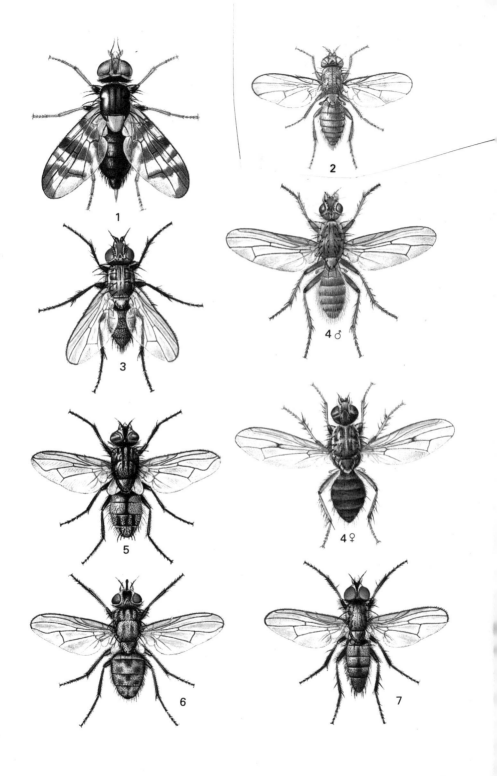

1

2

3

4 ♂

4 ♀

5

6

7

Phylum: **Arthropods — Arthropoda**

Class: **Insects — Insecta**

Order: **Two-winged flies — Diptera**

Family: **Bot-flies — Gasterophilidae**

1 Common Bot-fly *Gasterophilus intestinalis* — Length 12—15 mm. Parasite of horses and donkeys. Female lays several hundred eggs on the host's body, usually on the legs. When the animal licks its skin the eggs are transferred to the tongue where the larvae soon emerge. At first they remain on the tongue but then continue their growth in the stomach, passing out of the body with the faeces. The larva pupates either in the excrement or in the ground. Distribution: cosmopolitan.

Family: **Louse-flies — Hippoboscidae**

2 Deer-fly *Lipoptena cervi* — Length 5.2—5.8 mm. Found not only on red deer, as might be presumed from its scientific name, but also on roe deer, badgers and even Man. It is a parasite that sucks blood. When it first emerges it has two wings (wing measures about 6 mm), but these are shed as soon as it finds a host. Distribution: the Palaearctic region.

Family: **Blow-flies — Calliphoridae**

3 *Calliphora vicina* — Length 6—13 mm. Common chiefly in the neighbourhood of Man. Found on decaying animal matter. Female lays about 600 eggs on dead flesh. Larvae hatch shortly after and burrow inside the dead body, on which they feed. There they are often attacked by the predaceous larvae of other insects, e. g. Staphylinidae. Distribution: almost worldwide.

4 *Lucilia caesar* — Length 6—11 mm. Has metallic greenish-gold colouring, the same as several related and similar species. Flies from spring until late autumn. Very abundant around human dwellings. Settles on excrements, often also on flowers where is sucks nectar. Larvae found in decaying matter. Distribution: much of the Palaearctic region.

Family: **Sarcophagidae**

5 Flesh-fly *Sarcophaga carnaria* — Length 13—15 mm. Has striking chequer-board markings, which are also found in related species. Very common. Often found on flowers. Eggs are often dropped from a height into meat or decaying flesh, on which the larvae hatch and feed to complete their development. Distribution: Europe, Africa.

Family: **Tachinidae**

6 *Tachina fera* — Length 11—14 mm. Larvae are internal parasites of the caterpillars of the Black Arches Moth and Gipsy Moth. Distribution: the Palaearctic region.

7 *Phryxe vulgaris* — Length 5—8 mm. A beneficial species, as are most tachinids. Adults found on flowers. Larval stage is passed inside the caterpillars of butterflies and moths. Distribution: all Europe.

Family: **Hypodermatidae**

8 Ox Warble-fly *Hypoderma bovis* — Length 13—15 mm. Parasite on cattle. Female lays eggs on the hind quarters and legs of the host's body. Larvae bore inside and live under the skin. Distribution: the Palaearctic and Nearctic regions.

Order: **Fleas — Siphonaptera**

Family: **Pulicidae**

9 Human Flea *Pulex irritans* — Length 2—3,5 mm. Attacks Man as well as certain domestic and wild animals, sucking their blood. Female lays about 400 eggs. Distribution: cosmopolitan.

190

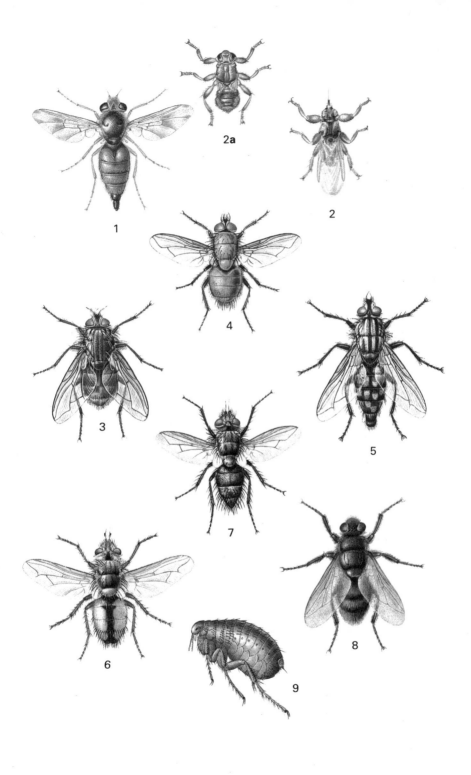

Phylum: **Moss animals — Bryozoa**

Family: **Sea-mats — Bicellariidae**

1 *Bugula neritina* — Height up to 100 mm. Looks more like a branching tuft of marine grass than an animal. Lives in large colonies. All individuals form a shrub-like zoarium (each individual in such a colony is called a zooid). *Bugula* is a marine species found chiefly on the hulls of ships and on buoys, in both shallow as well as deep water. Distribution: Atlantic Ocean, North Sea, English Channel, Mediterranean Sea.

Phylum: **Hemichordata**

Family: **Acorn worms — Ptychoderidae**

2 *Balanoglossus clavigerus* — Length 250 mm. Body elongated, wormlike, coloured yellow-brown. Front part furnished with a so-called 'acorn' — the proboscis. Lives singly in the littoral zone where it forms a U-shaped burrow in the sand, with its head near one end and its posterior near the other. It feeds on detritus mixed with sand and mud. Undigested remnants are eliminated together with sand and piled at the openings of the tunnel. At low tide the presence of these animals is revealed by the openings to the tunnels and by the piles of excrement. Distribution: Atlantic, English Channel, Mediterranean Sea; very abundant in places.

Phylum: **Echinodermata**

Class: **Sea cucumbers — Holothuroidea**

Family: **Holothuriidae**

3 Sea Cucumber *Holothuria tubulosa* — Length 250—350 mm. Body brownish-violet to brownish-red, covered with numerous spines. Found in the Mediterranean Sea at depths of as much as 100 metres. Often occurs in large groups.

Class: **Sea urchins — Echinoidea**

Family: **Echinidae**

4 Common or Edible Sea Urchin *Echinus esculentus* — Body about 160 mm in diameter, somewhat globular, red, studded with a great number of spines. Found along the coast at depths of as much as 50 metres, on rocks and amidst seaweed. Locally very abundant. Distribution: Atlantic Ocean (from Portugal to the North Sea).

Class: **Starfish — Asteroidea**

Family: **Asteriidae**

5 *Astropecten aurantiacus* — Body up to 300 mm in diameter. Upperside orange, underside yellow. Found on sandy sea bottoms at depths of 1—100 metres. Locally abundant. Distribution: Mediterranean Sea and Atlantic north to Portugal.

6 Common Starfish *Asterias rubens* — Body up to 500 mm in diameter, reddish-brown as well as dark violet. There are usually 5 broad arms, sometimes 4—6. Like other starfish it feeds on various molluscs. Very abundant at depths of 0—200 metres. Distribution: western coast of Africa and Europe, from Senegal to Greenland, North America.

Class: **Brittle stars, serpent stars — Ophiuroidea**

Family: **Ophiodermatidae**

7 *Ophioderma longicauda* — Body disc about 25 mm in diameter. Beautifully coloured. Found on rocky shores under stones at depths of 0—70 metres. Locally very abundant. Distribution: Mediterranean Sea and Atlantic north to Biscay.

1

2

4

5

3

7

6

Phylum: **Chordata**

Subphylum: **Vertebrates — Vertebrata**

Class: **Cyclostomes — Cyclostomata**

Order: **Myxiniformes**

Family: **Hagfishes — Myxinidae**

1 Common Atlantic Hag *Myxine glutinosa* — Length 25–40 cm, occasionally up to 50 cm. Body eel-like with atrophied eyes and four fleshy whiskers round the mouth and nostril. Skin smooth. Fin only at the caudal end of the body. A nocturnal species, found at depths of 20–800 metres on muddy bottoms. Feeds on animal life on the bottom but also attacks diseased fish or fish captured in nets, boring into their bodies and devouring the internal organs. The slimy mucus secreted by the skin provides protection against the effects of the digestive juices of the host. Distribution: both coasts of the Atlantic.

Order: **Petromyzoniformes**

Family: **Lampreys — Petromyzonidae**

2 Sea Lamprey *Petromyzon marinus* — Length up to 1 metre. Largest member of this order. A marine species that swims up rivers to spawn. Breeds in the shallow waters of rivers from March to June. Larvae have eyes covered with skin and toothless mouths with two lips; the mouth of adults is funnel-shaped with tiny, horny, rasping teeth and a large tongue that functions like a piston. In the sea adults are parasitic on fish, sucking up their blood and muscle tissues. Distribution: Found along the European coast from Scandinavia to the eastern shores of Italy, rare in the Baltic, absent in the Black Sea. Common also along the coast of North America (a smaller freshwater race is found in large lakes).

3 Wagner's Lamprey *Caspiomyzon wagneri* — Length up to 55 cm. Resembles the preceding species. Distribution: found in the Caspian Sea; during the spawning season swims up the Ural, Terek, Volga, Kura and other rivers. Spawns in sandy parts of river beds from September to November.

4 Danube Lamprey *Eudontomyzon danfordi* — Length 20–30 cm. A freshwater species parasitic on fish, attaching itself to their bodies with its suctorial mouth and feeding on their blood and muscles. Distribution: found in tributaries of the Danube and in rivers flowing south of the Danube into the Black Sea; absent from the mainstream of the Danube. Breeds in the shallow waters of rivers and streams.

5 Lampern *Lampetra fluviatilis* — Length 40 cm. Between September and November leaves the sea and swims far up rivers to their upper reaches. Spawning takes place from February to May; during migration it does not feed and after spawning dies. Larval stage lasts 2–3 years. Larvae live in the mud deposits on the bottoms of streams in calm backwaters and feed on organic matter. Distribution: abundant along the European coast from southern Norway to southern Europe; a freshwater form is found in Lake Ladoga and Lake Onega.

6 Brook Lamprey *Lampetra planeri* — Length 15–19 cm. A non-parasitic, freshwater species. Breeds from May to June in mountain streams. During the spawning season it excavates circular holes in the bottom of which the eggs are laid by the female while anchoring to stones with her suctorial mouth. These are fertilized by the male who twines himself round the female's body. After spawning the adults die. The larva lives 4–5 years in sandy-mud deposits, feeding on detritus and diatoms. Distribution: this species inhabits rivers flowing into the North and Baltic Seas; also found in northeastern Italy and Albania.

194

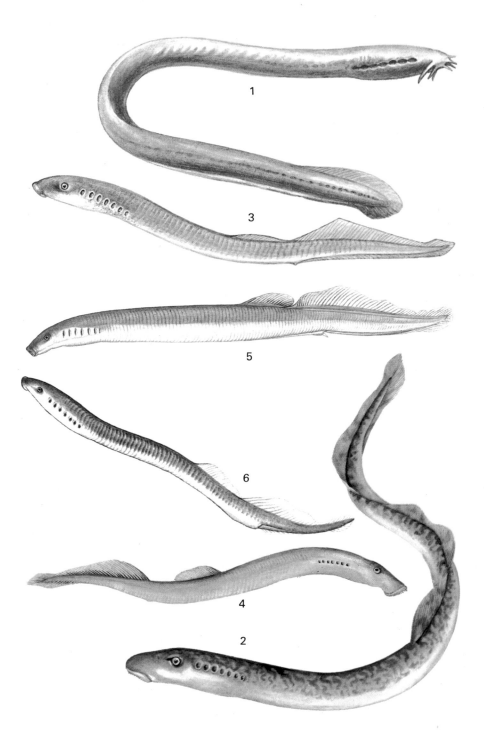

Subphylum: **Vertebrates — Vertebrata**

Class: **Cartilaginous fishes — Chondrichthyes**

Subclass: **Sharks and rays — Elasmobranchii**

Order: **Sharks — Selachii**

Family: **Mackerel sharks — Isuridae**

1 Common Atlantic Mackerel Shark or Porbeagle *Lamna nasus* — Length 1.5—3.5 metres, weight 100—150 kg. Fast and constantly swimming, viviparous shark that hunts chiefly herring and mackerel, but also smaller sharks, halibut, cod and octopus near water surface. Distribution: European, North American and north African Atlantic coasts as well as the Mediterranean Sea.

Family: **Thresher sharks — Alopiidae**

2 Common Thresher *Alopias vulpinus* — Length up to 6 metres. Brownish, greyish to black with markedly long upper lobe of tail fin. Often makes very long journeys at sea, usually swimming close to the surface. Hunts chiefly pelagic fish that travel in large shoals, swimming around such a shoal in ever smaller circles while threshing the water with its tail. Female bears 2—4 young. Entirely harmless to Man.

Family: **Smooth dogfishes — Triakidae**

3 Smooth Hound *Mustelus mustelus* — Length up to 2 metres. Viviparous shark found at depths of 20—100 metres. Feeds chiefly on crabs, lobsters, langoustes and smaller fish of the sea bottom. Jaws furnished with flat teeth similar to those of rays. Distribution: found along the coasts of Europe, except the Baltic and Black Seas. *M. asterias,* a related species, has a similar distribution.

Family: **Requiem sharks — Carcharhinidae**

4 Great Blue Shark *Prionace glauca* — Length up to 4 metres. Typical inhabitant of open seas where it often travels long distances. Feeds on fish that travel in shoals. Viviparous; newly-born young measure 50—60 cm. Distribution: common in all tropical and subtropical seas; extending to Gulf of Alaska and Japan. Occurs regularly but not very frequently in the northern parts of the North Sea. Dangerous to Man, though the extent to which this is so is usually exaggerated. In Japan it is hunted in large numbers as food.

Family: **Dogfish sharks — Squalidae**

5 Common Spiny Dogfish *Squalus acanthias* — Length up to 1.2 metres. Viviparous. Has a sharp poisonous spine in front of each of the two dorsal fins. Lives in large shoals often numbering as many as a thousand individuals. Hunts herring, mackerel, marine crustaceans, etc. Important species of commerce. Distribution: most plentiful shark of the North Sea.

Family: **Cat sharks — Scyliorhinidae**

6 Common Spotted Dogfish *Scyliorhinus caniculus* — Length up to 1 metre. Nocturnal. Hunts small fish, crustaceans, etc. Oviparous. Distribution: found along the coasts of Europe and north Africa, chiefly in sandy areas overgrown with seaweed at depths of 10—85 metres. The related species *S. stellaris* is common only south of the Bay of Biscay.

Family: **Angel sharks — Squatinidae**

7 Monkfish *Squatina squatina* — Length 1—2.5 metres. Shark with ray-like body. Overwinters in deeper waters; in summer it swims to shallow water where the female bears 10—25 live young. Feeds chiefly on fish of the sea bottom, crustaceans, etc. Distribution: found along the European Atlantic coast and in the Mediterranean Sea.

196

Subphylum: **Vertebrates — Vertebrata**

Class: **Cartilaginous fishes — Chondrichthyes**

Order: **Rays and skates — Rajiformes**

Family: **Electric rays, torpedoes — Torpedinidae**

1 Marbled Electric Ray *Torpedo marmorata* — Length up to 1.5 metres. Has a large electric organ on either side of the head with which it stuns its prey (produces a charge of 45—220 volts). Viviparous. External gills are not developed in the young. Feeds mainly on small fish, marine crustaceans and other invertebrates. Distribution: abundant in shallow waters along the European coast from the southern British Isles to the Mediterranean and along the northwestern coast of Africa.

Family: **Skates — Rajidae**

2 Thornback Ray *Raja clavata* Length 70—120 cm. Has many large spines on the back. Feeds on aquatic crustaceans and small fish. During the summer the female lays eggs encased in a four-cornered, protective sheath about 6 cm long; the young emerge after 4—5 months. Important fish of commerce which uses both the meat and the liver. Distribution: the coasts of all European seas.

Subclass: **Holocephali**

Order: **Chimaeriformes**

Family: **Chimaeras — Chimaeridae**

3 Rabbit Fish *Chimaera monstrosa* — Length about 1 metre, weight 2.5 kg. A deep-water species with large eyes, living on the bottom at depths of 200—500 metres. In front of the first dorsal fin there is a long poison spine, saw-toothed along its back edge. Feeds on small marine animals. Oviparous. Female regularly lays 2 eggs resembling those of a shark. Distribution: along the European and North American Atlantic coast.

Class: **Bony fishes — Osteichthyes**

Superorder: **Sturgeons — Chondrostei**

Order: **Acipenseriformes**

Family: **Sturgeons — Acipenseridae**

4 Atlantic Sturgeon *Acipenser sturio* — Length 3 metres, weight more than 300 kg. A large, migratory fish. Feeds on marine invertebrates and small, bottom-dwelling fish. In April and May it swims up rivers where it spawns in the swift current in deep hollows, laying up to 2.5 million eggs. Adult fish as well as fry stay only a short while in fresh water. In the 19th century it travelled up the Rhine as far as Basel, up the Elbe into the Vltava as far as Prague, up the Odra beyond Wroclaw and up the Vistula to Krakow. Found also in the Danube delta, very occasionally also further upstream. Overfishing as well as polluted rivers and the damming of upper streams contributed to its extinction in these rivers. Commercially of little importance in Europe nowadays (excepting the Black Sea region). Distribution: along the coast of most parts of Europe.

5 Sterlet *Acipenser ruthenus* — Length 50—60 cm. A small sturgeon with a long snout. Feeds on bottom-dwelling invertebrates. Spawns in May and June. Locally cultivated in ponds as a supplementary fish. Distribution: rivers that flow into the Black and Caspian Seas. In the Danube this species is found in reaches beyond Linz.

6 Giant Beluga *Huso huso* — Length 5—6 metres, weight more than 1 ton. Largest of the sturgeons. Migratory. Spends most of its life in the sea, spawns in large rivers. Prized not only for its tasty meat but also for its large number of eggs (roe) from which black caviar is processed. Distribution: common in rivers flowing into the Black Sea, Caspian Sea and the Sea of Azov.

Subphylum: **Vertebrates — Vertebrata**

Class: **Bony fishes — Osteichthyes**

Superorder: **Teleostei**

Order: **Eels — Anguilliformes**

Family: **Freshwater eels — Anguillidae**

1 European Eel *Anguilla anguilla* — Length up to 150 cm, weight 4 kg. Long, snake-like body with no pelvic fins; small scales embedded deep in the skin. Spawns in the Atlantic in the region of the Sargasso Sea. Young leptocephalus larvae resemble translucent willow leaves; they swim slowly with the Gulf Stream for several years, finally reaching the shores of Europe where they metamorphose, becoming small, snake-like elvers. Females swim up rivers, males remain at the river mouth. Females live in fresh water for several years, returning to the Atlantic to spawn, after which they die. Feed on crustaceans, small fish and aquatic insects.

Family: **Moray eels — Muraenidae**

2 Greek Moray *Muraena helena* — Length 1 metre. A long, slender fish. Found in the littoral zone, concealing itself in the hollows between corals, in underwater caves and similar crevices. Feeds chiefly on fish. Has been kept in marine aquaria since the days of ancient Rome. Has sharp teeth with poisonous glands at the base. Though dangerously poisonous it is highly popular with sportsmen. Distribution: abundant, particularly in the Mediterranean Sea.

Order: **Clupeiformes**

Family: **Herrings — Clupeidae**

3 Atlantic Herring *Clupea harengus* — Length 25—35 cm, very occasionally 40 cm. A slender, pelagic fish. Congregates in huge shoals that keep to deeper water by day and ascend to the surface of the sea by night. One of the most important sea fishes of commerce. Distribution: the northern Atlantic, in places where the warm southern ocean currents mingle with the cold northern currents.

4 Sprat *Sprattus sprattus* — Length up to 16.5 cm. Small sea fish that forms large shoals. Spawns in January—July by the coast. Eggs are pelagic. There are many different races. Tolerates marked fluctuations in the salinity of the water; found also in river mouths and in brackish waters. A very important fish of commerce; one- and two-year-old fish (about 10 cm long) are most often caught. Distribution: in the seas around the whole of Europe.

5 Sardine or Pilchard *Sardinus pilchardus* — Length 25—26 cm. Pelagic, shoaling fish. Feeds on planktonic crustaceans, pelagic fish eggs, small fry etc. Spawns in the open sea. After spawning sardines travel in vast shoals in search of food to the coasts — north in summer, south in winter. Distribution: in the seas around the whole of Europe.

6 Allis Shad *Alosa alosa* — Length up to 70 cm. Spawns in May and June, often far up rivers. Eggs float near the bottom. Young fish, 8—12 cm long, return to the sea where they live for several years feeding on crustaceans. When they reach a length of 30—40 cm they travel to fresh waters to spawn. Formerly an important fish of commerce (during the spawning season), now very rare in most European rivers. Distribution: along the European Atlantic coasts, western parts of the Baltic and Mediterranean Seas.

7 Twaite Shad *Alosa fallax* — Length 50 cm. Migratory fish that spawns in rivers but only in the lower reaches. Spawning season is in June and July. Biology similar to that of the preceding species. Distribution: along the European coast of the Mediterranean, in the Atlantic and the Baltic Seas.

200

Subphylum: **Vertebrates — Vertebrata**

Class: **Bony fishes — Osteichthyes**

Order: **Clupeiformes**

Family: **Anchovies — Engraulidae**

1 Anchovy *Engraulis encrasicholus* — Length rarely more than 16 cm. Marine fish with strikingly ventral mouth. Pelagic, travelling in large shoals and feeding on marine zooplankton. In summer it moves to the coast, in winter seeks deeper waters. Flesh often has a bitter taste. An important fish of commerce. Distribution: along the European Atlantic coast, in the Mediterranean and in the Black Sea.

Order: **Salmoniformes**

Family: **Trout and salmon — Salmonidae**

2 Atlantic Salmon *Salmo salar* — Length 1.5 metres, weight more than 50 kg. Large marine fish that in the summer and autumn ascends far up rivers to spawn. At this time males develop a markedly hooked lower jaw. Young salmon remain in the fresh water of the rivers 2—3 years. There they feed chiefly on small invertebrates, in the sea they feed solely on fish. In this century salmon have disappeared from most large European rivers due to the pollution and damming of the waters. They are still plentiful in Scandinavia, Scotland and Ireland.

3 Sea Trout *Salmo trutta trutta* — Length more than 1 metre. Ascends far up rivers to spawn. Experiments have shown that if they are prevented from returning to the sea these trout change into small brown trout and vice versa (young brown trout, if put in the sea, will grow into large, migratory sea trout). The biology and commercial importance is the same as that of the salmon.

4 Brown Trout *Salmo trutta fario* — Typical fish of Europe's mountain streams, rivers and lakes, characterized by bright and variable colouring. Its size depends on the environment. It feeds on aquatic insects and small aquatic invertebrates; large trout capture fish and other smaller vertebrates. Distribution: inhabits streams in mountains and foothills throughout all Europe; it is planted into cool ponds. Trout culture has a tradition of several hundred years in almost every part of Europe.

5 Rainbow Trout *Salmo gairdneri* — Length more than 60 cm, and attaining a weight of 4 to 5 kg. Native to the western USA. Introduced into Europe in the late 19th century. Planted in streams, dam lakes and suitable ponds.

6 Danubian Salmon *Hucho hucho* — Length up to 120 cm, weight 50 kg. Spawns in spring in water temperatures of 6—8 °C. Young feed on the larvae of aquatic insects. When they reach a length of 5—6 cm they begin to hunt small fish. Adults feed only on fish or other vertebrates. This species is a very good indicator of water pollution; its numbers have been rapidly decreasing in many rivers in recent years. Distribution: in the mountain and foothill streams that feed the Danube and its tributaries.

1

2

3♂

4

5

6

Subphylum: **Vertebrates — Vertebrata**

Class: **Bony fishes — Osteichthyes**

Order: **Salmoniformes**

Family: **Trout and salmon — Salmonidae**

1 Alpine Trout *Salvelinus alpinus* — Length 50—70 cm, weight 2 kg, very occasionally up to 4 kg. Ocean fish that feeds on invertebrates, insects and small fish. Spawns in autumn in fresh water; many mountain and northern lakes contain permanent, non-migrant fresh water forms. Young remain in freshwaters for 3—4 years. Distribution: northern seas. Many local geographic races occur in the lakes of Scandinavia, the British Isles and alpine glacial lakes.

2 Brook Trout *Salvelinus fontinalis* — Length 50 cm, weight more than 1 kg. Native of North America, introduced to European waters in the late 19th century. Biology similar to that of the Brown Trout and Alpine Trout, with which it often interbreeds. Planted in several European mountain streams, rivers and lakes.

Family: **Whitefishes — Coregonidae**

3 Freshwater Houting *Coregonus lavaretus* — Length 50—70 cm, weight 3—4 kg, very occasionally 130 cm and more than 10 kg. A deep-water fish that enters shallow water only during the spawning season in November. Feeds on plankton, insect larvae and small fish. Originally native to Lake Miedwie in Poland, it was introduced to many European ponds in the late 19th century.

Family: **Smelts — Osmeridae**

4 European Smelt *Osmerus eperlanus* — Length 30 cm. Ocean fish that ascends far up rivers during the spawning season in March and April. Spawns in sidestreams of rivers. The 4—5 cm long young return to the sea, where they live in deep water feeding on marine plankton and small fish. Locally of commercial value. Distribution: along the coast of Europe from northern Spain to southern Scandinavia; in the Baltic Sea to the Gulf of Bothnia.

Family: **Graylings — Thymallidae**

5 Common European Grayling *Thymallus thymallus* — Length 50 cm, weight more than 1 kg. Lives in shoals in the submountain sections of rivers with sandy and gravelly bottoms. Feeds on aquatic invertebrates and insects that fall on the surface. During the spawning season, from March to May, it ascends far upstream. Distribution: rivers of northern and central Europe and the Po River region. Absent in the southern parts of Europe and northern Scandinavia.

Family: **Pike, pickerel and muskellunge — Esocidae**

6 Northern Pike *Esox lucius* — Length 150 cm, weight 35 kg. Predaceous fish that from early youth feeds on fish fry, later on larger fish and other vertebrates. Found in lower reaches of rivers, in pools and backwaters overgrown with vegetation. Also travels far upstream into trout territory. Spawns early in spring in flooded meadows. A valuable fish of commerce; planted as a supplementary fish in carp ponds. Distribution: throughout Europe except the southern parts.

Family: **Mud Minnows — Umbridae**

7 Mud Minnow *Umbra krameri* — Length 8—10 cm. Brownish-red, irregularly spotted fish found in clear waters with abundant vegetation. Feeds on small invertebrates. In March the female constructs a nest of sand in which she lays the eggs, brooding over them until they hatch. Distribution: backwaters of the Danube from Vienna to the mouth of the river, in its tributaries, in the lower reaches of the Dniester and Prut rivers and in Lake Balaton and the Neusiedlersee.

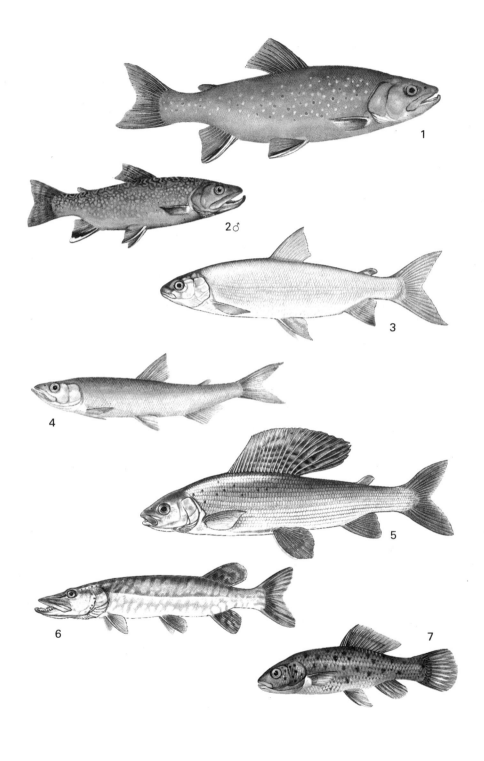

1

2♂

3

4

5

6

7

Subphylum: **Vertebrates — Vertebrata**

Class: **Bony fishes — Osteichthyes**

Family: **Marine hatchetfishes — Sternoptychidae**

1 Silvery Hatchetfish *Argyropelecus lychnus* — Length 9—10 cm. Deep-sea fish. Deep-bodied, laterally compressed, with large, telescopic eyes aimed upward at an angle. Around the eyes and along the lateral margins of the underside of the body there are numerous light organs called photophores. Found at depths of 350—700 metres, together with about 12 other closely related species. Distribution: chiefly in tropical and temperate regions of all oceans where it is important as food for tuna and other fish that forage at greater depths.

Family: **Lancetfishes — Alepisauridae**

2 Longnose Lancetfish *Alepisaurus ferox* — Length nearly 2 metres. Members of this family are among the largest of deep-sea predators. They have a long, high dorsal fin behind which is a small adipose fin. Large mouth is furnished with long, sharp, fang-like teeth. Diet consists mainly of other deep-sea fish. Quite often they swim to the upper layers where they are caught by fishermen. The study of their stomach contents has brought to light unknown species of deep-sea fish. Distribution: the depths of all seas and oceans.

Family: **Sawtailfishes — Idiacanthidae**

3 Ribbon Sawtailfish *Idiacanthus fasciola* — Length male 3—4 cm, female up to 30 cm. Marked sexual dimorphism. Male has atrophied digestive organs, teeth, and light organs which are reduced to a single photophore above the eyes. Male very short-lived, dies soon after spawning. Female long-lived. Larvae show no resemblance to the adult fish; they have the eyes set entirely off the head on long stalks and for a long time were believed to be a separate species. Distribution: the depths of all seas and oceans.

Family: **Viperfishes — Chauliodontidae**

4 Viperfish *Chauliodus sloani* — Length maximum 25 cm. Deep-sea fish with sharp, fang-like teeth. Noted for its interesting vertical migration; by night it sometimes comes up to the surface, by day it keeps to depths between 450 and 2,800 metres. Predaceous; feeds on fish of practically its own size. Distribution: all the seas from the equator to the poles.

Family: **Bristlemouths — Gonostomatidae**

5 *Cyclothone signata* — Length 5 cm. Member of a family that is the most numerous of deep-sea fishes. Eyes silver, light organs arranged in rows along the sides of the body. Biology little known as yet. Of interest is the fact that the planktonic eggs, about 0.8 mm in diameter, hatch into larvae resembling those of the herring family; photophores or light organs do not develop until at metamorphosis when the larva changes into a small fish. Distribution: the depths of all seas and oceans.

Family: **Lanternfishes — Myctophidae**

6 Spotted Lanternfish *Myctophum punctatum* — Length 10 cm. Deep-sea fish and a member of a large family comprising some 150 species. Breeding season is in winter. The transparent larvae remain together in groups near the surface until they attain a length of about 2 cm. Only then, following the change to the adult form, do they move downward into deeper water and develop light organs. Like many other species of this family they are important as food for sea-fish of commercial value. Distribution: the middle depths of the Atlantic and the Mediterranean Sea.

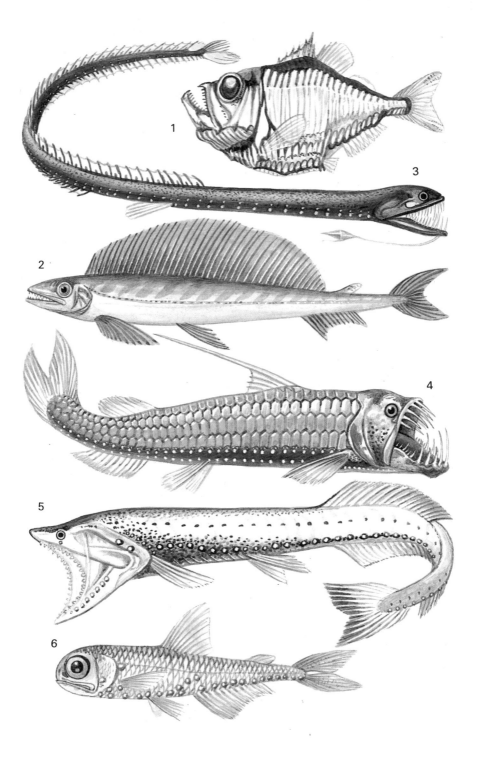

Subphylum: **Vertebrates — Vertebrata**

Class: **Bony fishes — Osteichthyes**

Order: **Cypriniformes**

Family: **Minnows and carps — Cyprinidae**

1 Roach *Rutilus rutilus* — Length 40 cm, weight 1 kg. One of the commonest fish in all types of fresh waters except mountain trout streams. Feeds on aquatic invertebrates, larger roaches also feed on aquatic vegetation. Spawns in April and May on aquatic vegetation; at this time the males develop conspicuous tubercles. Distribution: fresh waters of all Europe except the southern Mediterranean islands, northern Scotland and northern Norway. Also found in brackish waters and in the Baltic countries.

2 Danube Roach *Rutilus pigus* — Length 50 cm, weight 2 kg. Inhabits deeper waters. Differs from preceding species by having a greater number of scales along the lateral line and dark-coloured body tissue lining the abdominal cavity. Spawns in April and May. Distribution: the lakes of northern Italy (Lake Maggiore, Lake Lugano, etc.) and in the Po River region. The subspecies *R. pigus virgo* is found in the upper and middle reaches of the Danube and its tributaries.

3 Black Sea Roach *Rutilus (Pararutilus) frisii meidingeri* — Length 40 cm, weight 1.5 kg. Body long, cylindrical with small mouth and round, protruding snout. Migrant. Common in some alpine lakes. Feeds on molluscs, worms, insect larvae, aquatic vegetation and small fish. Distribution: the upper Danube system in Chiemsee, Traunsee, Attersee and Mondsee. A subspecies of *Rutilus (Pararutilus) frisii,* found in the northwestern river tributaries of the Black Sea.

4 Moderlieschen *Leucaspius delineatus* — Length 7—9 cm. Fish with slender, laterally compressed body occurring in large shoals in quiet and slow-flowing waters thick with vegetation. Feeds on plankton. Spawns in April and May. Eggs are laid in a band round the stems of aquatic plants and are watched over by the male. Distribution: central and eastern Europe, as far north as southern Sweden.

5 European Bitterling *Rhodeus sericeus* — Length 9 cm. Deep-bodied, laterally compressed. Common in calm waters of lower reaches of rivers, and in backwaters and pools. Feeds on planktonic crustaceans, insect larvae and worms. Spawns in April—June; at this time the females develop a long ovipositor with which the large eggs are deposited singly in the mantle cavity of freshwater clams or mussels into which the males inject milt. The fry is carried out from the mantle cavity of the mussel together with outflowing water. Distribution: all Europe except Denmark, Scandinavia, the British Isles and southern European peninsulas.

6 Nase *Chondrostoma nasus* — Length 40 cm, weight 1 kg. Has typical ventral mouth; the lips are covered with horny skin and have sharp edges. Feeds on films of algae covering rocks which it scrapes off with its horny mouth. Prefers rivers and lakes in foothills, often found in large shoals. Distribution: rivers that flow into the Baltic Sea from the south and into the Black Sea from the north and west. There are 17 other related species in Europe.

7 Minnow *Phoxinus phoxinus* — Length 6—10 cm. Lives in shoals in clean streams and mountain streams with sandy or stony bottoms. Feeds on various small invertebrates. Spawns between April and July. Distribution: all Europe from northern Spain and northern Italy; absent in northern Scotland, southern parts of Mediterranean peninsulas and extreme northern parts of Scandinavia.

208

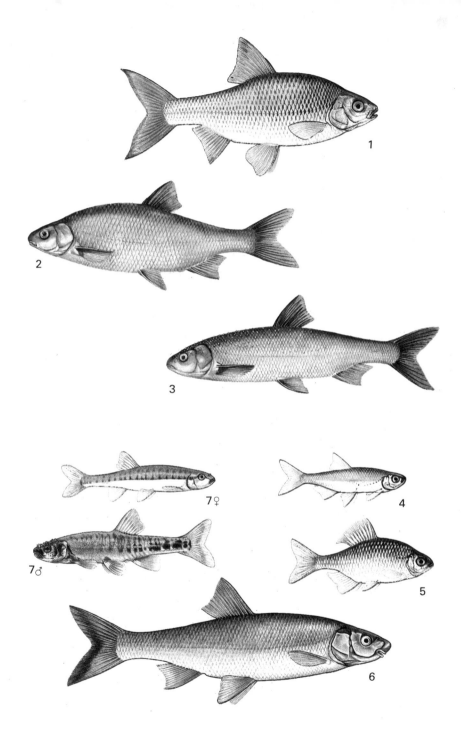

Subphylum: **Vertebrates — Vertebrata**

Class: **Bony fishes — Osteichthyes**

Order: **Cypriniformes**

Family: **Minnows and carps — Cyprinidae**

1 Dace *Leuciscus leuciscus* — Length 30 cm. Body almost circular in cross-section with small mouth and notched anal fin. Found in clear foothill and lowland rivers and streams. Feeds on insects, insect larvae and other invertebrates. Spawns between March and May on aquatic vegetation. Distribution: all Europe except the Mediterranean islands, Scotland and the extreme north of Scandinavia.

2 Ide or Orfe *Leuciscus idus* — Length 50 cm, weight more than 2 kg. Body deep and markedly flattened along the sides. Prefers smaller streams, often swims near the surface. Feeds on insects and other animals found on the bottom, larger specimens hunt fish. Spawns on vegetation and on stones near the shore. During the spawning season the male develops conspicuous tubercles on the head and body. Distribution: Europe from the Rhine as far as the Urals; absent in England, France, Switzerland, Norway and regions south of the Alps and the Danube.

3 Chub *Leuciscus cephalus* — Length 80 cm, weight more than 3 kg. Body long, cylindrical, with large scales edged with grey or red. Found in all types of flowing waters from the lower trout zone to lowland country, also in quiet water. Prefers shallow water with a firm bottom. Feeds on invertebrates and small fish, frogs and crayfish. Spawns in spring; at this time both sexes develop conspicuous tubercles. Distribution: Europe from southern Scotland and England as far as the Urals. Absent in Ireland, Denmark, northern Scandinavia and Mediterranean islands.

4 Rudd *Scardinius erythrophthalmus* — Length more than 30 cm, weight 1 kg. Common in coves and inlets on the lower reaches of rivers, in backwaters and pools with aquatic vegetation. Congregates in smaller shoals. Young rudds, up to about 7 cm long, feed on plankton, larger fish chiefly feed on aquatic vegetation. Spawns on aquatic vegetation. Distribution: all of Europe except the Iberian Peninsula, Scotland, western Norway, northern and central Sweden and the Crimea.

5 Asp *Aspius aspius* — Length 70—80 cm, weight 6—8 kg. Favourite game fish with long body and broad mouth, common in lower reaches of larger rivers and in established backwaters. Feeds on insects that fall on the water surface and on small fish, often attacking them with a loud splash and sometimes even leaping out of the water. Spawns in April—June on stony bottoms in flowing water. Distribution: Europe east of the Elbe in rivers flowing into the North, Baltic, Black and Caspian Seas. Absent in France, the British Isles, Denmark, Switzerland, Iberian Peninsula and southern Balkans.

6 Golden Tench *Tinca tinca* — Length 50—60 cm, weight 5—6 kg. Robust fish with small scales and strikingly small eyes. Male has longer and broader pelvic fins than female. Lives close to the bottom in slow-flowing rivers, established backwaters and inlets with muddy bottoms and dense aquatic vegetation. Feeds chiefly on bottom-dwelling animals. Tolerates marked lack of oxygen in water. Distribution: all Europe except northern Scandinavia and the USSR, Scotland, Dalmatia, and Crimea. Planted as a valuable supplementary fish in carp ponds.

210

Subphylum: **Vertebrates — Vertebrata**

Class: **Bony fishes — Osteichthyes**

Order: **Cypriniformes**

Family: **Minnows and carps — Cyprinidae**

1 Gudgeon *Gobio gobio* — Length 10—20 cm. Body elongated, spindle-shaped with large scales and short dorsal and anal fins. By the mouth are two short barbels, the throat is smooth and scaleless. Found on the bottoms of all types of fresh waters. Spawns in May and June in shallow water. Popular as bait in fishing for predaceous fish. Distribution: all Europe except the Iberian Peninsula, southern Italy, Greece, Norway, northern Scotland and northern Scandinavia.

2 Danube Gudgeon *Gobio uranoscopus* — Length 12—15 cm. Resembles the Gudgeon but has long barbels extending far behind the eyes; eyes set close to the top of the head and throat covered with scales. Partial to sections of rivers with a strong current; found on the bottom where it feeds on benthos. Distribution: upper and middle reaches of the Danube and its tributaries, in the rivers of Ruthenia, Slovakia, Rumania, etc.

3 Common Barbel *Barbus barbus* — Length 1 metre. Lives on the bottom in flowing sections of rivers. Congregates in shoals and feeds on the animals and vegetation of the bottom. Spawns in May and June. Distribution: western and central Europe; absent in Ireland, Denmark, Scandinavia and Italy. The smaller related Southern Barbel (*B. meridionalis*), only about 30 cm long, occurs sporadically from the northern parts of the Iberian Peninsula to Albania, Greece and the Peloponnesus. The Odra, Vistula, Danube, Dniester, Vardar and south Bulgarian rivers are inhabited by the subspecies *B. meridionalis petenyi*.

4 Bleak *Alburnus alburnus* — Length 15 cm. The belly behind the pelvic fins forms a smooth and scaleless keel. Found in deeper parts of slow-flowing waters in the middle and lower reaches of larger rivers. By day it swims near the surface where it feeds on insects that have fallen there. Spawns in May on aquatic vegetation. Distribution: north of the Pyrenees and Alps throughout the whole of Europe as far as the Urals. Absent in Ireland and Scotland, northern Scandinavia, Iberian Peninsula, Italy and Dalmatia.

5 Schneider *Alburnoides bipunctatus* — Length 14 cm. Resembles the Bleak but is more deep-bodied and has a double dark band bordering the lateral line (at least in the front part of the body). Found in shallow waters in the current of the upper reaches of rivers together with minnows. Feeds on insects and insect larvae. Spawns in May and June. Distribution: from France as far as the Caspian Sea, absent south of the Alps and Pyrenees, Denmark, northern Europe and the British Isles.

6 Silver or White Bream *Blicca bjoerkna* — Length 35 cm, weight 1 kg. Very deep-bodied, markedly flattened from side to side. Plentiful on the bottom in the lower reaches of larger rivers, in established backwaters and pools, inlets and ponds. Feeds on plankton, algae and larvae of aquatic insects. Spawns from late April to June on aquatic vegetation. Distribution: Europe north of the Alps and Pyrenees as far as southern Scandinavia, also in eastern parts of England and in rivers flowing into the Black Sea north of the Danube.

212

Subphylum: **Vertebrates — Vertebrata**

Class: **Bony fishes — Osteichthyes**

Order: **Cypriniformes**

Family: **Minnows and carps — Cyprinidae**

1 Common Bream *Abramis brama* — Length 75 cm, weight very occasionally more than 10 kg. Common fish of slow-flowing and quiet waters of the lower reaches of large rivers, valley reservoirs and lakes. The mouth is terminal and protractile. Found on the bottom, often in water overgrown with aquatic vegetation. Feeds on planktonic and benthic organisms. Spawns in the evening and at night in late April and May. Distribution: Europe north of the Pyrenees and Alps, absent from the southern and western parts of the Balkan Peninsula as well as from western and northern Scandinavia.

2 Zope or Blue Bream *Abramis ballerus* — Length 45 cm, weight 1.5 kg. Body deep, long and laterally compressed. Resembles the Common Bream but the terminal mouth aims upward at an angle. Occurs in smaller shoals. Feeds mainly on plankton. Spawns in April and May amidst aquatic vegetation. Distribution: lakes and lower reaches of rivers in the North and Baltic Sea region from the Elbe to the Neva, rivers of southern Sweden and Finland and in the Black Sea region from the Danube to the Ural River.

3 Danube or White-eyed Bream *Abramis sapa* — Length 30 cm, weight 700—800 gm. Resembles the preceding breams but the mouth is nearly ventral, the snout blunt and rounded. Feeds on small bottom-dwelling animal organisms, also on vegetation. There are migrant as well as resident populations; both spawn in April and May in river beds, but afterwards the migrant fishes return to the sea. Found in rivers flowing into the Black and Caspian Seas and Sea of Azov as well as in the Danube and its tributaries.

4 Common Carp *Cyprinus carpio* — Length 120 cm, weight more than 30 kg. Most popular fish of European pond culture, native to the Black and Caspian Sea region. The original wild form has a long scale-covered cylindrical body. It inhabits the Danube and some of its tributaries. Pond carp are deep-bodied. Spawns in May and June. The fry feed on zooplankton at first, later on bottom-dwelling animals. In Europe it is the most valuable of the freshwater fishes.

5 Common Carp *Cyprinus carpio* — Carp bred in ponds show marked deviations in the scale cover. The most common variety is the mirror carp with body irregularly covered with scales of different sizes. Another variety has a row of scales along the sides of the body and sometimes a similar line of scales along the base of the dorsal fin. Leather carp either have no scales at all or only a few individual scales below the dorsal fin and along the base of the other fins.

6 Grass Carp *Ctenophyryngodon idella* — Length more than 1 metre, weight 32 kg. Native to the middle and lower reaches of the Amur River and its tributaries and the waters of northern China. Several decades ago it was introduced to European ponds where it became established. Feeds chiefly on aquatic vegetation.

7 Silver Carp or Tolstol *Hypophthalmichthys molitrix* — Length up to 1 metre, weight 10 kg. A fish of the carp family native to East Asia. In the past decades it has been introduced to Europe where it has gradually become established. Feeds exclusively on plant plankton. Has a very rapid rate of growth.

214

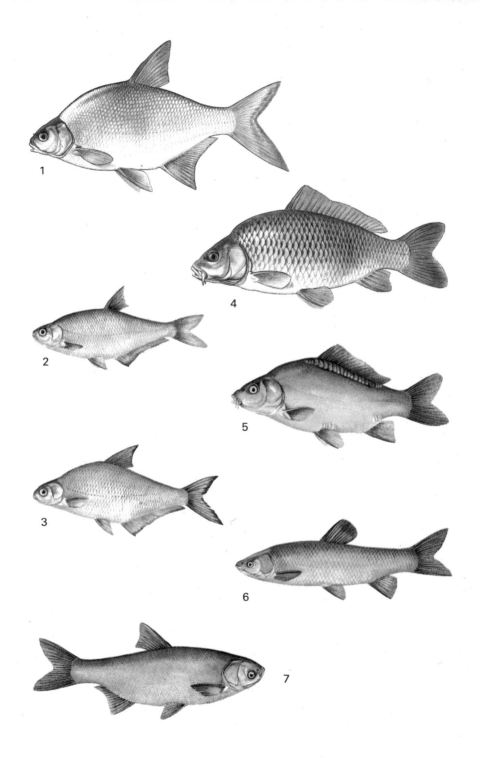

Subphylum: **Vertebrates** — **Vertebrata**

Class: **Bony fishes** — **Osteichthyes**

Order: **Cypriniformes**

Family: **Minnows and carps** — **Cyprinidae**

1 Ziege *Pelecus cultratus* — Length up to 60 cm, weight 1 kg. Typical fish of the upper layers; by day it keeps to deeper water, at night it rises to the surface. Feeds chiefly on insects floating on the surface, often also on the fry of other fish. Spawns in May and June. Eggs are pelagic. Distribution: brackish waters of the Baltic and Black Seas, the Caspian Sea and Lake Aral.

2 Zahrte *Vimba vimba* — Length 30—40 cm, weight more than 1 kg. A partial migrant. Inhabits lower reaches of larger, slow-flowing rivers. Feeds chiefly on bottom-dwelling invertebrates. Spawns in May and June on stony bottoms in flowing water. Distribution: Weser, Elbe and other rivers as far as the Neva, in southern Finland and in Sweden. It forms a number of geographic races.

3 Crucian Carp *Carassius carassius* — Length 40 cm, weight 1 kg. Resembles a small carp but has no barbels. Feeds chiefly on small benthic invertebrates. Inhabits backwaters and pools, swamps and hollows. Very tolerant of oxygen-deficient water. Found from England through northeastern France and in all rivers flowing into the North and Baltic Seas. The related Gibel Carp (*C. auratus gibelio*) is native to East Asia. The goldfish kept in aquariums are domesticated forms of the Goldfish *(C. auratus auratus)* of China, Korea and Japan.

Family: **Loaches** — **Cobitidae**

4 European Weatherfish *Misgurnus fossilis* — Length 35 cm, weight 150 gm. Elongated fish with dark longitudinal bands and 10 barbels around the mouth. Lives on the bottom of muddy waters, ponds and river inlets. In oxygen-deficient water it swallows air, absorbing oxygen from it as it passes through the digestive tract. Spawns in May. Fry have external filamentous gills which soon disappear. Distribution: in European rivers from the Seine to the Neva and from the Danube to the Volga. Absent in rivers flowing into the Arctic Ocean, in England, Scandinavia, Finland and southern Europe.

5 Stone Loach *Noemacheilus barbatulus* — Length 10—18 cm. Primarily a nocturnal fish with dark-marbled, cylindrical body and 6 barbels around the mouth. Lives on the bottom in flowing waters, ponds and lakes, usually hiding under stones or roots. Feeds on larvae of aquatic insects and other invertebrates. Spawns in May on sand or on stones in shallow water. Distribution: in European fresh waters except northern Scotland, northern Scandinavia, southern and central Italy and Greece.

6 Spotted Weatherfish or Spined Loach *Cobitis taenia* — Length 6—10 cm. Slender fish with head and body laterally compressed. Has 6 barbels round the lower jaw and a movable hinged spine beneath each eye. Burrows into the bottom mud of calm and slow-flowing waters. Feeds on bottom-dwelling invertebrates. Spawns in April and May. Distribution: Europe, except Norway, the northern parts of Sweden, Finland and USSR, Scotland, Ireland and the Peloponnesus.

7 Golden-spined Loach *Cobitis aurata* — Resembles the Spined Loach. Has 8 to 15 dark square spots on the sides and a leathery keel at the caudal end. In males the sides are markedly convex. Lives amidst stones and gravel in deeper flowing waters. Feeds on the bottom. Spawns in April and May in sandy and stony sections of rivers. Forms a number of geographic races. Distribution: Don and Danube river regions, Balkan rivers.

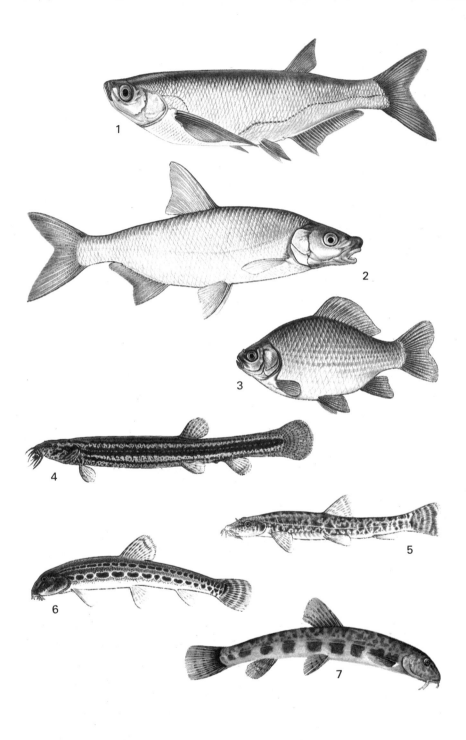

Subphylum: **Vertebrates — Vertebrata**

Class: **Bony fishes — Osteichthyes**

Order: **Catfishes — Siluriformes**

Family: **Eurasian catfishes — Siluridae**

1 Wels or European Catfish *Silurus glanis* — Length up to 3 metres, weight up to 300 kg; in Europe it generally attains a length of about 2 metres and weight of over 50 kg. One of the largest of Europe's freshwater fishes. Inhabits large rivers, dam reservoirs and lakes. Active at night when it forages for food near water surface; the day is spent on bottom of deep waters. Feeds on fish, small mammals and water birds. Spawns between May and July in shallow waters where the females make untidy nests of aquatic plants and roots. After mating the male watches over the eggs and later over the fry. Growth is very rapid. Distribution: European rivers east of the upper reaches of the Rhine, in the Elbe, Odra and Visla, and rivers flowing into the Black and Caspian Seas.

Family: **North American catfishes — Ictaluridae**

2 Brown Bullhead *Ictalurus nebulosus* — North American fish introduced to Europe at the turn of the century. Omnivorous, it consumes both plant and animal food. Spawns from April to June. Male watches over the eggs and later over the fry. In Europe it attains a length of 25—30 cm and a weight of about 1/2 kg; in its native habitat as much as 2 kg.

Order: **Lophiiformes**

Family: **Goosefishes and anglers — Lophiidae**

3 Anglerfish *Lophius piscatorius* — Length 1.7 metres, weight 40 kg. Bottom-dwelling fish found from the sea coast to depths of about 1000 metres. Feeds on fish, waiting concealed and motionless on the bottom and attracts its prey with a 'flag' — a flap of flesh hanging above the huge mouth at the tip of the fishing pole, modified from the first dorsal fin spine. Spawns between April and July at depths of about 400 metres. It lays over a million eggs which rest on a foam pad on which they float in the water, slowly rising to the surface. The larvae show no resemblance to the adult fish. Distribution: along the coasts of Europe, except the Black and Baltic Seas.

Order: **Gadiformes**

Family: **Codfishes — Gadidae**

4 Atlantic Cod *Gadus morrhua* — Length 150 cm, weight 40 kg. Common along the European coast of the Atlantic as well as far out at sea. Swims in large shoals. Feeds on herrings and other small ocean fish. Spawns usually in early spring. Important fish of commerce.

5 Ling *Molva molva* —Length 1.8 metres, weight 30 kg. Largest member of the genus. Feeds on various small sea fish. An important fish of commerce. Found at depths of 100—600 metres in the northeastern Atlantic.

6 Burbot *Lota lota* — Length 1 metre, weight 20 kg. Only freshwater member of the cod family. Lives concealed near the bottom and by the undermined banks of streams and rivers of the trout, grayling and barbel zone in Europe; occasionally also in lakes and rivers. It is a nocturnal predaceous species, feeding chiefly on fish and frogs. Spawns in winter. Females lay up to one million eggs. Locally, mainly in the northern regions, it is an important fish of commerce. Distribution: almost all of Europe north of the Balkans and Pyrenees.

5

1

3

6

2

4

Subphylum: **Vertebrates — Vertebrata**

Class: **Bony fishes — Osteichthyes**

Order: **Gadiformes**

Family: **Hakes — Merlucciidae**

1 European Hake *Merluccius merluccius* — Length 1 metre, weight 10 kg. Stout sea fish that dwells near the bottom by day, rising to the surface at night. Feeds on herrings, sprats, mackerels and other fish that congregate in large shoals. Spawns in spring. Eggs are pelagic. Important fish of commerce. Distribution: European seas except the Baltic and Black Seas.

Family: **Eelpouts — Zoarcidae**

2 European Eelpout or Viviparous Blenny *Zoarces viviparus* — Length 30—50 cm. Common fish of the sea bottom near the coast; found frequently also in brackish waters. Feeds on aquatic crustaceans, worms and small fish. Female bears live young. Distribution: the littoral zone of northern Europe from the north Norwegian coast south as far as the English Channel.

Family: **Cusk eels — Ophidiidae**

3 Bearded Ophidium *Ophidium barbatum* — Length 25 cm. Sea fish dwelling on sandy bottoms, often buried up to the head. Active by night. Feeds on invertebrates, for example, marine crayfish, polyps and molluscs, larger specimens feed on small fish. Distribution: Mediterranean Sea, the Atlantic European coast as far as Great Britain; also found in the Black Sea.

Family: **Cucumber and pearlfishes — Carapidae**

4 Pearlfish *Carapus acus* — Length up to 20 cm. Sea fish with laterally compressed body. Anal opening is located far forward in front of the pectoral fins below the throat. Spawns in summer. Eggs are small and elliptical. Lives inside sea cucumbers (Holothuria), feeding on their reproductive organs. If it causes excessive damage to the host's organs the sea cucumber throws it out by evisceration, regenerating replacements soon after. Distribution: the Mediterranean Sea.

Order: **Atheriniformes**

Family: **Flying fishes — Exocoetidae**

5 Flying Fish *Exocoetus volitans* — Length 18 cm. Distinguished by the large and long, wing-like pectoral fins and conspicuously elongated lower lobe of the tail fin. Usually swims in shoals just below the surface. When threatened by danger it flies with outspread fins above the water, taking advantage of the air currents. The length of such a flight is often as much as 200 metres. Spawns throughout the year in the open sea. Eggs float on the water. Found in all tropical waters, also in the western parts of the Mediterranean Sea.

Family: **Garfishes — Belonidae**

6 Garfish *Belone belone* — Length 80—100 cm, weight 1 kg. Travels in shoals in the open sea, in summer and autumn also found in the littoral zone, chiefly in the Mediterranean. Feeds mainly on marine crustaceans, octopuses and small fish. Its bones are coloured green. Spawns in summer near the shore. Eggs float freely; they are furnished with tendrils which results in their being caught on submerged objects. Distribution: the North Sea, Baltic Sea, Mediterranean and Black Seas.

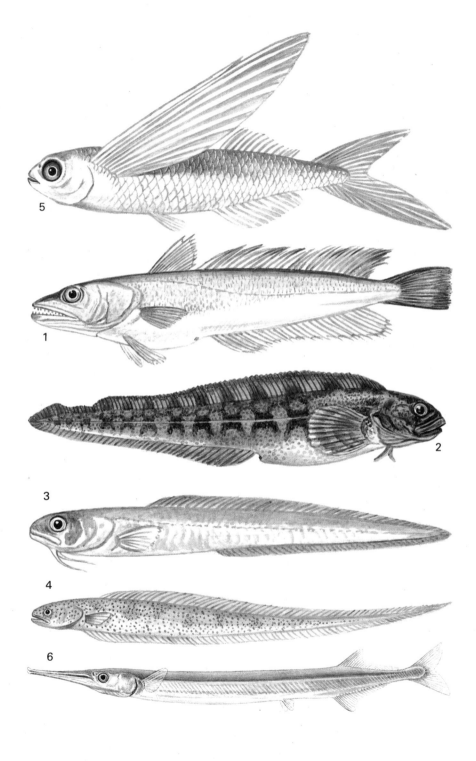

Subphylum: **Vertebrates — Vertebrata**

Class: **Bony fishes — Osteichthyes**

Order: **Zeiformes**

Family: **John dories — Zeidae**

1 John Dory *Zeus faber* — Length 70 cm, weight 20 kg. Fish of the open sea with rays of the first dorsal fin extended to form long trailing filaments. Feeds on fish and widely diverse marine invertebrates. Spawns in summer. Locally a popular and valuable market fish. Distribution: east Atlantic from the coast of Norway to the Mediterranean and Black Seas.

Order: **Gasterosteiformes**

Family: **Sticklebacks — Gasterosteidae**

2 Three-spine Stickleback *Gasterosteus aculeatus* — Length 4—10 cm. Small fish with free spines in front of the dorsal fin and bony plates along the sides. During the breeding season (April—June) the male constructs a nest of plant material. He watches over the eggs and, for a short while, the newly-hatched fry. Feeds at first on zooplankton, later on larger benthic particles. A circumpolar species of the cold and temperate zone of the northern hemisphere. Distribution: in Europe from the Black Sea, southern Italy and Iberian Peninsula to the northern coast of Norway.

Family: **Pipefishes and seahorses — Syngnathidae**

3 Seahorse *Hippocampus hippocampus* — Length 10—15 cm. Well-known marine fish found in places thick with seaweed both in the sea and in brackish waters. Feeds on marine plankton which it sucks up with the intake of water through the long tube-like snout. Spawns in spring and summer. Fertilized eggs are deposited by the female in the brood pouch of the male and fully developed young leave 4—5 weeks later. Distribution: the Mediterranean Sea; related species in the Black Sea and northeastern Atlantic.

4 Great Pipefish *Syngnathus acus* — Occurs in places along the coast where there is abundant seaweed, also in brackish waters and in the estuaries of large rivers. Usually lives at depths of less than 15 metres. Spawns in spring and summer. Eggs and young fry remain in the brood pouch of the male for about 5 weeks. Distribution: northeastern Atlantic from the Bay of Biscay to western shores of the British Isles. The subspecies *S. acus rubescens* lives in the Mediterranean and *S. typhle* lives in the Black Sea. Both are about 35 cm long. Another related species common in the Atlantic is *S. rostellatus,* measuring 15—17 cm in length.

Order: **Scorpaeniformes**

Family: **Scorpion fishes and rock fishes — Scorpaenidae**

5 Redfish *Sebastes marinus* — Length 1 metre, weight 15 kg. Found in the open sea and along the coast at depths of 100—400 metres. Bears live young. Important game fish. Distribution: north Atlantic, along the European and North American coasts.

Family: **Sculpins — Cottidae**

6 Miller's Thumb or Bullhead *Cottus gobio* — Length 15 cm. Freshwater fish, not very active. Feeds on insect larvae and small fish. Spawns in May on the underside of stones. Male watches over the eggs. Common in clear mountain streams and rivers. Distribution: Europe from England and the Pyrenees to the Caspian Sea; absent in southern Europe.

7 Alpine Bullhead or Mottlefoot Sculpin *Cottus poecilopus* — Length 15 cm. Differs from the preceding species by having horizontally striped pectoral fins. Distribution: in watersheds of the Arctic Ocean to the east of Scandinavia, in rivers flowing into the Baltic and in tributaries of the Danube and Dniester.

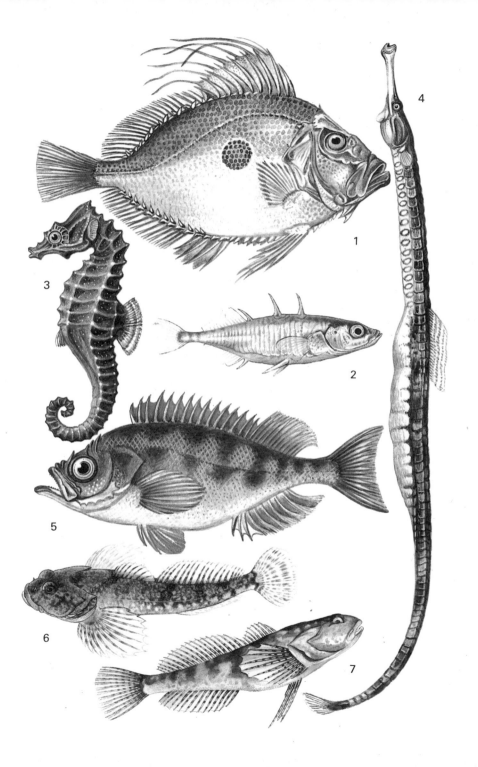

Subphylum: **Vertebrates — Vertebrata**

Class: **Bony fishes — Osteichthyes**

Order: **Scorpaeniformes**

Family: **Sculpins — Cottidae**

1 Fatherlasher or Shorthorn Sculpin *Myoxocephalus scorpius* — Length 30—50 cm. Marine sculpin inhabiting the littoral zone, sometimes enters river estuaries. Feeds chiefly on marine crustaceans and small fish. Spawns in winter. Eggs are laid in crevices between stones where they are guarded by the male. Distribution: northeastern Atlantic from the Bay of Biscay to Iceland and Greenland; the Arctic Ocean.

Family: **Snailfishes — Liparidae**

2 Sea Snail *Liparis liparis* — Length 15—18 cm. Occurs chiefly amidst growths of seaweed. Feeds on marine invertebrates, primarily crustaceans. Spawns in winter. Distribution: shallow coastal waters of the North Atlantic and Baltic Seas.

Family: **Lumpsuckers — Cyclopteridae**

3 Lumpfish or Sea Hen *Cyclopterus lumpus* — Length 60 cm. Ventral fins modified to form a sucking disk. Lives near the bottom from shallows to depths of about 300 metres. In late winter and early spring travels to shallow waters where it spawns in the splash zone. Eggs are laid amidst stones and in gravel and are guarded by the male for 1—2 months. Distribution: both sides of the North Atlantic, in Europe north of the Portuguese coast.

Order: **Tetraodontiformes**

Family: **Ocean sunfishes — Molidae**

4 Common Ocean Sunfish *Mola mola* — Length 3 metres. Fish of the open sea with flat, short, deep body and high dorsal and anal fins. Usually swims close to the surface. Feeds chiefly on marine crustaceans, octopuses, fish and marine algae. One of the most fertile fish, laying as many as 300 million eggs. Larva does not resemble the adult — it has a number of long spines for defence. Distribution: in tropical seas and in the temperate zone.

Order: **Perciformes**

Family: **Groupers and sea basses — Serranidae**

5 Sea Bass *Serranelus scriba* — Length 25 cm. Lives in shallow waters with rocky or sandy bottoms; common in growths of seaweed. Feeds on small fish, marine crustaceans and other invertebrates. Like other fishes of this family it is a hermaphrodite; the spawn and milt ripen at the same time. Spawns in early spring. Distribution: northeastern Atlantic, the Mediterranean and Black Seas.

Family: **Barracudas — Sphyraenidae**

6 Barracuda *Sphyraena sphyraena* — Length 1 metre. Slender ocean fish resembling the pike. Very aggressive, known to attack swimmers. Young fish travel in shoals, but adults often travel singly, near the shore where they hunt small fish. Distribution: the Atlantic as far north as the Bay of Biscay, in the Mediterranean and Black Seas.

Family: **Jacks, crevalles, scads and pompanos — Carangidae**

7 Horse Mackerel or Saurel *Trachurus trachurus* — Length up to 40 cm. Seafish forming large shoals in shallow water. Feeds on small fish, marine crustaceans and octopuses. Spawns in summer. Market fish. Distribution: the Atlantic, North Sea, western part of the Baltic, Mediterranean and Black Seas, usually far from the shore.

224

Subphylum: **Vertebrates — Vertebrata**

Class: **Bony fishes — Osteichthyes**

Order: **Perciformes**

Family: **Perches, walleyes and darters — Percidae**

1 European Perch *Perca fluviatilis* — Length 50 cm, weight 4 kg. One of the commonest of freshwater fishes. Found in inlets near banks with abundant aquatic vegetation; in the middle and lower reaches of rivers, in backwaters, lakes, ponds and valley reservoirs. Small perch feed on invertebrates, larger perch mostly on small fish. Young perch congregate in shoals, older specimens are solitary. Spawns in April and May. Eggs are laid in long strings twined around submerged objects. Distribution: all Europe except Scotland, the Iberian Peninsula, Italy, western Balkans and northern Norway.

2 Zander or Pike-perch *Stizostedion lucioperca* — Length more than 1 metre, weight 12 kg or more. Lives near the bottom in deeper sections of rivers with sandy or soil beds. Bred in ponds and planted into dam reservoirs, lakes and rivers. Spawns in April and May in shallow waters. Eggs are laid in nests on the roots of aquatic plants and are guarded by the male. Important freshwater fish with tasty meat. The related smaller *S. volgense* lives in rivers flowing into the Black and Caspian Seas from the Danube to the Ural.

3 Ruffe of Pope *Gymnocephalus cernua* — Length 10—15 cm. Common in the lower reaches of rivers, in dam reservoirs and in ponds. Feeds on small fish and invertebrates. Spawns between April and June on the bottom. Distribution: all Europe from England and northeast France eastward; absent in Ireland, Scotland, northern Norway, Iberian Peninsula, Italy and in the southern and western parts of the Balkan Peninsula.

4 Schraetzer *Gymnocephalus schraetser* — Length up to 24 cm. Found in swift, deep and sandy sections of rivers. Feeds on invertebrates and small fish. Distribution: Danube tributaries from Bavaria to the delta of the Danube. In some places plentiful, even in the mainstream of the Danube.

5 Zingel *Aspro zingel* — Length 50 cm. Slender fish found near the bottom of deeper, flowing waters. Feeds on invertebrates and small fish. By day hides in hollowed-out channels in deep currents. Spawns in April and May on the gravelly river bed. Distribution: tributaries of the Danube and Dniester.

6 Streber *Aspro streber* — Length 12—20 cm. Resembles the Zingel. Nocturnal, stays near the bottom in deeper, flowing sections of rivers. Feeds on various invertebrates. Spawns in spring. Distribution: Danube, Dniester and their tributaries. Ascends up the Danube as far as Austria and Bavaria.

Family: **Gobies — Gobiidae**

7 Mottled Black Sea Goby *Proterorhinus marmoratus* — Length 7—11 cm. Pelvic fins united to form a sucker. Nostrils elongated into fairly long tubes. Locally abundant in irrigation canals with dense vegetation. Feeds on small insect larvae and other invertebrates. Dwells near the bottom in brackish waters and rivers. Distribution: rivers flowing into the Black Sea.

226

Subphylum: **Vertebrates — Vertebrata**

Class: **Bony fishes — Osteichthyes**

Order: **Perciformes**

Family: **Gobies — Gobiidae**

1 Sand Goby *Pomatoschistus minutus* — Length 10 cm. Small goby abundant on sandy bottoms near the seacoast; young fish often live in river estuaries. As in all gobies the pelvic fins are united to form a sucker. Bottom-dwelling, feeds on small invertebrates. Spawns between March and July. Distribution: along the Atlantic coast from Spain to northern Norway, in the Mediterranean and Black Seas.

2 Black Goby *Gobius niger* — Length 15 cm. Found over sandy or muddy bottoms from the shore to depths of more than 50 metres, also in river estuaries. Spawns in spring. Distribution: along the coast of the eastern Atlantic, Baltic, Mediterranean and Black Seas. In the Mediterranean and the Black Sea it is caught for food.

Family: **Dragonets — Callionymidae**

3 Spotted Dragonet *Callionymus maculatus* — Length up to 14 cm. Found over sandy bottoms from the seashore to depths of about 300 metres. Feeds on marine worms, crustaceans, etc. Spawns in spring. Distribution: the northeastern Atlantic and the Mediterranean Sea. Along the European coast there are many other related species, often very brightly coloured and distinguished by marked sexual dimorphism.

Family: **Sunfishes — Centrarchidae**

4 Largemouth Bass *Micropterus salmoides* — Length 35—40 cm, weight more than 2 kg. North American freshwater fish. Bred in Europe since the 1880s in carp ponds and some alpine lakes. Lives in slow-moving or stagnant waters with dense vegetation. During the spawning season (May and June) male guards the eggs as well as the fry. Feeds on plankton in youth, later on insect larvae and small fish. Native of the USA and southern Canada.

5 Pumpkinseed *Lepomis gibbosus* — Length 15—20 cm. Brought to Europe together with the Largemouth Bass and planted out in places. Found in lakes and river inlets with abundant vegetation. Spawns in May and June. Eggs are laid in bowl-shaped depressions in the bottom and guarded by the male. Often nests in large colonies. Native to North America, from Dakota to the Gulf of Mexico; related species occur in the Antilles and in Central and South America.

Family: **Porgies, sea breams and snappers — Sparidae**

6 Gilt Head *Sparus auratus* — Length up to 70 cm. Found in the upper sea layers. Very rarely at depths of more than 30 metres. Congregates in small groups that hide among underwater rock formations. Feeds on marine crustaceans and echinoderms, which it crushes with its strong teeth. Breeds at greater depths during the winter. Locally important as a food fish. Distribution: the east Atlantic from the Bay of Biscay southward and in the Mediterranean.

7 Common Sea Bream or Axillary Bream *Pagellus centrodontus* — Length 40—50 cm. Marine fish occurring in large shoals in deeper waters between 150 and 500 metres. Important food fish. Distribution: the eastern Atlantic as far north as Ireland, very occasionally also in the North Sea.

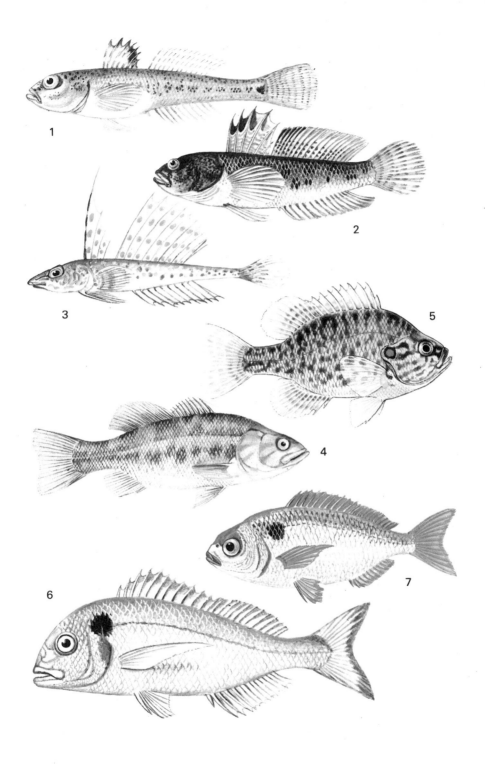

Subphylum: **Vertebrates — Vertebrata**

Class: **Bony fishes — Osteichthyes**

Order: **Perciformes**

Family: **Porgies, sea breams and snappers — Sparidae**

1 *Diplodus annularis* — Length 12—20 cm. One of the commonest fish of rocky coasts, often found also in brackish waters. Spawns between April and June. Eggs float freely in the water. Feeds chiefly on small marine crustaceans, worms, etc. Distribution: the Mediterranean, eastern Atlantic and Black Sea.

2 Dentex *Dentex dentex* — Length more than 1 metre. Predaceous marine fish feeding chiefly on fish. Occurs over rocky bottoms at depths of 10—200 metres; in spring more often near the coast, in winter at greater depths. A popular food fish. Distribution: eastern parts of the Atlantic as far north as the Bay of Biscay, very occasionally as far as the British Isles. In greater numbers in the Mediterranean.

Family: **Croakers or drums — Sciaenidae**

3 Umbrina *Umbrina cirrhosa* — Length up to 1 metre. Solitary fish found over sandy or muddy bottoms among submerged rocks. Feeds on crustaceans, worms, echinoderms and small fish. Spawns in June. Distribution: the eastern Atlantic, the Mediterranean and Black Seas.

Family: **Swordfishes — Xipiidae**

4 Swordfish *Xiphias gladius* — Length nearly 5 metres. Large fish with characteristic sword-like upper jaw, common in all tropical and warmer seas. Solitary, it lives in the open sea at depths ranging from the surface to about 600 metres. Fast swimmer, hunts various fish that travel in shoals. It charges into such a shoal, rapidly threshing about with its sword and then swallowing the fish that are dead and wounded. Spawns in summer. Eggs are pelagic. Meat is very tasty and it is therefore widely caught in southern Europe with nets as well as fishing poles. Distribution: most common in the Mediterranean. Occasionally found also in the northeast Atlantic, North Sea and western parts of the Baltic.

Family: **Thunnies — Thunnidae**

5 Great Bluefin or Atlantic Tuna *Thunnus thynnus* — Length up to 3 metres. During the summer often found close to the surface near the coast, in winter it descends to greater depths. Feeds chiefly on fish and cephalopods, young tunas on marine plankton. Spawns in summer. Eggs are pelagic. Important fish of commerce and also popular with sportsmen. Distribution: the Atlantic and the Mediterranean.

6 Skipjack Tuna *Katsuwonus pelamis* — Length 60—90 cm. Related to the preceding species. Occurs in shoals in the open sea. Spawns throughout the year. A very important fish of commerce, popular also with sportsmen. Distribution: the Atlantic as far as shores of Great Britain, in the Mediterranean and the Black Sea.

Family: **Mackerels — Scombridae**

7 Atlantic Bonito *Sarda sarda* — Length 80 cm. Occurs in large shoals near the surface by the coast. Feeds chiefly on schooling fish, cephalopods and other larger marine organisms. Migrates before spawning, travelling long distances. Spawns in summer. Important fish of commerce. Distribution: warmer parts of the Atlantic and the Mediterranean.

Subphylum: **Vertebrates — Vertebrata**

Class: **Bony fishes — Osteichthyes**

Order: **Perciformes**

Family: **Mackerels — Scombridae**

1 Atlantic Mackerel *Scomber scombrus* — Length 50 cm. Rapid and constantly swimming gregarious fish. In summer large shoals of mackerel occur near the shore, in winter they move to deeper waters. Feeds on marine crustaceans, various other invertebrates and small fish. Spawns in spring and summer. One of the most valuable fish of commerce. Distribution: the north Atlantic and Mediterranean, found also in the Black Sea.

Family: **Mullets — Mugilidae**

2 Striped Mullet *Mugil cephalus* — Length 50 cm. Occurs in small shoals near the seacoast, moves readily up rivers against the current. Feeds on small bottom-dwelling animals and plant parts. Males are smaller than females. Spawns in early spring. Distribution: seas and lower reaches of rivers from the Baltic along the entire coast of Europe, including the Mediterranean and the Black Sea.

Family: **Weeverfishes — Trachinidae**

3 Greater Weever *Trachinus draco* — Length 40 cm. Found over sandy bottoms, in which it is fond of burying itself; from the coast to depths of about 100 metres. On the gill covers and on the first dorsal fin there are sharp spines with grooves that contain venom. They are a menace to swimmers who may be dangerously wounded by them. The best way to counteract the effect of the venom is to immerse the wounded limb in hot water for some time — heat decreases the effect of the poison. Spawns in spring. Eggs are pelagic. Distribution: the coast of the northeast Atlantic, the Mediterranean and the Black Sea.

Family: **Wrasses — Labridae**

4 Rainbow Wrasse *Coris julis* — Length more than 25 cm. Occurs near coastal rock formations covered with seaweed to depths of about 120 metres. In winter descends to greater depths. Active only by day. Feeds on small marine crustaceans, molluscs, etc. Spawns in summer. Eggs are pelagic. Young differ in coloration from adults: young females have a blue patch on the lower edge of the gill cover; fish more than 20 cm in length are coloured olive-brown with a yellow longitudinal band on the sides. Distribution: the northwest Atlantic as far north as the southern shores of the British Isles, the Mediterranean.

5 Blunt-snouted Gold Sinny *Ctenolabrus rupestris* — Length 18 cm. Lives mostly amidst marine rock formations. Feeds on bottom-dwelling fauna. Spawns in summer. Eggs are pelagic. Adults probably die after spawning. Distribution: the northeast Atlantic, Mediterranean and the Black Sea.

6 Cuckoo Wrasse *Labrus ossifagus* — Length 35 cm. Males and females differ markedly in coloration, which is furthermore extremely variable. During the summer common amidst coastal rock formations at depths of about 10 metres where it digs hollows for the eggs. In winter descends to greater depths. Feeds on small bottom-dwelling marine invertebrates. Distribution: the northeast Atlantic coast and in the Mediterranean.

7 Gold Sinny or Corkwing *Crenilabrus melops* — Length 15—25 cm. Coloration very variable. Spawns between early spring and summer. Eggs are laid in nests made of seaweed. Common along the shores of all Europe as far north as the coast of Norway, also in the Mediterranean.

232

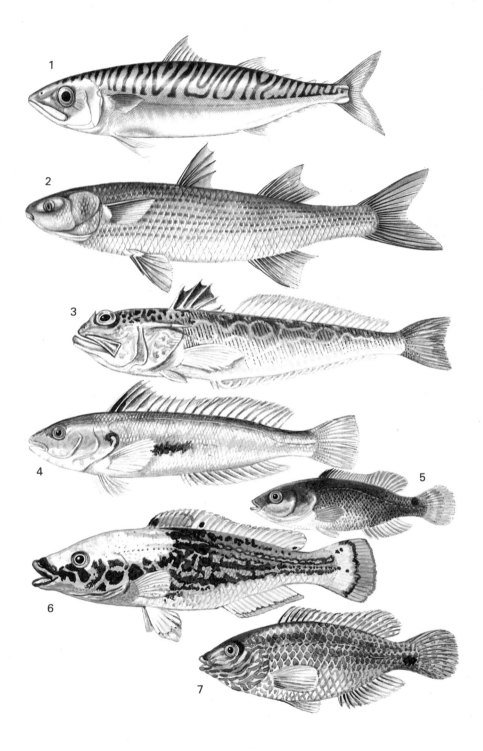

Subphylum: **Vertebrates — Vertebrata**

Class: **Bony fishes — Osteichthyes**

Order: **Perciformes**

Family: **Wolf fishes and wolfeels — Anarrhichadidae**

1 Atlantic Wolf Fish *Annarrhichas lupus* — Length 120 cm. Occurs at depths of 100—300 metres, younger fish in shallower waters. Feeds on marine crustaceans, molluscs and echinoderms. Distribution: northern parts of the north-east Atlantic from the extreme north as far as the British and French coast, the North Sea and western part of the Baltic.

Family: **Scaleless blennies — Bleniidae**

2 Shanny *Blennius pholis* — Length up to 16 cm. Occurs near rocky coasts, fond of burying itself in the mud or sand. Feeds on smaller animals and plant food. Eggs are laid under stones and in crevices between stones. They are guarded by the male who agitates the water with his fins to keep them provided with oxygenated water. Many related species are found along the coasts of all European seas. Distribution: the northeast Atlantic north of the Portugese coast.

Order: **Pleuronectiformes**

Family: **Right-eyed flounders — Pleuronectidae**

3 Atlantic Halibut *Hippoglossus hippoglossus* — Length 2.5—3.5 metres. Largest member of the family, found over sandy or rocky bottoms at depths of 50—2,000 metres. Feeds on fish, cuttlefish, and various marine crustaceans. Spawns between December and April at depths of 300—1000 metres. Has very tasty meat and is therefore an important fish of commerce. Distribution: the northeast Atlantic from the White Sea to the Bay of Biscay. Also in the North Sea and occasionally in the Baltic.

4 Plaice *Pleuronectes platessa* — Length 25—90 cm. Tolerates varying degrees of salinity and thus often found in brackish waters; it also enters rivers. Young plaice feed on small marine invertebrates (worms, crustaceans, etc.). Adult fish feed on larger prey, e. g. molluscs. Spawns in winter at great depths. Distribution: the north-east Atlantic, western parts of the Mediterranean and in the North Sea.

Family: **Soles — Soleidae**

5 Common European Sole *Solea solea* — Length 30—60 cm. Occurs in shallow waters near the coast, in deeper water usually at depths of 10—60 metres, very occasionally to depths of about 180 metres. Nocturnal fish. Feeds on marine molluscs, worms, crustaceans and small fish of the bottom. Spawns in winter. Important fish of commerce, popular for its tasty meat. Distribution: along the European coasts of the northeast Atlantic from Scotland to the Mediterranean, the southern parts of the North Sea and eastern parts of the Baltic.

Subphylum: **Vertebrates — Vertebrata**

Class: **Amphibians — Amphibia**

Order: **Tailed amphibians — Urodela**

Family: **Newts and salamanders — Salamandridae**

1 Fire Salamander *Salamandra salamandra* — Length 15—20 cm, in the Balkans up to 33 cm. Found from foothills to mountains up to elevations of more than 1,000 metres in broadleaved forests around clear streams rich in oxygen. Feeds on worms, slugs and various insects. Breeding period is in March and April, when it leaves its winter shelters on dry land. Female bears up to 60 live larvae that have external gills and live in water for 2—3 months after which they metamorphose and live on dry land. Distribution: central and southern Europe. In Europe it forms a great number of subspecies.

2 Alpine Salamander *Salamandra atra* — Length 14—16 cm. Lives in mountains at elevations of 800—2,000 metres in shady forests around mountain streams. Unlike the preceding species it does not bear aquatic larvae but gives birth directly to 2 fully developed young that live on dry land right after birth. Distribution: the Alps, the Jura in France and the mountains of Yugoslavia and Albania.

3 Crested Newt *Triturus cristatus* — Length 18 cm. Largest European newt, common in quiet or slow-flowing waters with dense aquatic vegetation. Breeding period is in March and April. Female lays 200—400 eggs singly on submerged leaves of grasses or aquatic plants. After 2—3 weeks these hatch into larvae with external gills that live in water for about 3 months, after which they metamorphose. Outside the breeding season adults live on dry land under stones, wood or amidst moss and feed on worms, snails and insect larvae. Distribution: central and southern Europe.

4 Smooth Newt *Triturus vulgaris* — Length 10—11 cm. Commonest European newt, found at lower elevations. Breeding period is in April and May. Female lays 200—300 eggs on aquatic vegetation or other submerged objects. Larvae hatch 2—3 weeks later. Distribution: all Europe; forms a great number of geographic races.

5 Alpine Newt *Triturus alpestris* — Length 8—11 cm. Typical mountain species. In early spring leaves its winter shelter and enters calm or flowing waters where mating takes place between March and May. Soon after mating adults return to dry land. Larvae have external gills and metamorphose after 2—3 months, at higher elevations they sometimes hibernate in water and metamorphosis takes place the following spring. This species is sometimes neotenic — occasionally it may attain sexual maturity and reproduce while still in the larval stage. Distribution: the mountains of central and southern Europe.

6 Carpathian Newt *Triturus montandoni* — Length 7—10 cm. Common in Carpathian mountain forests with small lakes with dense vegetation and slow-flowing mountain streams. Lives in water from March to June; after pairing lives on dry land. Hibernates in water. Breeding period is in late April and early May. Eggs are cemented to aquatic vegetation. As in other species of newts the male is smaller than the female. Distribution: northern Moravia and Slovakia, Hungary and the Rumanian Carpathians.

1

2

5 ♂

3 ♂

3 ♀

4 ♂

6 ♂

Subphylum: **Vertebrates — Vertebrata**

Class: **Amphibians — Amphibia**

Order: **Tail-less amphibians or frogs and toads — Anura**

Family: **Discoglossids — Discoglossidae**

1 Fire-bellied Toad *Bombina bombina* — Length 4.5 cm. Lives at lower elevations in calm, clear waters. Feeds on small aquatic animals. Female lays eggs singly or in small clumps on aquatic vegetation or submerged grass several times a year. Distribution: central and eastern Europe (north as far as southern Scandinavia, south as far as Vienna), northern Yugoslavia, Rumania and Bulgaria, to the southern parts of the USSR and Asia Minor.

2 Yellow-bellied Toad *Bombina variegata* — Length 5 cm. Common mainly in mountain regions. Feeds on small aquatic invertebrates, chiefly mosquito larvae. Hibernates on dry land in widely diverse places; throughout the warm seasons it lives in water. Distribution: central and southern Europe except the Iberian Peninsula. Within this area it forms several subspecies.

3 Midwife Toad *Alytes obstetricans* — Length 4—5 cm. Nocturnal, found mostly in mountain regions. Pairing takes place on dry land between early spring and late summer; male attracts females with his ringing voice. After mating male winds a string of eggs round the hind limbs, carrying them about with him for several weeks and taking care that they do not dry out. Shortly before the tadpoles emerge from the eggs the male returns to the water. Tadpoles hibernate in water and metamorphose the following year. Distribution: western parts of central and southern Europe.

Family: **Spadefoot toads — Pelobatidae**

4 Spadefoot Toad *Pelobates fuscus* — Length 5—8 cm. Active mostly by night, feeding on worms, snails and the like; by day it hides in holes. Partial to sandy areas. Can burrow in the ground very rapidly. Hibernates deep underground, often at depths of more than 2 metres. Pairing takes place in water between March and May. Often the tadpoles (larvae) do not develop into adults by winter and hibernate; they then measure up to 17 cm in length. Distribution: from central Europe to the east.

Family: **Toads — Bufonidae**

5 Common Toad *Bufo bufo* — Length 12 cm, in southern regions as much as 20 cm. Nocturnal, hiding under stones by day. Feeds on insects, worms, snails and spiders. Usually leaves its winter shelter on land in early March and enters water where mating takes place. Small tadpoles live in water for 3—4 months, after which they change into small toads that grow slowly. Males are smaller than females. Distribution: all Europe, Asia and northwest Africa from lowland to mountain elevations.

6 Natterjack Toad *Bufo calamita* — Length 6—8 cm. Active by night, feeding on various invertebrates. Lives in lowlands as well as at higher elevations. Does not move by leaping but by walking, for its hind legs are shorter than those of other toads. Pairing takes place in water in May. Hibernates deep in the ground. Distribution: all Europe from the Iberian Peninsula north to southern Scandinavia and east to the western parts of the USSR.

7 Green Toad *Bufo viridis* — Length 10 cm. Active both day and night. Feeds on insects, molluscs, worms and other invertebrates. Tolerates drought as well as salt water. Pairing takes place between April and the end of May. Tadpoles live in water 2—3 months. Males utter characteristic melodious sounds during the breeding season. Distribution: central and southern Europe, north Africa and all Asia from lowland to mountain elevations.

Subphylum: **Vertebrates — Vertebrata**

Class: **Amphibians — Amphibia**

Order: **Tail-less amphibians or frogs and toads — Anura**

Family: **Tree frogs — Hylidae**

1 Common Tree Frog *Hyla arborea* — Length 4—5 cm. Lives in moist regions with lush vegetation, during the breeding period (May) in water. Tadpoles metamorphose after 3 months; small frogs leave the water and climb shrubs and trees. Feeds on small insects which it often captures with a leap. Marked by ability to change colour, blending perfectly with its environment. Survives winter hidden under stones, in holes, etc., as well as on the bottom of calm bodies of water. Distribution: all Europe (except the British Isles), northwest Africa and Asia.

Family: **True frogs — Ranidae**

2 Edible Frog *Rana esculenta* — Length 10—12.5 cm. Has a dark-spotted belly. Lives round quiet and flowing waters at low and median elevations. Excellent swimmer. Feeds on insects, worms, small fish and other animals, hunting them on land as well as in water. Pairing takes place in early spring. Tadpoles change after approximately 4 months into frogs about 2 cm long. Hibernates in mud on the water bottom. Distribution: all Europe from England and France to the USSR and from Sweden to Sicily.

3 Marsh Frog *Rana ridibunda* — Length 17 cm. Thermophilous, partial to shallow banks of larger calm bodies of water at lower elevations. Belly a single colour with dark-grey dots. Feeds on various aquatic invertebrates, small fish and occasionally also other small vertebrates. Pairing takes place in April and May. Tadpoles change into frogs after 3—4 months. Hibernates in mud on the water bottom. Distribution: from north Africa to southern and central Europe, also western Asia.

4 Common Frog *Rana temporaria* — Length 10 cm. Very common frog of both lower and mountain elevations. In the Alps found even at altitudes of more than 3,000 metres. Feeds on various invertebrates. Pairing takes place at lower elevations in March, in the mountains in April or May. Tadpoles change into frogs after 2—3 months. Usually hibernates in mud on the water bottom, rarely on land. Distribution: central and northern Europe, all Asia.

5 Moor Frog *Rana arvalis* — Length 7.5 cm. Head sharply pointed. Lives in peat and swamp regions mainly at lower elevations, usually keeping close to water. Feeds on widely varied insects, spiders, snails, etc. Pairing takes place in March or April. Tadpoles metamorphose after 2—3 months. During the breeding season the male develops a bluish back and dark callouses on the first toe of each foreleg. In other members of the family differences between the sexes are not so conspicuous. Distribution: from northwestern France to Siberia, as far as the Arctic Circle. Absent in the Mediterranean and around the Black Sea.

6 Agile Frog *Rana dalmatina* — Length 7—9 cm. Lives in open broadleaved forests at lower elevations. Has the longest hind legs of all members of the genus. Differs from the Common Frog by its colouring, which is lighter, often brownish tinged with red. When danger threatens it makes 2—3 metre-long leaps. During the summer it lives on land, often far from water, feeding on various invertebrates. Pairing takes place in late March and early April when it congregates in forest pools. Tadpoles metamorphose after 2—3 months. Usually hibernates buried in mud on the water bottom. Distribution: from southern and central Europe as far north as southern Scandinavia.

Subphylum: **Vertebrates** — **Vertebrata**

Class: **Reptiles** — **Reptilia**

Order: **Chelonia**

Suborder: **Turtles, tortoises and terrapins** — **Cryptodira**

Family: **Freshwater turtles** — **Emydidae**

1 European Pond Terrapin *Emys orbicularis* — Length 30 cm. Feeds on invertebrates and small fish. Inhabits quiet or slow-moving waters at lower elevations, generally in the flood-plains of large rivers. Adult turtles always live in or near water, basking in the sun on the banks during the day. They are very shy. Hibernate buried in the bottom, emerging in late March and April. Breeding period is in May. Eggs are buried on dry land in sand which the turtles tamp down with the undershield (plastron). The young, 1.2—2 cm long, hatch after about 100 days. Distribution: north Africa, central and southern Europe, western Asia.

2 Striped-necked Terrapin *Mauremys caspica* — Length 30 cm. Common in fast-flowing streams as well as quiet pools. Diet consists of animal and plant food. Breeding period is between March and June, when the female lays 5—10 elongate eggs in holes in the ground, which she excavates with her hind legs. Young hatch after 70—100 days. Distribution: from north Africa through southern Europe to western Asia. In Europe it forms several subspecies.

Family: **Tortoises** — **Testudinidae**

3 Common European Tortoise *Testudo graeca* — Length 30 cm. Herbivorous. Inhabits shrubby regions from lowlands to foothills. Appears during the first warm days of March, mating immediately after. Female lays eggs in self-dug holes in the ground. Young hatch after 10—12 weeks. Distribution: southern Europe, north Africa, southwest Asia.

4 Hermann's Tortoise *Testudo hermanni* — Length 25 cm. Differs from the preceding species by having a spike at the tip of the tail and two plates, instead of one, on the dorsal shield above the tail. It also lacks the horny projection on either side of the femur at the base of the tail which is present in the Common European Tortoise. Its biology is identical with that of the above species. Distribution: western and eastern parts of southern Europe.

5 Margined Tortoise *Testudo marginata* — Length up to 35 cm. Herbivorous. Found on the dry sunny slopes of hillsides and often in dry stream beds. Awakens from its winter sleep in March, as a rule, and mates soon after. Newly-hatched young are about 3 cm long. In recent years its numbers have been rapidly declining in places where it was once numerous as a result of land cultivation and the disappearance of its natural environments. Distribution: southeastern Greece and Sardinia, where it was probably introduced.

Family: **Leather-backed turtles** — **Dermochelyidae**

6 Leatherback — *Dermochelys coriacea* — Length 2 metres, weight 600 kg. Typical turtle of the open sea. Feeds chiefly on marine animals. Moves to dry land only during breeding season in May and June, when it buries 90—150 eggs, about 5 cm large, in the sand near the shore. Young turtles hatch after about 2 months. Distribution: Atlantic, Pacific, Indian Oceans and the Mediterranean.

Subphylum: **Vertebrates — Vertebrata**

Class: **Reptiles — Reptilia**

Order: **Lizards and snakes — Squamata**

Suborder: **Lizards, geckos and iguanas — Lacertilia**

Family: **Geckos — Gekkonidae**

1 Kotschyi's Gecko *Cyrtodactylus kotschyi* — Length 10 cm. Nocturnal gecko, may be encountered outisde its hiding place also in the morning or late afternoon. Lives amidst large piles of stones, on rocks and on walls. Feeds on various invertebrates. Often found on the walls of buildings near lamps or lanterns, where it captures insects attracted to the light. Distribution: southern Europe and western Asia; a number of subspecies are known.

2 Moorish Gecko *Tarentola mauritanica* — Length 16 cm. Nocturnal; in spring may be encountered outside its hiding place by day, in summer active only in the evening and at night. The suction pads on its feet enable it to move swiftly and safely even on smooth, vertical surfaces. Eggs are laid in spring under stones and in cracks in walls. Young geckos, measuring 3–5 cm, hatch after 4 months. Distribution: abundant in western countries round the Mediterranean; sporadic distribution in southeastern Europe (e. g. in Dalmatia, Greece, Crete and Ionian Islands).

3 Turkish Gecko *Hemidactylus turcicus* — Length 8–10 cm. Partial to sunny regions where it may be found in rock crevices, on walls and under stones. Female lays 2 eggs. Incubation takes about 3 months. Distribution: the Mediterranean, north Africa and India-Pakistan; introduced by Man to the American continent.

Family: **Chameleons — Chamaeleonidae**

4 Mediterranean Chameleon *Chamaeleo chamaeleon* — Length 23–28 cm. Lives on branches of trees and shrubs amidst foliage, moving about with characteristic slow movements. Noted for its ability to change the colour of its skin from almost white to black. Eyes move independently of each other and can observe two separate objects at the same time. The tongue is long and can be projected to a great distance to catch insects. The tail is prehensile, serving to keep a hold on branches. Breeding period is in autumn, when the female lays about 30 elongated eggs, burying them in the ground. The young hatch the following summer after about 200 days. It is the only member of this tropical family found in the warm regions of Europe. Distribution: southern Spain and Portugal, Crete and the islands of Chios and Samos, north Africa, Syria, the Arabian Peninsula and Asia Minor.

Family: **Skinks — Scincidae**

5 Snake-eyed Skink *Ablepharus kitaibelii* — Length 10–11 cm. Common on dry, sunny and stony hillsides, often in oak leaves. Feeds on various insects and their larvae. Unlike most skinks it lays eggs. Several subspecies are known. Distribution: the Balkans, Aegean islands and western Asia. Southern Slovakia marks the northernmost limits of its range.

6 European Skink *Chalcides chalcides* — Length over 40 cm. Found on grassy hillsides. Hides under stones, in walls and under leaves. Feeds on insects, spiders and other invertebrates. Female bears 10–15 live young. Hibernates deep in the ground from early autumn to late spring. Distribution: northwest Africa and southwestern Europe.

Subphylum: **Vertebrates — Vertebrata**

Class: **Reptiles — Reptilia**

Order: **Lizards and snakes — Squamata**

Suborder: **Lizards, geckos and iguanas — Lacertilia**

Family: **Lizards — Lacertidae**

1 Green Lizard *Lacerta viridis* — Length 40—50 cm. Common at lowland as well as higher elevations in sunny, dry places with abundance of shrubs. Feeds on various insects, small lizards and mice. In spring the female lays 6—20 eggs from which small brownish lizards, 3—4 cm long, hatch 2—3 months later. Like other members of the genus *Lacerta* it sheds its tail when danger threatens. Distribution: central Europe and more southerly regions from northern Spain and France as far as Asia Minor.

2 Sand Lizard *Lacerta agilis* — Length more than 20 cm. Lives in warm, lowland country, foothills and mountains. Female lays 5—15 eggs between May and late June, burying them in holes about 6—7 cm deep. The young, 3—4 cm long, hatch after 8 weeks. Feeds on insects and other invertebrates, as well as young lizards. Distribution: almost all Europe except the extreme north, southern Balkans, Italy and the Iberian Peninsula. Common in several geographic races also in central Asia.

3 Viviparous Lizard *Lacerta vivipara* — Length 15—16 cm. Occurs in moist regions, in the north common in lowlands, in more southerly regions mainly in the mountains. Feeds chiefly on insects and other invertebrates. Distribution: almost all Europe, from the Pyrenees to the 70th parallel, and northern Asia as far as the Pacific Ocean.

4 Wall Lizard *Lacerta muralis* — Length 20—25 cm. Partial to dry, rocky and stony habitats. Feeds chiefly on insects. Breeding period is in May and June, mating often takes place a second and third time in the same year. Lays 2—8 eggs from which the young hatch after 8 weeks. Distribution: warmer parts of central and southern Europe and Asia Minor.

5 Ocellated Lizard *Lacerta lepida* — Length 50—90 cm. Largest member of the family. Found in lowlands as well as foothills in light, sunny areas with rocks, piles of stones, thickets and fruit trees. Very agile; when threatened by danger it can deliver a painful bite. Feeds on invertebrates and smaller vertebrates. Breeding period is in April and May. Female often lays more than 20 eggs from which the young hatch after 3 months. Distribution: northwest Africa, the Iberian Peninsula, southern France, northwestern Italy.

6 Grass Lizard *Lacerta taurica* — Length 20 cm. A small, very agile lizard found in dry, stony and grassy regions. Breeding period is in May. Lays 2—6 eggs. Distribution: southeastern Europe; Hungary, Rumania, the Balkans, Ionian and Aegean islands and the European part of Turkey.

Subphylum: **Vertebrates — Vertebrata**

Class: **Reptiles — Reptilia**

Order: **Lizards and snakes — Squamata**

Suborder: **Lizards, geckos and iguanas — Lacertilia**

Family: **Lizards — Lacertidae**

1 Steppe Racer *Eremias arguta deserti* — Length 20 cm. Noted for its ability to bury itself in the sand with lightning rapidity when danger threatens. Feeds on spiders, ants, various insects and other invertebrates. Lays 3—12 eggs once or twice during the summer. Distribution: sandy regions of eastern Rumania (coastal dunes) as far as the southern USSR.

2 Spanish Psammodromus *Psammodromus hispanicus* — Length 10—20 cm. Very swift and shy lizard found in dry, rocky regions and in coastal sand dune regions with sparse vegetation. Distribution: the Iberian Peninsula and southern France. The closely related *Ophisops elegans* is found in southeastern Europe and western Asia.

Family: **Lateral fold lizards — Anguidae**

3 Slow-worm *Anguis fragilis* — Length 45 cm; male is smaller than female. Found in lowlands as well as mountains, in moist regions under stones, tree trunks and in fallen leaves. Feeds on earthworms, slugs, spiders and various insects. Appears in April. Young are born in July and August as they hatch, the egg cover usually rupturing during their passage through the cloaca. Hibernates from October on, often in large groups, about 50 cm below the ground surface. Distribution: almost all Europe (except Ireland), north as far as the 66th parallel and east as far as northern Turkey and Iran. Also occurs in northwest Africa.

4 European Glass Lizard *Ophisaurus apodus* — Length more than 1 metre. Related to the Slow-worm. Found in sunny meadows, fields, scrub country, as well as around rock formations in the foothills. Feeds on snails, mice, voles, lizards, small birds and birds'eggs. If it captures a larger victim it stuns or kills it by rapidly spinning around its own axis, which is also done by the Slow-worm. Breeding period is in June and July, when the female lays 8—10 elongated eggs. The young hatch at the end of August. Distribution: the Balkans, Crimea, Asia Minor, Syria, Iran, Transcaucasia and Turkestan.

Suborder: **Snakes — Ophidia**

Family: **Blind snakes — Typhlopidae**

5 Worm Snake *Typhlops vermicularis* — Length 20—35 cm. Small, pink, burrowing snake resembling a large earthworm at first glance. Has two tiny black eyes and a sharp spine on the tail. Feeds on small invertebrates, chiefly ants and ant pupae. Lives in the ground and under stones, where it makes tunnels. Female lays 6 small eggs in May. Distribution: from southern Yugoslavia through the southern Balkans to central Asia. Also found on many Greek islands.

Family: **Boas — Boidae**

6 Sand Boa *Eryx jaculus* — Length 80 cm. Found in warm regions in stony places, usually under stones or in holes in the ground. Capable of burrowing into ground with lightning speed. Emerges only in the early morning and late afternoon to hunt lizards and mice, which are its main food. It kills its victims by coiling itself around their bodies and suffocating them. Breeding period is in June and July. Female usually bears 5—12 living young. Distribution: southeastern Europe, western Asia and north Africa.

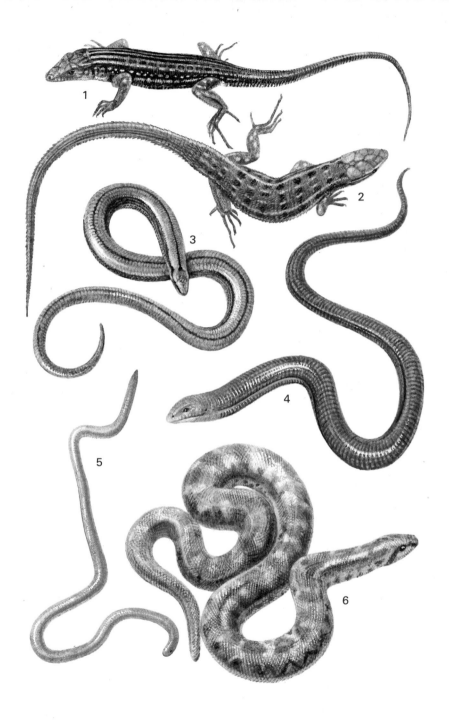

Subphylum: **Vertebrates — Vertebrata**

Class: **Reptiles — Reptilia**

Order: **Lizards and snakes — Squamata**

Suborder: **Snakes — Ophidia**

Family: **Colubrid snakes — Colubridae**

1 Grass Snake *Natrix natrix* — Length 1—1.5 metres. Common near water. Feeds chiefly on amphibians, mainly frogs, small rodents, fish and insects. Breeding period is in July and August. Female lays 6—30 eggs under leaves, in moss and similar hiding places. The young, measuring 10—15 cm, hatch after 2 months. Hibernates from November to the end of March under large stones, in holes and in other underground shelters. Distribution: all Europe, northwest Africa and western Asia.

2 Dice Snake *Natrix tessellata* — Length 150 cm. Found around fresh waters, mainly with an abundance of fish, which form the mainstay of its diet. Active by day and night. Swims very well and is adept at catching fish. Breeding period is in June and July. Eggs are laid among fallen leaves. Distribution: from southeastern France through Germany, all of Europe and Asia to northwest India and western China. In the south occurs as far as Egypt, in the north roughly to the 50th parallel (Germany, USSR), in places as far as the 54th parallel.

3 Smooth Snake *Coronella austriaca* — Length up to 75 cm. Found on dry, sunny, stony hillsides covered with vegetation; in southern Europe as high as 2,200 metres, in northern regions at lower elevations. Feeds on lizards, slow-worms, small snakes, rodents, birds and insects. Bites when in danger. Eggs are laid in August or September and the young, about 12—15 cm long, hatch shortly after. Distribution: almost all Europe except the southern parts of Italy and the Iberian Peninsula and the like. Distribution: southeastern Europe and western Asia.

4 Large Whip Snake *Coluber jugularis* — Length 2—3 metres. Largest European snake. Found in steppe and scrub country. Diurnal. Feeds on various small mammals, birds, lizards and snakes. Breeding period is in June and July. Female lays 7—15 eggs in holes in the ground, in rock crevices, and the like. Distribution: southeastern Europe and western Asia.

5 Balkan Whip Snake *Coluber gemonensis* — Length 120—140 cm. Found in dry regions with low shrub growth and in open, sunny oak woods. Feeds on rodents, lizards, birds, small snakes and insects. Distribution: the Balkans, particularly along the Adriatic coast, southern Greece, the Peloponnesus, also on Crete and the Greek islands of Euboia and Kythera.

6 Dahl's Whip Snake *Coluber najadum* — Length 120—130 cm. A very agile and attractive snake with characteristic pattern on the front part of the body. Feeds almost exclusively on lizards, sometimes also on various insects. Found in lowlands and foothills, being partial to places overgrown with thickets, often near streams. Usually lays only 3—5 eggs in holes in the ground, rock crevices or under stones. Distribution: the Balkan Peninsula, Asia Minor, Syria and northwestern Iran.

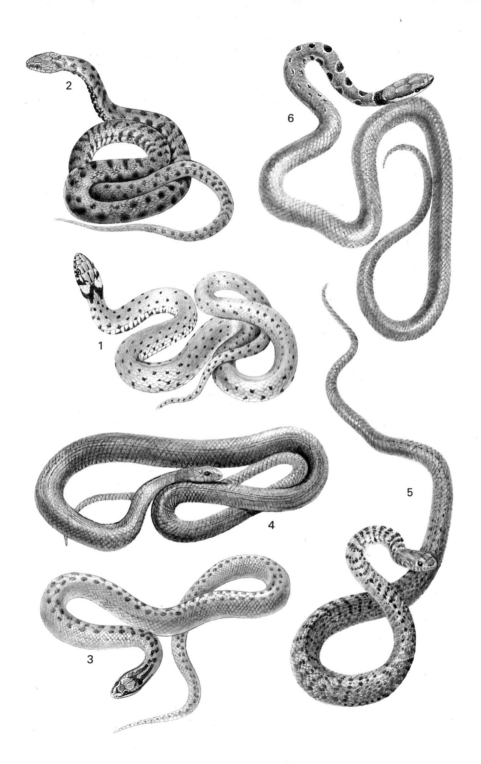

Subphylum: **Vertebrates — Vertebrata**

Class: **Reptiles — Reptilia**

Order: **Lizards and snakes — Squamata**

Suborder: **Snakes — Ophidia**

Family: **Colubrid snakes — Colubridae**

1 *Coluber hippocrepis* — Length 1.7 metres. A skilful climber; climbs up trees as well as houseroofs and drainpipes. Feeds on small birds and mice. In spring and early summer the female lays eggs in the ground, in rock crevices, under stones and among leaves. Distribution: the Iberian Peninsula, Sardinia, Spain, Portugal, northwest Africa.

2 Aesculapian Snake *Elaphe longissima* — Length 1.6—2 metres. Slender snake that climbs skillfully in the tops of trees and shrubs. Found on sunny, shrub-covered hillsides; in central Europe at lower elevations, in southern Europe also in mountains up to 2,000 metres. Feeds on small rodents, birds and lizards. In June and July female lays 5—8 eggs in decaying tree trunks, amidst leaves and in holes. The young, up to 20 cm long, hatch after about 2 months. Distribution: from northeastern Spain to the Balkans, northern parts of Asia Minor, the Caucasus ans northern Iran. In central Europe at places in France, Germany, Switzerland, northern Italy, Austria, Poland, Czechoslovakia and Hungary.

3 Four-lined Snake *Elaphe quatuorlineata* — Length 1.5—2 metres. Found on sun-warmed hillsides covered with thickets and in open woodlands, being partial to stony ground affording numerous opportunities for concealment. Feeds on small mammals, birds and birds'eggs. Active by day as well as after dusk. Breeding period is from spring to autumn. Female lays 6—16 elongated eggs, usually in July and August. Young hatch in September or early October. Distribution: southeastern Europe and western Asia.

4 Leopard Snake *Elaphe situla* — Length about 1 metre. One of the most brightly-coloured of European snakes. Partial to dry and warm, stony places covered with thorny thickets in foothills and mountains. Hides in an underground winter shelter in late October, remaining there until April. Feeds on small rodents, birds and lizards. In July and August the female lays 2—5 rather large eggs under stones or in dry, decayed wood and among leaves. Distribution: southern Italy, Sicily, western parts of the Balkan Peninsula, northern Sporades and Cyclades, Crete, Asia Minor, the Caucasus and the Crimea.

5 Montpellier Snake *Malpolon monspessulanus* — Length over 2 metres. Very swift snake. Has poisonous teeth at the back of jaws with which it cripples or kills captured prey: small mammals, birds, snakes and lizards. Found in warm, dry and sunny regions with low vegetation and thorny thickets; also around piles of stones near cultivated land, walls and ruins. Breeding period is in July and August. Female lays 4—18 elongated eggs. Young hatch in September and October. Distribution: southern Europe, north Africa and western Asia.

6 European Cat Snake *Telescopus fallax* — Length 1 metre. Snake with poisonous teeth at the back of the jaws. Found in dry, stony regions with low shrubs. Active in the evening and at night. Feeds chiefly on lizards and small mammals. Young feed mostly on insects and small lizards. Distribution: the Balkans, Greece and the Near East.

Subphylum: **Vertebrates — Vertebrata**

Class: **Reptiles — Reptilia**

Order: **Lizards and snakes — Squamata**

Suborder: **Snakes — Ophidia**

Family: **Vipers — Viperidae**

1 Adder *Vipera berus* — Length about 1 metre. Male is smaller than the female. Venomous; its bite may be fatal, particularly for children. Feeds chiefly on small rodents, often also on lizards, amphibians, small birds and insects. Found in moist as well as sunny places along forest streams, in clearings, on stony banks covered with vegetation, around buildings at higher elevations (more than 500 metres) and in mountains up to 2,000 metres (in southern Europe nearly up to 3,000 metres). In August or early September the female bears living young (the egg cover ruptures when passing through the cloaca). Distribution: all Europe, except the Iberian Peninsula, Italy, southern Balkans and Ireland. In northern Europe found as far as the 67th parallel.

2 Adder — black form *Vipera berus prester* — Besides the common greyish or brownish vipers with black or brown pattern on the back there is also an all-black form with the underside of the tail coloured yellow. This form often occurs in the mountains. Reddish-rufous vipers with brown zig-zag stripe on the back are designated as morpha *chersea*.

3 Nose-horned Viper *Vipera ammodytes* — Length up to 1 metre. Robust venomous snake with characteristic small 'horn' on the nose. Found in dry, sun-warmed places. Feeds on small rodents, occasionally also birds and lizards. In late August and September the female lays 4—20 eggs from which the young, measuring 15—20 cm in length, hatch immediately. Within its area of distribution it forms several subspecies, which apart from the size, number of scales and colour of the back also differ from one another in the colouration of the tip of the tail. Distribution: southeastern Europe and western Asia.

4 Asp Viper *Vipera aspis* — Length 70—75 cm. Found in foothills as well as mountains up to elevations of more than 2,600 metres. Occurs in dry, sun-warmed places with piles of stones, near crumbled walls, etc. Leaves its winter shelter in late March and April. Mating takes place soon after. In late August and early September the female lays 4—18 eggs from which the young emerge immediately. Feeds at first on young lizards, later almost exclusively on small mammals. Distribution: central and eastern parts of southern Europe. Besides the type form *V. aspis aspis,* common in northwestern Italy, France, northern Switzerland and southern Black Forest, there are several subspecies.

5 Blunt-nosed Viper *Vipera lebetina* — Length up to 1.5 metres. Robust viper found in rocky habitats, also in partly dried-out beds of mountain streams bordered by lush vegetation. Unlike the other European vipers it lays 15—20 eggs from which the young emerge after 4—5 weeks, i.e. in August and September. Feeds on small rodents, birds, lizards and snakes. It kills its prey by biting. Of all European venomous snakes it is the most dangerous to Man. Distribution: northwest Africa, some islands of the Greek Cyclades, Crete, and western and central Asia. The smallest subspecies *V. lebetina schweizeri* is found on the islands of Milos, Kimolos, Siphnos and Polinos in the Cyclades, another subspecies in Cyprus, still another in Iraq.

Subphylum: **Vertebrates — Vertebrata**

Class: **Birds — Aves**

Order: **Divers or loons — Gaviiformes**

Family: **Divers or loons — Gaviidae**

1 Black-throated Diver or Loon *Gavia arctica* — Length about 70 cm. Feeds chiefly on fish, molluscs, small crustaceans and insects. Found in the region of large northern lakes in the tundra and forest-tundra where it nests on the shore close to the water, often on small islands. In May—June the female usually lays 2 eggs. Both parents watch over the eggs and later also tend the nestlings. When the northern lakes freeze over, between October and April, they migrate to more southerly regions and overwinter on large rivers and lakes as well as the shores of the North, Mediterranean and Black Seas. Distribution: northern Europe, Asia, North America.

Order: **Grebes — Podicipediformes**

Family: **Podicipedidae**

2 Great Crested Grebe *Podiceps cristatus* — Length 48 cm. Prefers stagnant waters; common inhabitant of ponds. Feeds on small fish and various insect larvae. Nest is built of plant material and concealed in reeds, where it rests on the water. Between April and June the female lays 3—4 greenish eggs which both parents incubate. Both also tend the young. Nestlings have dark stripes and are carried about on their parents' backs. European populations overwinter in southern and western Europe; they travel to their winter quarters by night. Distribution: all Europe (except the extreme north), Asia, Africa, Australia.

3 Little Grebe *Podiceps ruficollis* — Length about 27 cm. Smallest of the grebes. Common on slow-moving waters and ponds but very shy, keeping hidden among the reeds. It feeds on various insects and insect larvae, hunting both on the surface and in the water. The nest is a floating structure made of plant material in which the female lays 5—6 pale-green eggs between April and June. Male and female take turns incubating and both tend the young. There are 2 broods a year. Distribution: all Europe, temperate regions of Asia, Africa and Australia.

4 Black-necked Grebe *Podiceps nigricollis* — Length 30 cm. Lives on ponds, lakes, pools and backwaters with dense vegetation. Feeds on aquatic insects and insect larvae. Nest is made of plant material; often nests in large colonies numbering up to several hundred pairs. In May and June female lays 3—4 greenish eggs. Both parents incubate and both tend the young. Migrates south short distances for the winter. Populations from central Europe winter in southern Europe. Distribution: all Europe (except the extreme north), Asia to western Siberia, North America, Africa.

Order: **Petrels and their allies — Procellariiformes**

Family: **Petrels and shearwaters — Procellariidae**

5 Fulmar *Fulmarus glacialis* — Length 47 cm. A widespread, pelagic bird that, apart from the breeding season, keeps to the open seas. It feeds chiefly on fish, and crustaceans. During the breeding season it nests in fairly large colonies on rocky coasts. In May or June the female lays a single large white egg in a small depression, sometimes lined with grass and feathers, on a rocky ledge. Both parents incubate and both tend the young. The nestlings are covered with down at first and remain in the nest for several weeks. Distribution: northern parts of the Atlantic, Pacific and Arctic Oceans.

Subphylum: **Vertebrates** — **Vertebrata**

Class: **Birds** — Aves

Order: **Pelicans and their allies** — **Pelecaniformes**

Family: **Cormorants** — **Phalacrocoracidae**

1 Cormorant *Phalacrocorax carbo* — Length 80—90 cm. Lives on fresh waters as well as at sea. Feeds on fish, which it consumes in large quantities; pursues its prey underwater. Nests in large colonies. The nest is built of twigs and grass stems in trees, on the ground, or on rock ledges. Between April and June the female usually lays 2—3 eggs. Both parents incubate and both tend the young. In September it leaves central Europe for the Mediterranean, returning again in early March. Distribution: from eastern North America through Europe to eastern Asia, including Africa, Australia and New Zealand.

Family: **Gannets and boobies** — **Sulidae**

2 Gannet *Sula bassana* — Length 94 cm. Seabird that spends almost its whole life on the open sea, occurring inland only rarely. Feeds chiefly on sea fish for which it dives, plummeting with wings folded from heights of 20—30 metres. Air sacs under the skin help soften the impact of the fall. Nests in large colonies. The nest is made of marine vegetation and is located on coastal cliffs. Between April and June the female usually lays 1 egg, which both parents take turns incubating. Both also feed the offspring. Distribution: the shores and islands of the north Atlantic including the British Isles.

Family: **Pelicans** — **Pelecanidae**

3 White Pelican *Pelecanus onocrotalus* — Length 160 cm. Feeds exclusively on fish. Nests in colonies. The nest is a huge pile of reeds jutting 1—1.5 metres above the surface and measuring up to 1.5 metres across. Between April and June the female lays 2—3 eggs, incubated mostly by herself. The young hatch after 33 days and are fed twice a day by both parents. Overwinters in Asia Minor, Egypt, southwestern Asia and India. Distribution: warm regions of Asia, northeast Africa, found in Europe in the region between the mouth of the Danube and the Sea of Azov.

Order: **Herons and their allies** — **Ciconiiformes**

Family: **Herons and bitterns** — **Ardeidae**

4 Grey Heron *Ardea cinerea* — Length about 90 cm. Common bird of lake and pond regions. Feeds chiefly on fish, less frequently on amphibians, small mammals, molluscs and insects, exceptionally will take young birds. Nests in trees, often in large colonies. The nest is made of strong twigs lined with finer material. Between March and May the female usually lays 4—5 eggs incubated by both parents. At first, parents put regurgitated food directly into the beaks of the young, later they regurgitate it into the nest. Populations from central Europe overwinter in southern Europe, those of western Europe are mostly resident. Distribution: Europe (north to the Orkneys), south and east Africa, central and southern Asia (as far as Japan).

5 Purple Heron *Ardea purpurea* — Length about 90 cm. Found mostly near water with thick stands of reeds. Feeds on fish, frogs, small mammals and insects. Usually nests in colonies. The nest is built in thick stands of reeds or cat-tails. In April or May the female lays 3—6 eggs, which both parents take turns incubating. The young are fed by the parents for about 6 weeks. Distribution: southern and eastern Europe (comparatively rare in central Europe), southern Asia, Africa.

Subphylum: **Vertebrates — Vertebrata**

Class: **Birds — Aves**

Order: **Herons and their allies — Ciconiiformes**

Family: **Herons and bitterns — Ardeidae**

1 Little Egret *Egretta garzetta* — Length 56 cm. Small, silvery-white bird found in swampy, lowland regions. Feeds on fish, amphibians and insects. Nests in colonies, often together with other birds of this family. The nest is built in trees and thickets. Between May and July the female lays 3—5 eggs. Both parents incubate and both tend the young. Distribution: almost all southern Europe, central and southern Asia, south and central Africa, Madagascar, the Sunda Islands, Philippines and northern Australia.

2 Bittern *Botaurus stellaris* — Length 76 cm. Found in large beds of reeds and low, shrubby willows and alders near small bodies of clean, shallow water. Feeds chiefly on insects, frogs, fish and small mammals. When danger threatens it assumes a characteristic reed-like pose with head erect and beak pointing upward. Generally nests in reed beds. In April or May the female lays 3—5 eggs. She incubates and tends the young alone. Distribution: Europe (as far as Sweden), Asia (as far as Japan), Africa. European populations winter from England through France to Greece. North and equatorial Africa mark the extreme limit of its wintering grounds.

3 Little Bittern *Ixobrychus minutus* — Length 36 cm. Smallest European member of this family. Found in the vicinity of quiet waters among reeds. Feeds on insects and insect larvae, small fish, amphibians. The nest is built among reeds close to the ground. In May or June the female lays 4—6 eggs, incubated by both parents which also tend the young. Migratory; it winters in Africa. Distribution: Europe (except Great Britain), Asia (as far as Siberia).

4 Night Heron *Nycticorax nycticorax* — Length about 60 cm. Inhabits lakes, ponds, pools and rivers bordered with trees and thickets. Usually nests in large colonies. The nest is located in trees, sometimes in reed beds. In May or June the female usually lays 3—5 eggs. Parents take turns to incubate and tending the young. Birds that nest in central Europe overwinter in tropical Africa. Distribution: southern Europe, warmer regions of central Europe, southeast Asia, Africa and America where it is found practically throughout the whole continent.

Family: **Storks — Ciconiidae**

5 White Stork *Ciconia ciconia* — Length up to 102 cm. Inhabits open country with bodies of water and small groups of trees. Builds its nest in single trees, on roofs, old chimneys and the like. In April or May the female lays 3—6 eggs which both parents take turns incubating; the female usually incubates at night. Parents feed the young with fish, frogs, small mammals, insects and worms. European storks overwinter in central and south Africa, Asia populations usually in southern India. They generally leave their nesting grounds in August, returning again in late March or early April. Distribution: Europe (except Italy, British Isles and northern parts of Scandinavia), southern and eastern Asia, Japan and north Africa.

Subphylum: **Vertebrates — Vertebrata**

Class: **Birds — Aves**

Order: **Herons and their allies — Ciconiiformes**

Family: **Storks — Ciconiidae**

1 Black Stork *Ciconia nigra* — Length 96 cm. Inhabits forested areas in lowlands, often also in mountains. Feeds chiefly on fish and amphibians, also on small mammals, reptiles and insects. The nest is built in old trees always near the trunk, sometimes also on cliffs. In late April or May the female lays 3—5 eggs. Both parents incubate and both tend the young. Distribution: Iberian Peninsula, central Europe, east as far as China and Sakhalin.

Order: **Waterfowl — Anseriformes**

Family: **Ducks, geese and swans — Anatidae**

2 Mallard *Anas platyrhynchos* — Length ♂ — 57 cm, ♀ — 49 cm. Inhabits water courses as well as calm water of all types, even in large cities. Feeds on aquatic vegetation and various aquatic invertebrates and small vertebrates. The nest is located in grass near water, under shrubs or (more rarely) in trees. In March or April the female lays 7—11 eggs which she incubates herself. Before leaving the nest she covers the eggs with a layer of down. As soon as they hatch the young ducklings follow their mother. They are good swimmers and divers. Distribution: all Europe, north Africa, Asia, North America.

3 Teal *Anas crecca* — Length ♂ — 36 cm, ♀ — 34 cm. Partial to waters overgrown with dense vegetation. Diet consists of both plant and animal food. The nest is built on the ground, often far from water in meadows and fields. In May the female lays 8—10 eggs which she incubates alone; she tends the young herself. In autumn teals gather in huge flocks. Flight is rapid, during migration a flock may travel as much as 100 km in one hour. European teals winter in southern Europe and north Africa. Distribution: Europe (except Italy, the Iberian and Balkan peninsulas), palaearctic Asia, the Nearctic region.

4 Garganey *Anas querquedula* — Length ♂ — 40 cm, ♀ — 36 cm. Inhabits waters with thick vegetation. The nest is built in thick sedges, thickets or in grass. Feeds on plants and aquatic invertebrates. Nests in flatlands and foothills, less frequently at higher elevations. Between April and June the female lays 7—12 eggs, incubating and tending the young herself. Winters in north and central Africa. Distribution: almost the whole Palaearctic region. Absent from the southern Mediterranean islands, Scotland and Ireland and in the more northerly parts of Scandinavia.

5 Gadwall *Anas strepera* — Length ♂ — 51 cm, ♀ — 48 cm. Inhabits shallow reservoirs with calm or slow flowing water and large expanses of open water. Feeds on aquatic plants and small animals. In May or June it lays 7—12 eggs in the nest carefully concealed on the ground near the shore. The female incubates and tends the young by herself. Central European populations migrate to southern Europe and north Africa for the winter. Distribution: Europe (from southern England and central Europe east to the Amur River region), central Asia, Iceland, North America, north Africa.

6 Wigeon *Anas penelope* — Length ♂ — 49 cm, ♀ — 44 cm. Found on large expanses of water bordered by thick vegetation. Feeds chiefly on plant food. Nests in May and June, usually near water. The nest is well concealed on the ground. Lays 8—10 eggs, incubated by the female alone. She also tends the young herself. In northwestern Europe it is usually resident, populations from north and eastern Europe winter on the shores of the North and Baltic Seas, around the Mediterranean and in north Africa. Distribution: the Palaearctic region.

Subphylum: **Vertebrates — Vertebrata**

Class: **Birds — Aves**

Order: **Waterfowl — Anseriformes**

Family: **Ducks, geese and swans — Anatidae**

1 Pintail *Anas acuta* — Length ♂ — 70 cm, ♀ — 57 cm. Inhabits inland bodies of water with thick vegetation. Feeds on small aquatic invertebrates and on plants. During the breeding season it seeks out lakes in more open regions, forest-tundra, swamps and marshland. When migrating it keeps mainly to the sea. Between April and June the female lays 7—11 eggs, which she incubates alone; she also tends the young by herself. Distribution: Scandinavia, more northerly parts of the USSR and North America.

2 Shoveler *Anas clypeata* — Length ♂ — 52 cm, ♀ — 48 cm. Inhabits calm bodies of water with thick beds of reeds. Diet consists of both animal and plant food. The nest is usually located in meadows near water. In April or May the female lays 7—10 eggs; she incubates and also tends the young herself. Shovelers which inhabit central Europe migrate to the Mediterranean as well as west to France, Holland, etc. for the winter. Distribution: central, western and northern Europe (excepting the extreme northern parts of Scandinavia), north and central Asia (east as far as Kamchatka), western North America.

3 Red-crested Pochard *Netta rufina* — Length ♂ — 57 cm, ♀ — 51 cm. Inhabits large freshwater lakes and ponds, either with thick vegetation or with islets, as well as shallow salt and brackish waters. Feeds chiefly on plants but will occasionally eat small aquatic animals. The nest is located on the ground and made of stems, twigs and leaves and lined with down. In May or June the female lays 6—13 eggs. She incubates and also tends the young by herself. Distribution: the southern Palaearctic region, also sporadically in central and eastern Europe.

4 Scaup *Aythya marila* — Length ♂ — 45 cm, ♀ — 40 cm. Female distinguished from the very similar Tufted Duck by the large white patch at the base of the bill. The diet consists of plant and animal food. The nest is located in shrubs or thick grass. In May or June the female lays 7—9 eggs. She incubates and tends the young herself. Nests in Iceland, Scotland, Scandinavia, northern USSR, North America. In central Europe it occurs only as a winter visitor, in great numbers during severe winters.

5 Tufted Duck *Aythya fuligula* — Length ♂ — 42 cm, ♀ — 38 cm. After World War II it spread throughout central Europe to such a degree that in many places it is now one of the commonest of ducks. Animal food forms the mainstay of the diet. It nests in May and June on large inland bodies of water bordered by thick vegetation, often in large colonies together with gulls and terns. In late May or June the female lays 8—10 eggs. She incubates and tends the young herself. In winter it migrates to western Europe and the Mediterranean; often, however, it overwinters on large rivers in cities. Distribution: central and northern Europe, northern Asia (east to Sakhalin).

1

2 ♂

4

3 ♂

5

Subphylum: **Vertebrates — Vertebrata**

Class: **Birds — Aves**

Order: **Waterfowl — Anseriformes**

Family: **Ducks, geese and swans — Anatidae**

1 Pochard *Aythya ferina* — Length ♂ — 46 cm, ♀ — 42 cm. A typical diving duck that forages mainly underwater. During the breeding season plant food prevails but during migration and the winter months animal food forms most of the diet. The nest is built in thick shoreline vegetation as well as on islands, usually near water. In May or June the female lays 7—10 eggs. Only the female incubates; she also tends the young by herself. Birds inhabiting central Europe fly west to the Mediterranean for the winter. Distribution: central and eastern Europe, British Isles, southern Scandinavia, central Asia (to Lake Baikal).

2 Ferruginous Duck *Aythya nyroca* — Length ♂ — 42 cm, ♀ — 40 cm. Inhabits bodies of calm water overgrown with vegetation but with small expanses of open water. The diet consists of animal as well as plant food. The nest is built on the ground near water. In May or June the female lays 7—11 eggs. She alone incubates and also tends the young. Central European populations often stay the winter, east European birds migrate to the Mediterranean, north Africa and the Middle East. Distribution: east Europe, southwestern Asia, found occasionally in central and western Europe where it nests infrequently.

3 Goldeneye *Bucephala clangula* — Length ♂ — 45 cm, ♀ — 41 cm. A northern duck. The diet consists almost exclusively of animal food, chiefly molluscs and insects. The nest is built in tree hollows. In April or May the female lays 4—14 eggs which she incubates herself. Nesting trees may be as far as 2 km away from water. The day after hatching the ducklings jump out of the nest to the ground in response to their mother's call. They are expert at diving soon after hatching. Distribution: northern Europe, northern Asia, North America. Recorded ocassionally in central Europe.

4 Eider *Somateria mollissima* — Length ♂ — 62 cm, ♀ — 56 cm. During the breeding season lives on stony, sandy or sparsely vegetated seacoasts, islands and inland lakes. Outside the breeding season it often lives far from land on the open sea. Feeds chiefly on molluscs. Generally nests in large colonies. The nest is located on the ground, usually close to water, often in an open place. In May or June the female lays 4—6 eggs which she incubates alone. After the ducklings have hatched they often join other families, thus forming larger groups. In winter it migrates to the coasts of western Europe, in severe winters as far as the Mediterranean. It has been appearing more often in central Europe in recent years. Distribution: northern Europe, Greenland, North America.

5 Red-breasted Merganser *Mergus serrator* — Length ♂ — 60 cm, ♀ — 52 cm. Found on the seacoast as well as on inland waters. Feeds chiefly on fish (both freshwater and seafish), crustaceans and aquatic insects. Nests in late May and June on the ground, often quite far from water, but always in a concealed place. The female lays 7—12 eggs which she incubates by herself. Young ducklings from several families often join to form a group led by a single female. Like other mergansers it is a winter visitor to central Europe where it occurs on ice-free, flowing waters. Distribution: Scandinavia, Iceland, southern coast of Greenland, Ireland, Scotland, northern Asia and North America.

Subphylum: **Vertebrates — Vertebrata**

Class: **Birds — Aves**

Order: **Waterfowl — Anseriformes**

Family: **Ducks, geese and swans — Anatidae**

1 Shelduck *Tadorna tadorna* — Length ♂ — 66 cm, ♀ — 62 cm. Found on flat, sandy or muddy seashores with dunes, river mouths and occasionally also on salty inland waters. Feeds almost exclusively on marine molluscs. The nest of down is located in burrows at least 1 metre long (rabbit burrows, etc.), occasionally under bushes, among stones or in tree cavities. In May or June the female lays 7−15 eggs which she incubates while the male stands guard. Both parents tend the young. Distribution: coast of the North and Baltic Seas, Mediterranean, Black and Caspian Seas. It occasionally occurs inland.

2 Greylag Goose *Anser anser* — Length ♂ — 83 cm, ♀ — 71 cm. Bill coloured a uniform flesh or orange-red. Found on larger bodies of calm water, on islets and in reed beds, in Scotland also found in peat moors and on small sea islands. Feeds exclusively on plant food. Paired birds remain together for life. In March or April the female lays 4−6 eggs which she incubates while her mate remains close by. Both parents tend the young. In Scotland it is resident while north and central European populations winter in the Mediterranean. Distribution: the Palaearctic region.

3 Lesser White-fronted Goose *Anser erythropus* — Length ♂ — 59 cm, ♀ — 52 cm. Occurs in the vicinity of lakes and rivers in the tundra and forest-tundra, on upland plateaus at high elevations and in lowland country near larger bodies of water. Its diet consists mostly of green plant parts and seeds. Nests in late May and June in elevated spots, among low shrubs in rocky places. Lays 4−5 eggs. The young are tended by both parents. It migrates across central Europe to its winter quarters on the coast of the Black and Caspian Seas, in Turkestan and Iran. It is the rarest of all the geese that migrate across central Europe. Distribution: northern Europe, Asia (east as far as the Gulf of Anadyr).

4 Bean Goose *Anser fabalis* — Length ♂ — 80 cm, ♀ — 73 cm. Bill is black with yellow or pink markings. Found in boggy forests and tundras, always near water. Usually found in large flocks but during the breeding season it lives in pairs. Feeds on plant food. In June or July the female lays 4−5 eggs which she incubates while the male stands guard. Both parents tend the young. During migration large flocks alight on the inland waters of central Europe; in mild winters they overwinter there while in severe winters they journey to southern Europe. Distribution: northern Scandinavia and northern Asia.

5 Brent Goose *Branta bernicla* — Length ♂ — 59 cm, ♀ — 56 cm. Found almost exclusively on the arctic seacoasts, mainly near river estuaries. Farther from the sea found only in the tundra around lakes and rivers. Feeds almost exclusively on mosses, lichens and grasses but occasionally eats crustaceans and molluscs. Nests in colonies on small islets near the coast, in fjords and in the tundra, always near water. In June the female lays 3−5 eggs which she incubates while the male stands guard. Both parents tend the young. In winter European birds converge around the Black and Baltic Seas, with an occasional bird straying inland. It is often found in the company of other species of northern geese. Distribution: northern Palaearctic.

Subphylum: **Vertebrates — Vertebrata**

Class: **Birds — Aves**

Order: **Waterfowl — Anseriformes**

Family: **Ducks, geese and swans — Anatidae**

1 Canada Goose *Branta canadensis* — Length ♂ − 99 cm, ♀ − 93 cm. North American species inhabiting lakes and bogs of the northern tundra, coastal swamps, prairies and semi-desert. Feeds mostly on plant food, particularly green plant parts and seeds. Introduced to England, Sweden and Denmark where it became naturalised in places. Nests on small islets or on the shore near water, sometimes also in old trees. In late April the female lays 5−6 eggs which she incubates by herself while the male stands guard. Both parents tend the young. It occurs in Europe during the migrating season or as a winter visitor from early October to late March.

2 Mute Swan *Cygnus olor* — Length ♂ − 159 cm, ♀ 155 cm. Neck characteristically S-shaped, bill orange-red with black knob at the base. The young are grey and do not possess the knob. The diet consists mostly of aquatic and bog plants, only occasionally of animal food. The nest is a conical structure located on islets or in reed beds. In April or May the female lays 5−9 eggs which she incubates herself while the male stands guard, often attacking intruders, even Man. In winter it congregates in ice-free waters and along the seacoast. Distribution: throughout the Palaearctic in regions with a mild climate from Denmark to Ussuri and the Pacific Ocean. It has become widespread and very common in many parts of Europe.

3 Whooper Swan *Cygnus cygnus* — Length ♂ − 150 cm, ♀ − 147 cm. The bill in adult birds is yellow at the base, extending forward and downward to form a wedge-shaped patch, black at the front. Found on open expanses of water and in swamps in the tundra, in river estuaries and on mountain lakes. The diet consists almost exclusively of plant food. Nests on small islets in lakes and in drier spots in swamps. In May or June the female lays 5−6 eggs which she incubates while the male stands guard. Both help to tend the young. Winters along the coast of the North, Baltic, Black and Mediterranean Seas. On rare occasions it migrates across central Europe between early October and April. Distribution: Iceland, northern Scandinavia, and northern Asia as far east as Kamchatka and Sakhalin.

4 Bewick's Swan *Cygnus bewickii* — Length ♂ − 119 cm, ♀ − 116 cm. Resembles the Whooper Swan, but differs in size and colour of the bill. This is yellow at the base; however the yellow does not extend below the nostrils, but terminates in an arc almost perpendicular to the longitudinal axis of the bill. Found on calm waters and in swampy regions in the tundra and in river estuaries. Nests on islets or on the tundra near water. In May or June the female lays 3−5 eggs which she incubates herself. Winters in Scandinavia, the British Isles and by the North and Baltic Seas. In northwestern Germany and northern France it is one of the commonest of swans between early October and early April. In summer it occurs in the extreme northern parts of the Soviet Union from the Kola Peninsula east to the mouth of the Lena River. The arctic regions of North America are the home of a closely related species — the Whistling Swan, *C. columbianus*.

Subphylum: **Vertebrates — Vertebrata**

Class: **Birds — Aves**

Order: **Birds of prey — Falconiformes**

Family: **Hawks, eagles and their allies — Accipitridae**

1 Griffon Vulture *Gyps fulvus* — Length 100 cm. In flight the wings are spread wide in a straight line and the feathers at the tip spread apart like fingers (emarginated). Feeds chiefly on carrion, which it usually watches out for when circling high in the sky. Nests in February — March, generally on cliffs. The nest is a huge construction of sticks and contains a single large egg. Incubation and tending the offspring are shared by both parents, a behaviour similar to that in all vultures. Some south European birds remain in their nesting grounds for the winter, others migrate to warmer regions. Only an occasional stray bird may be encountered in central and western Europe. Distribution: the Mediterranean, Balkan Peninsula, northeast and north Africa, southwest Asia.

2 European Black Vulture *Aegypius monachus* — Length 103 cm. Found in open country from lowland to mountain elevations. Feeds chiefly on carrion. Nests almost exclusively in trees. Between February and April the female lays a single egg. Distribution: southern Europe (Iberian Peninsula, Sardinia, Sicily), the Balkans, Asia (from the Middle East to China). Occasionally strays far north to northern France, Germany, Denmark and Poland.

3 Golden Eagle *Aquila chrysaetos* — Length 82 cm. The tarsi are feathered down to the toes. Found in vast lowland forests (in Asia), in Europe it has been forced into the mountains. It hunts mammals up to the size of a young goat (in mountains generally feeds on marmots), and will even eat carrion. Breeds in March and April. The nest is located on a cliff or tall tree. The female generally lays 2 eggs which both parents take turns incubating; they also share the duties of tending the young as do all birds of prey. Young eagles attain maturity after 3 years. A resident bird. Distribution: much of Europe, Asia, northwest Africa, North America.

4 Imperial Eagle *Aquila heliaca* — Length 75—80 cm. Inhabits open country with deciduous forests and extensive lowland areas. Hunts small and medium sized mammals. Between March and May the female usually lays 2 eggs which she incubates, mostly by herself. Both parents tend the young. Nests in trees, being partial to beechwoods. A resident bird. Distribution: southwestern and southeastern Europe and central Asia.

5 Lesser Spotted Eagle *Aquila pomarina* — Length 63 cm. Feeds on small mammals which it often hunts on the ground. The nest is located in tall trees. In April or May the female lays 1—2 eggs which she incubates, mostly by herself. The young are tended by both parents. A migratory bird, it flies to east Africa for the winter. Distribution: southeastern Europe, Asia Minor, Transcaucasia, northern Iran, India and northern Burma.

Subphylum: **Vertebrates — Vertebrata**

Class: **Birds — Aves**

Order: **Birds of prey — Falconiformes**

Family: **Hawks, eagles and their allies — Accipitridae**

1 Common Buzzard *Buteo buteo* — Length 51—56 cm. Found in countryside where woodlands are interspersed with fields and meadows. Feeds chiefly on voles. The large nest is usually located in tall trees in woods. In April or May the female lays 2—3 eggs, incubated by both parents, who also share the duties of tending the young. Some birds are resident, others migrant or dispersive. Migrant birds travel far from their nesting grounds in winter, on occasion flying from central Europe as far as northern Italy. Northern populations overwinter in central Europe. Distribution: Europe (except the extreme north of Scandinavia), Asia.

2 Sparrowhawk *Accipiter nisus* — Length 28—38 cm. As in all other members of this family the male is smaller than the female. Feeds on small birds, catching them by sudden attack in low flight; skillful at flying amongst trees. It lives and nests in dense forest stands, sometimes also in groves and parks. The nest is always located in a tree and can be identified by the scattered feathers below, for the female moults during the nesting period. In May she lays 4—6 eggs which she incubates herself. Both parents tend the young. At first the male brings food for his mate and later also for the nestlings, the female first tearing the flesh into small pieces and then feeding it to the young. A dispersive bird; some individuals fly as far as southwestern Europe for the winter. Distribution: all Europe, north Africa, central palaearctic Asia.

3 Goshawk *Accipiter gentilis* — Length 48—58 cm. Young birds have the underside covered with brown streaks whereas in adult birds it is marked with transverse bars. The male is smaller than the female. Found in wooded areas where it leads a secretive life. A resident bird. Hunts prey as large as a hen or rabbit. The large nest, built by both partners, is generally located high up in tall coniferous trees and close to the trunk. In April the female lays 3—4 eggs, incubated mostly by herself. The male supplies his mate and offspring with food. Distribution: Europe, Asia, North America.

4 Red Kite *Milvus milvus* — Length 62 cm. Inhabits lowland forests of all types. The tail is remarkably long and deeply notched. Feeds on small vertebrates, insects and carrion. The nest is located in trees and is occasionally lined with bits of paper, cloth and other debris. In April and May the female lays 3—4 eggs, incubated mostly by herself. Both parents tend the young. In the southern part of its range it is a resident bird, in more northerly parts it flies to the Mediterranean for the winter. Distribution: all Europe (nowhere is it plentiful), Middle East, northwest Africa.

5 Black Kite *Milvus migrans* — Length 57 cm. The tail is slightly notched. Found in woodlands of all types at lower elevations near calm and flowing waters. Feeds chiefly on small fish, even dead ones; also hunts small vertebrates. In April or May the female lays 2—4 eggs, incubated mostly by herself. The young are tended by both parents. Travels to equatorial Africa for the winter, some birds winter in the Mediterranean. Distribution: Europe (except the northern parts), most of Asia, Africa, Australia.

Subphylum: **Vertebrates — Vertebrata**

Class: **Birds — Aves**

Order: **Birds of prey — Falconiformes**

Family: **Hawks, eagles and their allies — Accipitridae**

1 White-tailed Eagle *Haliaeetus albicilla* — Length ♂ — 77 cm, ♀ — 90 cm. Has an unfeathered tarsus, wedge-shaped tail and powerful yellow beak. Adult birds have a white tail; in young birds it is brownish, often spotted with white. Feeds chiefly on fish but also on birds, mammals and carrion. Nests in forests and groups of trees near lakes and rivers, in the southern parts of the USSR it also occurs in dry steppe. In February or March the female lays 1—3 eggs. Both parents incubate and tend the young. Distribution: Europe, almost all northern and central Asia, southwestern Greenland.

2 Marsh Harrier *Circus aeruginosus* — Length 52 cm. Slender-bodied bird with long wings and a long tail. Marked difference between the sexes both in coloration and size (male is smaller). It lacks the white rump of the other harriers. Found near calm bodies of water with extensive reed beds, occasionally also in wet meadows. Feeds on small birds (young gulls) and mammals. Generally nests on piles of bent and broken reeds directly on the water. In April or May the female lays 4—5 eggs. She incubates these by herself while the male provides her with food. When the young have hatched both parents hunt prey but the nestlings are fed by the female. North European birds are migratory, south European birds are resident. Distribution: Europe (except the extreme north of Scandinavia), central and eastern Asia, north Africa, Australia.

3 Hen Harrier or Marsh Hawk *Circus cyaneus* — Length 47 cm. Found in swamp and marshland, peat moors as well as large damp meadows. Feeds mostly on small rodents. The nest, which is made of grass, heather and twigs, is always located on the ground. Between April and June the female lays 4—5 eggs. A migrant. European populations winter in the Mediterranean, north Africa and the Middle East. Distribution: almost all Europe, central Siberia, North America.

4 Montagu's Harrier *Circus pygargus* — Length 46 cm. Found in damp lowlands, bogs with reed beds and sedge. Feeds on small rodents, frogs, lizards and birds which it captures on the ground. The nest is located on the ground. In May or June the female lays 4—5 eggs. Distribution: Europe (except the northern regions, Ireland, southern Italy and Balkan Peninsula), Asia (to the Yenisei and south to northern Iran and Turkestan), north Africa.

5 Pallid Harrier *Circus macrourus* — Length 43—48 cm. Lives in open, dry regions, generally steppes. The diet is the same as that of Montagu's Harrier. The nest is located on the ground. In May or June the female lays 4—5 eggs. A migrant, it winters in Africa and the southern parts of Asia, appearing in central and western Europe in the autumn on its journey south. Distribution: eastern Europe, southwest Asia.

6 Honey Buzzard *Pernis apivorus* — Length 50—57 cm. Distinguished in flight from the Common Buzzard by the bars on the long tail, the narrow head and outstretched neck. The area between the cere and the eye is covered with bristles instead of feathers. Found in woodlands at moderate elevations up to 1,000 metres. Feeds chiefly on honey bees, bumble-bees and especially wasps. It builds its nest in trees, bordering the edge with green twigs. In late May and June the female lays 2 eggs, which both parents incubate; both also tend the young. A migrant; it winters in Africa, often travelling in large flocks. Distribution: almost all Europe and Asia.

Subphylum: **Vertebrates — Vertebrata**

Class: **Birds — Aves**

Order: **Birds of prey — Falconiformes**

Family: **Osprey — Pandionidae**

1 Osprey *Pandion haliaetus* — Length 55 cm. Its foot has a reversible outer toe so that prey can be seized with two toes in front and two at the back. The undersides of the toes have pads with a sandpaper-like surface which helps maintain a secure hold on the prey. Bound to water, it feeds chiefly on fishes. Builds a huge nest in the tops of trees. In April or May the female generally lays 3 eggs, which she usually incubates herself, the male providing her with food. A migratory bird, it winters in tropical and southern Africa. Distribution: almost all Europe and Asia, the Sunda Islands, Australia, Central and North America.

Family: **Falcons — Falconidae**

2 Hobby *Falco subbuteo* — Length 30—36 cm. Like all falcons it has a sharp notch in the upper bill, known as the 'tooth'. Inhabits open country with scattered woodlands and groves. Feeds chiefly on insects and small birds. Swift and skillful in flight. Nests in trees, often using the old nest of a crow. In June, the female lays 2—4 eggs. Both parents incubate and both tend the young. A migrant, it winters in eastern and southern Africa. Distribution: almost all Europe and palaearctic Asia.

3 Peregrine Falcon *Falco peregrinus* — Length 40—48 cm. As in all falcons the male is smaller than the female. Prefers open country from lowland to mountain elevations with thin woodlands, groves and thickets. In the north also found in tundra and rocky regions, both inland and on the coast. Feeds on birds the size of a crow or dove. Nests on cliffs or trees, sometimes on the ground — in the south from early March, in the north during May. The female lays 3—4 eggs, which both partners take turns incubating. A migratory or dispersive bird. Distribution: almost worldwide; in Europe, it is becoming increasingly rare.

4 Gyrfalcon *Falco rusticolus* — Length 51—56 cm. Differs from the Peregrine Falcon in that it lacks the moustachial streak. Found in open country with cliffs and woodlands as well as in hills. Nests on cliffs. In April or May the female lays 3—4 eggs, incubated mostly by herself. Distribution: northern Europe, Iceland, Greenland, arctic regions of Asia, North America. The occasional stray may be encountered in western and central Europe.

5 Merlin *Falco columbarius* — Length 27—30 cm. Smallest European falcon. Found chiefly in moorlands, the tundra and forest-tundra. Feeds on small birds captured in flight, and small rodents. Nests on the ground or in trees. In May or June the female lays 4—5 eggs. Both partners incubate and both tend the young. Winters in southern Africa and southern Asia. Appears in central and western Europe in winter during its migratory journey. Distribution: northern Europe, Asia, North America.

6 Kestrel *Falco tinnunculus* — Length 32—35 cm. Found in open country with fields and meadows and scattered groves and woodlands. Feeds chiefly on small mammals. Nests in old crows'nests, on cliffs, as well as in buildings. In April or May the female lays 5—7 eggs, which she incubates herself. The male provides her and later the nestlings with food. In northern Europe it is migratory, in southern Europe resident. Distribution: all Europe, Asia (except the northern regions), Africa.

278

Subphylum: **Vertebrates — Vertebrata**

Class: **Birds — Aves**

Order: **Birds of prey — Falconiformes**

Family: **Falcons — Falconidae**

1 Red-footed Falcon *Falco vespertinus* — Length 30 cm. Male differs markedly from female in colouring. Forms colonies in lowlands, steppes and forest-steppes. Feeds chiefly on larger insects. In May or June the female lays 4—5 eggs. Both parents tend the young. Distribution: eastern Europe, central Siberia and eastern Asia. It nests rarely and irregularly in central and western Europe.

Order: **Fowl-like birds — Galliformes**

Family: **Grouse — Tetraonidae**

2 Rock Ptarmigan *Lagopus mutus* — Length 34 cm. Winter plumage is white, summer plumage greyish-brown with white wings. In winter the legs and toes are covered with feathers. Makes its home in tundras and high mountains above the upper forest limit to the snow line. The diet consists mostly of plant food. Nests on the ground. In May or June the female lays 8—12 eggs which she incubates herself. Young birds remain with adults in large flocks. A resident bird which in Europe is found in glacial valleys in the mountains. Distribution: circumpolar to Spitzbergen and other arctic islands, the Alps, Pyrenees.

3 Black Grouse *Lyrurus tetrix* — Length ♂ — over 61 cm, ♀ — about 42 cm. Marked differences between the sexes both in size and coloration. Found in wooded regions at the edges of forests, in clearings, heaths and marshland. Feeds on buds, seeds, small insects, worms, snails, etc. During the breeding season males arrive at the courting grounds long before sunrise where they engage in characteristic combat (lec behaviour). The courting display ends shortly before sunrise. In May or June the female lays 7—12 eggs in the nest which is located on the ground. She incubates and guides the young to food by herself. Distribution: open taiga of northern Europe and Asia, mountains of central and western Europe.

4 Capercaillie *Tetrao urogallus* — Length ♂ — 94 cm, ♀ — 67 cm. Inhabits northern forests and, in more southerly regions, the larger mountain forests. Feeds on insects, leaves, pine needles and buds of trees. Has a distinctive and characteristic courtship display during which the male perches high up in a tree. Nests on the ground. Between April and June the female lays 5—8 fairly large eggs. She incubates and rears the young herself. Distribution: in central Europe it is plentiful only in large mountain forests, common in northern Europe and northern Asia as far as Lake Baikal.

5 Hazelhen *Tetrastes bonasia* — Length ♂ — 37 cm, ♀ — 34 cm. Male and female are almost identical. Found in mixed woodlands with thick undergrowth where it remains on the ground throughout the day. A resident bird. In summer it feeds on insects, worms, herbaceous plants and their seeds; in winter exclusively on seeds, fruit and buds. Nests on the ground. In May or June the female lays 7—10 eggs which she incubates herself. The young are reared by both parents. Distribution: Europe (except the southern parts), central and northern Asia.

Family: **Quails, partridges and pheasants — Phasianidae**

6 Rock Partridge *Alectoris graeca* — Length 35 cm. Found on dry, warm, stony hillsides. A resident bird. Nests on the ground. Between April and June the female lays 9—15 eggs, which she incubates herself. The young are reared by both parents. Distribution: the Alps, Italy, Balkans, southern, western and central Asia, east as far as China.

280

Subphylum: **Vertebrates — Vertebrata**

Class: **Birds — Aves**

Order: **Fowl-like birds — Galliformes**

Family: **Quails, partridges and pheasants — Phasianidae**

1 Grey Partridge *Perdix perdix* — Length 29 cm. Frequents fields and meadows in lowland as well as hilly country. The diet consists mostly of green plant food, in summer it also eats insects and other small invertebrates. Nests on the ground. In May or June the female lays 12—20 eggs. Only the female incubates (for 23—25 days) but the young are reared by both parents. Families remain together until the winter. A resident species and important game bird. Distribution: Europe (as far as southern Scandinavia), Asia Minor, central Asia.

2 Ring-necked Pheasant *Phasianus colchicus* — Length ♂ — 79 cm, ♀ — 60 cm. Marked sexual dimorphism. Naturalized in Europe; original home is central and eastern Asia. Found in foothills as well as lowlands in open country with fields and small scattered woods, in open woodlands, as well as beside water. Feeds chiefly on insects and insect larvae, green plant food and seeds. In May or June the female lays 8—15 eggs in a nest on the ground. She incubates and rears the young by herself. A resident species and important game bird. Distribution: throughout the warm and temperate regions of Europe (as far as southern Scandinavia; absent in the western part of the Iberian Peninsula, in the southern tip of Italy, Sicily and Greece), southern palaearctic Asia.

3 Quail *Coturnix coturnix* — Length 17 cm. Smallest European fowl-like bird. Found in steppes and fields, chiefly at lower elevations. The nest is located on the ground. In May or June the female lays 9—13 eggs. She incubates and rears the young by herself. Only migratory member of this family in Europe. Winters in Africa. Distribution: temperate and warm regions of Europe, Asia (east to Japan).

Order: **Cranes, rails and their allies — Gruiformes**

Family: **Cranes — Gruidae**

4 Common Crane *Grus grus* — Length ♂ — 122 cm, ♀ — 113 cm. Found in lowland bogs and barren swampy places in woods. The diet consists mainly of plant food. During the courtship display the partners 'dance'. The nest is large and flat and located in a dry spot. In April or May the female lays 2 eggs. Both partners incubate and rear the young. A migratory bird, it travels in large flocks to Africa for the winter. Distribution: Scandinavia, northern Germany and Poland, European part of the USSR, Asia as far as eastern Siberia.

Family: **Bustards — Otididae**

5 Great Bustard *Otis tarda* — Length ♂ — 102 cm, ♀ — 80 cm. Most robust European bird. Found in spreading lowland fields, meadows and steppes. The diet consists of plant food, mainly tender shoots. In autumn it congregates in flocks. The courtship display is impressive. In May or June the female usually lays 2 eggs in a shallow depression in the ground. She incubates and rears the young by herself. Distribution: southern parts of Europe and throughout steppe country across central Asia to the Pacific Ocean.

2 ♂

5 ♂

3

1

4

Subphylum: **Vertebrates — Vertebrata**

Class: **Birds — Aves**

Order: **Cranes, rails and their allies — Gruiformes**

Family: **Rails, coots and gallinules — Rallidae**

1 Coot *Fulica atra* — Length 38 cm. Common on calm waters overgrown with reeds, occurs on flowing water during winter. Feeds chiefly on aquatic plants for which it often dives. Nests in reed beds. The nest of aquatic vegetation floats on the surface and is attached to reed stems. Between March and June the female lays 7—15 eggs. There are usually 2 broods a year. Both parents incubate and both rear the young. A partly resident, partly migratory bird. Central European birds either stay the winter or migrate to western and southern Europe or north Africa. Distribution: almost all Europe (except the extreme northern parts), large parts of Asia, northwest Africa, Australia.

2 Moorhen *Gallinula chloropus* — Length 33 cm. Found on all types of water with dense vegetation. Feeds on plant seeds and insects. Birds live in pairs. The nest is built in dense waterside vegetation. Between April and June the female lays 7—10 eggs. There are usually 2 broods a year. Both parents incubate and rear the young. It is either resident (in more southerly parts) or migratory; moorhens from northern regions winter in southern Europe. Distribution: worldwide (except Australia and the northern parts of Europe).

3 Water Rail *Rallus aquaticus* — Length 28 cm. Found on the banks of calm bodies of water with dense growths of reeds, in wet meadows, marshes and moorland. Feeds on insects, insect larvae, and on the seeds of aquatic vegetation. The nest of flat leaves is always well concealed. Between April and August the female lays 6—11 eggs, incubated by both parents. The young are also reared jointly. There are often 2 broods a year. Sometimes stays the winter on its nesting grounds, sometimes passes it in north Africa and the Mediterranean. Distribution: Europe (except the northern regions), Asia (east to Japan), northwest Africa.

4 Spotted Crake *Porzana porzana* — Length 23 cm. Lives a concealed life in marshes and along the banks of calm bodies of water with dense vegetation. The nest is sometimes concealed among reeds but more often in clumps of sedge or grass. In May or June the female lays 7—11 eggs, incubated by both parents. The young are likewise reared jointly. There are 2 broods a year. A migrant, it generally winters in the Mediterranean region and in Africa. Distribution: all Europe (except the extreme north), Asia (east as far as the Yenisei).

5 Corncrake *Crex crex* — Length 27 cm. Unlike others of its kind it lives on dry land, occurring in damp meadows from lowland to hilly country, sometimes even in mountains. The nest is a lined hollow in the ground located in a dry spot. In June or July the female lays 7—12 eggs, incubated by both partners. The young are also reared by both parents. A migratory bird, it winters around the Mediterranean Sea and in tropical and southern Africa. Distribution: Europe (except the northern parts, Italy and the Iberian Peninsula), Asia (as far as Lake Baikal).

Subphylum: **Vertebrates — Vertebrata**

Class: **Birds — Aves**

Order: **Shorebirds, gulls and auks — Charadriiformes**

Family: **Oystercatchers — Haematopodidae**

1 Oystercatcher *Haematopus ostralegus* — Length 43 cm. Frequents coasts, islands and river estuaries. Occurs also in fields and meadows beside fresh water. Feeds on molluscs. Nests on the shore. The nest is a shallow depression, often lined with the shells of molluscs and other material. In May or June the female lays 3−4 eggs, incubated by both parents. Both parents share the duties of rearing the young. A resident or dispersive bird. Distribution: the coasts of all continents.

Family: **Plovers and their allies — Charadriidae**

2 Lapwing *Vanellus vanellus* — Length 32 cm. Found in damp meadows, swamps, fields, and on the banks of rivers and ponds. The diet consists of animal food. Between March and May the female lays 4 eggs. The nest is a depression in the ground, lined with grass. Both parents incubate and rear the young. North European birds fly south for the winter, west and south European birds stay the winter in their nesting grounds. Distribution: Europe (except northern Scandinavia), temperate parts of Asia.

3 Turnstone *Arenaria interpres* — Length 23 cm. Common on stony shores and rocky islands. In May or June the female lays 4 eggs in a depression in the ground. The parents take turns incubating. The young are reared by the male. Winters partly in the North Sea region, but mostly on the shores of Africa and southwestern Asia. Distribution: northern Europe, Siberia and adjacent islands, Greenland, northern North America.

4 Ringed Plover *Charadrius hiaticula* — Length 19 cm. Found on sandy and stony shores of seas and inland waters. Feeds on various insects and worms. The nest is generally a shallow, unlined depression. Between May and July the female lays 4 eggs, which she and her mate incubate in turn. The young are reared mostly by the male. There are 2 broods a year. Migrates to the coast of the Mediterranean Sea, Africa and southwest Asia for the winter. Distribution: more northern parts of Europe and Asia, North America, Greenland.

5 Little Ringed Plover *Charadrius dubius* — Length 15 cm. Found on barren shores of inland waters and on seacoasts. Feeds on various invertebrates. There are 2 broods a year between May and July. The nest is a shallow depression in the ground, lined sparsely with grass. The female lays 4 eggs. Both parents incubate and rear the young. A migratory bird, it winters in the Mediterranean region and in Africa. Distribution: Europe (except the northern parts), much of Asia, northwest Africa.

6 European Golden Plover *Pluvialis apricaria* — Length 28 cm. Inhabits tundras, northern marshes and moorland. Like others of its kind its diet consists of animal food. The nest is a depression in the ground lined with vegetation. Between April and July the female lays 4 eggs, incubated mostly by herself although the male occasionally relieves her. Both keep careful watch over the nest and the young. There are usually 2 broods a year. A migratory bird, it winters in the Mediterranean and in southwest Asia. Distribution: British Isles, Iceland, Scandinavia, southern coast of the Baltic, northern USSR as far as the mouth of the Yenisei.

Subphylum: **Vertebrates — Vertebrata**

Class: **Birds — Aves**

Order: **Shorebirds, gulls and auks — Charadriiformes**

Family: **Plovers and their allies — Charadriidae**

1 Dotterel *Eudromias morinellus* — Length 22 cm. Nests in stony and swampy northern tundras and in a few places in high mountains. The nest, which is a depression in the ground, is usually lined with moss, grass and other plant matter. In June or July the female lays 3 eggs. The duties of incubating and of rearing the young are performed by the male. A migratory bird, it winters in north Africa and the Middle East. Distribution: discontinuous. In Europe in the mountains of Scotland and Scandinavia, the southern Alps, Rumanian Carpathians, in Asia in northern and northeastern Siberia, the Urals, Taimir Peninsula and high mountains of central Asia.

Family: **Snipe, sandpipers and their allies — Scolopacidae**

2 Woodcock *Scolopax rusticola* — Length 34 cm. Common chiefly in broadleaved and mixed woodlands. Feeds on various invertebrates, hunting its prey on the surface and in the ground, probing the soil and pulling up worms with its long beak. The nest is a depression in the ground lined with old leaves. Between April and July the female lays 4 eggs, incubating and rearing the young by herself. There are 1 or 2 broods a year. Mostly a migratory bird, it winters in western and southeastern Europe and in the Mediterranean. Distribution: much of Europe (in Scandinavia as far as the Arctic Circle), Asia (east to Sakhalin and Japan), isolated nesting grounds on Atlantic islands, in the Caucasus, and in the Himalayas.

3 Common Snipe *Gallinago gallinago* — Length 27 cm. Common in marshland, round ponds and in damp meadows. Nesting habits similar to those of the Woodcock. Migrates to Africa for the winter, sometimes stays the winter in its nesting grounds. Distribution: same as that of the Woodcock but extending farther north, also found in North America.

4 Curlew *Numenius arquata* — Length 58 cm. Largest European wader. Found in damp meadows and marshland that is not unduly waterlogged; in eastern Europe and Asia it also occurs in dry steppes where it is generally restricted around water. Feeds on insects, worms, and molluscs which it captures in the mud with its long beak. In April or May the female lays 4 eggs. Both parents incubate and rear the young. Mostly a migratory bird, it winters in the Mediterranean and Africa. Distribution: in Europe the same as the preceding species, in Asia as far east as the Amur River.

5 Black-tailed Godwit *Limosa limosa* — Length 40 cm. Inhabits meadows near water. It forages for food (insects, worms, molluscs) in mud. Nests on the ground among dense vegetation; the depression is lined with dry grass. In April or May the female lays 4 eggs. Both parents incubate and rear the young. A migrant, it winters in the Mediterranean. Distribution: isolated occurrences in central and western Europe, continuous from northern France east across all of Asia to Kamchatka.

6 Spotted Redshank *Tringa erythropus* — Length 31 cm. Generally found in boggy places. Nests in May and June. The 4 eggs are incubated by both parents. The young are likewise reared by both parents. Winters in the Mediterranean, passing regularly through central Europe. Distribution: northern Scandinavia, all of northern Siberia.

288

Subphylum: **Vertebrates — Vertebrata**

Class: **Birds — Aves**

Order: **Shorebirds, gulls and auks — Charadriiformes**

Family: **Snipe, sandpipers and their allies — Scolopacidae**

1 Redshank *Tringa totanus* — Length 28 cm. Commonest European member of this genus. Inhabits wet, boggy regions, peat moors and meadows near water. Feeds on insects, worms and molluscs. Nests in April or May. The hollow, in which 4 eggs are laid, is extremely well concealed in the shoreline vegetation. Both parents share the duties of incubating and rearing the young. Winters in the Mediterranean and on the coast of western Europe, in northern and also on occasion in central Africa. Distribution: throughout most of Europe, Asia (as far as the Amur).

2 Green Sandpiper *Tringa ochropus* — Length 23 cm. Found in old woodlands in marshy places, and along the banks of watercourses. Feeds on aquatic insects and spiders. Nests in trees in the old nests of other birds, often quite high up. Between April and June the female lays 4 eggs, incubated mostly by herself. Sometimes winters in western Europe and the Mediterranean, but usually in Africa. Distribution: eastern Europe, southern Scandinavia, the Caucasus, Asia (as far as eastern Siberia).

3 Wood Sandpiper *Tringa glareola* — Length 20 cm. Occurs chiefly in tundra and forest swamps. Feeds on aquatic insects and spiders. The nesting hollow, well concealed amongst vegetation, is lined with leaves and other plant material. In May or June the female lays 4 eggs. Both parents incubate and both rear the young. A migratory bird, it winters from the Mediterranean south to south Africa and in southern Asia. When migrating it may often be seen beside fresh waters throughout Europe. Distribution: northern Europe and Asia (east to Kamchatka and the Amur River region).

4 Common Sandpiper *Tringa hypoleucos* — Length 20 cm. Inhabits flat, shrub-covered, muddy and sandy shores of lakes and ponds. Prefers flowing waters. The nest is a depression lined with plant matter and well concealed in the shoreline vegetation. In May or June the female lays 4 eggs. The duties of incubation and rearing the young are performed mostly by the male. A migratory bird, it occasionally winters in the Mediterranean and western Europe, but mainly in Africa, Madagascar, and southern Asia as far as Australia. Distribution: all Europe, Asia as far as the Japanese islands; North America is the home of the closely related Spotted Sandpiper *(Tringa macularia).*

5 Knot *Calidris canutus* — Length 26 cm. Inhabits dry and rocky lowlands and grassy tundra. One of the most northerly nesting of birds. The eggs are laid in June. A migratory bird, it winters in the Mediterranean, by the Black Sea, in Australia, South America, southern Asia and west Africa; occasionally on the coast of the North Sea. Distribution: the Arctic region.

Subphylum: **Vertebrates — Vertebrata**

Class: **Birds — Aves**

Order: **Shorebirds, gulls and auks — Charadriiformes**

Family: **Snipe, sandpipers and their allies — Scolopacidae**

1 Dunlin *Calidris alpina* — Length 19 cm. Always found beside water. In central Europe it occurs in meadows near water and in marshes; in the north found on tundra. Feeds on small invertebrates and seeds. Between late April and June the female lays 4 eggs. The nesting hollow is concealed in vegetation and lined with plant material. Both parents share the duties of incubation and of rearing the young. European birds sometimes winter in the southern region of the North Sea and on the coast of western Europe but more usually in the Mediterranean region and north Africa. Distribution: northern Europe, Asia, America.

2 Ruff *Philomachus pugnax* — Length ♂ — 25 cm, ♀ — 23.5 cm. Marked differences between the sexes. Inhabits damp lowland meadows, marshes or, in northern regions, the tundra. During the migratory season it may be seen on the banks of ponds in central and western Europe. Feeds on worms, insects and often seeds. When courting the cocks gather in large numbers and perform feigned combats. The nest is a shallow depression in the ground sparsely lined with vegetation. In May or June the female lays 4 eggs. She incubates and also rears the young by herself. Winters in tropical and south Africa, sometimes no farther south than the Mediterranean region, very occasionally also in western and central Europe. Distribution: shores of the North and Baltic Seas from the French coast northward, northern Asia.

Family: **Stilts and avocets — Recurvirostridae**

3 Avocet *Recurvirostra avosetta* — Length 43 cm. Found on coasts, near brackish waters and river estuaries. Feeds on insects, molluscs and crustaceans which it captures with sweeping movements of its beak. Nests in colonies. The nesting hollow in the ground is sparsely lined with vegetation. Between April and May the female lays 4 eggs. Both parents incubate and rear the young. Northern populations are migratory and winter in Africa and southern Asia, south European populations are often resident. Distribution: western and southern Europe, coast of the North and Baltic Seas, in the hinterland from Neusidlersee east to Mongolia and India; local populations occur in tropical Africa.

4 Black-winged Stilt *Himantopus himantopus* — Length 38 cm. Inhabits shallow salt and fresh waters with muddy bottoms. Feeds on insects, small molluscs and worms. Generally nests in large colonies. The nest, a mere scrape in the ground near water, is sparsely lined with vegetation. In May the female lays 4 eggs. Both parents take turns incubating and both rear the young. Birds of more northerly regions migrate to Africa and southern Asia. Distribution: southern Europe, central and western Europe, occasionally central and southern Asia, Africa, the Nearctic, Neotropical and Australasian regions.

Family: **Phalaropes — Phalaropidae**

5 Red-necked Phalarope *Phalaropus lobatus* — Length 17 cm. Bird of the north. Found in wet grassy places on the shores of lakes and rivers, coasts and in marshes. Feeds chiefly on insects and crustaceans. The female, which is larger and more brightly coloured than the male, selects the nesting site. In May she lays 4 eggs in a hollow in the ground which is lined with vegetation, leaving the duties of incubating and rearing the young to the male. A migrant, it winters in west Africa, by the Indian Ocean, in Malaysia and the Moluccas. Distribution: northern Europe, far northerly parts of Asia and North America.

Subphylum: **Vertebrates — Vertebrata**

Class: **Birds — Aves**

Order: **Shorebirds, gulls and auks — Charadriiformes**

Family: **Thick-knees — Burhinidae**

1 Stone Curlew *Burhinus oedicnemus* — Length 41 cm. Found in large fields, sandy areas and steppe with sparse vegetation. Feeds on insects, molluscs and small vertebrates which it hunts at night. Between April and June the female lays 2 eggs in an unlined depression in sand. Both parents incubate and both rear the young. There are 2 broods a year. Winters in western and southwestern Europe, northwest and east Africa. In southern Europe it often stays the winter. Distribution: temperate regions of Europe, southwest and southern Asia, north Africa.

Family: **Gulls and terns — Laridae**

2 Great Black-backed Gull *Larus marinus* — Length 74 cm. Nests in colonies on rocky coasts and some inland lakes. Feeds on various vertebrates and invertebrates as well as carrion. The nest is made of plant material. In May or June the female lays 2—3 eggs. As with all gulls, both parents incubate and tend the young. Distribution: northern Europe, Spitsbergen, Greenland, Labrador. It often strays far south.

3 Herring Gull *Larus argentatus* — Length 56 cm. Found on coasts and the shores of inland lakes. Feeds on various marine animals, birds' eggs, birds, carrion, as well as refuse. Nests in large colonies. The nest, lined with vegetation, is located on cliffs, on gravel, in grass, reed beds and even on the roofs of buildings. In May or June the female lays 3 eggs. In the moderate and southern parts of Europe it is resident, northern populations journey as far as the coast of Africa for the winter. When migrating it may often be encountered inland. Distribution: coasts of the whole northern hemisphere and some inland lakes.

4 Common Gull *Larus canus* — Length 41 cm. Found on coasts as well as the shores of inland lakes, in marshes and marshy tundra. Feeds on various vertebrates and insects. Nests in large colonies. The nesting habits are similar to those of the Herring Gull. North European birds generally winter on the shores of the North and Baltic Seas, birds of central Europe are sometimes resident and sometimes migrant, the latter migrate to the Mediterranean for the winter. Distribution: northern Europe (from England and Ireland northwards), central Asia, northwestern parts of North America.

5 Little Gull *Larus minutus* — Length 30 cm. Smallest of the gulls. Found on the shores of fresh waters with abundant vegetation as well as on seashores. Feeds chiefly on insects. Nests in colonies, often together with the Black-headed Gull and the Black Tern. The nest, made of plant material, is located on cliffs, clumps of sedge, bent and broken reeds, sandflats, etc. In May or June the female lays 2—3 eggs. Generally winters in the Mediterranean, the Black Sea and western Europe. Distribution: locally on the coast of the North and Baltic Seas (from the coast of Finland through the European USSR to Siberia).

Subphylum: **Vertebrates — Vertebrata**

Class: **Birds — Aves**

Order: **Shorebirds, gulls and auks — Charadriiformes**

Family: **Gulls and terns — Laridae**

1 Black-headed Gull *Larus ridibundus* — Length 37 cm. A well-known and common European gull. Found on calm inland waters with thick vegetation and on the coast. Feeds on insects, worms and small fish. Nests in colonies. The nest is made of plant material. Between April and June the female lays 3 eggs. Winters partly on the water in large cities and in harbours, partly in western Europe, southern Asia and north Africa. Distribution: throughout most of Europe (except Italy, the Balkans and the Iberian Peninsula), Asia to Kamchatka.

2 Kittiwake *Rissa tridactyla* — Length 40 cm. Nests on rocky coasts but outside the breeding season it keeps to the open seas. Feeds chiefly on fish and crustaceans. Nests in large colonies, often together with other sea birds. Between May and July the female lays 2 to 3 eggs. North Atlantic populations winter mainly in the Atlantic between 40° and 60° N, in the North and Baltic Seas and often in the Mediterranean. Distribution: northern coast of Scandinavia, British Isles, Denmark, France, the Hebrides, northern coast of Asia and North America.

Family: **Skuas — Stercorariidae**

3 Arctic Skua or Parasitic Jaeger *Stercorarius parasiticus* — Length 46 cm. Has typical elongated central tail feathers. Feeds mostly on fish and small rodents. Often pursues other sea birds and robs them of their prey. Nests in tundra, usually by the seashore or near lakes and rivers, always in large colonies. In May or June the female lays 2 eggs in an unlined hollow. Both partners incubate and tend the young. A migrant, it winters on the shores of South America, west Africa, Australia and in the Persian Gulf. Distribution: holarctic.

4 Great Skua *Stercorarius skua* — Length 59 cm. Feeds on fish, robbing other sea birds of their catch, and on the eggs and young of sea birds. Nests either singly or in small colonies, usually close to the sea. The nesting habits are similar to those of other skuas. In winter it occurs farther south, sometimes as far south as Gibraltar and Italy. Distribution: coast of the north Atlantic and other northern seas.

Family: **Gulls and terns — Laridae**

5 Black Tern *Chlidonias niger* — Length 25 cm. Only tern with completely black breeding plumage except for the white under tail coverts. Like all terns it has a long forked tail. Inhabits inland waters. Feeds chiefly on insects but also on fish. Nests in colonies. The nest, made of aquatic plants, is located on bent, floating reeds or other floating plants. In May or June the female lays 3 eggs. Both partners share the task of incubating and tending the young. A migratory bird, it winters in tropical Africa. Distribution: Europe (as far as southern Finland), Asia Minor, central Asia, western Siberia, North America.

6 Common Tern *Sterna hirundo* — Length 35 cm. Found on the shores of fresh waters and on muddy islets as well as on seacoasts. Feeds on fish, crustaceans and insects. Nests in colonies, often together with gulls. The nest is made of dry plant material. Between May and July the female lays 3 eggs which are incubated by both partners. The young are likewise tended by both. A migrant, it winters in the Mediterranean and Africa. Distribution: throughout most of Europe, Asia, North America.

296

Subphylum: **Vertebrates — Vertebrata**

Class: **Birds — Aves**

Order: **Shorebirds, gulls and auks — Charadriiformes**

Family: **Gulls and terns — Laridae**

1 Arctic Tern *Sterna paradisea* — Length 38 cm. Inhabits flat seashores, islets, and the shores of inland waters in the tundra. Feeds on small fish, crustaceans and sometimes also on insects. Nests in colonies. The female usually lays 2 eggs in an unlined depression in the ground. Both partners incubate and tend the young. Skims the water but has never been known to alight on the surface. A migrant, it undertakes long flights south; from the extreme north of Europe it travels along the coast of west Africa and along the coast of North and South America to the Antarctic. Distribution: during the breeding season it occupies the northernmost parts of Europe, Asia and North America.

2 Sandwich Tern *Sterna sandvicensis* — Length 40 cm. Found on shores with sparse vegetation and on islets close to the shore. Feeds on fish. Nests in colonies. In May or June the female lays 2—3 eggs in a shallow depression in sand which is only sparsely lined with plant stems. Both partners incubate and both tend the young. A migrant, it winters on the coasts of west and south Africa, the Red Sea and Persian Gulf. Distribution: southern Sweden, British Isles, France, Denmark, Holland, the Mediterranean, Black and Caspian Seas, eastern coast of North America. Occasionally strays inland.

Family: **Auks — Alcidae**

3 Razorbill *Alca torda* — Length 42 cm. Found on coastal cliffs and solitary islands. Feeds on fish and crustaceans. Nests in colonies. Between April and June the female lays a single egg directly on the bare rock, under a boulder or in a rock crevice. Both partners share the duties of incubating and rearing the young. Winters on the coast of the western Baltic, North Sea, western part of the Mediterranean Sea and in northwest Africa. Distribution: North Atlantic — Iceland, Spitsbergen, Scandinavia, Ireland, Great Britain, eastern North America, Greenland. Southernmost breeding grounds are in Brittany.

4 Guillemot *Uria aalge* — Length 43 cm. Feeds chiefly on fish, to a lesser degree on crustaceans, molluscs and insects. Nests on coastal cliffs and islands in large colonies, often together with the Razorbill. In May or June the female lays a single egg directly on the bare rock. Both partners incubate and tend the young. At the age of 25 days the young bird leaps from the cliff into the sea. After the breeding season it migrates long distances, often as far as the coast of west Africa and the western Mediterranean. Distribution: North Atlantic and Pacific, Arctic Ocean. Its range extends far south, as far as Portugal.

5 Black Guillemot *Cepphus grylle* — Length 35 cm. Found near the coast and sometimes on islands with thick vegetation. Feeds mostly on small fish but also on crustaceans and worms. Nests singly or in small colonies. In May or June the female generally lays 2 eggs in a rock crevice or under a boulder, but usually rears only a single nestling. Both partners share the duties of incubating and tending the offspring. Winters on the coast of the North and Baltic Seas, sometimes also on the French coast of the Atlantic. Distribution: circumpolar in the far north.

298

Subphylum: **Vertebrates — Vertebrata**

Class: **Birds — Aves**

Order: **Shorebirds, gulls and auks — Charadriiformes**

Family: **Auks — Alcidae**

1 Puffin *Fratercula arctica* — Length 30 cm. Has a large parrot-like bill which is particularly striking during the breeding season when it swells at the base and becomes brilliantly coloured. Feeds on fish, molluscs and crustaceans. Found on grassy slopes by the seashore and on islands where it nests in large colonies in burrows which it excavates. In May or June the female lays a single egg incubated alternately by the male and female. The offspring is also reared by both. Winters by the North Sea, North Atlantic, northwest coast of Africa and western Mediterranean, occasionally by the Baltic Sea. Distribution: North Atlantic, northern parts of North America, Greenland. Brittany marks the southern limit of its breeding grounds.

Order: **Pigeons and their allies — Columbiformes**

Family: **Pigeons and doves — Columbidae**

2 Stock Dove *Columba oenas* — Length 33 cm. Found in old, mostly broadleaved or mixed woodlands with plenty of natural hiding places. Feeds on seeds. Has 2—3 broods a year. Between April and July the female lays 2 eggs in the nest which is located in a tree hollow. Both partners incubate and tend the young. At first the young feed on 'pigeon's milk' regurgitated from the crop of the adult birds, later they are fed half-digested fruits and seeds. In western and southern Europe it is a resident bird, in central Europe it usually migrates to southern Europe. Distribution: Europe (except northern Scandinavia), western Asia (as far as the Irtysh River), northwest Africa.

3 Rock Dove *Columba livia* — Length 33 cm. All breeds of domestic pigeons originated from this dove. Found in rocky, sparsely vegetated country from the coast to inland areas. Feeds on seeds. Nests on high cliffs, preferably in caves. Between April and July the female usually lays 2 eggs. Distribution: southern Europe, north Africa, Middle East, Asia Minor and southern Asia (to Japan).

4 Wood Pigeon *Columba palumbus* — Length 40 cm. Has a white patch at the bend of the wing which in flight looks like a white bar. Adult birds also have white patches on either side of the neck. Found in all types of forests and in parks and gardens. Feeds chiefly on acorns and beechnuts, also on berries and small snails. The nest is located in tree tops. Sometimes it occupies an old crow's or raptor's nest. Between April and August the female lays 2 eggs. North European populations winter in western and central Europe and the Middle East; south European birds are usually resident. Distribution: Europe (except the north), western and southern Asia, northwest Africa.

5 Turtle Dove *Streptopelia turtur* — Length 27 cm. Tail has a narrow white terminal band which is clearly visible in flight. Found in open mixed and broadleaved woodlands as well as in thickets. Nests low down in trees or in thickets. Between May and July the female lays 2 eggs. A migrant, it winters in north Africa and in the Mediterranean. Distribution: Europe (except Scandinavia), western Asia and north Africa.

6 Collared Turtle Dove *Streptopelia decaocto* — Length 28 cm. Tail has a broad white terminal band. Found in parks, gardens, broadleaved and mixed woods. Feeds on berries, seeds and various plant material. Nests from March to October in trees and on buildings. The female lays 2 eggs 3—4 times a year. A resident bird. Distribution: originally restricted to southern and eastern Asia and the Balkan Peninsula but since 1930 it has spread northward and westward.

300

Subphylum: **Vertebrates — Vertebrata**

Class: **Birds — Aves**

Order: **Owls — Strigiformes**

Family: **Barn owls — Tytonidae**

1 Barn Owl *Tyto alba* — Length 34 cm. Has a striking, heart-shaped facial disc. Found near human habitations. Nests in towers, in ruins and barns. Feeds on voles and other small mammals, birds and insects. The nesting season begins in April and sometimes lasts until July and in years when the vole population is very high it nests through autumn and even winter. The female lays 4—7 (or more) white eggs in an unlined scrape. Both partners incubate and both tend the young. A resident or dispersive bird. Distribution: all Europe (as far as southern Scandinavia), the Middle East, southern Asia, Africa, part of North America, South America, Australia.

Family: **Typical owls — Strigidae**

2 Eagle Owl *Bubo bubo* — Length 66—71 cm; female is slightly larger than the male. Largest European owl. Found in lowland and mountain regions where it nests in rock formations or stony hillsides. If there are no rock formations it nests in hollow trees or the nests of raptors. Feeds on mammals and birds as large as a badger or capercaillie hen. Strictly nocturnal hunter. Between March and May the female lays 2—4 eggs on bare rock. She incubates them by herself while her mate hunts and brings her food. Both partners tend the young. A resident or dispersive bird. Distribution: throughout most of Europe, Asia and north Africa.

3 Snowy Owl *Nyctea scandiaca* — Length 57 cm. Inhabits tundra, in lowlands and mountains. Feeds on small mammals, mainly lemmings. Nests on the ground. Between April and June the female lays 3—8 eggs, which she incubates by herself. Both partners tend the young. Generally a resident bird but in severe winters it journeys south. Distribution: holarctic.

4 Tawny Owl *Strix aluco* — Length 38 cm. Inhabits woodlands with old, mainly broadleaved trees, parks, treed avenues and large gardens. A characteristic feature are the dark-brown eyes (similar to those of the Ural Owl). Feeds chiefly on rodents and other small mammals, birds and larger insects. Nests in cavities and abandoned nests of raptors, occasionally even in buildings and holes in the ground. In March or April the female lays 3—4 eggs which she incubates herself. The young are tended by both parents. There are 1—2 broods a year. A resident bird. Distribution: Europe (except Ireland, Iceland and northern Scandinavia), western Siberia, southern Asia, north and northwest Africa.

5 Ural Owl *Strix uralensis* — Length 61 cm. Inhabits old forests in lowlands as well as mountains. Nests in tree hollows and abandoned nests of raptors. The diet is the same as that of the Tawny Owl. Often hunts in the daytime. Between March and May the female lays 3—4 eggs which she incubates by herself. The young are tended by both parents. A resident bird. In severe winters it is often found in the vicinity of towns and villages. Distribution: northern Europe, Siberia to Sakhalin and Japan. Isolated nesting grounds in the Alps, Carpathians and other European mountains.

Subphylum: **Vertebrates — Vertebrata**

Class: **Birds — Aves**

Order: **Owls — Strigiformes**

Family: **Typical owls — Strigidae**

1 Pygmy Owl *Glaucidium passerinum* — Length 16.5 cm. Smallest European owl. Found in coniferous woods at both lowland and mountain elevations. Feeds on small mammals and perching birds. Hunts by day and night. The song is a series of soft melodious whistles. Nests in tree holes, often in holes made by woodpeckers. In April or May the female lays 4—6 eggs which she incubates herself while her mate hunts for food. In central Europe it is a resident bird. North European populations migrate to warmer climes for the winter. Distribution: northern Europe and Asia as far as the Amur region. Occurs sporadically in some mountain massifs of central and southern Europe.

2 Little Owl *Athene noctua* — Length 22 cm. Found in parks, gardens, cemeteries, treed avenues and copses. Feeds on small mammals, birds and insects. Nests in hollows in walls and trees, in nestboxes and rabbit holes. In April or May the female lays 4—5 white eggs which she incubates herself while the male brings her food. Both parents tend the young. A resident or dispersive bird. Distribution: throughout most of Europe, Asia (as far as northern China, India and Iraq), north Africa.

3 Long-eared Owl *Asio otus* — Length 36 cm. Resembles the Eagle Owl. Found in forests, mainly coniferous and mixed woods, less frequently in broadleaved forests. Feeds on small mammals, chiefly voles and mice. Utilizes the abandoned nests of crows, magpies and even squirrels. Between March and June the female lays 4—6 eggs which she incubates herself. The male provides her, and later also the young, with food. There are 2 broods a year. It is either resident, dispersive or migratory, depending on the supply of food, often journeying far to the west or southwest. Distribution: Europe (except extreme northern parts), central Siberia, northwest Africa, North America.

4 Short-eared Owl *Asio flammeus* — Length 37 cm. Inhabits open country, tundra, marshland, steppes, where it seeks out marshy places. Feeds on small mammals which it hunts mostly in daytime. It is the only owl that builds its own nest on the ground among reeds, grass or field crops. In April or May the female lays 4—7 eggs which she incubates herself. The male provides her, and later the young, with food. A dispersive or migratory bird, depending on the food supply. Often undertakes long journeys as far as tropical Africa and southern Asia. Distribution: almost all Europe, central and northern Asia, North America, central part of South America.

5 Tengmalm's or Boreal Owl *Aegolius funereus* — Length 25 cm. The legs are thickly covered with feathers which reach as far as the talons. Inhabits deep coniferous forests at both lowland and mountainous elevations. Feeds on small mammals and songbirds. Nests chiefly in tree holes, often those abandoned by woodpeckers. Between March and May the female lays 4—6 eggs which she incubates herself while the male provides her, and later the young, with food. In autumn it leaves mountain regions for lower elevations. Distribution: central Europe (discontinuous, in mountain regions), northern Europe, Asia, North America.

Subphylum: — **Vertebrates** — **Vertebrata**

Class: **Birds** — **Aves**

Order: **Cuckoos and their allies** — **Cuculiformes**

Family: **Cuckoos** — **Cuculidae**

1 Cuckoo *Cuculus canorus* — Length 33 cm. The characteristic call is made only by the male. Found in open, mixed groves with dense undergrowth of thickets. Feeds on caterpillars and insects. A brood parasite, it lays its eggs in the nests of other birds (one to a nest) between May and July. The eggs often resemble those of the foster parents in size and coloration. The female lays a total of 15—20 eggs. The young hatch after 12 1/2 days, their first instinct being to remove from the nest the eggs as well as the rightful progeny of the foster parents, so that it remains alone in the nest without any rivals. A migratory bird, it winters in tropical and south Africa. Distribution: all Europe, Asia, throughout most of Africa.

Order: **Nightjars and their allies** — **Caprimulgiformes**

Family: **Nightjars** — **Caprimulgidae**

2 European Nightjar *Caprimulgus europaeus* — Length 27 cm. Inhabits open and dry woodlands containing a high percentage of conifers, forest margins and peat-moors. A crepuscular and nocturnal bird, it feeds on nocturnal insects, chiefly moths. Between May and July the female lays 2 eggs directly on the ground; it does not build a nest. Both partners incubate and both tend the young. A migratory bird, it winters in southern Asia and Africa. Distribution: throughout most of Europe, Asia (as far as Lake Baikal and Afghanistan), northwest Africa.

Order: **Kingfishers and their allies** — **Coraciiformes**

Family: **Hoopoes** — **Upupidae**

3 Hoopoe *Upupa epops* — Length 28 cm. Found in open country with scattered copses, also in gardens and in the vicinity of buildings. Feeds on insects. Nests in tree holes, crevices in walls and piles of stones. Between May and July the female lays 6—8 eggs; there are sometimes 2 broods a year. The eggs are incubated solely by the female; the male provides food. When the young are 15 days old the female begins to help with the feeding. During the nesting period the female and young exude a foul-smelling secretion from the preen gland which they squirt at the enemy when threatened by danger. A migratory bird, it winters in tropical Africa. Distribution: throughout most of Europe, central and southern Asia, most of Africa.

Family: **Rollers** — **Coraciidae**

4 Roller *Coracias garrulus* — Length 30 cm. Inhabits open country with scattered copses and open woodlands. Feeds chiefly on larger insects, less frequently on small rodents and lizards. Nests in tree holes and cavities in walls. Between May and July the female lays 4—5 eggs. Both parents incubate and both tend the young. A migratory bird, it winters in east Africa. Distribution: most of Europe, southwest Asia, northwest Africa.

Family: **Kingfishers** — **Alcedinidae**

5 Kingfisher *Alcedo atthis* — Length 16.5 cm. Found in the vicinity of calm and flowing waters. Feeds on small fish and aquatic insects. Nests in burrows which it digs in sand or soil banks. Between April and July the female lays 6—7 eggs. Both partners share the duties of incubation and tending the young. There are 2 broods a year. A partial migrant. Distribution: much of Europe, Asia, north Africa.

Subphylum: **Vertebrates — Vertebrata**

Class: **Birds — Aves**

Order: **Kingfishers and their allies — Coraciiformes**

Family: **Bee-eaters — Meropidae**

1 Bee-eater *Merops apiaster* — Length 28 cm. Occurs in open country, often near streams and rivers. Feeds on flying insects, chiefly bees and wasps. Nests in colonies in burrows which it digs in sand or soil banks. In June or July the female lays 4—7 eggs. Both partners incubate and both tend the young. A migratory bird, it winters in Africa. Distribution: central, southern and southeastern Europe, the Middle East, southwest Asia, northwest Africa.

Order: **Woodpeckers and their allies — Piciformes**

Family: **Woodpeckers and wrynecks — Picidae**

2 Wryneck *Jynx torquilla* — Length 16 cm. Found in open woodlands in lowland and hilly country, in treed avenues, parks and larger gardens. Feeds mainly on ants and their larvae, also on other insects. Nests in holes vacated by other animals. In May or June the female lays 7—10 eggs in the bottom of the hole. Both parents share the duties of incubation and tending the young. A migratory bird, it winters in tropical Africa and India. Distribution: throughout most of Europe, Asia (as far as Japan), Algeria.

3 Black Woodpecker *Dryocopus martius* — Length 45 cm. Largest European woodpecker. Found chiefly in vast coniferous forests at both lowland and mountain elevations. Feeds on the larvae of insects living in wood, also on ants and their larvae. For nesting it seeks out large old trees in which it excavates a deep hole with its beak. In April or May the female lays 4—5 eggs. Both parents incubate. A resident bird; the young are dispersive. Distribution: throughout most of Europe, Asia (as far as Japan and Kamchatka).

4 Green Woodpecker *Picus viridis* — Length 32 cm. Found in broadleaved woods, parks, treed avenues and larger gardens. Feeds chiefly on ants and their larvae, less frequently on other insects. It excavates a nesting hole in the trunk of broadleaved trees in which the female lays 5—7 eggs in April or May. Both partners incubate and both tend the young. It is a resident, or at most a dispersive bird. Distribution: throughout most of Europe and the Middle East.

5 Grey-headed Woodpecker *Picus canus* — Length 25 cm. Found in open broadleaved as well as mixed woods and also large, quiet parks at lower elevations as well as in mountains. Rarer than the Green Woodpecker. It has similar nesting habits. In warmer regions it is resident, in northern Europe dispersive. Distribution: most of Europe (absent, for instance, in the west), western, eastern and southeastern Asia.

4 ♂

5 ♂

2

3 ♂

1

Subphylum: **Vertebrates — Vertebrata**

Class: **Birds — Aves**

Order: **Woodpeckers and their allies — Piciformes**

Family: **Woodpeckers and wrynecks — Picidae**

1 Great Spotted Woodpecker *Dendrocopos major* — Length 23 cm. Found chiefly in coniferous forests, but also in treed avenues, parks and large gardens. Feeds on insects that live under bark as well as in wood, on the seeds of conifers and on nuts. The nesting holes are excavated in soft or rotting wood in trees that are still standing. In May or June the female lays 5—6 eggs. Both partners incubate and both tend the young. A resident bird, but north European populations are migratory, flying to more southerly regions for the winter. Distribution: throughout most of Europe and much of Asia (as far as Kamchatka and southeastern China), northwest Africa.

2 Lesser Spotted Woodpecker *Dendrocopos minor* — Length 14.5 cm. Smallest woodpecker. Occurs in broadleaved and mixed woods, large gardens and parks; mainly at lower elevations, less often in hilly country. Feeds chiefly on beetles and their larvae, less often on ants. In winter it also feeds on seeds. Nests in holes which it drills in trees. In April or May the female lays 5—6 eggs. Both partners incubate and both tend the young. In more temperate regions it is resident, north European populations winter in central Europe. Distribution: throughout most of Europe (except Ireland and Scotland), Asia (as far as Kamchatka and northern Japan), northwest Africa.

3 Middle Spotted Woodpecker *Dendrocopos medius* — Length 21.5 cm. Found at lowland elevations in broadleaved forests with plenty of old hollow trees, in parks and in large old gardens. Does not occur in coniferous forests. The diet is the same as that of the Great Spotted Woodpecker. Nests in holes made by other woodpeckers. Between April and June the female lays 5—6 white eggs. Both parents incubate and both tend the young. A resident or dispersive bird. Distribution: all Europe (except the southern part of the Iberian Peninsula, the British Isles and northern Scandinavia), the Middle East.

Order: **Perching birds — Passeriformes**

Family: **Larks — Alaudidae**

4 Crested Lark *Galerida cristata* — Length 17 cm. Has a prominent crest on the head. Originally a bird of the steppes, it occurs now in cultivated steppes and fields. Feeds on seeds, parts of green plants and insects. The nest, made of stems, grasses, roots, sometimes also hairs and feathers, is located on the ground. Between April and July the female lays 3—5 eggs. There are 2 broods a year. Only the female incubates but both parents tend the young. A resident bird, it overwinters in the neighbourhood of its nesting ground. Distribution: almost all Europe (except the British Isles, most of Scandinavia and northern parts of the European USSR), Asia (as far as Korea, west Pakistan and Arabia), north Africa.

5 Woodlark *Lullula arborea* — Length 15 cm. Occurs in large, low stands with sparse grass, e. g. heaths, clearings in pinewoods, etc. Its lovely, melodious song is usually heard at night. The nest is a deep hollow in the ground lined with roots, moss, hairs, etc. Between April and June the female lays 4—5 eggs which only she incubates. Both parents tend the young. There are 2 broods a year. Winters partly in western Europe but mostly in the Mediterranean. Distribution: almost all Europe (except Ireland, Scotland, northern Scandinavia and European part of the USSR), the Middle East, northwest Africa.

310

1

2

3

4

5

Subphylum: **Vertebrates — Vertebrata**

Class: **Birds — Aves**

Order: **Perching birds — Passeriformes**

Family: **Larks — Alaudidae**

1 Skylark *Alauda arvensis* — Length 18 cm. Found in fields, meadows and other treeless places in lowlands and mountains. The feeding and nesting habits are similar to those of the Crested Lark. Winters in southern Europe; some central European birds and west European populations stay the winter in their nesting grounds. Distribution: almost all Europe, Asia, northwest Africa.

Family: **Swallows and martins — Hirundinidae**

2 Swallow or Barn Swallow *Hirundo rustica* — Length 18 cm. Occurs in the vicinity of human habitations, from lowlands to mountains up to the tree line. Feeds chiefly on insects, which it captures in flight. Nests under eaves or inside buildings close to the roof. The nest is an open quarter-sphere made of mud mixed with saliva and strengthened with grass stems and straw. Between May and August the female lays 4—5 eggs. She incubates but both parents tend the young. There are 2—3 broods a year. A migratory bird. Distribution: almost all Europe (except the extreme northern parts), Asia, north Africa, North America.

3 House Martin *Delichon urbica* — Length 13 cm. Like the swallow, it occurs in human habitations, often in large numbers even in cities. Feeds on insects. Nests in colonies. The nest of mud is a covered quarter-sphere and is located under eaves and cornices. Between May and August the female lays 5 eggs. Both partners share the duties of incubation and tending the young. There are 2 broods a year. A migratory bird, it winters in Africa and Asia. Distribution: northwest Africa, in Europe and Asia its range is almost identical to that of the swallow.

4 Sand Martin or Bank Swallow *Riparia riparia* — Length 12 cm. Inhabits open country with calm or flowing waters. Feeds on flying insects. Nests in colonies. The nest is a deep tunnel dug into vertical sand or clay banks. The tunnel ends in a chamber lined with feathers, in which the female lays 5—6 white eggs between May and July. There are 2 broods a year. Both partners incubate and tend the young. A migratory bird. Distribution: almost identical with that of the swallow. Wintering grounds are the same for both.

Family: **Wagtails and pipits — Motacillidae**

5 Yellow Wagtail *Motacilla flava* — Length 16.5 cm. The throat is never black. Inhabits wet meadows and fields in lowlands. Feeds on insects. Nests on the ground. Between May and July the female lays 5—6 eggs. Only the female incubates, both parents tend the young. There are 2 broods a year. A migrant, it winters in tropical Africa and tropical Asia. Distribution: almost all Europe (except the extreme northern parts), part of north Africa, Asia (north of the Himalayas), Alaska. Throughout its range it occurs in 22 different geographical races.

6 Grey Wagtail *Motacilla cinerea* — Length 18 cm. The male's throat is black. Found beside rivers and streams in foothills, mountains and often also in lowlands. Feeds on insects. Nests in cavities in river banks. Between April and July the female lays 5—6 eggs. Both parents incubate and tend the young. There are 2 broods a year. Winters in southern Europe and north Africa. Distribution: almost all Europe, Asia (north of the Himalayas), northwest Africa.

6 ♂

5

1

4

2 ♂

3 ♂

Subphylum: **Vertebrates — Vertebrata**

Class: **Birds — Aves**

Order: **Perching birds — Passeriformes**

Family: **Wagtails and pipits — Motacillidae**

1 Pied or White Wagtail *Motacilla alba* — Length 18 cm. Found in open country, usually near water. Often nests in the neighbourhood of farms where the livestock attracts large numbers of insects, on which it feeds. The nest, made of twigs, leaves, roots and moss, is located in cavities or cracks. Between April and August the female lays 5—6 eggs. There are 2—3 broods a year. Only the female incubates, but both parents tend the young. A migratory bird, it winters in the Mediterranean, Africa and Middle East. Distribution: all Europe, almost all Asia, Africa.

2 Tawny Pipit *Anthus campestris* — Length 16.5 cm. Occurs in open sandy country, fallow land and fields. Feeds on insects. The nest, made of roots and moss, is located on the ground. Between May and July the female lays 4—5 eggs, which she incubates alone. Both parents tend the young. A migratory bird, it winters in north and central Africa and southern Asia. Distribution: Europe (except the British Isles, Scandinavia and more northerly parts of the European USSR), southern USSR, steppe regions of Siberia, central Asia, north Africa.

3 Water Pipit *Anthus spinoletta* — Length 16 cm. Inhabits high mountains above the forest limit and sea coasts. Feeds mostly on insects. Nests on the ground under overhanging grass, a stone or dwarf shrub. Between May and July the female lays 4—6 eggs, which she incubates alone. Both partners feed the young. Most birds fly south for the winter. Distribution: Europe, Asia, North America.

4 Tree Pipit *Anthus trivialis* — Length 15 cm. Found in open woodlands from lowland to mountainous elevations. Feeds on insects. The nest of plant fragments is concealed in a clump of grass. Between May and July the female lays 5 eggs, which she incubates alone. Both parents tend the young. Winters in Africa and the Mediterranean. Distribution: almost all Europe, Asia (as far as northeastern Siberia and northern parts of Asia Minor).

Family: **Waxwings — Bombycillidae**

5 Bohemian Waxwing *Bombycilla garrulus* — Length 18 cm. Inhabits northern forests with dense shrub layer. In summer feeds chiefly on mosquitoes, in winter on various berries. The nest, made of lichens, mosses, twigs and moss, is located in trees. In May or June the female lays 4—6 eggs which only she incubates. Both parents tend the young. A dispersive as well as migratory bird. During the winter it may be encountered, almost every year, in central Europe, usually in large flocks. Distribution: north polar region.

Family: **Shrikes — Laniidae**

6 Red-backed Shrike *Lanius collurio* — Length 18 cm. Commonest of all shrikes. Inhabits dry open country with numerous shrubs, forest margins, gardens, etc. Feeds on insects, occasionally on small vertebrates and berries. Nests in bushes 1—2 metres above the ground. Between May and July the female lays 4—6 eggs which only she incubates. Both parents tend the young. Winters in Asia and Africa. Distribution: almost all Europe, much of Asia.

314

Subphylum: **Vertebrates — Vertebrata**

Class: **Birds — Aves**

Order: **Perching birds — Passeriformes**

Family: **Shrikes — Laniidae**

1 Great Grey Shrike *Lanius excubitor* — Length 25 cm. Largest European shrike. Inhabits open scrub land, gardens, etc. Feeds on insects and small vertebrates, often impaling its victims on sharp thorns near the nest. Nests in trees and tall thorny shrubs. Between April and June the female lays 5—7 eggs, which she incubates. Both parents tend the young. Distribution: Europe (except the British Isles, Italy and the Balkans), Asia, north Africa, North America.

Family: **Dippers — Cinclidae**

2 Dipper *Cinclus cinclus* — Length 18 cm. Found along streams and rivers in foothills and mountains. Feeds on aquatic insects, crustaceans and molluscs. Hunts food underwater; runs about on the stream bed using its wings to help move against the current. When it emerges, the water runs off its oiled wings immediately. The nest, made of moss and aquatic plants, is located close to the water. Between April and July the female lays 4—6 eggs. Both parents incubate and tend the young. There are 2 broods a year. A resident and dispersive bird. Distribution: discontinuous, almost throughout all Europe, the Middle East and central Asia, Africa.

Family: **Wrens — Troglodytidae**

3 Wren *Troglodytes troglodytes* — Length 9.5 cm. Found in woods, parks and gardens with thick undergrowth. Feeds on insects. Nests in thickets, along brooks, in piles of underbrush, etc. Between May and July the female lays 5—7 eggs, which she incubates. Both parents tend the young. Northern populations are migratory. Distribution: about 38 races throughout the northern hemisphere.

Family: **Accentors — Prunellidae**

4 Dunnock *Prunella modularis* — Length 18 cm. Inhabits broadleaved and mixed woods, parks with thick undergrowth. In summer feeds mostly on insects, in winter on small seeds. Between April and July the female lays 4—5 eggs. There are 2 broods a year. The female incubates, both partners tend the young. The well concealed nest is placed low down in thickets. Winters in western and southern Europe, north Africa, Asia Minor, the Caucasus. Distribution: almost all Europe, Asia Minor. Found in the mountains of Europe is the related Alpine Accentor (*Prunella collaris*) and rarely, the Siberian Accentor *(Prunella montanella)* of Siberia.

Family: **Old World warblers — Sylviidae**

5 River Warbler *Locustella fluviatilis* — Length 15 cm. Found along rivers and backwaters, in damp overgrown meadows, etc. Feeds on insects. The nest is located directly on or close to the ground. Between May and July the female lays 4—5 eggs. There are 1—2 broods a year. Winters in tropical Africa. Distribution: Europe (from eastern Germany north to southern Sweden, south to the Black Sea), western Siberia.

6 Grasshopper Warbler *Locustella naevia* — Length 13 cm. Found in dry habitats with thick vegetation, also in willow and alder carrs in marshy meadows. Feeds on insects. Leads a secretive life. Nests close to the ground. Between May and July the female lays 5—6 eggs. Both parents incubate and tend the young. There are 1—2 broods a year. Winters in southern Europe, north Africa and southwest Asia. Distribution: Europe (north to southern Scandinavia), southwestern Siberia.

Subphylum: **Vertebrates — Vertebrata**

Class: **Birds — Aves**

Order: **Perching birds — Passeriformes**

Family: **Old World warblers — Sylviidae**

1 Great Reed Warbler *Acrocephalus arundinaceus* — Length 19 cm. Largest European member of this genus. Lives concealed in reed beds, on the edges of lakes and ponds. Feeds on insects. The nest, a basket expertly woven of grass stems, hangs between strong reeds which serve as supports. Between May and July the female lays 4—5 eggs. Both partners incubate and tend the young. Distribution: Europe (except Scandinavia and the British Isles), southwest Asia, northwest Africa.

2 Reed Warbler *Acrocephalus scirpaceus* — Length 13 cm. Commonest European member of this genus. Found amidst reeds bordering ponds, as well as in bushes far away from water. Feeds on insects. The nest resembles that of the Great Reed Warbler. Between May and July the female lays 4—5 eggs. Both partners incubate and tend the young. There are 1—2 broods a year. Winters in tropical Africa. Distribution: Europe (except Scotland, Ireland, most of Scandinavia), southwest Asia, northwest Africa.

3 Icterine Warbler *Hippolais icterina* — Length 13 cm. Inhabits parks, gardens, broadleaved woods. Feeds on insects, berries and fruit. The nest is located in the fork of a branch or a branch next to the trunk. The outer walls are often camouflaged with bits of birch bark, the inside is lined with soft material. In May or June the female lays 5 eggs. Both partners incubate and tend the young. Winters in tropical and south Africa. Distribution: Europe (from central France eastward), western Siberia.

4 Barred Warbler *Sylvia nisoria* — Length 15 cm. Found on sun-warmed banks, in thickets along paths, in forest margins and along streams, in parks and gardens. Feeds on insects, berries and fruit. The nest is located in thickets. In May or June the female lays 5—6 eggs. Both parents incubate and tend the young. A migratory bird, it winters in east Africa and southern Arabia. Distribution: central Europe, Asia (as far as Mongolia and Iran).

5 Blackcap *Sylvia atricapilla* — Length 14 cm. Found in coniferous forests, groves and parks in both lowlands and mountains. Feeds on insects, berries and fruit. The nest is located in thickets. Between May and July the female lays 5—6 eggs. There are 2 broods a year. Both partners incubate and tend the young. Winters in southern Europe and Africa, as far south as the equator. Distribution: Europe (except northern Scotland), western Siberia, the Middle East, northwest Africa, Atlantic islands.

6 Whitethroat *Sylvia communis* — Length 14 cm. Found in thickets, hedgerows, etc. Feeds on insects and berries. The nest is a loosely woven construction placed close to the ground. Between May and July the female lays 4—6 eggs. There are 2 broods a year. Both partners incubate and tend the young. Winters south of the Sahara. Distribution: almost all Europe (except northern Scandinavia), Asia (as far as Lake Baikal), northwest Africa, Mediterranean islands.

5 ♂

3

1

2

4 ♂

6

Subphylum: **Vertebrates — Vertebrata**

Class: **Birds — Aves**

Order: **Perching birds — Passeriformes**

Family: **Old World warblers — Sylviidae**

1 Lesser Whitethroat *Sylvia curruca* — Length 14 cm. Inhabits thickets, hedgerows, forest margins, parks and gardens. Feeds on insects and berries. Between May and July the female usually lays 5 eggs. Both partners incubate and tend the young. Winters in tropical Africa. Distribution: Europe (except the Iberian Peninsula, southern Italy, Ireland, northern Scandinavia), Asia (as far as eastern Siberia and northern China).

2 Chiffchaff *Phylloscopus collybita* — Length 11 cm. The legs are black-brown. The song is a characteristic, monotonously repeated 'chiff-chaff'. Found in woodlands with dense undergrowth. Feeds on insects. The nest is located either on the ground or in thickets close to the ground. Between April and July the female lays 6−7 eggs, which she incubates by herself. Rearing the young is also mainly her responsibility. There are 2 broods a year. Winters by the Mediterranean Sea, in the Middle East and north Africa. Distribution: Europe, Asia (as far as eastern Siberia), the Middle East, northwest Africa.

3 Willow Warbler *Phylloscopus trochilus* — Length 11 cm. Resembles the Chiffchaff, but has brown legs. Found in all types of forests, parks, often in willow groves. Feeds on insects. The nest is located on the ground. Between April and June the female lays 6−7 eggs, which she incubates by herself. Both parents tend the young. Winters in the Middle East and south Africa. Distribution: northern parts of the Palaearctic region.

4 Wood Warbler *Phylloscopus sibilatrix* — Length 13 cm. Largest member of this genus. Found in open broadleaved and mixed woodlands in lowland regions, particularly in beechwoods. Feeds on insects and berries. Nests on the ground. In May or June the female lays 6−7 eggs, which she incubates by herself. Both parents tend the young. Distribution: most of Europe, western Siberia.

5 Goldcrest *Regulus regulus* — Length 9 cm, weight 5−6 gm. Smallest European bird. Found mainly in spruce and pine woods. Feeds on insects and spiders. The bowl-shaped nest, which is almost closed at the top, is located in trees. In May or June the female lays 8−10 eggs which she incubates by herself. Both parents tend the young. There are 2 broods a year. A resident bird; in winter it usually only travels short distances. Distribution: almost all Europe, central and eastern Siberia, Korea, Manchuria, North America, isolated regions of palaearctic Asia.

Family: **Old World flycatchers — Muscicapidae**

6 Spotted Flycatcher *Muscicapa striata* — Length 14 cm. Found in parklands with sparse vegetation, forest margins, treed avenues, etc., often near human habitations. Perches in an elevated spot whence it darts from time to time to catch an insect, immediately returning to its post. Nests in crevices, often under eaves. Between May and July the female lays 5 eggs. Both partners incubate and tend the young. There are 1−2 broods a year. Winters in tropical and south Africa. Distribution: all Europe, Asia (to Lake Baikal), northwest Africa.

Subphylum: **Vertebrates** — **Vertebrata**

Class: **Birds** — **Aves**

Order: **Perching birds** — **Passeriformes**

Family: **Old World flycatchers** — **Muscicapidae**

1 Pied Flycatcher *Ficedula hypoleuca* — Length 13 cm. Found in open, sun-dappled broadleaved woodlands, riverine groves, parks, etc. where there are plenty of hollow trees. Feeds on flying insects, in late summer also on berries. Nests in tree holes and man-made nestboxes. In May or June the female lays 5—8 eggs, which she incubates by herself. Both parents tend the young. A migrant, it winters in north and central Africa. Distribution: most of Europe (except certain southern regions), western Siberia, northwest Africa.

2 Collared Flycatcher *Ficedula albicollis* — Length 13 cm. Distinguished from the Pied Flycatcher by the white neck-band and white rump. Feeds on flying insects. The habitat and nesting habits are similar to those of the Pied Flycatcher. Winters in tropical Africa. Distribution: Europe (from eastern France through Poland to the Kharkov region of the USSR, Italy, Sicily, the Balkans), western Siberia, the Caucasus, Crimea, Turkey, Iran, Israel.

Familly: **Thrushes and their allies** — **Turdidae**

3 Whinchat *Saxicola rubetra* — Length 13 cm. Inhabits rolling, open hill country with isolated bushes and streams. Feeds on insects. The nest is well concealed on the ground. In May or June the female lays 5—6 eggs, which only she incubates. Both parents tend the young. Winters in equatorial Africa. Distribution: Europe (except the southern parts of Italy, the Iberian Peninsula and the Balkans), western Siberia, southwest Asia.

4 Wheatear *Oenanthe oenanthe* — Length 14 cm. Found in quarries, sandpits, amongst rocks, stone screes in mountains. Feeds on insects, spiders and snails. The nest is concealed in a hole or crevice on or just above the ground. In May or June the female lays 5—6 eggs, which she incubates by herself. Both partners tend the young. A migrant, it winters in tropical Africa. Distribution: all Europe, North America, Greenland.

5 Redstart *Phoenicurus phoenicurus* — Length 14 cm. Found in broadleaved and mixed woods, parks and gardens, wherever it can find holes for nesting or man-made nestboxes. Is fond of perching in an elevated spot. Continually twitches its tail and is hardly ever still. Feeds on insects and berries. There are 2 broods a year. Between May and July the female lays 6—7 eggs which only she incubates. Both parents tend the young. Winters in tropical Africa and southern Arabia. Distribution: Europe (except southern Italy and Greece), northwest Africa, Asia (east as far as Lake Baikal), the Middle East.

6 Black Redstart *Phoenicurus ochruros* — Length 14 cm. Originally a native of mountain cliffs, it is now often found in cities. Feeds on insects and berries. Nests in crevices under roofs, in holes in walls, etc. Between April and July the female lays 5—6 eggs which she incubates by herself. Both parents tend the young. South and west European birds are resident, central and east European populations winter in the Mediterranean and north Africa. Distribution: central and southern Europe, the Middle East, central Asia, northwest Africa.

322

Subphylum: **Vertebrates — Vertebrata**

Class: **Birds — Aves**

Order: **Perching birds — Passeriformes**

Family: **Thrushes and their allies — Turdidae**

1. European Robin *Erithacus rubecula* — Length 14 cm. Often found in places that are perpetually dim — forest undergrowth and dense thickets, which may explain the rather large eyes. Also found in gardens, etc. Feeds on insects, spiders, worms and berries. Nests in a hollow on the ground, between roots, or in a hole in a wall. Between April and June the female lays 5—6 eggs which she alone incubates. Both partners tend the young. There are 2 broods a year. Winters in north Africa, Asia Minor, central and southern Europe. Distribution: Europe (except the extreme north of Scandinavia and European USSR), the Middle East, Asia Minor, the Caucasus, northwest Africa.

2 Nightingale *Luscinia megarhynchos* — Length 17 cm. Found in lowland regions in broadleaved or mixed woods which have a dense undergrowth and a thick litter of dry leaves, in parks and in large neglected gardens. Noted for its beautiful song. Sings during the day, often at high noon, as well as at night. Feeds on insects and berries. The nest is located either directly on or close to the ground. In May or June the female lays 4—6 eggs, which only she is responsible for incubating. Both partners tend the young. Winters in southern Arabia and tropical Africa. Distribution: western and central Europe, northwest Africa, the Middle East, central Asia.

3 Bluethroat *Luscinia svecica* — Length 14 cm. Found in swampy areas and marshland covered with reeds and bushes, in inundated river valleys, etc. Feeds on insects and berries. The nest is located in thickets on or just above the ground. Between April and June the female lays 5—6 eggs. A migratory bird, it winters in north and northeast Africa. Distribution: almost all Europe, Asia. In Europe there are two races: *L. svecica cyanecula* (illustrated here), which inhabits western, central and southern Europe, northern and central Asia, and *L. svecica svecica* which inhabits northern Europe and the USSR.

4 Rock Thrush *Monticola saxatilis* — Length 19 cm. Found on bare sun-warmed rocks from lowland to mountainous elevations, in old quarries and ruins. Feeds on insects, spiders, snails, and berries. Nests in inaccessible rock crevices. In May or June the female lays 4—5 eggs which she incubates alone. Both partners tend the young. A migratory bird, it winters in tropical Africa. Distribution: southerly parts of Europe (north as far as Poland), northwest Africa, the Middle East, central and eastern Asia.

5 Song Thrush *Turdus philomelos* — Length 23 cm. Found in woods with dense undergrowth, large gardens and parks. Nests in bushes, trees and recesses in buildings. The nest is made from various herbaceous plants and lined with a mixture of mud, animal faeces and wood shavings cemented with saliva, thus forming a smooth hollow. Between April and July the female lays 4—6 eggs which she incubates by herself. Both parents tend the young. There are 2 broods a year. Winters in western and southern Europe, north Africa and Asia Minor. Distribution: most of Europe, the Middle East, western Asia.

324

1

2

3

5

4

♂

♀

Subphylum: **Vertebrates — Vertebrata**

Class: **Birds — Aves**

Order: **Perching birds — Passeriformes**

Family: **Thrushes and their allies — Turdidae**

1 Mistle Thrush *Turdus viscivorus* — Length 27 cm. Largest European thrush. Found in coniferous and mixed forests from lowland to mountainous elevations, in western Europe often in large parks. Feeds on insects, snails, worms, and berries. The nest is located high up in trees. Between April and June the female lays 4—5 eggs which only she incubates. Both parents tend the young. There are 2 broods a year. Birds of southern regions are resident, northern populations winter in southwestern Europe and northwest Africa. Distribution: all Europe (except northern Norway, northwest Africa, the Middle East, eastern Asia.

2 Fieldfare *Turdus pilaris* — Length 26 cm. Found mostly in coniferous forests, sometimes also in larger parks. Feeds on insects, earthworms, snails, berries and fruit. Nests in colonies, in trees. Between April and June female lays 5—6 eggs which she incubates by herself. Both partners tend the young. There are 2 broods a year. Mostly a migrant, it winters in western and southern Europe. Distribution: discontinuous in northern Europe and Asia.

3 Blackbird *Turdus merula* — Length 26 cm. As late as the 19th century it was still an inhabitant of forests but now it is one of the commonest of birds even in the centre of large cities, in gardens, parks, etc. The nest is located in trees, thickets, niches of buildings, etc. The nesting and feeding habits are similar to those of the Fieldfare. There are 2—3 broods a year. North European birds winter in southern Europe, west and central European birds are usually resident. Distribution: most of Europe (except Scandinavia, Iceland and European USSR), northwest Africa, the Middle East, southeast Asia.

4 Ring Ouzel *Turdus torquatus* — Length 24 cm. Found in rocky and scrub country, open coniferous and broadleaved forests near the tree line in mountains, stands of dwarf pine and sparsely vegetated mountain slopes. The diet is the same as that of the Blackbird. Nests in low trees and on the ground. Between April and June the female lays 4—5 eggs. Both partners incubate and tend the young. A migratory bird, it winters in the Mediterranean. Distribution: discontinuous — Great Britain, the Pyrenees, Alps, Carpathians, Scandinavia, the Caucasus, Asia Minor.

Family: **Parrotbills and bearded tits — Paradoxornithidae**

5 Bearded Tit *Panurus biarmicus* — Length 17 cm. Inhabits large reed beds bordering rivers, lakes and brackish waters. Feeds on insects, in winter also on seeds. The nest is located among thick reeds just above the water surface. Between April and July the female lays 5—7 eggs. There are 2 broods a year. Both partners incubate and tend the young. In southern regions it is resident, in the north dispersive. Distribution: locally in Europe, southwest and eastern Asia.

Subphylum: **Vertebrates — Vertebrata**

Class: **Birds — Aves**

Order: **Perching birds — Passeriformes**

Family: **Long-tailed tits — Aegithalidae**

1 Long-tailed Tit *Aegithalos caudatus* — Length 14 cm (including the 7.5 cm-long tail). Found in broadleaved and mixed woods, gardens and parks. Feeds on small insects. The nest, located low in thickets, is a closed, egg-shaped structure with small side entrance; it is woven of moss, spider-webs and lichens, camouflaged with bits of bark and twigs. Between April and June the female lays 6—12 eggs which she probably incubates by herself. Both partners tend the young. There are 2 broods a year. Generally stays the winter. Distribution: Europe (except the extreme northern regions), the Middle East, Siberia (to Kamchatka and China).

Family: **Penduline tits — Remizidae**

2 Penduline Tit *Remiz pendulinus* — Length 11 cm. Found along calm and flowing waters bordered with dense reeds and thickets. Feeds on insects, in winter on seeds. The nest is usually located on branches overhanging the water. It is a closed globular structure, with tube-like entrance at the side, woven of grass stems, plant down and animal hairs. In May or June the female lays 6—8 eggs. There are 1—2 broods a year. Only the female incubates and tends the young. A resident bird. Distribution: much of Europe, central Asia, southern parts of Siberia, central China, Japan.

Family: **Typical tits — Paridae**

3 Great Tit *Parus major* — Length 14 cm. Found in all types of woods, parks and gardens from lowland to mountainous elevations. Feeds on insects, oily seeds and fruit. The nest is located either in natural crevices or holes in walls, cracks in beams, etc. Between April and June the female lays 8—10 eggs which she incubates by herself. Both partners tend the young. Generally stays the winter in the nesting grounds; sometimes travels southward. Distribution: almost the entire Palaearctic region.

4 Blue Tit *Parus caeruleus* — Length 12 cm. Found in groves, parks, gardens, open mixed woods. Feeds on insects, berries, in winter chiefly on oily seeds. The nest is located in tree holes and other cavities. There are 2 broods a year. Between April and June the female lays 10—12 eggs which only she incubates. Both parents tend the young. A resident bird. Distribution: Europe (to central parts of Scandinavia and southern Finland), northwest Africa, the Middle East.

5 Coal Tit *Parus ater* — Length 11 cm. Inhabits coniferous woods and coniferous parts of mixed woods; avoids large forests. Feeds on insects, in winter on various conifer seeds. The nest is located in tree cavities, in holes under stumps and roots, in rock crevices and in nestboxes. Between April and June the female lays 8—10 eggs which she incubates by herself. Both partners tend the young. There are 2 broods a year. West European and central European populations are resident, north European birds winter in central Europe. Distribution: Europe (except the northern regions), Asia (east to Kamchatka and southeastern China), the Middle East, northwest Africa.

Subphylum: **Vertebrates — Vertebrata**

Class: **Birds — Aves**

Order: **Perching birds — Passeriformes**

Family: **Typical tits — Paridae**

1 Azure Tit *Parus cyanus* — Length 14 cm. Lives concealed amidst dense thickets, in marshland, tundra, woods with thick undergrowth, etc. The nesting habits and diet are similar to those of the Blue Tit. Usually resident, sometimes dispersive. It is a rare visitor in central and western Europe during the winter months. Distribution: isolated in western and central Europe. From eastern Europe to the Amur.

2 Marsh Tit *Parus palustris* — Length 12 cm. Found in broadleaved and mixed woods, parks and large gardens. Feeds on insects and insect eggs, in winter on seeds. The nest is located in tree holes and nestboxes. In April or May the female lays 7—10 eggs which she incubates by herself. Both partners tend the young. There are 2 broods a year. Distribution: Europe (from England and southern Scandinavia eastward), the Caucasus, eastern Asia.

3 Willow Tit *Parus montanus* — Length 12 cm. Inhabits mostly coniferous forests in both lowland and mountainous regions. The diet is the same as that of the Marsh Tit. Nests in cavities. In May the female lays 6—8 eggs which she incubates by herself. Both partners tend the young. There are 1—2 broods a year. A resident bird. Distribution: northern Europe, North America, northern Asia.

4 Crested Tit *Parus cristatus* — Length 12 cm. Found in coniferous forests from lowland to mountainous elevations, in western Europe also in broadleaved woods. The diet is the same as that of the Marsh Tit. Nests in cavities. Between April and June the female lays 7—10 eggs, which she alone incubates. Both parents tend the young. There are 2 broods a year. It is a resident or, at most, a dispersive bird. Distribution: Europe (to western Siberia).

Family: **Nuthatches — Sittidae**

5 Nuthatch *Sitta europaea* — Length 14 cm. Found in open woodlands, parks and large gardens with big old trees. Excellent at climbing trees, both upwards and downwards. Unlike woodpeckers it does not use its tail as a prop, and goes downwards head first. Feeds on insects, insect eggs, oily seeds, and berries. Nests in tree holes; if the entrance is too large it reduces it using mud mixed with saliva. In April or May the female lays 6—8 eggs which only she incubates. Both parents tend the young. A resident bird. Distribution: almost all Europe (except Ireland, northern Scotland and more northerly parts of Scandinavia), Siberia, southern Asia, northwest Africa.

330

Subphylum: **Vertebrates — Vertebrata**

Class: **Birds — Aves**

Order: **Perching birds — Passeriformes**

Family: **Treecreepers — Certhiidae**

1 Treecreeper *Certhia familiaris* — Length 13 cm. Found in very large coniferous and mixed woodlands. Feeds on insects, insect eggs and larvae. Nests in crevices, under loose bark, etc. Between April and July the female lays 5—7 eggs which she incubates by herself. The young are tended by both parents. There are 2 broods a year. A resident bird. Distribution: Europe (north to 60—61° N.), Asia (to 57° N.), southern parts of North America.

2 Short-toed Treecreeper *Certhia brachydactyla* — Length 13 cm. Resembles the preceding species. Feeding and nesting habits are similar to those of the Treecreeper but there is only 1 brood a year. A resident bird. Distribution: southern, central and western Europe, Tunisia, Algeria, Asia Minor, the Mediterranean islands.

Family: **Buntings — Emberizidae**

3 Snow Bunting *Plectrophenax nivalis* — Length 17 cm. Found in tundra, rocky country near the seashore and northern mountains up to the snow line. Feeds on insects and seeds. The nest is located on the ground in rock crevices, between stones, etc. In June or July the female lays 5—6 eggs which she incubates by herself. In winter it leaves its far northern breeding grounds, flying south to the coast of the Baltic and North Seas, etc. Distribution: northern Europe, arctic regions of Asia, North America.

4 Corn Bunting *Emberiza calandra* — Length 18 cm. Found in dry, open country in lowlands, in fields and meadows with isolated trees and bushes. Feeds on seeds and insects. The nest is located on the ground. In May or June the female lays 4—5 eggs which she incubates. The young are tended by both parents. There are 2 broods a year. A resident or dispersive bird; some populations overwinter in southern Europe. Distribution: Europe (east to the Ukraine), Asia Minor, central Asia, locally in north Africa.

5 Yellowhammer *Emberiza citrinella* — Length 17 cm. Commonest member of the family. Found in open countryside with fields and meadows, in thickets, hedgerows and in edges of broadleaved forests. Feeds on seeds, berries and insects. Nests on or close to the ground. Between April and July the female lays 4—5 eggs. Both parents incubate and tend the young. There are 2 broods a year. North European populations travel to the southerly parts of their breeding range for the winter. Distribution: Europe (north of central Spain, northern Italy and the Balkans), western Siberia.

6 Reed Bunting *Emberiza schoeniclus* — Length 15 cm. Found in damp, mainly marshy regions with reeds, and in shoreline reed beds. Feeds on insects, molluscs, crustaceans, seeds. The nest is located in a dry spot on the ground. Between May and July the female lays 5—6 eggs, incubated mostly by herself. The young are tended by both parents. There are 1—2 broods a year. A resident bird, in northern regions dispersive. Distribution: Europe (except Greece and the Mediterranean islands), much of Asia.

Subphylum: **Vertebrates — Vertebrata**

Class: **Birds — Aves**

Order: **Perching birds — Passeriformes**

Family: **Buntings — Emberizidae**

1 Lapland Bunting *Calcarius lapponicus* — Length 15 cm. Found in tundra and on the summits of mountain ranges above the tree line. Feeds on insects and seeds. The nest is located on the ground, amidst low vegetation and dwarf shrubs. Between May and July the female lays 4—6 eggs. Overwinters in warmer regions that are not too distant (only rarely in central Europe). Distribution: the Arctic region, Scandinavia, Kamchatka.

Family: **Finches — Fringillidae**

2 Hawfinch *Coccothraustes coccothraustes* — Length 17 cm. Found in open broadleaved woodlands, parks and large gardens. Has a characteristically large, cone-shaped bill. Feeds chiefly on seeds; fond of cracking cherry pits. Usually nests high up in trees. In May or June the female lays 4—6 eggs. Both parents incubate and tend the young. Mostly a resident bird; northern populations often journey as far as the Mediterranean for the winter. Distribution: Europe, Asia, northwest Africa.

3 Chaffinch *Fringilla coelebs* — Length 15 cm. Found in all types of woodlands, hedgerows, parks and gardens, often close to dwellings. Feeds on seeds and insects. The nest is located in trees and bushes. Between April and June the female lays 4—6 eggs, incubated by herself. The young are reared by both parents. There are 2 broods a year. Mostly a migratory bird, it winters in southern Europe; however many individuals (mostly males) stay the winter in the nesting grounds. Distribution: all Europe, western Siberia, the Middle East, northwest Africa.

4 Brambling *Fringilla montifringilla* — Length 15 cm. Found in northern beech and spruce woods. Feeds on insects, seeds and berries. The nesting habits are similar to those of the Chaffinch. Winters partly in southern Scandinavia but mostly in central and southern Europe. Migrates in large flocks. Distribution: northern Europe, northern Asia (to Kamchatka).

5 Greenfinch *Carduelis chloris* — Length 15 cm. Found in parkland with bushes, old gardens, smaller mixed woodlands, etc. Feeds on seeds and berries. Nests in bushes and trees. Between April and June the female lays 5—6 eggs, which she alone incubates. The young are reared by both parents. There are 2 broods a year. Partly a resident bird, partly a migrant, journeying to more southerly regions for the winter. Distribution: Europe (except northern Scandinavia), the Middle East, northwest Africa.

6 Goldfinch *Carduelis carduelis* — Length 12 cm. Very attractively coloured. Found in open country with scattered trees, in parks, open woodlands, and vineyards. Feeds on seeds (mainly of thistles) and insects. Adept at climbing on vegetation, particularly thistles. The nest is located in the tops of trees, mainly broadleaved species. Between May and July the female lays 5—6 eggs, which only she incubates. The young are tended by both parents. There are 2 broods a year. A dispersive bird; north European populations often migrate for the winter to western and central Europe or as far as the Mediterranean. Distribution: Europe (north as far as southern Sweden), western Asia, northwest Africa.

Subphylum: **Vertebrates — Vertebrata**

Class: **Birds — Aves**

Order: **Perching birds — Passeriformes**

Family: **Finches — Fringillidae**

1 Linnet *Carduelis cannabina* — Length 13 cm. Found on dry fallow land, pastureland with juniper bushes, in cemeteries, parks, etc. Feeds on seeds. The nest is generally located close to the ground, in a tree or bush. Between April and July the female usually lays 5 eggs, which she incubates by herself. The young are reared by both parents. It is partly dispersive, partly migratory, wintering in northern Italy and southern France. Distribution: Europe (to southern Sweden and Finland), western Siberia, the Middle East, northwest Africa.

2 Serin *Serinus serinus* — Length 12 cm. Native to the Mediterranean region. From the beginning of the 19th century it spread northward. Found in the neighbourhood of human habitations, in gardens, parks and the margins of broadleaved and mixed woodlands. Feeds on seeds. The nest is located in trees and shrubs. Between May and July the female lays 4—5 eggs which she alone incubates. The young are reared by both parents. There are 2 broods a year. Birds nesting in the northern part of the range are migratory, wintering in southern, central and western Europe, those of other regions are resident. Distribution: Europe (except most of Scandinavia), Asia Minor, northwest Africa.

3 Crossbill *Loxia curvirostra* — Length 17 cm. The female is yellowish-green. Found in areas with conifer trees. Feeds almost exclusively on conifer seeds, which it extracts from fir cones with its peculiar crossed bill. Also eats wild fruits and insects, occasionally. Female builds substantial nest of twigs, lined with grasses, in a conifer tree, and lays 3—4 eggs during February or March. Only the female incubates the eggs, but both partners feed the nestlings. One brood. Not a migrant, but highly dispersive, especially in poor seasons for conifer seeds. Distribution: most of northern Palaearctic (not extreme north), including permanent population in Scotland; mountainous areas of southern Europe and east Asia; southern Canada and northern USA, south to Mexico in the west.

4 Bullfinch *Pyrrhula pyrrhula* — Length 15 cm, northern race 17 cm. The male has a striking red breast, the female is greyish-brown. Found in coniferous and mixed forests with a dense undergrowth of thickets, in parks, very occasionally also in gardens. Feeds on seeds. The nest is generally located fairly high-up in conifers. Between May and July the female lays 4—5 eggs which she incubates by herself. The young are reared by both parents. There are 2 broods a year. A resident bird; northern populations winter in central to southern Europe. Distribution: almost all Europe (north from the Iberian Peninsula and Italy to northern Scandinavia), northern Asia (to Japan and Kamchatka).

Family: **Weavers and their allies — Ploceidae**

5 Snow Finch *Montifringilla nivalis* — Length 18 cm. Found in rocky regions at the limit of permanent snow and ice in high mountains, often near glaciers. Feeds on seeds and insects. The nest is located in rock crevices or under stones in screes. Between May and July the female lays 5—6 eggs. Both partners share the duties of incubating and tending the young. There are 1—2 broods a year. Winters near the nesting grounds but descends to lower elevations. Distribution: high mountains of Europe and Asia.

6 House Sparrow *Passer domesticus* — Length 15 cm. Unlike the Tree Sparrow, it shows sexual dimorphism. Associate of man, in small villages as well as large cities. Feeds on seeds, buds and insects. It nests in various places, in holes in walls, etc. Between April and August the female lays 5—6 eggs. Both partners share the duties of incubating and rearing the young. There are 2—3 broods a year. A resident bird. Distribution: worldwide.

336

Subphylum: **Vertebrates — Vertebrata**

Class: **Birds — Aves**

Order: **Perching birds — Passeriformes**

Family: **Weavers and their allies — Ploceidae**

1 Tree Sparrow *Passer montanus* — Length 14 cm. The male and female have similar plumage. Found in farming regions with orchards, in parks and in country gardens. The diet is the same as that of the House Sparrow. Nests in various cavities and nestboxes. Between April and August the female lays 5—6 eggs. Both partners incubate and both tend the young. There are 2—3 broods a year. A dispersive bird, at least in the northern and eastern populations. Distribution: almost all Europe (except the western and southern Balkans, northern Sweden and Finland), northern Asia.

Family: **Starlings — Sturnidae**

2 Starling *Sturnus vulgaris* — Length 21 cm. Originally an inhabitant of broadleaved forests with hollow trees, it is now found also in treeless regions. Nests in holes in walls, under eaves and in nestboxes. Feeds on insects, worms, snails and fruit. Between April and June the female lays 5—6 eggs. Both partners incubate and tend the young. There are 1—2 broods a year. In western and southern Europe it stays the winter, otherwise it migrates, wintering in western and southwestern Europe and the Mediterranean region. Distribution: Europe (except the Iberian Peninsula, southern France and west coast of the Balkan Peninsula), Asia (to Lake Baikal).

Family: **Orioles — Oriolidae**

3 Golden Oriole *Oriolus oriolus* — Length 24 cm. Found in groves and broadleaved woods in lowlands and foothills, sometimes also in open pine stands and large parks. Feeds on insects and various fruits. The hammock-shaped nest is suspended between the forks of slender terminal branches, usually high up in the treetops. Between May and July the female lays 3—5 eggs. Both partners share the task of incubating and rearing the young. A migratory bird, it winters in central and southern Africa. Distribution: Europe (to southern Scandinavia, absent in the British Isles), western and southern Asia, northwest Africa.

Family: **Crows and their allies — Corvidae**

4 Jay *Garrulus glandarius* — Length 34 cm. Found in all types of woods from lowlands to mountains. Feeds on acorns, beechnuts, berries, insects, worms, birds'eggs and small vertebrates. The nest is located high up in the treetops. In April or May the female lays 5—6 eggs. Both partners incubate and tend the young. A resident or dispersive bird. Distribution: Europe (to central Scandinavia), Asia, northwest Africa.

5 Nutcracker *Nucifraga caryocatactes* — Length 32 cm. Found in taiga and in coniferous forests in mountains, often above the upper tree line. Feeds on the seeds of conifers, berries, fruit, insects, snails, etc. Fond of the nuts of cembra pine, often burying them in the ground above the tree line, thus contributing to the spread of forest into the mountains. The nest is located in the crowns of conifers. In March or April the female lays 3—4 eggs which only she incubates. The young are reared by both parents. A resident, dispersive or invasive bird, descending in winter from the highest parts of the mountains to lower elevations. Distribution: Scandinavia, European USSR, the Alps, Carpathians, Balkan mountains, Siberia, central Asia.

Subphylum: **Vertebrates — Vertebrata**

Class: **Birds — Aves**

Order: **Perching birds — Passeriformes**

Family: **Crows and their allies — Corvidae**

1 Magpie *Pica pica* — Length 46 cm, the tail making up more than half of the length. Found in open parkland country, fruit orchards, shrub-covered fallow land and hedgerows with tall trees. The nest, protected by a kind of roof, is located low down in thickets or high up in tree-tops. In April or May the female lays 5—7 eggs, which she incubates by herself. The young are tended by both parents. A resident bird. Distribution: all Europe, much of Asia, northwest Africa, North America.

2 Jackdaw *Corvus monedula* — Length 33 cm. Found in open countryside with groups of old trees, in built-up areas, and in rocky terrain. Feeds on insects, worms, snails, small vertebrates and seeds. Generally nests in colonies. The nest is located in holes, crannies, etc. In April or May the female lays 5—6 eggs which she incubates by herself. Both partners tend the young. North and east European populations usually winter in western Europe or the Mediterranean region, in western and southern Europe it is a resident bird. Distribution: Europe (to central Scandinavia), western Asia, northwest Africa.

3 Raven *Corvus corax* — Length 63 cm. Largest member of the crow family. Found in the north in shrub-covered tundra, on seacoasts, in open country with woodlands and hedgerows, in the south in both mountainous and lowland regions. Feeds on insects, vertebrates, carrion, fruit. The nest is located in tall trees or on cliffs. In March or April the female lays 4—6 eggs which she incubates by herself. The young are reared by both parents. A resident bird. In western and central Europe it is quite rare, occurring in greater numbers only in the Alps and here and there in the Carpathians. Distribution: almost all Europe, Asia, north and east Africa, North and Central America.

4 Rook *Corvus frugilegus* — Length 46 cm. Adult birds have bare white skin round the base of the bill. Found in farm country with scattered groups of trees, in recent years also in built-up areas. Does not occur in mountains. Feeds on insects, worms, small vertebrates, berries, fruit. Nests in large or small colonies, high up in trees. In March or April the female lays 3—5 eggs, which she incubates. The young are reared by both parents. In eastern Europe it is migratory, in central and western Europe resident or dispersive. Distribution: Europe (from the British Isles eastward), eastern Asia.

5 Carrion Crow *Corvus corone corone* — Length 47 cm. Found in open countryside in fields and meadows with scattered hedgerows and groups of trees, in continuous forests, open groves and in parks. Feeds on small vertebrates, birds'eggs, insects, worms, carrion, and fruit. In April or May the female generally lays 5 eggs, which she incubates alone. The young are fed by both parents. A resident or dispersive bird. Distribution: western Europe to the Elbe and Vltava rivers, Vienna, and across the Alps to northern Italy, northern and central Asia (to Kamchatka and Japan).

6 Hooded Crow *Corvus corone cornix* — Length 47 cm. Differs from the preceding subspecies by having partially grey plumage. Its biology is identical with that of the Carrion Crow. Distribution: eastern Europe, eastern Siberia.

340

Subphylum: **Vertebrates — Vertebrata**

Class: **Mammals — Mammalia**

Order: **Insectivores — Insectivora**

Family: **Hedgehogs — Erinaceidae**

1 European Hedgehog *Erinaceus europaeus* — Length 30 cm. Found in woods among undergrowth, on shrub-covered hillsides, in gardens and parks in cities and villages. Occurs high up in the mountains (in the Alps up to 2,000 metres). Feeds on various insects, slugs, worms, spiders and even small vertebrates. The nest is built in undergrowth and lined with moss and straw. It produces 7—10 young. It hibernates in the nest. Distribution: western Europe as far east as the lower reaches of the Odra, in Bohemia and the Alps.

2 East European Hedgehog *Erinaceus concolor* — Size and life habits are the same as those of the preceding species. Until recently it was considered to be a geographic race of the European Hedgehog, from which it differs by displaying two colours in the young and in having a white patch on the breast. The dark colouring on the head between the nose and eyes is not continuous whereas in the European Hedgehog it forms 'spectacles'. Distribution: from central Europe east to northwest China, Korea, and the Ussuri River region in the USSR.

Family: **Shrews — Soricidae**

3 Common Shrew *Sorex araneus* — Length of body 65—85 mm, tail 32—47 mm. Found in damp places where it feeds on insects, slugs, worms and spiders. It consumes its own weight of food daily. Lives in burrows which it digs or more often in abandoned holes made by other small mammals. In winter it often enters buildings. The underground nest is lined with grass and other soft plant material. There the female bears 5—10 young, 2—4 times a year. Distribution: almost all of Europe and Asia.

4 Alpine Shrew *Sorex alpinus* — Length of body 62—80 mm, tail 54—75 mm. Found mostly in low mountains and the dwarf-pine belt of high mountains with moist microclimates. Occurs around mountain streams and springs. Like other shrews it is primarily nocturnal. Bears 6—8 young, once or twice a year. Feeds on insects, worms and snails. Distribution: most of Europe's higher mountain ranges including the Alps where it lives up to elevations of 3,300 metres.

5 Pygmy Shrew *Sorex minutus* — Length of body 45—66 mm, tail 32—46 mm, weight 3—5 grams. Smallest European insectivore. Found in damp coniferous and mixed woods from lowland regions to the upper limit of forests in mountains. Digs shallow underground burrows where the female bears 4—10 young, 1—3 times a year. It feeds chiefly on insects, spiders, worms and snails and also on oily plant seeds. Distribution: it occurs as several races in Europe and the Palaearctic regions of Asia.

6 European Water Shrew *Neomys fodiens* — Length of body 70—96 mm, tail 47—77 mm. Found on the shores of streams, rivers, lakes and ponds from lowland to mountain elevations. Digs burrows near water, the opening at one end always being located underwater. The nest is lined with grass and moss. The breeding period is from April to late August or September. There are 2—4 litters a year, each consisting of 4—7, sometimes as many as 11 young. Active mostly by night, when it hunts aquatic insects, snails, small fish and frogs underwater. An excellent swimmer. Distribution: throughout Europe, in the Alps up to elevations of 2,500 metres; in Asia as far as the Ussuri River.

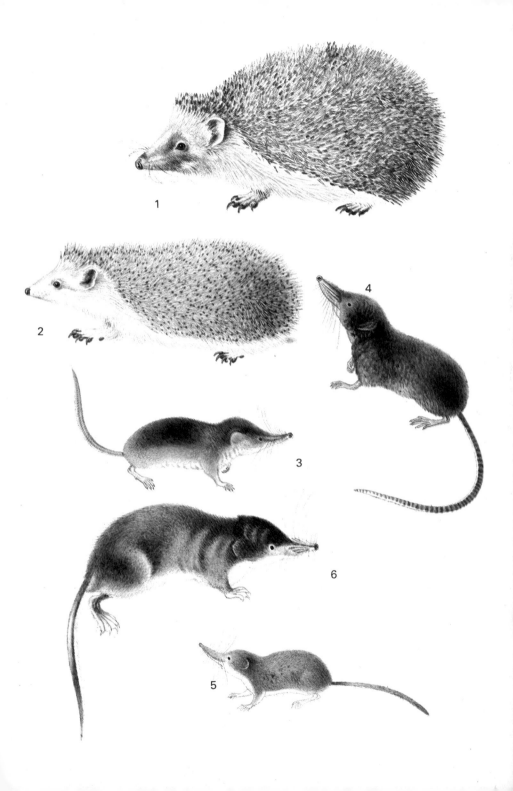

Subphylum: **Vertebrates — Vertebrata**

Class: **Mammals — Mammalia**

Order: **Insectivores — Insectivora**

Family: **Shrews — Soricidae**

1 Greater White-toothed Shrew *Crocidura russula* — Length of body 64—95 mm, tail 33—46 mm. Found chiefly in human habitations, fields, gardens and cemeteries; in mountains up to elevations of 1,600 metres. Feeds mainly on insects, occasionally on plant seeds. The breeding season is from April to September. There are 2—4 litters a year, each comprising 3—10 young. Distribution: the more southerly regions of Europe (north as far as central and southern Germany and Poland); the warmer regions of Asia, east to Korea and Japan. It also occurs in northwest Africa, in Kenya, Sudan and Angola.

2 Lesser White-toothed Shrew *Crocidura suaveolens* — Length of body 53—83 mm, tail 25—44 mm. Found in shrub-covered clearings in steppe-like lowland regions, in parks and in buildings. Feeds on various invertebrates, small vertebrates and carrion. Nests in burrows, usually those made by rodents. There are 2—4 litters per year, each consisting of 2—6 blind and naked young. When they are 4—5 weeks old they are led about by their mother, each holding firmly on to another by the fur at the base of the tail. Distribution: throughout Europe north to the Baltic Sea, temperate regions of Asia east to China and Korea. Occurs also in northwest Africa and perhaps in the eastern and southwestern parts of the African continent.

3 Bicolor White-toothed Shrew *Crocidura leucodon* — Length of body 63—90 mm, tail 28—39 mm. Common in fields and in the vicinity of buildings. Lives in holes, generally in scrub country. There are 2—3 litters a year, each comprising 3—9 young, which the female leads about in the same manner as the White-toothed Shrew. The diet is also similar. Distribution: southern and central Europe north to the Baltic; in the Palaearctic regions of Asia it forms several geographic races.

4 Savi's Pygmy Shrew *Suncus etruscus* — Length of body 36—52 mm, tail 24—29 mm, weight 1.5—2.5 grams. Smallest mammal of the world. Found in damp places near water. Feeds on insects and other invertebrates. Has 5—6 litters a year, each consisting of 2—5 young. Distribution: regions bordering the Mediterranean, Transcaucasia, Turkestan.

Family: **Moles — Talpidae**

5 Russian Desman *Desmana moschata* — Length of body about 215 mm, tail 170 mm. Found near large rivers, chiefly along backwaters with thick vegetation. Feeds on insects, molluscs, crustaceans, small fish and plants. Lives in burrows with an underwater entrance. Has 2 litters a year, each comprising 1—5 young. A fur animal protected by law. Distribution: native to the USSR, along the lower reaches of the Volga, Don and the Ural River region; introduced to several places in the European part of the USSR.

6 Pyrenean Desman *Galemys pyrenaicus* — Length of body 110—135 mm, tail 130 mm. Found near water, chiefly in places with lush shoreline vegetation. It digs burrows in the bank with entrance underwater; the nesting chamber is always above water level in a dry section. Little is known about this species. Due to overhunting its numbers are constantly declining. Distribution: along rivers and streams in the Pyrenees and other places in northern Spain and Portugal.

Subphylum: **Vertebrates — Vertebrata**

Class: **Mammals — Mammalia**

Order: **Insectivores — Insectivora**

Family: **Moles — Talpidae**

1 European Mole *Talpa europaea* — Length of body 130—170 mm, tail 23—38 mm. Found in great numbers in damp places in meadows, clearings, parks and forest margins up to elevations of 2,000 metres. Lives underground, using its shovel-like forefeet to dig a series of tunnels, at the same time making its well-known molehills on the surface. Feeds chiefly on earthworms, slugs and grubs. Produces a single litter of 4—5 young. Distribution: Europe, from southern Sweden to Spain, Italy, Sicily and northern Greece and from Great Britain to the Urals and Caucasus. Occurs also in Asia as far as Lake Baikal and the Lena River region.

Order: **Bats — Chiroptera**

Family: **Horseshoe bats — Rhinolophidae**

2 Horseshoe Bat *Rhinolophus hipposideros* — Length of body 38—45 mm, wingspan 190—250 mm. By day it stays in colonies in attics, church steeples, ruins, caves, emerging in the evening. Like all bats it feeds on insects which it captures in flight. The breeding period is from May to June. It usually produces 1—2 young. Distribution: most of Europe, south Africa, the Middle East, central Asia.

3 Greater Horseshoe Bat *Rhinolophus ferrumequinum* — Length of body 58—70 mm, wingspan 330—400 mm. Spends the day in caves, underground shafts, rock cavities and ruins in warmer areas. In winter it often forms large colonies, in summer it leads a solitary life or occurs in small groups. It hunts prey in slow flight fairly close to the ground until after dusk. In mid-June it usually bears a single young. Distribution: Europe, Great Britain, central Germany, Austria; north as far as Slovakia and Ruthenia; Asia as far as China and Japan. It is also found in northwest Africa.

Family: **Vespertilionid bats — Vespertilionidae**

4 Common Noctule *Nyctalus noctula* — Length of body 60—80 mm, wingspan 320—460 mm. Found in lowlands and foothills in woods and parks with plenty of old hollow trees, where it hides during the day in summer. Winter is spent in tree hollows or other shelters. It often travels long distances to the south for the winter. In late May it produces 2 young. Distribution: throughout Europe (north as far as southern Scandinavia and Finland), Asiatic USSR, northern China and northwest Africa.

5 Long-eared Bat *Plecotus auritus* — Length of body 47—51 mm, wingspan 220—260 mm. Found in the neighbourhood of human habitations. It emerges after dark and flies slowly, close to the ground. Hunts prey in parks, gardens, forests and forest margins. In May or June 1—2 young are born. During the summer females form small colonies of 5—20 individuals, the males remain solitary. Distribution: lower elevations and mountains of northern Europe (in the Alps up to 1,850 metres); in more southerly regions only found in the mountains; Asia as far as Japan.

6 Brown Bat *Myotis myotis* — Length of body 60—80 mm, wingspan 350—430 mm. One of the commonest bats, found chiefly around human habitations, less often in caves. Females form large colonies in summer. In May or June it bears a single young. Distribution: Europe (the Ukraine marks its easternmost limits), Turkey, Lebanon, Syria and north Africa.

Subphylum: **Vertebrates — Vertebrata**

Class: **Mammals — Mammalia**

Order: **Bats — Chiroptera**

Family: **Vespertilionid bats — Vespertilionidae**

1 Daubenton's Bat *Myotis daubentoni* — Length of body 46—51 mm, wingspan 210—250 mm. Found in the immediate vicinity of water. In summer it hides by day in tree holes, attics or wall crevices. Winter is usually spent in caves, abandoned shafts or various crannies. Females form large colonies in summer. In June it usually produces a single offspring. Feeds on insects which it captures close to the water's surface. Distribution: throughout Europe north to central Scandinavia; Asia east to Korea and Japan.

2 Barbastelle *Barbastella barbastellus* — Length of body 42—52 mm, wingspan 240—275 mm. In summer it hides in hollow trees or wall crevices by day, leaving its shelter at dusk. Hunts insects, mostly in forests and in forest clearings. In June produces 1 or, very occasionally, 2 young. Overwinters in caves, abandoned mine shafts, cellars and ruins. Distribution: throughout Europe (north as far as southern Sweden and Norway); western parts of the USSR, Asia Minor and in northwest Africa.

3 Common Pipistrelle *Pipistrellus pipistrellus* — Length of body 33—45 mm, wingspan 180—230 mm. Common in lowlands as well as higher regions (in the Alps up to 2,000 metres). Originally a tree-dweller, it is now often bound to human habitations, where it sleeps in summer under loose plaster, behind window-shutters, pictures and in wall crevices. It forms large colonies in summer. Produces 1—2 young, which are fully independent within two months. Distribution: throughout Europe (except the extreme north); Asia and northwest Africa.

Order: **Primates**

Family: **Guenon-like monkeys — Cercopithecidae**

4 Barbary Ape *Macaca sylvanus* — Length of body 75 cm. This is the only European monkey. It lives in bands, often close to human habitations. The strongest male is always head of the band. Feeds on vegetation as well as eggs and small animals. Produces 2 young, which are fully grown after about 4 1/2 years. Lives in places where the temperature often drops below freezing point and adapts easily to rugged climates. Several attempts were made to introduce this monkey to central Europe. Since 1969 it has lived in a preserve in the Vosges, containing animals brought there from the Atlas Mountains of Morocco. It is native to north Africa, whence it spread as far as Gibraltar.

Order: **Carnivores — Carnivora**

Family: **Weasels and their allies — Mustelidae**

5 Weasel *Mustela nivalis* — Length of body 130—240 mm, tail 50—70 mm. The female is always smaller than the male (as in most other carnivores). Lives in forests, clearings, fields, gardens and near human habitations. Found high up in mountains, in the Alps up to 2,700 metres. Usually occupies the burrows of voles and mice but also inhabits fallen hollow trees. Usually produces 4—7 young. Feeds chiefly on mice and voles, sometimes also on sousliks, rabbits and ground-nesting birds. Distribution: throughout Europe (except Ireland), Asia (as far as Japan and Korea), north Africa and North America.

6 Ermine or Stoat *Mustela erminea* — Length of body 240—290 mm, tail 80—90 mm. Very adaptable, has no special habitat requirements. Found both in lowland and mountain regions, in the Alps up to 3,000 metres. In winter its fur becomes entirely white, except the black tip of the tail. Distribution: throughout Europe, most of Asia, northwest Africa and North America.

Subphylum: **Vertebrates — Vertebrata**

Class: **Mammals — Mammalia**

Order: **Carnivores — Carnivora**

Family: **Weasels and their allies — Mustelidae**

1 European Mink *Lutreola lutreola* — Length of body 320—400 mm, tail 120—190 mm. Found in the vicinity of rivers and streams with thick herbaceous vegetation along the banks. A nocturnal animal, it conceals itself in holes on the banks of watercourses by day. Feeds on smaller aquatic vertebrates and aquatic invertebrates. Mates in March or April and produces 2—7 young in May or June. Distribution: occurs as several geographic races in France, Austria, Poland, Finland, Hungary, Yugoslavia, Rumania, the European USSR and western Siberia.

2 European Polecat *Putorius putorius* — Length of body 400—440 mm, tail 130—190 mm. Partial to human dwellings. Found from lowlands to mountains, in the Alps up to 2,000 metres. Very adaptable, it may be encountered in fields as well as forests and along water. Feeds on small and medium-sized mammals, such as hares, and on ground-nesting birds. Often kills poultry and feeds on eggs in coops. When threatened with danger it discharges a foetid liquid from the anal gland at the base of the tail. In May or June the female bears 4—5 young. The family remains together till the following spring. Distribution: throughout Europe, Asia and northwest Africa.

3 European Badger *Meles meles* — Length of body 600—850 mm, tail 110—180 mm. Inhabits forests from lowland to mountain elevations. Digs long, deep tunnels in concealed places; the nesting chamber is lined with moss. Here it passes the winter in false hibernation and in summer it conceals itself by day. It is active at night. The diet consists of varied animal and plant food. Mates in July. The young are not born until February to April of the following year. The litter consists of 1—5 but usually only 2 young. Distribution: throughout Europe except the extreme north and throughout most of Asia.

4 Pine Marten *Martes martes* — Length of body 480—530 mm, tail 230—280 mm. Inhabits forests from lowlands to mountains. Active mostly at night, concealing itself by day in tree holes, old birds' and squirrels' nests. Excellent tree climber. Feeds on small rodents, birds, birds'eggs, various insects and sweet fruit, but sometimes it captures even larger prey such as hares and rabbits. In April it produces 2—6 young. Distribution: throughout Europe and western Siberia to the lower reaches of the Ob and Irtysh rivers, the Caucasus, Transcaucasia and most of Asia.

5 European Marten *Martes foina* — Length of body 450—500 mm, tail 250—270 mm. Differs from the Pine Marten by usually having a white patch on the throat and breast, extending to the forelegs; in the Pine Marten the patch is generally yellow and terminates in a wedge between the forelegs. Found in forest margins, rock formations and ruins. Its biology is similar to that of the Pine Marten but it is also active during the day. Both are important fur animals. Distribution: throughout Europe (except Scandinavia, Great Britain and northern parts of the European USSR), Asia as far as northern China and Mongolia.

6 Glutton or Wolverine *Gulo gulo* — Length of body 700—830 mm, tail 160—250 mm. Inhabits taiga and forested tundra. Feeds chiefly on rodents such as lemmings, but it also attacks hares, foxes, martens, various birds and fish. It also eats plant food, being fond of various fruits. It has been known to hunt certain large animals such as Roe Deer, young Red Deer, for which it lies in wait in trees. Distribution: northern regions of Europe, Asia, North America.

Subphylum: **Vertebrates — Vertebrata**

Class: **Mammals — Mammalia**

Order: **Carnivores — Carnivora**

Family: **Weasels and their allies — Mustelidae**

1 Common Otter *Lutra lutra* — Length of body 650—800 mm, tail 350—500 mm. Found along streams and rivers, excavating simple burrows in the banks. Occurs also on the seacoast and in mountains up to elevations of 2,500 metres. Mostly nocturnal. Feeds on fish, less frequently on crayfish, amphibians, aquatic mammals and birds. Produces 2—5 young once a year. A rare fur animal. Occurs as 10 geographic races throughout Eurasia.

Family: **Bears — Ursidae**

2 Brown Bear *Ursus arctos* — Length of body 170—250 cm, tail 6—14 cm, height at shoulder 100—110 cm, weight 150—300 kg, very occasionally as much as 400 kg. Largest European carnivore. In Europe it is nowadays found in mountains and foothills, in mixed and coniferous forests where there are plenty of suitable places for concealment. The diet is a mixed one. In some cases it feeds only on flesh, attacking large wild game as well as grazing sheep and cattle. Passes the winter in its den in false hibernation. In winter the female bears 1—2 small-sized young. Distribution: occurs as several geographic races throughout Europe, Asia and North America.

3 Polar Bear *Thalarctos maritimus* — Length of body over 2.5 metres, weight 400—600 kg. Inhabits regions of permanent ice and snow around the North Pole. Feeds chiefly on young seals. In winter the female bears young in dens excavated in snow, the walls of which are turned into ice by her warm breath thus providing an excellent thermal insulation. In many places its numbers have been greatly reduced by hunting so that nowadays it occurs in great numbers only in Greenland and on the coast and islands of arctic North America and Asia.

Family: **Weasel cats — Viverridae**

4 Genet *Genetta genetta* — Length of body 47—58 cm, tail 41—48 cm. Found on rocky slopes covered with dense thickets. Active mostly by night; by day sleeps in hollow trees or rock crevices. Hunts small vertebrates, being partial to brown rats. There are 1—2 litters a year, each consisting of 2—4 young. Distribution: Africa; in Europe it inhabits the Iberian Peninsula and southern France.

Family: **Foxes and their allies — Canidae**

5 Wolf *Canis lupus* — Length of body 100—165 cm, tail 35—50 cm. Lives in packs; in summer these consist of a single family, in winter of several families. The strongest male is the leader of the pack. In summer the Wolf feeds on small animals and various fruits, in winter hunts large prey in packs. Between March and May the female usually bears 4—6 young in the den, keeping constant guard over them during the first few days while the male keeps her provided with food. Nowadays it occurs only rarely in mountain regions of central Europe; in eastern Europe it is also found in lowlands. Almost extinct in western Europe, occurring rarely in the Pyrenees and the Apennines. Also found in Scandinavia, the Carpathians, the Balkan Peninsula, Asia (as far as Japan and Korea) and North America.

6 Jackal *Canis aureus* — Length of body 85—105 cm, tail 20—24 cm. Lives in pairs or small groups, mostly in thick vegetation around water in lowland regions. Starts hunting after sundown. Feeds on rodents, amphibians, fish, carrion, insects and fruit. In April or May the female bears 4—9 young in den excavated by her. Distribution: southeastern Europe, Asia and Africa.

Subphylum: **Vertebrates — Vertebrata**

Class: **Mammals — Mammalia**

Order: **Carnivores — Carnivora**

Family: **Foxes and their allies — Canidae**

1 Red Fox *Vulpes vulpes* — Length of body 65—76 cm, tail 35—44 cm. Found chiefly in forests, copses and field thickets, often in places with rock cavities. Lives singly or in families. Feeds mostly on various vertebrates but also on insects, worms, molluscs and fruit. Mates in January or February. The female bears 3—8 young in a den lined with hair. Distribution: the Palaearctic (except the extreme northern parts) and Nearctic regions.

2 Arctic Fox *Alopex lagopus* — Length of body 50—70 cm, tail 30 cm. Two forms exist: one is light brown in summer and white in winter, the other is greyish-blue throughout the year. Lives in small groups. Feeds on small rodents, fish cast up by the sea, fruits, and in the far north often on food left by polar bears. The female bears 4—8 young in a lined den, usually in May. Distribution: around the North Pole and the tundra of northern Asia and North America.

3 Corsac Fox *Alopex corsac* — Length of body 50—60 cm, tail 30 cm. Resembles the Red Fox but has comparatively longer legs. A typical inhabitant of the steppe, semi-desert and desert. It feeds chiefly on small steppe rodents, birds and birds' eggs, occasionally also on larger animals such as hares, sousliks and marmots. The female bears 2—11 young in abandoned badger or fox dens. Distribution: mainly in Asia but extending west into Europe as far as the Ukraine.

4 Raccoon-Dog *Nyctereutes procyonoides* — Length of body 65—80 cm, tail 15—25 cm. Found in broadleaved woodlands intersected by streams, in scrub country and in cultivated steppes. Lives in pairs or families. Usually active at night, remaining concealed by day either in a self-dug hole or in a badger or fox den. In May the female bears 6—8 young which are reared by both parents. Feeds on vertebrates as large as a rabbit, birds' eggs, various invertebrates and fruits. Distribution: native to the Amur and Ussuri region of the USSR, China and Japan. In the 1930s it was introduced as a fur animal to the European USSR whence it spread to Finland, Sweden, Poland, Czechoslovakia, Germany, Rumania and Hungary.

Family: **Cats — Felidae**

5 Wild Cat *Felis silvestris* — Length of body 79—94 cm, tail 29—35 cm. Found mainly in warm, broadleaved woods, less frequently in mixed woods in foothills and mountains. Apart from the breeding season it lives singly, concealing itself by day in hollow trees, rock crevices, disused burrows. Generally hunts in the evening and at night when it feeds mostly on small mammals, birds and reptiles. Occasionally it will take larger prey such as hares. In April or May the female bears 2—6 young which she suckles for about a month, after which she feeds them flesh. Distribution: Europe, Asia and Africa.

6 European Lynx *Lynx lynx* — Length of body 90—130 cm, tail 15—20 cm. Found in the larger submontane and mountain forests. The den is located in thickets, among rocks or in tree cavities. Emerges to hunt at dusk. Feeds on small and larger mammals (as large as a Roe Deer), birds and occasionally on reptiles and amphibians. In May or June 2—3 young are produced. In western Europe it is now almost extinct. Occurs in central and eastern Europe and in Asia.

Subphylum: **Vertebrates — Vertebrata**

Class: **Mammals — Mammalia**

Order: **Pinnipedia**

Family: **Walruses — Odobaenidae**

1 Walrus *Odobaenus rosmarus* — Length: male 4.5 metres, weight more than 1000 kg. The female is much smaller. Found on the coasts of the Arctic seas where it usually lives in pairs. Feeds on molluscs, crustaceans, fish and even baby seals. Generally produces a single offspring. If danger threatens both parents protect the young, this behaviour resulting in a strong family unit. Distribution: Greenland, Spitsbergen, northern Siberia, North America.

Family: **True or earless seals — Phocidae**

2 Common Seal *Phoca vitulina* — Length 165—180 cm, occasionally as much as 2 metres; females are smaller. Spends most of its life in water although it is fond of resting on sandy and clay shores. An expert swimmer, venturing as far as 50 km from the shore. Also sleeps in water. Feeds chiefly on fish, marine crustaceans, molluscs and other invertebrates. Mates in August, when it congregates in large herds on the shore. After 11 months the female bears a single young which is immediately capable of swimming and diving. Distribution: off the coasts of the north Atlantic, rarely found off the coast of the North, Baltic and Black Seas. Often swims up rivers.

3 Ringed Seal *Phoca hispida* — Length 150—185 cm. Feeds on marine invertebrates and fish. In March or April the female generally bears a single young. The young are covered with a thick coat of fur which makes life in water impossible. Only when this has been replaced by the normal hairy coat, some twenty days later, can they enter the water. In Europe it is common in the eastern part of the Baltic, becoming rarer farther westward; it is rarely found in the North Sea. It also occurs off the northern coast of Europe, Asia, North America, in the Arctic and in Lake Saima and Lake Ladoga.

Order: **Rodents — Rodentia**

Family: **Tree squirrels — Sciuridae**

4 Red Squirrel *Sciurus vulgaris* — Length of body 20—24 cm, tail 16—20 cm. Found in woodlands, parks and gardens, often in the immediate vicinity of man. Spends most of its life in trees where it feeds on seeds, hazel nuts, fruit, the bark of young shoots and buds; occasionally it eats insects, birds'eggs and even nestlings. On the ground it gathers nuts, berries and mushrooms. It stores food for the winter in caches in tree hollows or in the ground. It builds a nest in trees where the female bears 3—8 young twice a year. Distribution: occurs as many subspecies throughout the Palaearctic.

5 Marmot *Marmota marmota* — Length of body 53—73 cm, tail 13—16 cm. Found high in mountains, mainly in subalpine and alpine meadows and on rock screes. Lives in families or in colonies. Digs deep holes in which it sleeps, retreats from danger and hibernates for 6 months or more. The diet consists of plant food. Distribution: Europe, particularly the Alps and Carpathians.

6 European Souslik *Citellus citellus* — Length of body 195—240 mm, tail 60—70 mm. Found in cultivated steppes, meadows and sometimes also in clearings. Lives in colonies and digs an inclined tunnel in the ground up to 2 metres long with a grass-lined side chamber. Active by day only during the warm months. Hibernates in winter. Feeds on grass seeds, cereal grains, young shoots and insects. Mates in April or May and produces 6—8 young in late May or June. Distribution: Eurasia and North America.

Subphylum: **Vertebrates — Vertebrata**

Class: **Mammals — Mammalia**

Order: **Rodents — Rodentia**

Family: **Tree squirrels — Sciuridae**

1 European Flying Squirrel *Pteromys volans* — Length of body 135—205 mm, tail 90—140 mm. Glides to the ground by means of extensible skin fold which can be spread out like an aerofoil between the fore and hind feet. Found in mixed woods and groves of aspen where it builds the nest in holes 3—4 metres above the ground. Feeds chiefly on the seeds of trees but also eats grass seeds, strawberries, mushrooms and tree buds. Hides in the nest by day, emerging in the evening to forage for food. There are 1—2 litters a year, each generally consisting of 2—4 young. Distribution: mainly an inhabitant of northern Asia; in Europe it is found only in Scandinavia, Finland and European USSR.

Family: **Beavers — Castoridae**

2 European Beaver *Castor fiber* — Length of body 70—100 cm, tail 30—35 cm. Inhabits calm and flowing water in open woodlands. Lives in families or colonies in underground holes dug in banks, with entrances below the water level, or in so-called lodges. Builds dams to raise the water level. These are constructed of mud, stones and tree trunks felled and trimmed by gnawing with its sharp incisors. Feeds on aquatic plants and the bark of trees. In April or May the female bears 2—4 young. Within historic times the beaver was widespread throughout Europe's forest belt but has since become extinct. Nowadays it is found only in Scandinavia, France, Germany, Poland and the European USSR.

Family: **Cricetid rats, mice and voles — Cricetidae**

3 Common Hamster *Cricetus cricetus* — Length of body 210—340 mm, tail 25—65 mm. Common in cultivated steppes in both lowlands and foothills. A solitary, nocturnal rodent that lives in underground burrows expanding into a nesting chamber and a food chamber. In winter it hibernates. Feeds on grain, plant shoots and even small rodents and young birds. There are 2—3 broods a year, each consisting of 4—12 young. Distribution: Europe from France southward; Asia as far as the Yenisei River.

4 Norway Lemming *Lemmus lemmus* — Length of body 130—150 mm, tail 15—19 mm. Digs a complex system of corridors at a shallow depth in the ground and builds a spherical nest of shredded vegetation. Active throughout the winter. Lives on plant food. Produces 4—10 young, 3 times a year. At irregular intervals, generally every four years, a rise in population number is followed by mass migration resulting in most of the animals falling prey to their enemies or drowning in rivers or in the sea. Distribution: the mountains and tundra of Scandinavia, Finland and the northern regions of the USSR.

5 Water Vole *Arvicola terrestris* — Length of body 120—211 mm, tail 60—130 mm. Found in damp places on the shores of flowing and calm bodies of water, in damp lowland meadows and wet high mountain meadows. Swims and dives well. Mostly active by day. Digs burrows or builds a spherical nest above ground in the roots of willows or clumps of sedge. Feeds on aquatic plants, tree roots or vegetables. Produces 2—8 young, 3—5 times a year. Distribution: almost all of Europe and the Asiatic USSR.

6 Muskrat *Ondatra zibethicus* — Length of body 260—400 mm, tail 190—250 mm. Found on the banks of flowing and calm bodies of water. Native of North America but was introduced to central Bohemia in 1905 whence it spread to many European countries. Lives in pairs or families in underground corridors which it digs in banks; the entrances are below water level. The diet consists of both plant and animal food. There are 3—4 broods a year, each consisting of 7—8 young. Distribution: nowadays it is widespread throughout much of Europe, the Asiatic USSR, Mongolia and China.

358

Subphylum: **Vertebrates — Vertebrata**

Class: **Mammals — Mammalia**

Order: **Rodents — Rodentia**

Family: **Cricetid rats, mice and voles — Cricetidae**

1 Pine Vole *Pitymys subterraneus* — Length of body 80−105 mm, tail 26−40 mm. Found in forest margins, among dense vegetation along the banks of streams and in various damp situations with thick growths of herbaceous plants at higher elevations, including high mountains. Lives in underground corridors. Produces 2−3 young, 3−5 times a year. Feeds on vegetation, fruits, seeds, mushrooms. Distribution: throughout most of Europe except Scandinavia and the northern parts of the European USSR as well as certain Mediterranean islands.

2 Snow Vole *Microtus nivalis* — Length of body 110−113 mm, tail 43−68 mm. Found in alpine meadows and adjacent screes at the alpine and subalpine level (in the Alps at 2,300 metres); very occasionally also found at lower elevations. The diet consists solely of plant food. Lives in a system of underground corridors. The nest of dry grass is located under a stone or in a rock crevice. Active by day and throughout the winter. Produces 5−6 young, 2−3 times a year (in June and August). Distribution: European mountains and the mountains of Asia Minor.

3 Common Vole *Microtus arvalis* — Length of body 90−120 mm, tail 35−40 mm. Very common in fields from lowland to mountain elevations. Lives in colonies in underground corridors where the nest and food stores are also located. Feeds on grain, plant shoots and roots as well as small animals. Capable of a high rate of reproduction: there are 3−7 broods a year, each consisting of 4−10 young, which are capable of reproduction within six weeks after birth. Thus, in warm and fertile years populations may become very large. Distribution: throughout most of Europe and Asia except the northern regions.

4 Bank Vole *Clethrionomys glareolus* — Length of body 85−110 mm, tail 35−55 mm. Typical inhabitant of woodlands. Partial to places with dense vegetation. Makes two types of holes, one serving as a hiding place, the other for breeding. Feeds chiefly on vegetation, mushrooms, insect larvae. Produces 3−5 young, 3−4 times a year. Distribution: Europe (except the extreme south), western Siberia and Asia Minor.

Family: **Palaearctic mole rats — Spalacidae**

5 Lesser Mole Rat *Spalax leucodon* — Length of body 150−240 mm; tail is very short. Completely blind; the atrophied eyes are covered with skin. Found in dry flatlands as well as in mountains. Mountain specimens are usually smaller than those of lowlands. Lives underground where it tunnels long corridors with the aid of its strong head and large incisors. The mounds of earth on the surface are smaller than those of the European Mole. Produces a single litter of 1−4 young. Feeds on plant roots. Distribution: Hungary, the Balkans, western Ukraine, Transcaucasia and Asia Minor.

Family: **Old World rats and mice — Muridae**

6 European Harvest Mouse *Micromys minutus* — Length of body 82−108 mm, tail 70−100 mm. Common in damp lowlands on the edges of swamps, in wet meadows and on the shores of streams and ponds. A gregarious rodent that is active mostly by day. Builds a spherical nest of grasses or the stems of aquatic and shoreline vegetation. The nest has a single entrance. Feeds on plant and animal food. A good climber. Produces 3−7 young, 2−3 times a year. Distribution: throughout Europe (except the extreme north), Asia, east to Japan and north Vietnam.

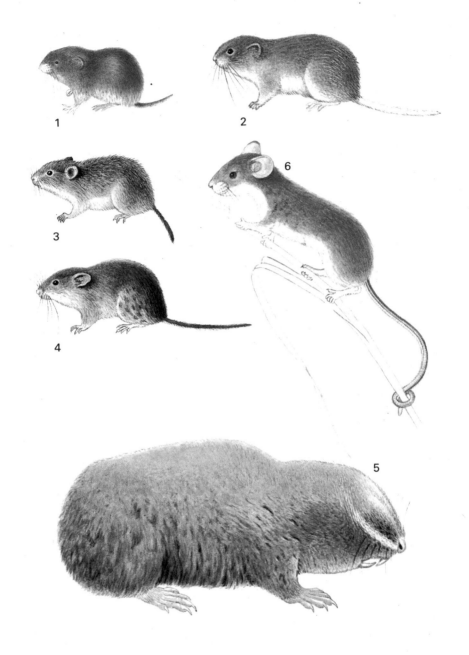

Subphylum: **Vertebrates — Vertebrata**

Class: **Mammals — Mammalia**

Order: **Rodents — Rodentia**

Family: **Old World rats and mice — Muridae**

1 Striped Field Mouse *Apodemus agrarius* — Length of body 80−115 mm, tail 65−92 mm. Common along the edges of forests, and in thickets and copses in lowlands and foothills. Found in rather moist environments but avoids large forests. Digs underground tunnels where the nest and foodstore are located. Feeds on seeds and a variety of invertebrates such as insects and worms. There are 3−4 litters a year, each consisting of 5−7 young. Distribution: western, central and eastern Europe (not recorded from Great Britain or France), Asia east to China and Korea.

2 Yellow-necked Field Mouse *Apodemus flavicollis* — Length of body 98−116 mm, tail 90−127 mm. Found in woodlands, chiefly in rather damp locations. Lives in underground holes, in tree cavities and birds' nests; in winter it enters human habitations. An expert at climbing and jumping. Feeds mostly on oily seeds, insects and worms but occasionally will eat green plant food. Produces 4−8 young, 2−4 times a year. Distribution: throughout Europe far to the north (including the Shetlands, Hebrides and Scandinavia); Asia, to Korea and China.

3 Wood Mouse *Apodemus sylvaticus* — Length of body 82−108 mm, tail 70−100 mm. Common along the edges of woods, in copses, cemeteries, parks and gardens; in winter it enters buildings. Mostly nocturnal. The diet is similar to that of the preceding species. Lives in holes in the ground; sometimes builds a nest of grass and moss on the ground, inside a bird's nest or elsewhere in trees. There are 2−4 broods a year, each consisting of 2−9 young. Distribution: throughout Europe, Asia and north Africa.

4 Lesser Field Mouse *Apodemus microps* — Length of body 77−101 mm, tail 55−95 mm. Found in forest margins, in small copses and in shrub clearings, in warm and dry places, chiefly in lowland regions. Very occasionally found in foothills and rarely at higher elevations. The diet consists of plant food and small animals. Distribution: southeastern parts of the European USSR and adjacent steppes; its range extends to Czechoslovakia.

5 House Mouse *Mus musculus* — Length of body 72−100 mm, tail 67 − 95 mm. Synanthropic; in summer found in fields, while in winter it usually moves to human habitations, into haystacks and farm buildings. Lives in families or larger communities in underground holes. Feeds on grain and refuse. There are 4−8 litters a year, each consisting of 4−8 young which are fully grown by the age of 1 1/2 months. Distribution: native to the steppes of Asia and southern Europe, now worldwide.

6 Black Rat *Rattus rattus* — Length of body 158−252 mm, tail 190−240 mm. Often mistaken for the Brown Rat. However, it is found in drier places and in the higher storeys of buildings. It is more slender and smaller than the Brown Rat and usually coloured grey or black. More discriminating in diet than the Brown Rat, feeding chiefly on plant food, mainly seeds, cereal grains and fruit. There are 3−6 litters a year, each consisting of 5−10 young, which are fully developed at the age of three months. Native to tropical Asia. As an associate of man it has spread throughout much of the world where it occurs in numerous geographic races.

362

Subphylum: **Vertebrates — Vertebrata**

Class: **Mammals — Mammalia**

Order: **Rodents — Rodentia**

Family: **Old World rats and mice — Muridae**

1 Brown Rat *Rattus norvegicus* — Length of body 190—270 mm, tail 130—230 mm. Differs from the Black Rat mainly by having a strong and shorter tail and short ear lobes. Found in buildings usually near water, in sewage systems, cellars, sties or storehouses. Found in large groups or in families. Forages for food mainly at night. It is an omnivore and an unpleasant pest. There are 3—6 litters a year, each consisting of 6—10 young, which are fully grown and capable of reproduction at the age of 2—3 months. Distribution: native to palaearctic Asia whence it spread with Man throughout the world.

Family: **Dormice — Gliridae**

2 Edible Dormouse *Glis glis* — Length of body 130—180 mm, tail 100—150 mm. Has a long bushy tail and resembles a small grey squirrel. Found in broadleaved woodlands, chiefly beechwoods, in parks, gardens and cemeteries. Chiefly nocturnal. Lives in families or small groups. The nest of moss is located in hollow trees, holes in walls, under eaves, in nestboxes or on the ground. There it hides by day and also hibernates in winter. Feeds on seeds, nuts, young tree shoots, bark and insects. Produces a single litter of 3—6 young. Distribution: throughout Europe (except the northern regions) and Asia.

3 Garden Dormouse *Eliomys quercinus* — Length of body 105—147 mm, tail 80—135 mm. The tail has a characteristic brush-like tip. Found in gardens, parks and broadleaved woodlands from lowland regions to foothills. Nocturnal. The nest is located in hollow trees, in the ground or in rock crevices. Feeds on small vertebrates, invertebrates, seeds and fruits. In May or June the female bears 2—8 young. Distribution: central and southern Europe (Poland, northern Germany and central regions of the European USSR mark the northern limits of its range), north Africa.

4 Forest Dormouse *Dryomys nitedula* — Length of body 80—115 mm, tail 70—100 mm. Found in broadleaved forests (very occasionally also in mixed and coniferous forests), in clearings and gardens, from lowlands to elevations of 1,500 metres. Nocturnal. The nest is located in trees and bushes. Feeds on nuts, fruit and invertebrates. In May or June the female bears 3—6 young. Distribution: from Italy, Switzerland and Germany far eastward into Asia. Absent in western Europe and Scandinavia.

5 Common Dormouse *Muscardinus avellanarius* — Length of body 75—86 mm, tail 55—77 mm. Found in broadleaved and mixed woodlands, less frequently in coniferous forests. Nocturnal. Lives in small colonies. Constructs two types of nests: the one built in summer is round, 3—5 cm in diameter, and located in shrubs, trees as well as in haylofts or attics of mountain chalets. The winter nest is located on the ground. Feeds on the seeds of trees, hazel nuts, forest fruits and insects. There are one or two litters a year, each consisting of 3—5 young. Distribution: throughout Europe and Asia Minor.

Family: **Jumping mice — Zapodidae**

6 Northern Birch Mouse *Sicista betulina* — Length of body 50—75 mm, tail 76—108 mm. Found in mountain meadows and fields. In the mountains of central Europe it is a glacial relic. Nocturnal. The nest of grass and moss is located on the ground or in tree cavities close to the ground. Feeds on grass seeds, fruits and insects. The breeding season is in June or July, when the female bears 2—6 young. Distribution: northern, central and eastern Europe, Siberia and the Caucasus.

Subphylum: **Vertebrates — Vertebrata**

Class: **Mammals — Mammalia**

Order; **Rodents — Rodentia**

Family: **Jerboas — Dipodidae**

1 Fine-toothed Jerboa *Allactaga jaculus* — Length of body 190—250 mm, tail about 280 mm. Found in steppe and semi-steppe. Nocturnal, hiding in underground burrows by day. Constructs four types of burrows: the first, the so-called permanent burrow, consists of a living chamber and 1—2 storerooms; the second serves as a place of concealment by day; the third has a short corridor and is a place of concealment by night, and the fourth, the so-called winter burrow, is up to 2 metres deep and is used for hibernation. Feeds on seeds, plant shoots and insects. Distribution: Asia, east to the Altai, westward only to the Ukraine.

Family: **Old World porcupines — Hystricidae**

2 Porcupine *Hystrix cristata* — Length of body 57—68 cm, tail 50—68 mm. Found in dry flatlands and at the foot of mountains in dense thickets. Spends the day in burrows, emerging to forage for food at dusk. The diet consists of plant food. In May the female bears 1—4 young which have short quills pressed close to the body. The quills of adult porcupines are 30—40 cm long and it appears that these may be ejected against the enemy in case of grave danger. Distribution: north Africa, very occasionally also Italy and Sicily.

Family: **Nutrias — Myocastoridae**

3 Coypu *Myocastor coypus* — Length of body 40—80 cm, tail 40—50 cm. Has webbed toes on the hind legs. Found along flowing or calm bodies of water with plenty of aquatic vegetation. Digs a shallow burrow in the shore with a half-submerged entrance. Feeds on aquatic vegetation. The female bears 5—12 young twice a year. Native to South America, whence it was introduced to Europe after World War I.

Order: **Lagomorphs — Lagomorpha**

Family: **Piping hares — Ochotonidae**

4 Steppe Pika *Ochotona pusilla* — Length of body 150 mm, the tail is rudimentary. Found in valleys with lush vegetation but also ascends high up into the mountains. Lives in colonies. Digs burrows about one metre long terminating in a living chamber. Does not hibernate but stays the winter in the burrow without emerging above ground. It prepares stores of food for the winter. Distribution: chiefly Asia, the area round the upper reaches of the Volga, the southern Urals, northern Kazakhstan, Burma, Asama, Kashmir and China. It also occurs in eastern Europe.

Family: **Hares and rabbits — Leporidae**

5 European Hare *Lepus europaeus* — Length of body 550—650 mm, tail 75—100 mm. Found in cultivated steppes and forest margins both in lowland regions and foothills. Solitary. Feeds on vegetation, in winter it nibbles the bark of young trees and shrubs. The female usually bears 2—3 young, 3—4 times a year. Distribution: throughout Europe except the northern regions, much of Asia and Africa. Introduced to North America.

6 Blue or Varying Hare *Lepus timidus* — Length of body 460—610 mm, tail 40—80 mm. A northern hare whose fur is white in winter and dark in summer. Habits are similar to those of the European Hare. The female generally bears 6—8 young, 2—3 times a year. During the Ice Age it occurred in the more southerly parts of Europe and has survived as a glacial relic in certain mountain ranges where several geographic races can be recognized: one is found in the mountains of Scotland, another in Ireland. A fairly small race occurs in the Alps between 1,300 and 3,500 metres.

366

Subphylum: **Vertebrates — Vertebrata**

Class: **Mammals — Mammalia**

Order: **Lagomorpha — Lagomorpha**

Family: **Hares and rabbits — Leporidae**

1 European Wild Rabbit *Oryctolagus cuniculus* — Length of body 350—450 mm, tail 40—73 mm. Found in dry forest margins, shrubby hillsides and similar environments from lowlands to elevations of about 600 metres, even higher in the southern part of its range. Often lives in large colonies. Digs a system of underground tunnels which serves as its permanent home. Emerges at dusk and feeds on plants. Produces 4—12 young, 4—7 times a year. Distribution: native to northwest Africa and Spain. Spread by Man throughout central and eastern Europe, Australia and New Zealand.

Order: **Even-toed ungulates — Artiodactyla**

Family: **Old World pigs — Suidae**

2 Wild Boar *Sus scrofa* — Length of body 110—180 cm, tail 15—20 cm, height at shoulder 85—115 cm. Generally found in oak and beech woods next to fields and meadows, mainly in foothills and mountains. Lives in herds and is mostly nocturnal. By day it remains in marshy places hiding in thickets. The diet consists of plant and animal food. In March the female bears 4—12 striped young in a previously prepared bed. Distribution: throughout Europe, Asia and north Africa (to the Sudan).

Family: **Deer — Cervidae**

3 European Elk or Moose *Alces alces* — Length of body 250—270 cm, tail 12—13 cm, height at shoulder up to 235 cm. Found in damp broadleaved forests at lower elevations. In summer the females and young live together in families, in winter they are found in moderately large herds headed by an elder female. Old males are solitary. Feeds on the leaves, shoots and bark of trees and shrubs and other plants. In May or June it generally produces 2 young. Distribution: Scandinavia, Poland, the USSR, almost all of northern Asia and North America.

4 Fallow Deer *Dama dama* — Length of body 130—160 cm, tail 16—19 cm, height at shoulder 85—110 cm. Found in broadleaved woodlands and meadows at lower elevations. Females and young generally form herds separate from the males. The female usually bears 1—2 young in June. Feeds on herbaceous plants, the leaves and bark of trees, acorns, chestnuts and beechnuts. Distribution: native to the Mediterranean region and Asia Minor. Since medieval times it has been introduced to preserves in western and central Europe.

5 Red Deer *Cervus elaphus* — Length of body 165—250 cm, tail 12—15 cm, height at shoulder 150—165 cm. Found in wooded regions in foothills and mountains. Lives in small herds, the females and young together and the males separately. Feeds on herbaceous plants, leaves, young shoots and bark of trees, beechnuts, acorns and various field crops and fruit. The rutting season, when the males often engage in fierce combat, takes place from late August to October and generally lasts about 4 weeks. In June the female bears 1—2 young. Important game animal. Distribution: several geographic races are recognized throughout Europe north to central Scandinavia, in Asia to the Sea of Japan and in northwest Africa and in North America.

6 Roe Deer *Capreolus capreolus* — Length of body 95—135 cm, tail 2—3 cm, height at shoulder 65—75 cm. Found in all types of forests from lowlands to mountains; in some places also found in open cultureland. During the summer it lives in families of females and young, in winter it lives in larger herds. Males generally live singly. The rutting season is from mid-July to mid-August. The young are born the following May or June. Feeds on herbaceous plants, leaves, buds and bark of trees. Distribution: almost all of Europe and palaearctic Asia.

Subphylum: **Vertebrates — Vertebrata**

Class: **Mammals — Mammalia**

Order: **Even-toed ungulates — Artiodactyla**

Family: **Deer — Cervidae**

1 Reindeer *Rangifer tarandus* — Length of body 130—220 cm, tail 7—20 cm, height at shoulder 110—120 cm. Differs from other members of the deer family in that both male and female have antlers. Found in northern tundras as well as in forests, also high up in mountains. Lives in herds throughout its life, small ones in summer, very large herds in winter sometimes numbering several thousand heads. Feeds on herbaceous plants, young twigs and leaves of trees, shrubs and lichens. The rutting season is in autumn. In the following May or June the female bears 1—2 young. It is kept in a semi-wild state and used for its meat, skin and milk, and as a working animal. Distribution: northern parts of Europe, Asia and North America.

Family: **Horned ungulates — Bovidae**

2 Mouflon *Ovis musimon* — Length of body 110—130 cm, tail 5—10 cm, height at shoulder up to 95 cm. Found in warm, mixed or broadleaved forests with glades and meadows; fond of warm and sunny southern slopes. Lives in moderately large flocks headed by an old female. Feeds on vegetation, the leaves and shoots of trees, chestnuts and acorns. In March or April it produces 1—2 young. Distribution: native to the Mediterranean, where it has survived in Corsica and Sardinia; introduced to many west and central European countries, Yugoslavia and the Crimea where it has become successful.

3 Chamois *Rupicapra rupicapra* — Length of body 110—113 cm, tail 7—8 cm, height at shoulder 70—80 cm. Found in high mountains up to the region of permanent ice and snow. Lives in herds consisting of females and young. These are joined on occasion by the males, who otherwise live in smaller groups or singly. Extremely good at climbing and leaping. The diet consists of plant food. The mating season is in November and December. In May or June the female bears 1—2 young. Distribution: the Cantabrian Mountains, Pyrenees, Alps, Apennines, Carpathians, high mountains of the Balkans, the Caucasus, Transcaucasia and the mountains of Asia Minor.

4 Wisent or Aurochs *Bison bonasus* — Length of body 310—350 cm, tail 50—60 cm, height at shoulder 85—200 cm. Found in broadleaved and mixed forests with lush undergrowth of thickets and forest meadows. Lives in herds headed by a male. Usually grazes at dusk. Feeds on grass and herbaceous plants, the leaves, shoots and bark of trees and shrubs. The breeding season is in August when the males engage in fierce combat. In May or June the female bears a single young. Distribution: at one time it was common in forests throughout much of Europe but by the Middle Ages it had been almost exterminated; nowadays it occurs only in some countries in preserves (Poland, the USSR) and in zoos.

5 Ibex *Capra ibex* — Length of body 130—135 cm, tail about 13 cm, height at shoulder 65—80 cm. Inhabits high mountains from the upper forest limit to the snow line. Lives in herds comprising females, young males and young. Adult males either live separately in small bands or singly. Jumps expertly over rocks. Feeds on mountain plants and in winter also on moss. In June the female bears 1—2 young. Distribution: known by several geographic races in the mountains of Europe (Alps and Caucasus), palaearctic Asia and Africa (Egypt, Sudan and Ethiopia).

Subphylum: **Vertebrates — Vertebrata**

Class: **Mammals — Mammalia**

Order: **Even-toed ungulates — Artiodactyla**

Family: **Horned ungulates — Bovidae**

1 Saiga Antelope *Saiga tatarica* — Length of body 130—135 cm, tail 8—12 cm, height at shoulder ♂ up to 70 cm, female shorter. Steppe-dweller that lives in herds in lowlands and in mountains on upland plateaus. The diet consists of plant food. Grazes in the early morning and afternoon. During the dry period in summer it often travels great distances in search of food and water. The rutting season is in November and December. At this time a great number of females congregate round the males who engage in fierce combats, often ending in the death of one of the combatants. In May or June the female bears 2 or sometimes only a single offspring. Distribution: in former times it was to be found over a wide area from the Carpathians to Mongolia and northeastern China. Nowadays it is confined to the Ukraine and several places in Asia.

2 Wild Goat *Capra aegagrus* — Length of body 100—110 cm, tail 20 cm, height at shoulder 95—100 cm. Inhabits rocky terrain among scattered trees and shrubs. Leaps with great agility. Females and young congregate in small herds; old males live singly while younger males live in small groups. Feeds on plants, in winter on moss and the needles of dwarf pine. In April or May the female bears 1—3 young. Distribution: the mountains of Greece, Asia Minor, the Caucasus, the Middle East and western India. Experimentally introduced to certain other mountains as well as lower hills.

3 Spanish Ibex *Capra pyrenaica* — Length of body 145—160 cm, tail 12 cm, height at shoulder ♂ — 75 cm, ♀ — 65 cm. Life habits similar to those of the Ibex of the Alps and Caucasus. Lives in herds, old males live singly. Distribution: Pyrenees.

Order: **Whales, dolphins and porpoises — Cetacea**

Suborder: **Mysticeti**

Family: **Rorquals — Balaenopteridae**

4 Common Rorqual Whale *Balaenoptera physalus* — Length 18.5—25 metres. On each side of the upper jaw there are 320—420 whalebones which serve as a sieve in foraging for food. Found in the Arctic seas; in winter it often swims far south to tropical and subtropical seas. Forms schools of 6—10 individuals. Feeds chiefly on small fish and invertebrates. The female bears a single young up to 4 metres long. When pursued, it swims at speeds of more than 30 km per hour. Submerges for lengthy periods, often for 15 minutes. Hunted by Man and is therefore declining in numbers from year to year. Distribution: common along the shores of Europe and regularly occurs in the Mediterranean Sea.

Family: **Right whales — Balaenidae**

5 Bowhead *Balaena mysticetus* — Length 15—21 metres, occasionally reaching 24 metres. On each side of the upper jaw there are 300—360 whalebones each measuring up to 350 cm in length. Feeds on marine invertebrates and small fish. The young are born in arctic waters. Produces only a single offspring. Females and young live in schools. Swims more slowly than rorquals, but is able to remain submerged for 30—60 minutes. Distribution: the Bowhead is a typical inhabitant of the Arctic seas around icefloes. At one time it was common but its numbers have been greatly depleted by overhunting. Very occasionally it occurs off the northern coast of Europe.

Subphylum: **Vertebrates — Vertebrata**

Class: **Mammals — Mammalia**

Order: **Whales, dolphins and porpoises — Cetacea**

Suborder: **Odontoceti**

Family: **Dolphins — Delphinidae**

1 Common Dolphin *Delphinus delphis* — Length 18—26 metres. Lives in large or small schools. Expert swimmer, covering up to 35 km in one hour. The diet consists mainly of fish, but it also feeds on cephalopods, molluscs, medusas and other marine invertebrates. Distribution: common along the entire European Atlantic coast, in the Mediterranean and Black Sea, the Indian Ocean and northern Pacific. Does not occur in the Arctic seas.

2 Bottlenosed Dolphin *Tursiops truncatus* — Length 2.5 metres. Lives in schools. Feeds chiefly on marine fish. Generally produces a single offspring, very occasionally two. The gestation period is about 12 months. The young are tended by the mother for one year. The Bottlenose is the most commonly kept cetacean in oceanariums and is the subject of intensive research. Adult specimens have a fairly large brain weighing 1500—1800 grams. Distribution: in coastal waters of the tropical and temperate zone of the Atlantic north to the shores of Great Britain and northern France; also fairly common in the Mediterranean Sea.

3 Common Killer Whale *Orcinus orca* — Males often measure up to 10 metres, females 3.8—4.6 metres. Each jaw is furnished with 20—28 strong sharp teeth. A gregarious whale and one of the fiercest of marine animals. Feeds on whales and dolphins, seals, sea lions, and fish. Hunts in groups exhibiting a high degree of 'pack behaviour'. Distribution: all seas and oceans, chiefly in the northern hemisphere. Often found also along the European Atlantic coast, very occasionally even making its way far up rivers into the interior.

4 Northern Pilot Whale *Globicephala melaena* — Length 6—7 metres. Predatory. Often congregates in large schools headed by an old and experienced male. The female bears a single young once every 2—3 years. Found in the Arctic Ocean and northern parts of the Pacific and Atlantic, off the Faroe and Shetland islands, and occasionally also in the Mediterranean.

5 Sperm Whale *Physeter macrocephalus* — Length up to 25 metres. Found mostly in tropical seas whence, however, it roams far north and south. Forms schools numbering 15—20 individuals. In former times, when it was far more numerous than nowadays, schools often numbered as many as several hundred individuals. Feeds chiefly on cephalopods and fish, diving for them to great depths. Also hunts giant deep-sea octopuses. A new-born Sperm Whale, measuring 3.5—4 metres, suckles for about six months. The Sperm Whale is one of the most highly valued of cetaceans; practically all of it is processed for commercial purposes. Very much in demand is ambergris — a dark, wax-like substance found in the guts of diseased or dead Sperm Whales and used in the perfume industry. Often visits the shores of Europe and occasionally also enters the Mediterranean.

Index of Common Names

380

Index of Latin Names

389